W9-CUV-502

Modern Project Management

Foundations for Quality and Productivity

THE DATA PROCESSING HANDBOOK SERIES

Modern Project Management: Foundations for Quality and Productivity

Forthcoming

Quality Data Processing: The Profit Potential for the 80s
The Installation and Management of a Project Methodology

THE DATA PROCESSING HANDBOOK SERIES

Modern Project Management
Foundations for Quality and Productivity

CLAUDE W. BURRILL
IBM Systems Science Institute

*✳ **LEON W. ELLSWORTH**
IBM Systems Science Institute

*Yours for —
Leon W. Ellsworth*

BEA

BURRILL-ELLSWORTH ASSOCIATES, INC.
Tenafly, N.J.

Third printing, June 1981

Library of Congress Cataloging in Publication

Burrill, Claude W
    Modern project management

    (The Data processing handbook series)
    Bibliography: p.
    Includes index.
    1. Electronic data processing—Management.
I. Ellsworth, Leon, 1922-   joint author. II. Title.
III. Series: Data processing handbook series.
QA76.9.M3B87   658'.05   79-24457
ISBN 0-935310-00-2

To Agnes and Kathleen

CONTENTS

6. ADJUSTING FOR SIZE   147

7. EFFECTIVE PROJECT COMMUNICATION   161

8. INTRODUCING CHANGE   175

9. PROJECT SELECTION AND REVIEW   199

14. ESTIMATING—THE DELPHI METHOD   313

15. NETWORKS—THEORY   329

16. NETWORKS—PRACTICE   373

17. PEER REVIEWS   387

18. PROJECT CONTROL TOPICS   397

19. AUDITING A PROJECT METHODOLOGY   415

APPENDIX D: FORMS, REVIEWS, GUIDES, AND CHECKLISTS 507

PREFACE

Computer software is big business. The United States alone will spend about $50 billion in 1980 to develop and maintain software, and all indications are that expenditures will increase with time. Costs are staggering, but so is the impact of computer systems. It is very difficult to think of *any* daily activity that is totally independent of computer systems. Most things we touch are involved with order entry systems, billing systems, production systems, and so on. Some birth registers are automated, and presumably even coffins are under tight inventory control by computers.

Because software is now so very important to our lives, anything that can be done to improve systems will have a multiplier effect throughout the economy. At a time when our society is buffeted by energy shortages and inflationary pressures, productivity gains are badly needed. The software industry is in a position to have a significant impact on our economy by improving the software development process and the quality of software systems. In writing this book, our hope is that we can help to bring about such improvements.

Writing a book is a project, not unlike an application development project. It has its purpose, scope, objectives, due date, quality standards, and other components of a data processing project. Following is a report on some aspects of our project and the product it produced.

Project Objectives

The mission of Burrill-Ellsworth Associates is to foster quality and productivity in data processing. The purpose of this book is to lay the foundations for quality and productivity by addressing the application development area. The scope of the book is limited to the methods and procedures of application development. Our objective is to provide practical information and guidance for accomplishing data processing projects. To meet this objective, we present our material in two ways. In the main part of the book (Chapters 1-20) we take a tutorial approach and describe, explain, and discuss various topics relating to project methodology. In the second part (Appendices A-D) we use a handbook approach to provide lists, forms, policies, procedures, and other components of a methodology.

Our book is written primarily for data processing professionals who are involved with the management of data processing projects: Project Managers, Data Processing Managers, and their supporting staffs. In testing our material, however, we discovered another group that finds our material useful. This is the group of students and data processing professionals who want to expand their knowledge beyond purely technical topics, perhaps with the view of moving ultimately into management. A third group finding this material useful is the organization's auditors. This group has a vital interest in procedures, standards, documentation, and many other topics we address. Finally, there are some users of data processing systems who want to delve into the project process. They find the book useful because knowledge of data processing is not required for most of the material.

Project Team

People have asked how we ever let ourselves be recruited onto the team for this project—why did we ever write this book? The main reason was to condense our experience and material into a form most useful to our students, thereby improving the quality and productivity of the educational process.

During the past five years our assignments at IBM involved us in studying, discussing, teaching, and thinking about the project area. We had much information, but it lacked a coherent structure. The writing of this book gave us the opportunity to organize our ideas, and it forced us to think about areas that otherwise we could have overlooked quite easily.

Over the years we have discussed data processing projects with hundreds of people. We have benefited from teaching project methodology to over 1,700 students from more than 200 organizations. We have examined the project handbooks of many organizations. From all of these sources we have learned much about the best current practice for managing data processing projects. In this book we attempt to organize this practical know-how into a logical structure. To this we add our own ideas, particularly in areas such as function analysis, peer reviews, and transactional estimating where there were gaps in existing practice.

Project Problems

There is a well-established tradition in data processing to spend more time discussing project problems than accomplishments. As respectors of tradition, we want to discuss two of our major problems. The first concerns "data." That we had such a problem will not surprise most of our readers because they often hear about problems involving data entry, data transmission, data integrity, data redundancy, data security, and so on. But we faced a more serious problem: Is "data" singular or plural? Pluralists argue that the dictionary settles the question, and they cite the existence of "datum" to squelch opposition. Singularists usually fall back on common usage—"everybody" says "data is" rather than "data are." We vascillated between these two views as our publication or due date approached. Then, just in the nick (or, in the vernacular, neck of time), we were saved by *The New York Times.* A distinguished columnist, William Safire, wrote in the June 3, 1979, issue that it is acceptable to treat "data" as singular. In fact, he stated, "I think 'the data is' is widely accepted and 'the data are' is passe." Clearly we had little choice but to move with the *Times* and treat "data" as singular. The alternative would have required a change in our book title from *Modern Project Management* to *Passe Project Management,* and somehow this did not appeal.

The second major problem is the singleton "s" as used in conjunction with the pair "he." There seemed to be four alternatives: To write (1) "she," (2) "(s)he," (3) "he," and (4) "he or she." A fifth alternative ("she or he") was considered briefly, but somehow it got lost in the design process. We also were offered "he and/or she" and other variants by helpful colleagues, but we decided that such help we didn't need.

The major risk with alternatives (1) and (3) is possibly offending some readers. These are readers who, on seeing use of alternative (1) or (3), would jump to the conclusion that the authors merely reacted in an antichauvinistic or chauvinistic manner, respectively, without clear recognition that two sexes exist and both, for the most part, are literate.

A problem with alternative (4) is that it is extremely tiresome to read "he or she" line after line. The major consideration, however, is its effect on productivity. With alternative (4), readers do more work, but they receive no more information.

Alternative (2) seems too cute, and how cute can one be when describing methods and procedures? And what if a trend should develop? (Wo)men might write about child(ren), (p)residents, (s)trip report(s)—soon it would come to (every)one attempting to (s)top everyone else.

The "s" and "he" problem, of course, leads to corollary difficulties with the use of "er" and/or "im" with "h." Taken with our first problem, a simple statement about the correctness of a person's data leads to consideration of "her data are correct," "his data is correct," "his or her (as the case may be) report contains correct data," and so on.

Our quandary over the second problem was resolved when, in a flash inspiration, we (by which is meant the "royal we," that is, one of us) recalled the trusty rule that gained us acceptable marks in college: If you don't know the answer to a multiple choice question, always select the third alternative. And that is how "his data is correct" came about—right or wrong. (Incidentally, if you feel strongly about this subject, merely look on alternative (3) as the "invisible 's' " alternative. It is just as logical to write "he" and pronouce it "she" as it is to write "knot" and pronounce it "not."

Product Test

A data processing product is subjected to various tests before it is delivered; so should it be with a project methodology. During development of our material, it was our good fortune to be able to work with Computer Management, Inc. They tested our material by applying it to their projects, and they made many constructive comments for improvement. Although we are grateful to them for advice and assistance, it should be recognized that Computer Management is in no way responsible for omissions or shortcomings in our material.

Because Computer Management performs data processing work under contract for other organizations and is dedicated to quality products, smooth-running projects are essential to their success. This made them an ideal group for giving our material a rigorous test. Results of this test can best be described by quoting parts of a letter from J. Frank Smith, Jr., President of Computer Management:

> I could go on and on about the many advantages we feel we have received in the use of your techniques and management systems you suggested. I will merely highlight a few we believe have made a very tangible and substantial contribution toward the success of our systems as well as the profitability of our company.
>
> The phased approached to systems development activity has enabled us to:
>   1. Provide a structure for effective communications with user management . . . .
>   2. We have been able to deliver systems with a high degree of quality, on schedule, with a significant reduction in minor maintenance . . . .
>   3. The development activity can now be measured through a series

of well-defined, deliverable products. This allows a continuous evaluation of the progress in each project. . . .

4. We have been able to develop an historical data base through which we have improved our estimating techniques for future projects.

User's Guide

Chapters 1 through 7 should be read in sequence, and they should be read before reading other parts of the book.

Chapters 8 through 20 are independent. They can be read in any order except that Chapter 16 is best read after Chapter 15. The cost of chapter independence is some minor redundancy, but in our judgment this cost is far outweighed by the benefit.

The appendices are not just supplements to the text; they have independent value. We suggest, however, that as you use material in the appendices that you read related sections in the text.

Modern Project Management is a comprehensive book about the data processing application development process. It provides a practical project methodology that is consistent with the principles of Peter Drucker and Douglas McGregor, and it explains how this methodology benefits both the workers and the organization. *Modern Project Management* is an indispensible handbook and reference for all who strive to improve the quality of data processing systems and the productivity of the development process.

ACKNOWLEDGMENTS

We have been helped by so many people that it is not possible to acknowledge them individually. To all who have given us assistance, time, and ideas we express our profound thanks. Especially we want to thank our students, whose comments have helped us to shape our material. And we want to thank Computer Management for helping us test our material in "the real world."

Our debt to three people is so great that a blanket acknowledgment will not suffice. All of our colleagues at the IBM Systems Science Institute have been helpful, but we particularly acknowledge the contribution of Walter Cameron. Walt taught with us for two years and helped evolve many of our ideas. We also thank Frank Howard, Senior Vice President of Computer Management, for the ideas, advice, and time he gave to us. Finally, we wish to thank our editor, Jane Tonero of Editorial and Graphic Services. Her patience and expert guidance were instrumental in converting our manuscript into a finished book.

Modern Project Management
Foundations for Quality and Productivity

1

THE DATA PROCESSING PROJECT

1-1 THE CONCEPT OF A PROJECT

It is convenient to think of work as falling into two categories: continuing efforts and single-time efforts. Continuing efforts are those on-going, repetitive tasks that involve the operation of an existing process or procedure. This is the work associated with the terms production and operations. Working on an assembly line is the standard example of continuing effort, but other examples are directing traffic, operating a keypunch, and running a computer center.

A single-time effort, on the other hand, is one that is intended to be performed only once. Single-time efforts are called *projects,* and they are used to produce a process or a unique product. Unlike continuing efforts, which suggest permanence and routine, projects are temporary and involve creativity. Examples of projects are easy to find:

Develop a new product line
Establish a process for evaluating employees
Build an office building
Repair an automobile
Write a term paper
Upgrade a production facility
Update a standards manual
Produce a payroll system

The classification of a particular work effort as a continuing effort or a project is somewhat arbitrary, and it reflects the attitude of the person making the classification. For example, maintenance of an existing computer

1

program is usually treated as a continuing effort and is managed as such. However, there is a growing tendency to look upon maintenance as a project and subject it to standard project procedures.

It is not uncommon for a work effort that is basically a project to be misclassified as a continuing effort. Doing this almost guarantees that the work effort will continue indefinitely. A good example of this is the Government's handling of Indian affairs. What should basically have been viewed as a single-time effort extending over a number of years was established as a continuing effort; as a result the problem has persisted. One cannot blame a group for considering its activities to be continuing efforts—after all, the first goal of any group must be survival if possible. But the organization empowered to establish the group and to fund it must make a clear classification and must recognize the one-time nature of the work to be done by many of the groups they establish. This obviously applies to governments, but there is ample evidence from many business organizations that it applies to them, too.

Projects are the means society and organizations use to create, to change, and to build. They are the basic agent used for innovation and renewal. Operation of a process is a continuing effort, but the construction or modification of a process is a project. Some areas, such as engineering and construction, have a well-developed procedure or methodology for implementing projects. In other areas, the understanding of projects is minimal and project methodology is ad hoc or nonexistent. But one thing is clear: Because of the importance of projects, society and organizations must understand the process and learn to manage it successfully, or they will be forced aside by those who do.

1-2 DP PROJECTS

This book concerns data processing (DP) projects. Henceforth, when we speak of a project, it is the DP project that we have in mind.

In most organizations, the Data Processing Department (DPD) is an important agent for change, and the project is the vehicle for accomplishing this change. A typical project might involve the development of a new application or system, the enhancement of an existing system, or the modification and installation of a software package. Occasionally, an unusual project is encountered, such as moving a data center, documenting an existing program, or installing a standard methodology to guide all future projects. As noted above, maintenance of existing programs is usually not treated as a project, but it is often more effective if it is.

The importance of projects in the past can readily be seen by observing the large investment most organizations have in DP software and systems and by realizing that it took many projects to put all of this in place. The future importance of projects can be surmised by looking at expectations for data processing growth. This growth was recently projected by the SILT Committee of SHARE,[1] which is an organization of computer users. Some of their figures are as follows.

It is estimated that there were 220,000 programmers in the United States in 1975. This number is projected to grow to 330,000 by 1985. Total annual expenditures for data processing amounted to $41 billion in 1975, and this will grow to $164 billion in 1985. This means that, whereas data processing amounted to about 3.2% of the gross national product in 1975, it will be about 8.3% of the gross national product in 1985. This quadrupling of DP expenditures in the United States will be matched by a roughly comparable rate of growth in the rest of the world.

From this projected rapid growth in data processing, it can be seen that DP projects will continue to be vitally important to all organizations. But certain implications can be drawn about the nature of the projects themselves. First, products produced will increase in size and complexity during the next decade. The SILT Committee projects a thousand-fold increase in the amount of machine-accessible stored data in the next ten years; this implies a large increase in the number of data-based systems. Communications-based systems should proliferate with the large-scale use of satellite communications because this should bring an order of magnitude drop in the cost of transmitting large amounts of data. Distributed intelligence and the ubiquitous minicomputer will result in a growth of distributed systems. All of this suggests larger, more complex systems; in fact, the SILT Committee believes that the next ten years will see a doubling in the number of major systems. These large, complex systems will, in turn, generate large, complex development requirements.

Second, one can expect an increased demand on projects to produce data processing systems that are reliable and available. It is estimated that in 1975 about 30% of the labor force depended in a direct way on computers to do their job. By 1985, this figure will increase to 70% of the labor force. With the bulk of workers dependent on data processing, delays and errors will not be tolerated. Quality software will have to become the norm, and this will place heavy demands on projects to ensure the delivery of quality products.

A third implication of rapid growth is increased involvement of all parts of the organization in DP projects. Gone are the days when most projects

---

[1]*Data Processing in 1980-1985*, T. A. Dolotta, et al. New York: John Wiley and Sons, 1976.

involved only the project team and a single user. Tomorrow's systems will involve many functional areas and will raise complex security, privacy, and legal questions. This means that many groups and organizations will be involved with projects, including:

> Formal project selection group
> Project personnel
> Project management
> DP operations
> DPD management
> User management
> General management
> Data administration
> Internal audit
> Legal
> Security

Increased size, complexity, involvement of many areas, and the demand for quality will all generate an increased need for effective project management. Much of the project work will be done by people who do not report to the Project Manager, so his job will become more like that of an orchestra conductor than of a supervisor. The need to coordinate diverse efforts and to cope with complexity will result in more attention being paid to planning, tracking, controlling, and auditing project work.

1-3 THE TRADITIONAL SITUATION

Traditionally, DP projects have been beset with problems. Chief among them were:

> The development cycle has been too long
> Many projects have been completed late
> Cost overruns have been common
> Deliverable products have been poor in quality, having incorrect or missing function and in need of correction immediately after installation
> Maintenance has been a problem, partly because of poor documentation and unreadable code

Nor is the future without its potential problems. One ominous sign can be seen by comparing future hardware costs with future people costs. The

SILT Committee anticipates that the productivity or cost/performance of hardware will improve by a factor of 100 during the 1975-1985 time period, while the productivity of programmers is expected to improve by only a factor of 1.33. These figures amount to a 60% annual improvement in hardware productivity as compared with only a 3% annual improvement in productivity of project personnel. While we believe the 60% figure may be somewhat high and the 3% somewhat low, one thing is clear: There is an obvious need for a significant improvement in project performance. In fact, the SILT Committee states that the two most critical problems between now and 1985 are (1) to improve the productivity of the applications software development process, and (2) to improve the quality of the end product of that process.

There are many reasons for these typical DP problems. Among those frequently voiced are:

Systems complexity is continually increasing
There is little theoretical foundation for building systems
There is a tendency in DP not to adopt solutions found by others
Poor project management
Poor project methodology, resulting in poor estimating, planning, controlling, etc.

Little can be done to prevent systems from growing more complex, but the other factors are being addressed in many quarters. Five years ago it was true that most projects came in late, over budget, and did not deliver all that was promised. Today the situation is dramatically different in many organizations. By evolving an effective project methodology, improving management techniques, and adopting improved implementation methods, a significant number of shops now bring projects in on time, within budget, and produce quality products. This performance must become the norm for tomorrow if the mission of DP is to be fulfilled.

We believe that many of the problems associated with DP projects are a natural outcome of growth and success. Organizations pass through different stages of growth much the same as do humans, and what is required at one stage might be inappropriate at the next. Let us see how this applies to the typical DP Department.

Data processing is a relatively new industry and most DP shops have been going through a period of "adolescence" during which emphasis has been on start-up and rapid growth. A few years ago most shops were young and relatively small. Most projects were for simple systems involving a single user. As a result, communications and control were simple and direct. Emphasis was on creating systems quickly, and this could best be achieved by encouraging individual action. Informality of management and communication was the rule.

Procedures and practices that worked well in the old environment are now straining under the burdens brought by growth and success. Changes in the size of organizations, the increasing complexity of systems, more involved organizational interactions, and an increased awareness of the vital role played by DP all require a modification in project methods. The more mature status of most DP shops brings with it a requirement for stronger management, more administrative controls, and functional specialization. Formal communication and formal procedures are needed in place of the more relaxed approach of yesterday. Thus, the new methods are required to cope with the new status of DP, and the so-called crisis is merely an indication that the industry has grown from adolescence into adulthood.

1-4 THE EFFECTIVE PROJECT

Our aim with this book is to lay the groundwork for effective projects— projects that lead to improved productivity and quality output. One of the basic tasks of management is to make work productive; another is to make workers achieving.[2] An effective project is one in which both of these objectives are accomplished.

Productive project work implies a quality project product, an on-time product, and effective and efficient use of resources. This is usually described by saying that the objective of a project is to produce a quality product, on time, and within budget.

The requirements to accomplish productive project work include:

An environment that fosters work
Properly defined work requirements
Effective plans and controls
Proper and stable work procedures
Adequate resources

Let us explore these requirements briefly.

Work does not take place in a vacuum; for it to be productive, it must be done in a suitable environment. This does not mean just the physical surroundings, but also the psychological environment generated by the people,

---

[2] *Management: Tasks, Responsibilities, Practices,* Peter F. Drucker. New York: Harper and Row, 1974, page 40.

procedures, and policies of the organization. Most of us have had the unhappy experience of working in an atmosphere where nothing could be accomplished. At times, most of us have taken an important piece of work home because we could not get it done at the office. From such experiences it is easy to see the necessity of an environment that fosters work.

For productive work it is also necessary to specify clearly the job to be done; this means defining the output of the work effort and prescribing standards against which completed work can be measured. Most of us at one time or another have been asked to work against a vague work objective—to perform when we were not told what was required. We know from this that if work is to be productive, it must be aimed at the result to be achieved.

The required output of a project is usually obtained by performing a number of related tasks. Just which tasks are required is something that must be determined by analyzing the work objective. These required tasks must then be synthesized into a process for producing the desired output. This effort of analysis and synthesis leads to a plan for accomplishing the work. Control tasks must be embedded into this work process to gather information for reporting work progress. As we have already observed, traditional problems with projects often stemmed from the failure to perform this planning and control function effectively. We have all seen projects where there wasn't time to plan the project and do it right, but there was time to do it over when faced with failure.

The work itself must be done by appropriate procedures, which should be standardized for all projects. This includes standards for all aspects of project work, including design, coding, testing, documentation, and management.

Finally, for the work effort to be productive it is necessary to supply the resources of people, equipment, time, and so on that the project requires. We all know the result of skimping on resources: late projects and poor quality. In the end the required resource is usually expended, but it is often charged to maintenance and repair rather than to the project.

The second management task mentioned above is to produce an achieving project worker, one who produces a quality product effectively and efficiently and at the same time receives personal satisfaction and reward from his efforts. Management usually recognizes the need for the first of these attributes, but the second is often overlooked.

Among the requirements for project workers to be achieving are:

A well-defined job
The knowledge and skills necessary to do the job or provisions for
    obtaining them
Proper facilities and materials

Free and open communications, both formal and informal
Opportunity for satisfaction and reward from contribution to organiza-
    tional goals

It is unreasonable to expect a worker to be achieving if he does not
know what is expected of him. But a well-defined job is not enough; a
worker must also know how to do it. This means that management must
supply not only the tools and facilities to do the job, but must also make provisions for gaining skills that are required for work assignments.

Workers obviously must have access to the formal project communications that relate to their job, but informal communication must be maintained, too. One of the most critical requirements in this area, and one that
is very often neglected, is communication of the data needed by workers to
control their own work. People do not work well when kept in the dark.
The mushroom theory of management ("Keep them in the dark and throw
dung at them") rarely works, particularly with the level of knowledge workers
who populate DP projects.

Finally, the reason most people work is for the personal satisfaction
and reward, both tangible and intangible, that they get from doing a job well.
What is required is an atmosphere where such personal rewards can be obtained by doing what is required to satisfy organizational and project goals.

To make projects effective, it is necessary to examine project work,
project workers, and project working. This book focuses on the first of these
and mainly concerns the project work process. Thus we shall take up such
topics as identification of work activities, estimating resources, planning
work, establishing control systems, tracking progress, and assessing work
output.

The creation of an effective work process is a prerequisite to successful
project management; and insofar as project managers are concerned with the
project work process, this book deals with management subjects. However,
we do not focus on project workers, therefore we do not discuss job structuring, employee evaluation, motivation, compensation, informal communication, and similar topics. Also, we are not primarily concerned with the working process, so we do not discuss techniques for better design, coding, testing,
and so on.

In the pages to follow, we shall develop a general project process and
methodology that can be adapted to most projects and most organizations.
This is developed with the typical DP application project in mind, but the
basic underlying concepts are applicable to any project, from writing a term
paper to landing a man on the moon. The methodology developed will help
managers to make work productive by calling for clear project specifications,
improved work procedures, and effective plans and controls. It will help to

make workers achieving by calling for well-defined jobs and improved project communications.

1-5 FORMAL PROJECT METHODOLOGY

A project is a formally established, single-time work effort with the following characteristics:

An established beginning or start date
A well-defined purpose and scope
A formally established, documented cost-benefit basis
A well-defined project product, including product performance criteria
Well-defined project completion criteria
An established endpoint or completion date

A project is established to produce some product or deliverable. Because of the complexity of the typical product, a rather elaborate process must be established to produce it. The distinction between the final product and the production process seems clear and one that is easily made, but experience shows otherwise. Because the two get confused, an example will help to highlight the difference.

Consider the project of building a house. This involves deciding on the location and type of house required, the design of the house, and actual construction. All of these work activities have to do with the actual product—the house. It is work that must be done whether the house is custom-built or mass produced in a factory and assembled on-site. But there is other work that must be done, too. It is necessary to hire workers, plan the order of work, make work assignments, and track work progress—all of this has to do with the process of construction. Although it is work that must be done, it does not contribute directly to the deliverable. Instead, it is work that has to do with the process used to build the deliverable.

In the same way, DP projects involve writing specifications, designing, coding, testing, documenting, and other activities that are directly related to building the project product. But a project involves other tasks that have to do with the process used to produce the product: planning, controlling, estimating, hiring, assigning work, and so on. The latter activities are sometimes described as those that have to do with the system used to build the system being delivered.

A project methodology has to do with the process used to build the deliverable; it concerns the way one plans, estimates, controls, etc. Since a methodology will be developed in this book, we should define more formally what is meant by the term.

A *methodology* is a formal collection of explicit or referenced principles, policies, methods, procedures, practices, and definitions detailing how something is to be accomplished and specifying how this defined process interfaces with related processes. Thus, a project methodology states how an organization's DP projects will be accomplished and specifies the interfaces with other organizational groups and systems, such as general management, accounting, internal audit, personnel, DP operations, and user organizations.

A procedure will be described as *formal* if it has been established by an organization and transmitted in writing. Thus a formal DP project methodology is a written statement about how projects are to be conducted.

In recent years, many organizations, both large and small, public and private, have established formal methodologies for their DP projects. These vary greatly in detail, but they are similar in basic features and resemble the methodology presented here. Among the benefits of such a formal project methodology are:

Aids in project selection

Allows phased commitment of resources, thereby helping to control risk

Involves management in critical decisions by specifying approval points

Promotes communication by standardizing procedures and terminology

Facilitates cost accounting and financial reporting

Causes necessary documentation to be created during the process, not after the fact

Improves product quality by specifying reviews and enforcing standards

Cuts costs by standardizing the production process

Involves users in a formal way

Facilitates proper data collection

Provides a rational basis for estimating by enabling project-to-project comparisons

Enables management and control of projects

In short, a formal project methodology is beneficial because it increases productivity and helps to ensure product quality.

One large pharmaceutical house reported a 75% reduction in project development costs as a result of installing a formal project methodology.

A large software development organization reported that as a result of following a formal project methodology over 95% of their projects in a given year were completed on time, within budget, and meeting specifications.

Of course the benefits are not always as dramatic as in these two examples, but in most organizations they are substantial. The larger the project, the more compelling the argument for a formal methodology. And even if improved productivity and quality were not reason enough, the growing requirements for security and auditability make such an approach to project management essential.

1-6 THE SYSTEM LIFE CYCLE

Although the project is the main focus of this book, we must recognize that it is only one step in a complex process. Before a project is started, work must be done to establish need and set priorities. After a project is completed, the project product, also referred to as a *system,* must be used and evaluated. Figure 1-1 shows the major stages in the complete life cycle of a DP system. Let us review these stages so we can fix some of the ideas and terms that will be used throughout the book.

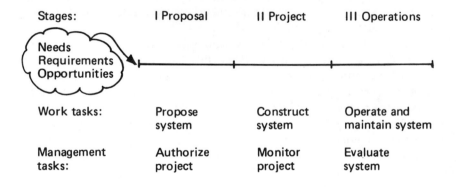

Figure 1-1. Stages in the system life cycle

The first major stage for a system is the Proposal Stage. During this period, needs, requirements, and opportunities for DP services are identified. This is done by various groups, including Business Opportunity Analysis, end users, and the DP Department. Ideas for proposed systems are documented and submitted to a management committee. We shall call this group the *Project Selection Committee,* but it is variously known as the Management Committee, the Automation Committee, or the Review Committee.

The Project Selection Committee must evaluate all proposals for DP services. This committee must select those proposals that are to be imple-

mented and must assign each accepted proposal a priority. In keeping with organization resources, the Project Selection Committee funds specific proposals and authorizes work to start. This action marks the end of the Proposal Stage and the start of the next stage for each authorized system.

The second major stage for a system is called the Project Stage. The major work task in this period is the construction of the proposed system. The major management task is the monitoring of the project. This is done to determine if work is progressing satisfactorily and to judge if continuation of the project is in the best interest of the organization. The Project Stage comes to an end when the developed, tested, and approved system has been installed and is operational.

The third stage of a system is the Operation Stage. The first two stages mainly involve cost; the third stage is the period when the organization benefits from the system by using it to do productive work.

From the view of developers, the main task in the Operations Stage is maintenance (repair and enhancement) of the system. The primary management task is the continual evaluation of the system during operations to determine if the system meets specified requirements and if there is a need for major revision, replacement, or withdrawal of the system. The end of the Operation Stage is marked by the withdrawal of the system or by its replacement by a successor system.

The entire set of stages for a system is often referred to as the *system life cycle* to acknowledge the fact that this "cradle to grave" process is repeated from system to system. In the same way, the steps of the Project Stage is referred to as the *project life cycle,* and those of the Operation Stage as the *operation and maintenance life cycle.*

Each stage of a system requires an appropriate methodology—that is, a collection of principles, policies, methods, procedures, practices, and definitions relating to the work of that stage. In this book, we are concerned mainly with a methodology for the Project Stage, and this will be developed in detail. The methodology for the Proposal and Operation Stages will be touched on lightly in Chapter 9.

1-7 SUMMARY

- A project is a single-time effort used to produce a process or a unique product.
- DP products promise to increase in size and complexity, and they will face increased demands for reliability from all sectors of the organization.
- The increased demands made on DP products underscore the need

for effective means to manage the development effort.

- A formal project methodology helps management with the task of making project work productive and workers achieving.
- The need for more formal project procedures is, in part, a natural outcome of the maturity of data processing.
- The DP project, which is the main focus of this book, is only one of three steps in a complex process that starts with the proposal of a system and ends with its operation.

2

FORMAL PLANNING

2-1 INTRODUCTION

If we had to say in one word what this book is about it would be: Planning. It is about achieving project results on purpose rather than by accident.

The contrast between a planned project and a "happening" can be illustrated by considering two different ways of building a house. One approach is to hire a carpenter and put him to work. He makes decisions and orders supplies as the need arises, and the owner checks periodically to see if his dream is being realized. As misunderstandings surface, bits of work have to be torn out and redone. Some problems don't get spotted early enough, and then the owner has the difficult choice of making a costly revision or living with a mistake. Eventually the project converges on a compromise dictated by economic reality and the desire to see no more of the workers.

Of course, the other way to build is to precede construction work with detailed planning. This generally doesn't prevent all headaches, but it does help to minimize misunderstanding, cuts down on actual construction time, and is more likely to result in a project that fulfills the owner's expectations. The cost of planning, which is an added activity under this mode of operation, is usually saved many times over through elimination of rework and wasteful idle time.

The analogy between constructing a building and constructing a DP system is a helpful one to keep in mind as you read this book. In particular, the contrast between building a house with and without plans illustrates quite clearly the difference between building a DP system by following a clear, formal methodology and by doing it in the old-fashioned way. As we introduce other ideas that may seem new for DP, try to think of them as they

15

might apply to engineering or construction, and you will probably recognize that many have been common practice in those areas for years. Incidentally, none of the ideas discussed in this book is completely new—all have been used successfully for years by some DP shops. What we are attempting to do is to bring these ideas together and coordinate them to give everyone an opportunity to learn what we believe to be the best of current practice.

Since this book is about DP project planning, we start by discussing planning in general. In this chapter we discuss what planning is and what it is not. We review briefly the general concept of a plan and how planning is practiced in organizations. Then we relate these general concepts to planning in the DP area and to planning of DP projects.

2-2 PLANNING AND PLANS

Every organization plans to some extent, but not all of them plan in a formal way. A *formal* planning procedure is one that is

A written procedure
A procedure that is uniformly and regularly applied
A procedure that calls for written output

Hereafter when we use the term planning, it is formal planning that we have in mind.

Planning is a process that starts with a mission, fixes goals and objectives to be reached, develops plans and procedures for reaching them, establishes an organization for achieving this, and assigns responsibility and accountability to see that it is done. It is an iterative process cycling between goals on the one hand and resources on the other, between what one wants to do and what one is able to do.

The output of the planning process is a *plan.* Note that we say *a* plan rather than *the* plan because there are many suitable ways to attain a given set of objectives. For a plan to be meaningful, it must result in work. As work is performed, it is monitored by the control system and progress is compared to plan. Thus the planning process meets the control process through work. Planning is a continuous process, not just a one-time effort. If the control system signals a problem, it is often necessary to adjust plans to the new reality.

Planning is a decision-making process. As you plan, you are deciding what should be done and, by the same token, what should not be done. Planning is very hard work. In fact, planning is one of the most difficult and complex mental tasks that a person undertakes. Because it involves making innumerable and difficult choices, planning cannot be left to underlings, but must engage those individuals with the responsibility for implementation and results.

Planning is a major management function. This is true for all levels from project management to top management. If anything, its importance is increasing because of the complexity of most undertakings and the time required to accomplish them. Also, the huge impact most undertakings have on the entire organization dictates that every effort be made to accomplish them successfully.

To understand what planning is, we might look at some of the things it is not. It is not predicting. That is, it is not a statement about what *will* take place; rather it is a statement about what we *want* to take place. A plan is like a route laid out on a map; it shows where we want to go, but it is not a prediction that we will definitely get there. Like a well-marked route, we have confidence that if we follow the plan we will end up where we want to be, but we recognize that we may encounter unmarked detours on the way.

Planning is also not an attempt to eliminate risk. With or without a plan, there are unforeseen events that can plague any project. Planning cannot prevent these, but it can help to reduce their impact and to control risk.

Planning is not a process of making future decisions, of crossing one's bridges before coming to them. Rather it is a matter of assessing the future impact of present decisions. As events unfold, it will be necessary to make fresh decisions, and these result in new plans. Planning amounts to a careful assessment of the impact of decisions before they are made.

The success of a DP project depends to a large extent on the quality of the planning that goes into the project. And there is no question about the fact that successful project planning can best be achieved in an organization whose atmosphere is conducive to this activity. Project planning requires support from upper management and other organizational areas, and the entire effort will be frustrated when this support is lacking. Because projects interface with so many functional and organizational areas, project planners need outside backing to coordinate all project activities. Also, planning procedures should be consistent from project to project, and this cannot be achieved without proper help from upper management. Unfortunately, it is not uncommon to find people who would like to plan their projects properly but who are stymied by lack of support from above. These people face a slow, frustrating, up-hill battle to install planning, but their success can have a major impact by setting an example for other areas to follow.

Just as project planners need upper management support, so must the project planners understand the requirements of upper management and the type of planning that goes on in other organizational areas. Project plans must mesh with other organizational plans, and this can be achieved only if project management is aware of what is going on outside their area.

Recently there has surfaced another important reason for people in DP to have an understanding of general planning. Many organizations are building information systems to support their planning efforts, and frequently these systems are designed by DP personnel. Effective design obviously requires that these designers have some familiarity with the planning process.

Fortunately, project planning is not fundamentally different from general organizational planning. The details differ, but the basic content of a good project plan is the same as the content of, say, an organization's five-year plan. Because all organizational plans are fundamentally the same and because it is important for project planners to understand the total planning picture, a quick review of general planning will serve as an introduction to project planning.

2-3 CONTENTS OF A PLAN

A general plan for any organization is a comprehensive document, and its parts can be grouped in many different ways. It is convenient to discuss the parts of a general plan under the following six headings.

1. Identity and mission. Every general plan should have statements describing the identity and basic mission of the organization. These answer such questions as: Who are we? What business are we in or what is our purpose? Basically, how should we operate? The statements of identity and mission are usually supported by basic policy statements for the organization. These policies cover many aspects, but five are of paramount interest in connection with DP systems, namely, the policies on quality, data, privacy, security, and audit. Examples of these five policies are given in Appendix C, together with a sample of a modern mission statement for a DP Department.

2. Ends. The next part of a general plan is a statement of the goals and objectives, of what is to be accomplished by the organization. A comprehensive plan would have goals and objectives for the organization as a whole, for divisions, departments, groups, and for individuals. Goals and objectives for these different levels must be consistent and in keeping with the organization's mission. They must be operational and related to the work done at the different levels. Also, the goals and objectives must be such that individuals can relate to them and become committed to them.

The terms "goals" and "objectives" have different meanings to different authors. As we use the terms, an objective is short in range and is a target that is expected to be met. It is usually quantitative so that actual performance can be measured and compared to the objective. Objectives can be considered as steps toward the achievement of goals.

Goals provide direction and guidance to the organization rather than specific objectives. Because of this, they are often descriptive or qualitative rather than quantitative. Goals are long in range; in fact, they are often modified before being reached. Goals flow from the mission statement. They help to concentrate the efforts of the organization and to keep the entire group pulling together.

A comprehensive plan for an organization would have goals and objectives in each major area, including:

Marketing
Innovation
Human resources
Physical plant and resources
Financial resources
Productivity
Social responsibility
Profitability

Goals and objectives for these areas must be coordinated so as to be consistent and nonconflicting. Setting such goals and objectives is no small task, but it is essential if the organization is to survive.

3. Means. Another part of a plan is to tell how goals and objectives are to be met. This amounts to a description of the continuing efforts and single-time efforts designed to bring about these ends.

A continuing effort is a routine designed to meet certain objectives. Often it is related to current products or procedures, and it is likely to continue for some time without major change. Frequently, continuing efforts are the current source of cash and profits for the organization.

A single-time effort or project is work designed to bring about change. It is directed toward goals and objectives that involve renewal and new direction. Single-time efforts are usually a cost to the organization, but are necessary as a means of building revenue-producing programs for the future.

4. Resources. To implement efforts, an organization requires resources of money, people, equipment, time, and so on. A plan should contain a statement of the resources required over time, and an indication of where these resources are to come from and how they are to be allocated to meet requirements.

5. Action plans. Detailed plans of various kinds are necessary to convert plans to controlled action. These detailed plans consist of schedules, budgets, assignments, procedures, and so on.

6. Reaction plans. A general plan includes a means for controlling organizational work to keep all efforts according to plan. This includes a means for data gathering and evaluation and the necessary procedures for re-planning to correct for omissions, changes, and problems of various kinds.

2-4 ORGANIZATIONAL PLANNING

These are the basic parts that a plan should contain, which exist, in varying degrees, in all good plans. But a plan is not a static document. It is always subject to change and modification in light of new information. Therefore, important as it is to have a comprehensive plan, it is equally im-portant to have a planning process or procedure and a knowledgeable group of people to carry out this procedure on an iterative basis.

The planning process, like any other organizational activity, must be directed and managed. There is no standard structure for doing this, but there are some general guidelines that help to promote success. It is impor-tant that the planning group not be autonomous and isolated from the busi-ness of the organization. Establishment of a separate planning group that works in isolation and submits its results for management approval is a sure way to disaster. Worse yet is to have a group of outside experts do the planning. Planning cannot be done *for* an organization, it must be done *by* it. It is important that the planning group involve managers and specialists as well as planners, and that they maintain continuous contact with the areas for which they are planning.

It is important, too, that the planning group report to some person with authority for carrying out the plan. Otherwise the plan lacks credibility or becomes distorted under the influence of the functional area to which the planning group does report. The planning group should be established in such a way that planning is a continual process, not just an occasional activity. This is not an easy requirement to meet because some members of the plan-ning group will be managers with other responsibilities, but it is nevertheless important.

For a successful planning effort, every member of the organization, and particularly every manager, should know the purpose and nature of planning. They should understand that it is part of the job of every professional. The person who is least likely to understand this is not the top executive or even the project leader—it is the project worker. Until they stop to think about it, most professional workers do not realize that planning and control of work are part of their jobs. They think that all of the previous discussion about plans and planning is only for the boss and those above. But individual workers must decide on the tasks that must be performed if they are to ac-complish their objective, they must string these tasks into a productive process, they must set a timetable for work units to be completed, and they must control units of work to see that they are accomplished on time and within resource constraints. All of this is planning and control. Admittedly, an individual worker may not formalize his plan into a written document, but all true professionals engage in planning. And the basic components of an individual's plan are exactly the same as those listed above for any organizational unit.

(While we are discussing individuals, let us briefly depart from the main topic of this book to address the question: If planning works well for organizations, why doesn't it also work well for individuals in their personal lives? The answer is that it does. At present most individuals run their careers in the same way that projects were run in the past—vague objectives, no clear concept of requirements, attention to certain details and neglect of others, and a general drift toward what one hopes will be a successful result. An alternative approach is to develop a personal plan—a formal, written document for one's career. The components of such a plan are just those that are listed above, starting with identity and mission and ending with reaction plans for feedback and control. In a gathering of fellow professionals you will find that a very small percent—less than 5% of the typical group of DP project workers—have such personal plans. But those that do have them are usually enthusiastic; this is something for you to think about.)

2-5 PROJECT PLANNING

The parts of a plan for a DP project parallel those of a general plan as follows:

General Plan	Project Plan
Identity and mission	Project purpose and scope
Ends	Project objectives and management goals
Means	The controlled, stable project process
Resources	Money, people, equipment, time, . . .
Action plans	Networks, schedules, budgets, test plans, conversion plans, work assignments, . . .
Reaction plans	Contingency plans, data gathering, reporting, replanning, . . .

Throughout the book various tools used in producing the parts of a project plan will be discussed.

An organization should have two types of plans: standing plans and single-use plans. *Standing plans* are for recurrent situations; an example would be standards for performing a given task. *Single-use plans,* as the name suggests, are for a specific situation. The relationship among standing plans, single-use plans, and project products is illustrated in Figure 2-1.

A formal project methodology is a standing plan for all projects within an organization. It describes the tasks and procedures required to do any project. To accomplish a particular project, it is necessary for project management to use the standing project methodology as a guide and to build a single-use plan meeting the requirements of the particular project. The resulting project plan, therefore, can be viewed as a blueprint for a particular project that has been constructed according to the standards spelled out in the formal project methodology. Use of a formal project methodology helps to simplify the construction of plans for particular projects; instead of "reinventing the wheel" for each project, it provides a starting point for project planning. This helps to ensure the completeness of these plans, and it provides a standard framework that makes project-to-project comparison possible.

2-6 PROS AND CONS OF PLANNING

This book is about project planning, and we would not be writing it if everyone were doing a good job of it at the present time. But it must be acknowledged that this is not the case; in fact, there is considerable hostility to planning in some quarters. Among the reasons usually given for *not* planning are:

> "It takes too much time. We're too busy with our current crisis to spend a lot of time on planning."

> "Planning is too expensive. We don't have the resources to waste on all this peripheral activity, but must put our manpower on the major project activities."

> "Planning doesn't allow flexibility. Our situation is dynamic and we can't be locked into a static pattern. It's much more important to keep one's options open."

> "Plans are always based on unreliable assumptions. Just as soon as the assumptions fail, the plan is useless and all the effort spent on it is wasted."

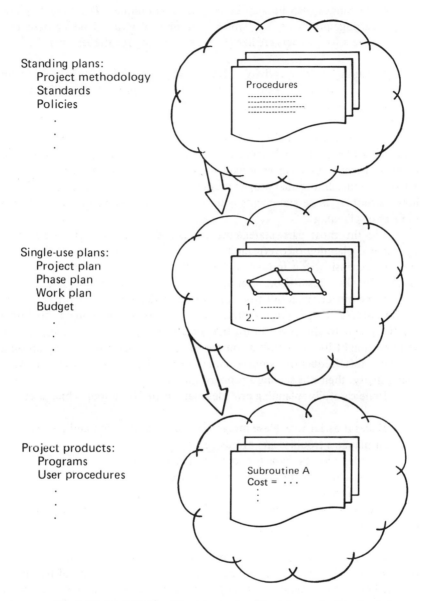

Standing plans:
    Project methodology
    Standards
    Policies

Procedures

Single-use plans:
    Project plan
    Phase plan
    Work plan
    Budget

1. --------
2. ------

Project products:
    Programs
    User procedures

Subroutine A
Cost = · · ·

Figure 2-1. Relationship among standing plans, single-use plans,
and the project products

"One cannot plan because every project is unique. There are very few recurring problems for which standing plans can be constructed. Planners for projects are like generals preparing for the last war."

"Planning stifles creativity. Design and programming are more art than science. Planning keeps people in a box and prevents them from finding the best way to build the system."

Each of us, no doubt, can add to this list because we have all heard statements like these. It's important to know the various reasons for not planning because you are very likely to encounter some of them when you attempt to install a formal project methodology. It's also important to know how to counter these statements and to be able to give convincing arguments in favor of planning.

For the most part, statements against planning are really statements against bad planning or overplanning. There is no question that some plans are too expensive, too inflexible, too stifling, and take too much time to create. But these result from a misapplication of planning principles.

Some objections result from a failure to understand the realities and objectives of planning. For example, one purpose of planning *is* to bridle creativity and to direct it toward the goals of the project. Although a programmer might like to polish a routine or find a novel way to accomplish a function, this frequently is not a requirement. If planning helps to prevent such activity, then it is serving a proper function.

Done carefully, planning provides many benefits, among which are:

Makes it easier to achieve integrated, purposeful action and results
Anticipates troubles and avoids delays
Provides a logical basis for coordination and control
Helps achieve economy and avoids rework
Facilitates management
Encourages development of sound individual goals and objectives
Helps to assure quality project products

In the final analysis, the test of whether planning is worthwhile or not is the same as the test that should be applied to any expenditure of resources: Do the benefits sufficiently outweigh the costs? As with many other aspects of a project, the use of planning is dysfunctional at both extremes—too little planning is not good and too much planning is not good. Just how much is useful and just which tools are most effective are highly dependent on the organization. No two shops are the same, and no two have the same planning requirements. You can evolve what is best for your organization by introducing innovations and by carefully measuring the costs and benefits that result.

2-7 SUMMARY

- The basic theme of this book is that project success is linked with effective formal project planning.
- Project planning is similar to general organizational planning, and a project plan has the same basic components as a general plan for an organization.
- The components of any plan can be grouped into: identity and mission, ends, means, resources, action plans, and reaction plans.
- Project leaders must understand the planning process to guide their projects and to know how project plans fit into general organizational plans. As an added benefit, they will find that this understanding helps them in making their own personal plans.
- Objections to planning usually are reactions to bad planning or overplanning, but these objections must be understood if they are to be overcome.

CONTROL OF WORK

3-1 INTRODUCTION

Proper project control is vital if the project purpose is to be accomplished. The design and operation of an effective control system is a nontrivial undertaking. One part of such a system is a mechanism for the collection and distribution of the information required for control, and the construction of this mechanism can be a significant development project in its own right. Frequently such mechanisms are computerized. Some organizations have spent many man-years building software packages for project control, and there are dozens of proprietary packages on the market that are designed for this purpose. Unfortunately, however, the emphasis in building or installing such a system is too often on the mechanics of control. A great deal of effort is put into the details of design without ever taking a hard look at the fundamentals of control.

Before building or installing a control system it is essential to understand the basic concepts of control. What is control? What is controlled? How is it controlled? What are the components of a control system? What does control cost? In this chapter fundamental questions such as these will be explored. Then in Chapters 4 and 5 we shall see how control principles are applied to a project.

3-2 FUNDAMENTALS OF CONTROL

Modern organizations have inherited a number of terms from the past that confuse, mislead, or rile many people. *Manager* and *manpower* sound chauvinistic to many ears. *Workers* suggest that its counterpart, managers, do not work. But the most misleading term in common usage is *control*. The problem with this word is that it has many meanings, most of which are at odds with the way it is used in describing an aspect of managing work.

The word control can refer to power, as when one is in control of a political party. Closely related is the meaning of authority, command, or domination; Hitler held control over continental Europe during most of World War II. Another meaning of control is to restrain, to curb, to discipline, or to confine; this is what we have in mind when we speak of flood control or the control of a team of horses. These various meanings differ somewhat, but there is a common thread running through them all: They all suggest something or someone being held by a strong force.

There is another meaning of control, however, and that is to guide or to steer. An automatic pilot can be used to control an airplane; a thermostat controls the temperature in a room; feedback control and process control are standard engineering concepts. This meaning of control has to do with following a prescribed course toward some objective.

The notion of guidance, of following a prescribed course, is the meaning of control that we have in mind when we speak of an organizational control system. Unfortunately, however, the other meanings of control often interfere with a clear understanding of this concept. Because control means domination or restraint to many people, there is a tendency to build control systems that reflect these meanings. Features are installed that have more to do with keeping the workers in line than with getting the work done; this results in control systems that act more as constraining forces than as guidance mechanisms. Quite often such features are counterproductive, and then the control system fails to meet its basic objective of helping to make work productive. To correct for this failure, more constraints are added to the system; the result is a more costly but less effective control system and even less productive work. If repeated, this spiral of more constraint and less productivity can lead to real disaster.

Because there is so much confusion in this area, let us begin our discussion of control and control systems by reviewing seven fundamental principles that underlie these concepts. These fundamentals will be stated in a general way to stress the fact that they apply to any work process. Later we shall see how they apply to the DP project, but you might like to reflect on that question as you read along.

1. Work Controlled

Work is controlled—not workers. The first and most fundamental principle of control is that one controls work, not workers. The objective is to get the work done, not to make the workers toe the line. It is easy to see how these objectives were confused back in the days when most work involved simple, mechanical tasks. If a worker could dig a ditch at the rate of two feet an hour, then the way to have twenty feet dug in a day was to make sure that the worker put in an honest ten-hour day. A time clock and an overseer for the worker indirectly controlled the true objective: completed work.

This confusion between controlling work and controlling workers is still with us today. Many organizations strictly enforce office hours for all DP personnel (quite irrespective of how much unpaid overtime is worked), and many strictly prescribe the number and duration of coffee breaks. Until very recently, the keypunch operators in one organization could not leave their stations without a supervisor's approval; as they walked around they had to carry paddle boards containing a notice to the effect that they had permission to be outside their area. Interestingly enough, some restrictive control standards are imposed on DP organizations by the workers themselves through their organized labor unions, which attempt to bring shop controls (with which they are familiar) into the office environment.

Probably the confusion between controlling work and controlling workers has always caused problems, but there is no question about the effect it has today. This is particularly true with knowledge workers, which includes the people in data processing. Attempts to constrain and regiment knowledge workers generally lead to resentment and an atmosphere that stifles creativity—just the opposite of what is required. What one is striving for is an atmosphere where workers can be productive. Control should be viewed as a tool that a worker can use to work more effectively and efficiently. It is a tool to control his work, not him.

2. Completed Work

Control is based on completed work. To determine if any work process is achieving its objectives, it is necessary to look at the product that is produced. To determine if a bottle-forming machine is functioning properly, one looks at the number and quality of bottles being made. To determine if an airplane is flying along the proper path, the position of the plane is checked. In the same way, the control of any work process is based on feedback from completed work.

For a complex work activity, this principle does not mean that one waits until the entire activity is completed and then looks to see if the result is satisfactory. Instead, it is necessary to subdivide the complex activity into a number of small tasks and to apply the principle to each task. This means that each task must have a well-defined output, and there must be standards for judging the completed work.

The job of dividing a complex activity into a number of small tasks is not an easy one. Often it is difficult to define the small tasks in such a way that each has a definite output. In such situations there is a temptation to structure tasks so that the output is not completed work, but an *estimate* of completed work. This is definitely not the same thing. It is one thing to produce a specified report, it is another thing to do one-half the coding of a particular module. The object of a work activity is to produce a product, not an estimated fraction of a product. A system built on control from estimates fails to focus on the true objective.

Feedback information is required on both quantitative and qualitative aspects of completed work. It is not enough to know that a process is forming 100 bottles a minute, we must also know that the bottles are of acceptable quality. One can usually measure the amount of resource used by a work process and the time the work effort takes, and so it is relatively easy to control these aspects of work. The quality of an output presents a more difficult challenge. Certain aspects of quality can be measured, and most would agree that the more falling into this category the better. But nonmeasurable aspects cannot be ignored, and a control system must have a means of checking on these aspects of completed work, too.

3. Motivation and Self-Control

Control of complex work is based on motivation and self-control. For a complex work activity, the range of response to control signals is so great that it cannot be preprogrammed. There is no mechanical system that can cope adequately, therefore control must be exercised by some person. Basically, there are two choices: Either control is exercised by the person who does the work, or it is exercised by someone else.

Control of work by someone other than the worker presents many serious problems. The control process is complicated by the need for communication and coordination between the controller and the worker. There is a real danger that the effort will degenerate into control of the worker rather than the work, or at least there is danger of it being viewed this way by the worker. Such a view can lead to stifling of creativity and can otherwise hamper the worker's effort. One more problem is that an outside controller has a difficult time knowing the complex work process well enough to put in reasonable checkpoints for assessing progress and to make sensible adjustments as required. Another way to put this is that the person who knows the work effort best is the one who does it. The worker is in the best position to establish a reasonable course to follow, he is the first to sense deviations from what is expected, and he can make adjustments much more quickly than an outsider can. All of these facts point to the conclusion that self-control by workers is by far the most reasonable system for a complex work process, particularly one involving knowledge workers.

To illustrate this concept of self-control, consider the activity of coding and testing a module that might result in, say, 40 lines of code. The individual to whom this is assigned has a deadline for the completed task. To meet this, he must decide how much time to allocate to the design of logic, to coding, to testing, and to documentation. Then he must keep track of his progress and adjust his effort so as to complete the activity on time. In effect, he controls his own work effort. He probably does not do this in a formal, written way, but nevertheless the control function is part of his job.

We do not mean this example to suggest that self-control is restricted to the worker level. Individuals at all levels of an organization have work assignments, and self-control of work applies at all levels. For example, part of the work of a Project Manager of a DP project might be to produce a project plan. To do this he must pace his activity so as to produce a plan of acceptable quality at the proper time—that is, he must control his own work. (We might note that a formal project methodology provides a standard for assessing the quality of his work product—the project plan.)

Self-control is part of the job of every knowledge worker—it is one of the things he is paid to do. This fact is not recognized widely enough, partly because it is rarely written into the job description. As we did above, it is customary to say that the job is to code and test a certain module; hardly ever is it stated that the job is to code and test a module *and* to control the work. Is it any wonder that some workers believe that control is somebody else's problem? One way to improve the control of any complex activity is to state clearly that work control is part of each job. Most knowledge workers would intuitively understand this concept and would welcome the open acknowledgment of their control responsibilities. Moreover, emphasis on control at the level of the individual helps to promote understanding and appreciation of the overall control system.

Worker and management awareness that self-control is part of each job is an important step toward an effective control system, but it certainly is not the only step. As with any other aspect of the job, self-control functions best when the worker is motivated and has the desire to make it successful. Certainly it is necessary to have proper procedures, standards, and other formalities, but the most important part of any control system is the people. The best set of control procedures in the world won't work well unless the people involved are motivated to make it work. By its nature, this book tends to focus on the mechanical aspects of control. In doing so, we do not mean to suggest that this is all there is to it. Quite the contrary, the entire topic of motivation and human engineering of control systems is so vast and so important that a discussion would take us far outside the scope of our effort.

4. Capturing Control Data

Controls for capturing control data must be built into the work process. For control it is necessary to gather data concerning aspects of completed work. We cannot judge whether or not a bottle-forming machine is producing at the proper rate and quality unless we first gather data about the output of the process. Various mechanisms or *controls* are needed to capture control data, and the act of gathering the data is itself a work activity. In order to capture control data, these controls and their operation must be built into the work process.

Because the operation of controls adds an additional burden to the work effort, controls should be designed so as to interfere with work as little as possible. In particular, care should be taken to capture only data that is required for control. It should be captured in the simplest practical manner, and should be captured only once except in very unusual circumstances.

Many people equate controls with forms and reports. For most projects these are an important means of data capture; but data, particularly on qualitative aspects of work, is also captured through inspection, consultation, review, and other judgmental processes. It is just as important to have these mechanisms in the work process as the more standard controls such as time cards and machine logs.

Many workers look upon controls as a nonproductive overhead that only interferes with the major work effort. Because of this attitude, it is important that controls be human engineered so as to minimize adverse reaction to them.

5. Distributing Control Data

Control data must go to the person who does the work. If our object is to control work, then control data must be related to the work process if it is to have an impact. This means that control data must go to the person who actually does the work.

Consider the example of a pilot who is flying an airplane. Suppose that at some point in time the location of the plane is determined, this is compared to the flight plan, and a calculation is made to ascertain the deviation from course and the adjustment required to get back on course. Now suppose that this control data is given not to the pilot but to his manager. It doesn't make sense, does it? But the equivalent of this is common practice in many organizations.

It is not uncommon for a worker to receive little or no control data concerning his work effort. As far as the impact that data can have on his work, there might as well not be a control system. This lack of data could be ascribed to a faulty control system design, but more often it stems from the failure to realize that workers must control their own work. On the other hand, it is not uncommon for a manager to receive more control data than he can possibly use, including all of the data relating to the work of his people. The idea here probably is that the manager needs this data to control his subordinates and to evaluate them. Thus the work control system becomes confused with the employee evaluation system.

6. Routine Controlled

A control system is designed for the routine. A thermostatic control system for regulating the temperature in a room is designed to control the running of the furnace. If the temperature varies too much, the thermostat can turn the furnace on or off. However, it cannot make adjustments for a dry boiler, an exhausted fuel supply, a broken pipe, a clogged chimney, or a failure in the electric supply that powers the thermostat. It cannot control for these extreme events because it was not built for this purpose. It was built to handle the routine hour-by-hour task of turning the furnace on and off, and the extreme events must be handled by other means. This example illustrates the next fundamental principle: A control system is designed to cope with the routine; exceptions must be given special handling.

This principle is familiar to those who design computer systems. Usually the effective approach is to design a system to handle the bulk of routine situations and to allow for exceptions to be handled outside the system. An effective procedure can be constructed for coping with ordinary variation, but a system that attempts to handle everything is never completed—there is always something new that has to be considered.

To build an effective control system, it is necessary to decide what is routine and what is not, what is to be handled by the system and what is to be tagged for special treatment. What is routine depends on the range of response that can be made to control data; it depends on the scope of action and the authority of the worker using the data.

A worker needs three things from management to control his work: a clearly defined assignment or objective, control data regarding his work effort, and a statement of his authorized range of response to this control data. Let us illustrate this last requirement.

Suppose that the task of coding and testing a certain module is assigned to a worker. If minor adjustments in his work plan must be made to accommodate changes in machine availability or interference from outside the project, the worker can be expected to make them. If, on the other hand, he uncovers a design flaw that significantly increases the scope of his assignment, he probably does not have the authority to add resources to his effort or to alter his completion date. For him this is an exception that must be passed to others for handling.

We can now see that self-control by the worker does not mean that he is the only one who is concerned with controlling the work. Rather it is that he controls the work within an authorized range of response. Exceptions that fall outside his authority are passed to others. There are two important points here. First, self-control is not an all or nothing affair; it requires a careful analysis of what is routine for the worker and what is not. Second, a procedure must be established for handling exceptions; this leads to our next principle.

7. Levels of Control

Control of a complex work process is achieved through levels of control. An effective control system for a complex work process is built on the notion that there are different levels of control. Each control level has its objectives, its control data requirements, and its range of response to control signals. As one moves up the levels of control, the objectives become broader and more far-reaching and the range of response becomes wider. The need for control data, on the other hand, lessens. This changes from a need for a large amount of detailed data to a need for a small amount of highly aggregated data. Lower levels of control tend to have short-term horizons, upper levels have long ones. Lower levels of control look more at trees, upper levels at the forest.

What is exceptional at one level of control may be routine at the next higher level. This means that only the most pressing control problems find their way to the top level of control.

Levels of control can be illustrated by considering a motor transport company. A driver who is assigned the task of driving a truck from one point to another needs control data about the position of his truck on the road, his speed, the position and the speed of other traffic, weather and lighting conditions, mechanical condition of the truck, and so on. The dispatcher of the company has different control requirements. He is not concerned with the mile-by-mile progress of the truck, but only on the time that it passes key checkpoints and on the time and condition on arrival at the final destination.

The general management of the company has still different control requirements. They are not concerned with individual trips of the truck, but with
the total time the truck is used during the month, average cost per mile, and
so on. A flat tire is probably an exceptional event to the driver. He would
not attempt to respond directly to the exception, but would pass the data to
the dispatcher. The dispatcher's range of response probably allows him to
address the problem by sending a repair truck to the scene. General management's concern about the flat tire would be limited to the effect it had on
fleet down-time and total maintenance cost.

Control of work in an organization is usually related to the organizational structure; that is, the levels of control correspond to the levels of
management. (This is not always the case. For example, the financial department might have control over certain aspects of work and yet not be in the
management chain.) It is often useful to distinguish four general control
levels: workers, supervisors or lower level management, middle management,
and upper management. For a particular work process, such as the process
of implementing an application program, each of these levels has its particular
work assignments and objectives, each has its control requirements, and each
has its range of response to control data. The control system must be such
that these various control objectives and requirements are coordinated and
the correct control data flows to each level.

3-3 COMPONENTS OF A CONTROL SYSTEM

A *control system* is a system for guiding a work process toward some
objective. To understand the components of such a system, it is helpful to
focus on some specific example, for instance, the system used to govern the
speed of a steam engine, or the budgeting mechanism used to control the flow
of funds in an organization, or the system used to control the temperature of
a room. This last example is as simple as any and is familiar to everyone, so
let's look at it. After we have explored this simple system, our observations
can be applied to the examination of a control system for a DP project.

Let us consider a room that is heated by a furnace. Assume the temperature in the room is controlled by means of a thermostat that can turn the
furnace on and off as required. Let us examine, first, the basic work process
and, second, the system used to control it.

The basic work process is to produce heat. As with any work process,
it has certain inputs and outputs. The basic input to the process is fuel, and
the basic output is heat. (We shall ignore other inputs, such as oxygen, and
other outputs, such as exhaust.) The basic work process and its major inputs
and outputs are depicted in Figure 3-1.

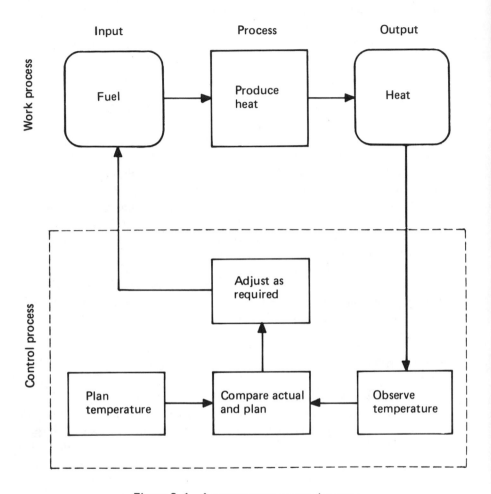

Figure 3-1. A temperature control system

The control system for regulating temperature works as follows. The user of the system decides on the temperature that is desired and sets this on the thermostat. The thermostat records the actual temperature, compares this with the desired temperature, and turns the furnace on or off as required. Thus there are four basic steps to the control system: planning or projecting the temperature that is desired; observing the actual temperature that has resulted from the work process; comparing the actual temperature with planned temperature; and adjusting the process if required. These four components of the control system are depicted in Figure 3-1.

Although Figure 3-1 refers to a specific work process, it illustrates the four basic activities of any control system. The four activities are:

1. Planning performance
2. Observing actual performance
3. Comparing actual and planned performance
4. Adjusting as required

Often the first of these four activities is referred to as *planning,* and the last three are referred to as *controlling.* The planning and controlling activities taken together constitute the control system.

We introduced these four fundamental components of a control system by examining a simple work process because we did not want to obscure the picture with the details of a complex situation. But now that we have the fundamentals in mind, let us see how they apply to a DP project.

3-4 COMPONENTS OF A PROJECT CONTROL SYSTEM

The description of a control system for a project is complicated by three factors: (1) The difficulty of distinguishing between the basic work process and the control process, (2) the concept of self-control, and (3) the various levels of control.

The first factor—to distinguish between the basic work process and the control process—caused no difficulty in our example of a furnace. For a complex work process such as a DP project, the distinction between these two types of tasks blurs. Some examples will illustrate what we mean. Is the activity of testing code a basic work task or a control task? Obviously the reason one tests is to help verify the quality of the program or system being tested. The test does not produce a project deliverable in the same way that designing and coding do, and in that sense it is a control activity. On the other hand, it is a traditional activity on projects and is usually regarded as "part of the job" rather than "overhead," and from this point of view it might be regarded as a basic work task. If we assume that test is a basic work task, then what about the test plan or script for testing? Is the preparation of this a basic work task or are we now into planning, which is part of the control system? And what about preparation of the drivers (for bottom-up development) or stubs (for top-down development)? These are not deliverable products, so how should they be classified? What about the management of change? If you regard this as a control activity, then you must ask

how it differs from product specification during the problem definition stage
of the project.

The second problem in describing a project control system involves the
concept of self-control. If each worker is responsible for controlling his own
work, then every work task is a combination of basic work and control functions. This means that the line between these two types of activities is completely blurred. We can still speak of the control system, but cannot specify
the specific control activities.

The third complication in describing project control has to do with
levels of control. The project control system as viewed by top management
is quite different from that as viewed by the Project Manager. And the system
viewed by a project worker is still different. What might be a basic work task
for one individual is part of the control system for another.

A View of Control

Since it isn't possible to cover everything at once, in this chapter we
shall concentrate on the project control system as viewed by the Project
Manager. This is probably the view that most people have in mind when they
discuss project control systems. In describing a project control system, we
shall generally omit reference to self-control. This is a basic concept, but precisely because it is all pervasive it will not be discussed at every turn. This
means that as far as levels of control are concerned, further discussion in this
chapter of the control system at the worker level will be omitted. Also
omitted is a discussion of control by management above the project level
since this topic is covered in Chapters 4 and 9.

The distinction between basic work tasks on the one hand and planning
and control tasks on the other will be maintained. We believe this is a useful
distinction because it helps to provide a framework for viewing control. Also,
it is a traditional distinction and one that might help some individuals to define their project tasks. As a practical matter, we believe the distinction is
not vital. The classification of a particular activity as a basic or as a control
task is not as important as the fact that there is a conceptual distinction. The
following classification is, therefore, the one we shall use in our discussion.

> Basic tasks include:
>   Specification
>   Analysis
>   Design
>   Coding, including support code
>   Testing, including construction of test plans

     Revision work
     Conversion
     Documentation
     Training
     Site preparation
   Planning and control tasks include:
     Estimating
     Scheduling
     Assigning work
     Tracking and reporting progress
     Reviewing
     Revising plans

   These lists are not complete and cannot be complete until all project work has been listed, but we believe that they convey our point of view. Basic work tasks are those that might be done on a project of any size, even one that is so small that formal planning is minimal. They are tasks that are normally done by the project workers. On the other hand, planning and control tasks tend to be activities that are done by the project leader or by a staff assistant on a large project. They are activities directly relating to directing the project effort.

   Figure 3-2 depicts the project control system and its relation to the basic project activities—the "actual work" of the project. The latter activities are related in an IPO (input, process, output) manner to the inputs of the project (requirements, resources, . . .) and the project deliverables (programs, documentation, . . .). The arrows in the figure indicate the major data flows among the depicted activities.

   Now, let us discuss the four components of the control system: planning, observing, comparing, and adjusting.

Planning

   Planning involves an analysis of work into the tasks that are required to produce the project product and a synthesis of these tasks into a productive work process. It requires estimating the time and resources required for these tasks, assigning and scheduling them, and establishing points at which progress is to be reviewed. Planning involves setting goals for each work activity and coordinating these with the project objective. It is based on the existence of preestablished standards for each piece of work and defined measures by which workers can direct their own effort.

   The planning activity results in the plans, schedules, budgets, and

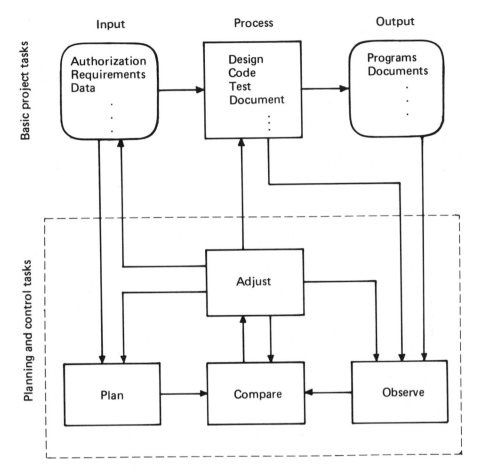

Figure 3-2. A project control system

review points that provide the blueprint for the project. Most of this material will be specific to the particular project for which the planning is being done. However, some planning can be done in a general way and applied across all projects; for example, the division into project phases, networks at a highly aggregated level, and the requirements for various reports.

When people say they have problems with project control, many times the difficulty lies in the failure to do an adequate job of planning. Control is not possible without planning, and it is next to impossible with bad planning.

Because planning and controlling are so closely interrelated, the procedures for performing these functions must be designed in tandem.

Observing

Unlike the simple furnace example discussed earlier, it is not sufficient to control a project by looking at final output. It is necessary to divide such a complex process into a large number of small tasks and to monitor each of these separately. This means that the control system focuses on points within the project as well as on the final project deliverables. We have attempted to indicate this in Figure 3-2 by showing arrows into the "Observe" function from both the "Process" function and the project "Output."

Most observation of actual performance is done by people; the major exception is the mechanical recording of computer runs. Observations are made individually or in review groups. An example of the former is the weekly appraisal by an individual of his work, and an example of the latter is a peer review of a product for quality. Observations of actual performance are reported in such records as time cards, task completion reports, machine logs, progress reports, review reports, and trouble reports. The forms to be used for these reports and the reporting procedure should be standardized so that they can be applied uniformly to all projects.

If there is a general problem in the area of observing project progress, it is probably that too much data is collected rather than too little. In fact, if control problems arise, the typical reaction is to collect more control information and to require more reports. Often this is the wrong direction to take. A more useful approach is to make a careful assessment of what is absolutely essential for control and to avoid the collection of extraneous data. The collection and handling of data is costly, and it must be justified by the usefulness of the information it provides. Moreover, this justification, or at least the need for and use of data, should be explained to the project team. To omit this step may result in unreliable data and an undermining of the control function.

Comparing

The method of comparing actual performance to plan depends on whether or not you are dealing with an aspect of work that can be quantified. For quantifiable aspects, such as elapsed time and resource utilization, comparison is usually made by computing the *variance*. This is the difference between planned performance and actual performance:

$$\text{Variance} = \text{Planned} - \text{Actual.}$$

Certain aspects of work cannot be quantified, or at least we do not have effective means for doing so at present. Many characteristics of quality fall into this category. For nonquantifiable aspects of work, actual performance must be recorded on the basis of judgment, and comparison to plan is made in the same way. Usually judgment is binary: The product is satisfactory or it is not; it meets requirements or it does not. This means that, just as in the previous case, variance for nonquantifiable aspects of work is the difference between plan and actual, except it is not a mathematical difference but a judgment that the product differs from plan or it does not.

An illustration may help to explain the control of nonquantifiable aspects of work. Consider the work of documenting a system. The plan for a piece of this task might call for a document describing a specified part of the system and meeting certain standards. Observation might be done at a review where completeness and quality of the document are examined and recorded. Comparison would amount to judging whether or not the document is complete and meets standards.

The comparison of actual performance to plan is summarized in various reports and charts. Formats of these documents should be standardized and applied from project to project. This not only saves the project team the time required to design forms and reporting procedures, but it also serves other important purposes. Uniform reports make it easier to compare one project to another. This facilitates upper management control in a multi-project environment, and it also helps to make estimates for future projects more reliable.

One mark of a good control system is that comparisons of actual performance to plan are presented to management in an effective way. This means that a proper balance is struck between presenting so much detail that important signals are obscured and presenting so little that important problems are overlooked. And it means that control data is presented in such a way as to convey maximum information without undue effort on the part of the recipient.

Adjusting

The fourth function of a control system is to make adjustments if circumstances require it. For simple systems, this function is accomplished by establishing a prescription to be followed when actual performance deviates from plan. For example, for a heating system the prescription is that the system is turned on if the temperature falls below a certain minimum, and it is turned off if the temperature rises above this point. This type of control is not possible for systems as complex as a DP development project. Here it is necessary to resort to what in cybernetics, which is the science of control, is termed *implicit control*: Instead of prescribing the control procedure for every possible situation, arrangements are made to ensure that an appropriate reaction can be found to situations that arise. As a practical matter, this means that the responsibility for reaction must be lodged with some individual, and it is up to that person to make necessary adjustments.

To determine whether or not an adjustment should be made, variance of actual to plan is compared with a predetermined standard. If the variance is excessive, then a response is required. The action that is taken depends on the authority and range of response of the individual having responsibility for the work. If his range of response does not permit him to address the problem properly, a signal is sent up the line until a level of control is reached that can handle the problem. For example, a programmer might be allowed a one-day leeway to complete his work effort; if it goes beyond that, the Project Manager might get in on the act. And a Project Manager might be allowed to slip the project by up to a week, but beyond that his manager becomes involved. And so on up the levels of control.

Adjustments can be made anywhere in the entire system: in the inputs to the project, such as resources or specifications; in the way the basic project activities are performed; in the project plan; or in the control system itself. We have attempted to indicate this in Figure 3-2 by showing arrows from the "Adjust" function to all parts of the system except the final output.

3-5 CHARACTERISTICS OF A PROJECT CONTROL SYSTEM

It is possible to construct a project control system with all of the basic components just described and satisfying all of the fundamental principles listed earlier and still have a dud. This is because the components and fundamentals address only the basic aspects of control systems; they do not address their character or focus. To be effective, a control system must focus on six characteristics.

1. Objectives

A control system must focus on objectives. A control system can be ineffective because it fails to focus on the objectives of the organization. If it misses what is important, it will not do what was intended even if it has all of the "correct" parts and supplies reams of control data.

The designer of a control system must ask: What is important to the organization? What is it attempting to do? Which aspects of work are most important to track and control? What are the critical points in the process where controls should be inserted? The control system should be based on these considerations and trivia should be avoided.

The important is controlled. But it is also true that the controlled is important. If a control system emphasizes budgets, then budgets become the primary concern of all workers. An organization may state that part of a manager's job is to improve people; but if no provision is made to control this task, the manager takes it as a cue that the organization isn't really serious. A common failure of project control systems is to slight the quality of work. The reason for this is fairly clear—quality is much harder to control than time or resource utilization. But whatever the reason, if control of time and resource is stressed, then it is not surprising to find that projects come in on-time and within budget at the expense of product quality.

2. Response

A control system must focus on response. A control system is not useful unless there is an appropriate response to control signals. If control data does not result in action, then the control system is ineffective even if it focuses on the key objectives.

To trigger a proper response, a control system must deliver the right data to the right people, and it must deliver this data in a form that is useful. It does no good to have important data if it is buried in a report and escapes the attention of the worker. To achieve a response, it is necessary to know who is responsible for action, what actions can be taken, what are the control requirements, what controls are needed to meet these requirements, and how control data can best be presented.

3. Timeliness

A control system must focus on timeliness. Not only must control data reach the right person, but it must be timely. There are two aspects to timeliness. First, there should not be a long delay between the collection of data and its presentation to the recipient. A control system that takes forever to generate reports is soon bypassed and falls into disuse.

The second aspect of timeliness is not quite so obvious; it is related to the frequency of reports. Each individual on a project has a time frame within which he operates; that is, he has discretion to work for a certain period of time without delivering a product. The time frame for a programmer might be four to six days, while that of a Project Manager might be three or four weeks. The higher in the level of control, the longer the time frame. To be effective, a control system must be keyed to the time frames of the various individuals. For example, a weekly cycle for routine reports might be reasonable for a programmer, whereas a monthly one might be right for the Project Manager. For the Project Manager to receive real time data might be just as bad as to have a cycle that is too long. Reports containing fresh data and geared to the worker's time frame are most useful.

4. Human Factors

A control system must focus on human factors. A control system is used by people, and it should focus on people. This is a large and extremely important topic, and we shall touch on only a few of the human factors that are involved.

A control system should be easy to use. This means no jargon and no complex procedures. Instructions should be clear and simple. Forms should be kept to a minimum and designed for ease of use. Above all, the system should be designed for the convenience of people, not machines. Data should be collected well and presented well. As an example of the wrong approach, one organization asks workers to complete two weekly reports containing overlapping data; instructions even state that the two reports must agree! Input should be done once and by simple means. Data should be presented in clear, uncluttered reports. Summary reports should be provided and exception reporting used when appropriate.

A control system should be explained to those who use it, particularly to those who must provide data. If workers do not understand the system, they may be suspicious of it. This can lead to circumvention or subtle forms of sabotage, such as insertion of faulty data or late filing of reports. Explaining the system helps to gain worker support, but it can have another positive result: If the workers understand what the control system is designed to do, they may suggest better ways to do it.

5. Flexibility

A control system must focus on flexibility. It is not possible to establish a single procedure that can be used to control all projects because there is such a wide range of control requirements. Requirements differ not only by company size and the size of the DP department, but also by project size, by the character of the project, and by the project organization. A successful control system must be flexible enough to meet these differing requirements.

One way to achieve flexibility is to establish a control system for medium projects, to use only a portion of this system for small projects, and to augment it for large projects. This will be explored in Chapter 6.

A control system must also be flexible over time. Control requirements change as the organization and people change, the control system must also change or it will soon become outmoded. To avoid rigidity, responsibility must be fixed and procedures designed to review the control system periodically and to make necessary modifications.

6. Simplicity

A control system must focus on simplicity. Complex control systems present problems. Some are so bad that they are not used. Others are used, but they are counterproductive because the presence of unnecessary controls promotes an attitude that inhibits control. But the worst problem with complex systems is that they direct attention to the mechanics of the system rather than to work and results, and the outcome is bureaucracy.

Unnecessary controls do not give more control, but they do add to the cost of the control system. Thus unncesssary controls contribute increased costs and decreased benefits.

A control system should be simple. One should strive for the smallest control effort that produces the required result. Each piece of input data and each report should be examined to see if it is necessary. If not, it should be eliminated.

The fact that a control system is simple, however, does not mean that it is small or that the control activity can be accomplished with little time or effort. Indeed, a very common error in DP is to assume that something as complex as the typical project can be managed with a trivial control system. This just cannot be; it requires a substantial control mechanism to control a complex system. Moreover, proper control requires sufficient data to resolve the ambiguities that arise because of random errors in the reporting system, that is, it requires a certain amount of redundancy. All of this means that a significant amount of project resource must be devoted to planning and controlling if the project is to meet its objectives. How much resource is a question we take up next.

3-6 RESOURCES FOR PLANNING AND CONTROL

What percent of the total project effort is expended in the area of planning and control on the typical DP project? The authors have asked this question of hundreds of people from dozens of different DP organizations, and the answers ranged from a low of 0% ("We don't plan at all, we start right in coding") to a high of 50%. The median response was about 15% for an average-size project. Most respondents indicated, however, that they thought their present planning and control efforts were inadequate and that the percent devoted to these activities should be larger.

The effort devoted to planning and control depends on project size, of course. For very large projects, with correspondingly more people and interactions, it is necessary to increase the percent of effort devoted to these activities, and it is not unreasonable to spend 30% of the total effort in this area. But for very small projects, too, the percent of time spent on planning and control can rise above the average because, although the basic work activity is not large, certain irreducible minimum of planning and control is required. This variation of planning and control effort with project size is depicted in Figure 3-3.

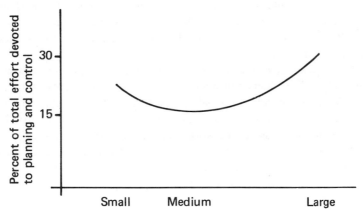

Figure 3-3. Planning effort relative to project size

The percent of effort devoted to planning and control also depends on the technology employed on the basic project activities. This percentage will undoubtedly increase if a change is made from traditional development technology to the improved productivity techniques (HIPO's, structured programming, top-down development, etc.). These techniques have the effect of reducing the effort required for basic work activities. This makes for smaller projects and reduces the total effort for planning and control, but probably not by the same factor as for the primary work activities. Therefore, as a percent of the total effort, the planning and control effort will increase.

If we look to the future, two trends seem likely. Development projects will probably become larger and more complex, and most organizations will probably adopt some of the improved productivity techniques. As just indicated, both of these developments will tend to increase the percent of effort devoted to planning and control. This fact, coupled with the general belief that these activities have not received proper emphasis in the past, suggests that it is not unreasonable to expect that 20% to 25% of the total effort will be devoted to planning and control in the near future.

3-7 WORK BREAKDOWN

The basic tool for constructing a control system is *work breakdown,* that is, the division of work into a number of pieces. The division process can be applied successively so that pieces are divided into smaller pieces, then these into still smaller pieces, and so on. For example, the total task of accomplishing a project can be divided into pieces, which are usually called phases. These phases can then be divided into smaller work efforts, these can be further subdivided, and so on.

Work breakdown is beneficial for two reasons. First, it reduces complexity. The job of doing and managing one large task is replaced by a number of jobs, each for doing and managing a small task. Even though there are many more small tasks to be done, each is more tractable so the total effort is less. The second reason that work breakdown is beneficial is that it allows *short-interval scheduling.* Work can be broken into pieces of short duration, and each of these can be assigned a definite due date. This allows close monitoring of project progress, prevents problems from building up undetected, and provides increased ability to recover from mistakes and to respond to change.

To be effective, work breakdown requires careful analysis and planning; how to break down work is discussed in Chapter 12. Here we want to point out that in applying the process it is necessary to answer questions such as the following for each task at each level of breakdown:

What is the task—what are its inputs, outputs, and standards for performance?
Who authorizes it and how is this done?
Who assigns work and tracks progress?

How much time and resource should it take?

What aspects of the task should be controlled; how should they be controlled?

Who has responsibility for performing the task, assessing its quality, and reporting its completion?

The answers that are supplied to these questions will have a significant impact on the procedures and practices for accomplishing projects. Thus, in addition to being a basic control tool, work breakdown shapes the entire project methodology.

Current practice for dividing a DP project into smaller work units usually establishes three levels of work breakdown: phases, standard tasks, and work units. *Phases* are major divisions of a project. They usually relate to major project tasks, such as designing, coding, and testing. *Standard tasks* are basic work activities of a phase. They are the smallest unit of work assigned a separate accounting identity for the purpose of estimating and resource control. *Work units* are tasks of short duration, usually some part of a standard task. These are packages of work that are assigned to specific individuals to be done. A methodology that examines these different levels of work more closely is presented later in this book, and examples of phases and standard tasks appear in Appendix A. At this point, only general characteristics of these different levels of work breakdown will be described.

The levels of project work bear a relationship to the levels of project control. Upper management maintains control of a project at the phase level. It requires reports from DP management at the completion of each phase, and makes decisions on this data. DP management must track progress in more detail; for this purpose they receive reports from the Project Manager at major checkpoints within the phase. These checkpoints are usually keyed to the completion of important standard tasks. The Project Manager must have still more detail, and he obtains this by controlling at the work unit level. (For self-control of his work, a worker breaks his work units into still smaller pieces. This last subdivision is usually done informally, which is why we do not include it in our levels of work breakdown.)

There is a fundamental difference between phases and standard tasks on the one hand and work units on the other. Once established, the phases and standard tasks for an organization are fixed and do not vary from project to project. On the other hand, work units depend on the particular project and the job to be done. The project methodology does not define the work units; it merely establishes standards or guidelines describing how they should be defined for a particular project. Thus phases and standard tasks are part of the methodology or standing plan; work units are established as part of a specific plan or single-use plan.

3-8 PROJECT PHASES

Phases divide a project into a number of subprojects, each of which is subject to review at the funding level. These reviews give management an opportunity to see if the project is meeting requirements.

Most organizations establish from five to ten phases for projects. They are usually established so that they follow sequentially—one phase is completed before the next one begins. The work output for one phase becomes a fundamental input to the phase that follows.

The specific phases selected by an organization are not nearly as important as the fact that definite phases have been fixed and clearly defined. For best results, the phases should be established as a standard to be used on all projects and by all functional areas. This is in marked contrast to the traditional approach where each project has usually been left to develop its own version of a life cycle. But many advantages accrue from having a standardized approach; some of the more important benefits are the following.

Control. Phases allow for effective control at the funding level. They provide a series of checkpoints at which upper management can review the project for quality and adherence to plan. Phases provide management an opportunity to reassess their project objectives and to make necessary and timely corrections in the direction the project is taking.

Communication. One of the first benefits to appear from a standard set of phases is that people start to talk the same language. Very quickly members of the project team, the users, and even upper management learn the precise purpose, objective, and deliverables of each phase. It becomes possible to tell someone that "We're in the middle of the phase Design Product "[1] instead of being required to give a detailed explanation of what has or has not been done. The elimination of confusion and the constant need to explain terms is a major benefit of standard phases.

User Involvement. In addition to easing communication problems, having a standard set of phases promotes user involvement. In part this stems from a better understanding of the process and their role in it; but it also stems from the realization that, by endorsing the methodology, upper management has indicated that they expect participation.

Documentation. With standard phases, each phase has required output, and this must be produced before the phase is completed. The benefits of this are many. Plans for the project must be produced in writing, thus preventing a "seat-of-the-pants" management style. System requirements must

---

[1] Observe that *Design Product* is a description of work in a "verb-object" form. We shall follow the convention of using this form to describe all work at all levels of work breakdown.

be stated in writing before the architecture is specified, thus saving the costly process of modifying the system to meet ever-changing requirements. Much system documentation must be built before the system is actually built; for example, design documentation is produced before coding begins, and program documentation is produced before testing begins. This avoids the traditional problem that the documentation doesn't get done because the project is late.

Quality. Having a standard set of phases enhances product quality in many ways. The precise output requirements of each phase help to ensure that the product is complete and that all required documentation has been produced. The required periodic reviews and checks by users help to assure completeness and compliance with standards. More generally, the fact that the project is conducted in a standardized, businesslike manner helps to promote an atmosphere conducive to quality workmanship.

Estimating. One of the important benefits of a standard set of phases is that it provides a basis for making better estimates. This will be discussed in greater detail in Chapter 13. At this point we merely observe that if every project is developed in a different way, if there is no standardization from project to project, then the time and cost of a past project may not relate at all to the time and cost of a future one. To build an effective estimating procedure it is necessary first to have a standard way of doing projects, and the first step in this direction is a standard set of phases.

3-9 STANDARD TASKS

The work to be done in a project phase can be subdivided into a number of pieces called standard tasks. But since tasks can be subdivided into smaller tasks and these into smaller still, it is not at all obvious at what level of subdivision the standard tasks lie. To answer this question, let us examine the meaning we attach to the word "standard" and the relation standard tasks have to the accounting system.

Remember that standard tasks for an organization are specified in their project methodology and do not vary from project to project. This means that a standard task is activity that might be conducted on *any* project as contrasted with an activity that is specific to a particular project. Code Modules is a generic activity; Code Module 6.15 might be an activity on a particular project. Design System Test is a generic activity, whereas Design Test of Programs X and Y is specific. Thus, the word "standard" refers to a general or generic activity as contrasted with one that is tailored to a particular project.

But saying that a standard task is a generic activity still does not completely define it. The task Document System is a generic activity; however, so is a part of it, such as Document User Procedures. To get a clearer understanding of standard tasks, we need to look more closely at the way data on completed work is used.

Data on work is collected for control purposes, but it is also used for estimating future work. For instance, often we have to estimate the time and resource requirements for a project phase. Based on historical data, we might estimate for units of phase work and summarize these to produce an estimate for the phase. To apply this approach, it is necessary to fix the units of work on which to base the estimates and to keep them uniform from project to project.

A typical project involves literally hundreds of individual work assignments, and we could preserve historical data on actual time and cost for each of these. However, this would not be too useful for estimating future projects. Many individual assignments are specific to a given project; for estimating purposes it would be more useful to collect data at a generic level so that project-to-project comparisons are possible. If reported data is too voluminous, it will probably be aggregated or averaged before it is used; this, too, means that full detail is not needed for estimating future projects. What is needed is a level of work that is not so highly aggregated that useful information is lost, but not so detailed that the reporting system becomes cumbersome or that it focuses on tasks that are specific to a particular project.

The appropriate level of work breakdown that we seek is what we mean by a standard task. Since it is the basis for estimating time and cost, the cost accounting and time reporting systems should be tied to these units. In fact, a formal definition is that *standard tasks* are the smallest units of work having distinctive numbers in the organization's chart of accounts for projects. They are basic units of work for estimating time and resources and for making project-to-project comparisons.

The definition of standard task allows considerable latitude for interpretation, and there is a wide variation among organizations in the number of standard tasks they recognize. Each organization should construct its own list of standard tasks, perhaps using our list in Appendix A as a guide. As each project is undertaken, it is possible that additional tasks will be encountered that are not on the original list. By adding these new tasks, a fairly complete list can be developed in a short time.

Not all standard tasks will apply to every project, however. The task of Prepare Site may not be necessary for a project that is to make use of an existing installation. On the other hand, it would be an extremely important task for a communication-based project that involved the installation of new terminals at several locations. The list of standard tasks should be regarded as a checklist that can be used to make certain that nothing is omitted from a particular project.

Bear in mind that the standard tasks are part of a methodology that is a standing plan, and a standing plan is a guide for the construction of a single-use plan for a specific project. As applied to the standard tasks, this means that some of them may not apply, and others may have to be shifted from one phase to another. For example, the phase in which equipment is ordered can vary considerably from project to project, and it is necessary to make the appropriate adjustment when planning for a specific project. Still other standard tasks are general and will need to be detailed, and the amount of detailing can vary considerably with the project. Tasks relating to training are sometimes examples of this.

The benefits from having standard tasks so closely parallel the benefits for project phases that we will not go into them in detail. We have seen their use in planning, estimating, and control. It is also easy to see that they play an important role in communication, documentation, user involvement, and the promotion of quality.

3-10 WORK UNITS

A *work unit* is the smallest piece of project work that is given formal recognition. It is an activity that is assigned to an individual or group who is expected to perform the work and is responsible for its quality. A work unit is short in duration; a useful standard is that it is an activity to be accomplished by one person in four to six days.

Work units are specific to a particular project. They are shaped not only by the job to be done but also by the skills and ability of the people who are to do them. The project methodology does not list work units, but it does establish standards for defining them. Part of the job of the project planner is to specify work units, and this is done in keeping with the standards for the organization.

A work unit is usually a portion of a standard task. For instance, Build Programs might be a standard task for an organization. This might be subdivided into a number of work units, each of which would call for the building of a specific module. (By "build a module" we mean to start with the design HIPO and to flowchart, code, test, and integrate the module into the evolving system; this, of course, assumes top-down development.)

If work units are portions of standard tasks, and if standard tasks are the smallest activities with distinctive accounting numbers, does this mean that we do not estimate and track the time and resource requirements for work units? Not at all. But it is necessary for us to explain what might at first seem to be a contradiction.

Accounting data is collected at the standard task level because these are generic activities. From the Accounting Department point of view, this is sensible because it means that the chart of accounts does not have to be changed for each project. What it means to Data Processing is that this accounting data can be used to make project-to-project comparisons. This is why we stressed that data on standard tasks is used to make estimates for future projects.

It is also necessary to make estimates for work assigned to people. When a work unit is assigned to an individual, it is necessary to estimate how long the task will take and then to track actual progress. (The mechanism for doing this and for reconciling various estimates is discussed in Chapter 5.) In fact, the work unit is the basic piece of work that the Project Manager uses to track project progress. Data on actual performance is collected at the work unit level for tracking a project and for measuring worker achievement. This data is aggregated at the standard task level for entry into the planning data base and for use in estimating future projects.

3-11 DESIGNING A PROJECT CONTROL SYSTEM

The heart of a project methodology is the project control system. It provides a foundation for the other tools and techniques used to guide projects, it embodies a control philosophy that shapes the work environment, and it establishes the basis for project interaction with other management systems. Because it plays such a central role, the project control system usually must be tailored to the organization that is to use it. No two organizations have the same work environment, management structures, and control requirements: For this reason, there is no universal control system that can be applied to all. A project control system should be designed to meet the needs of a specific organization, and it should be designed with attention and care.

The design of a control system is no small undertaking, and it is best handled as a project in its own right rather than by being submerged in some other project. Such an approach will pay for itself in the long run because it will save the need to reinvent the wheel for each project. In this section, some of the points that must be considered when designing a control system will be discussed.

Objectives. The place to begin designing is with a written statement of the objectives of the control system. People differ in their view of such systems; not everyone understands the seven fundamentals of control listed in Section 3-2. The time to get these differences out in the open is at the beginning of the project. The relation of the control system to those of accounting and personnel evaluation should also be clarified at this time.

Policies and Procedures. A number of general questions must be answered before starting with the details of design. This list will suggest the type of basic policy questions that should be addressed:

What philosophy of control should be used? Emphasis on self-control? A tight and highly structured system? What is our basic attitude about people and how does this influence the design of the control system?

What should be the levels of control? What responsibility and range of response at each level? Power to authorize? Tolerance to risk?

To what projects does the control system apply? How will the system adjust to differences in project size, type, etc.?

Who is to be served by the system? Project Managers? DP management? Upper management? User departments?

Who has control responsibility? How are activities of user departments to be controlled?

How are controls to be introduced? Will use of the system be optional or mandatory?

What will be the reaction of people to the system? How should this influence the design? Documentation? Training requirements?

Control Aspects. A question with far-reaching implications is: What aspects of work are to be controlled? The usual development project is responsible for producing a project on time, within budget, that meets specifications. Thus there should be control on at least three aspects of work: time, money, and quality. Many organizations, however, prefer to control two additional aspects, although they can be subsumed under monetary control: personnel cost and equipment cost.

Four of these five aspects can be quantified quite easily, and this eases the task of designing a system to manage them. The exception is quality, and for this reason it should receive the greatest attention in designing the management system. Unfortunately just the opposite is what usually happens — stress is placed on the quantifiable, and the nonquantifiable is slighted. This is one of the primary reasons for project failure.

Work Breakdown. Actual design of the control system starts with the definition of project phases. The phases are the backbone of the system, and it is necessary to decide such matters as:

What phases should be used?
What are the inputs and outputs of each phase?
What should be the procedures for authorization and approval of phases?
What are the standard tasks of each phase?

Planning. It is necessary to make a plan for each aspect of work that is to be controlled. Therefore, for each control aspect it is necessary to decide on how this plan is to be made, by whom, and with what frequency. This means making decisions about the kind of plans, schedules, budgets, and review points that will be required.

Controlling. For each aspect of work to be controlled, it is necessary to decide on how control is to be implemented. For each aspect this involves answering such questions as:

What is the generic work of each worker?
What are the key objectives of the organization, and how do they relate to the control system?
What data is needed for control? Is it really needed?
How is the data to be collected? By whom?
How is the data to be reported? To whom?
What is to be the range of response to divergence of actual from plan? What is routine and what is exceptional?

Specific Details. After answers have been obtained to general questions of the type listed above, it is necessary to get down to the specific details of the management system. This means the details of planning and control, including such matters as: design of forms, distribution list for reports, frequency of reports, sign-offs, and interfaces with accounting and personnel systems.

Control of the System. In designing a management control system, thought should be given to the question of how the system itself will be monitored. Some mechanism should be included for the evaluation of the system and the modification as required. One of the deliverables from any project should be an evaluation of the control system as it was applied to that particular project together with specific suggestions for its improvement. It should also be decided how data obtained from the postinstallation review of the product will be used to help improve the project control system.

3-12 OTHER TYPES OF CONTROL

This chapter is primarily on the control of work and the system required to do this. However, there are two other types of control that are encountered in connection with projects: control of documents and control by internal auditors. We will touch on these topics at this point; each is discussed more fully later on.

The documents involved with a project can be divided into two categories. One collection of documents relates to the project methodology, that is, it describes how projects are implemented in the organization. The bulk of these documents is gathered in a collection called the *Project Handbook.* Some of these, such as standards for design or programming, are not actually in the Project Handbook, but are in separate manuals that are referenced by the Handbook. The Project Handbook is the primary source of information on how projects are conducted, and it provides a framework for controlling documentation relating to this process.

The other category of project documentation is all of the material that relates to a specific project. This includes the authorization document, statement of objectives, specifications, design, coding, test plans and results, training plans and materials, plans, reviews, and so on. The amount of project-related documentation on even a medium-size project can be tremendous. Control of this documentation is achieved by using a *Project Workbook.* Essentially, this is a structure for the documentation—a filing system. At the end of the project, the Project Workbook is a complete record of all paper that flowed on the project.

Both the Project Handbook and the Project Workbook are discussed in detail in Chapter 7. The important point to remember for now is that the Project Handbook contains information relating to the way *any* project is conducted, and the Project Workbook contains the documentation for a specific project.

The other type of control encountered on a project is control by internal auditors (or by external auditors if the organization is small). Auditors are interested in controlling the project for two reasons: To see that the organization's assets are safeguarded and that the assets are being used effectively. Thus, auditors are concerned that funds spent on a project can be accounted for and that they are spent wisely. In particular, this last concern means that auditors are interested in the effectiveness of the methodology used to implement projects.

To some extent control by auditors overlaps the concepts of control discussed in this chapter. But their point of view is different, and for this reason we shall go more deeply into the topic of audit control. This is done in Chapter 19.

3-13 SUMMARY

- A project requires a system for controlling work.
- Some of the fundamental principles that underlie control are:

  Work is controlled—not workers
  Control is based on completed work
  Control of complex work is based on motivation and self-control
  Controls for capturing control data must be built into the work
      process
  Control data must go to the person who does the work
  A control system is designed for the routine
  Control of a complex work process is achieved through levels of
      control

- A control system involves four basic activities:

  Planning performance
  Observing actual performance
  Comparing actual and planned performance
  Adjusting as required

- An effective control must focus on:

  Objectives
  Response
  Timeliness
  Human factors
  Flexibility
  Simplicity

- Effective control requires effort and resource. Control typically accounts for 15% of the total project efforts, and this percentage is likely to increase in future years.
- The basic tool for constructing a control system is work breakdown. Current practice for subdividing projects calls for three levels of work breakdown: phases, standard tasks, and work units.
- Design of a project control system is itself a project of considerable importance. Designing a system calls for careful consideration of requirements ranging from the objectives of the system to specific details and a method for controlling the control system itself.
- In addition to work, projects also are involved with document con-

trol. A *Project Handbook* is used for controlling documents relating to the project methodology, and a *Project Workbook* for those relating to specific projects.
- The Internal Audit Department controls a project to see that organizational assets are safeguarded and used effectively.

4

PROJECT METHODOLOGY

4-1 INTRODUCTION

We have two major objectives in this chapter. The first is to look more closely at the concept of a project methodology. We shall describe in general terms what a methodology encompasses and how it fits in with other aspects of the organization. As you read our description you may think we have included many more factors in our system than are typically encountered in practice. This may be true, but keep in mind that we are describing a general methodology and this *is* very extensive. After all, a methodology touches on all of the many facets of a project. Just which facets a particular methodology focuses on is another matter.

Because our discussion of a general methodology is, by its very nature, somewhat abstract, our second objective is to make the discussion more concrete by presenting an example of a project methodology. We shall present some specific phases, standard tasks, procedures, and so on that are typical of the best current practice. Although we are primarily trying to explain and illustrate ideas, what we present will be sufficiently detailed so that it can be used as a starting point for the development of a methodology for a specific organization.

The methodology presented here comes from two sources. Over a number of years we have examined the project methodologies used by many organizations. We have discussed these systems with people who have used them and have learned about their good and bad features. From all of this we have gained a fairly good idea of the best procedures in current practice, and this empirical knowledge is one source of the methodology presented.

Empirical knowledge—what works in the "real world"—is a necessary basis for a methodology, but it alone is not sufficient. It provides a collection of useful tools, but it does not provide a conceptual basis for unifying these tools. This unification was provided by the second source of our methodology, which was logical derivation. By using function analysis (Chapter 12), we made a careful assessment of the work involved in the project process, both the work required to build the product and the work required to manage the project. We examined the various organizational requirements and built project procedures to match these requirements. By using analytical techniques we constructed a methodology that is consistent, but at each step we checked to see that our procedures were in line with those that work well in actual practice. Thus our methodology is a blend of formal derivation and practical know-how.

As you read about our methodology, keep in mind that it is only an example. Parts of it may be suitable for a particular organization, and other parts may not be. But this is true of any methodology. It is always necessary to customize a methodology to an organization because it must fit in with other management systems, the size and other characteristics of the organization and its projects, and, most important of all, the experience, requirements, and ideas of the people who are to use it.

The various appendices of this book detail many of the topics discussed in this chapter. In particular, they present a base project methodology, that is, a minimal methodology that can be installed by an organization that is just adopting a formal project process.

Throughout the chapter we shall focus only on the project itself. We assume that the project selection and authorization has already taken place (a topic discussed in Chapter 9), and we go on from there.

4-2 BASIC FEATURES OF A METHODOLOGY

Earlier we stated that a methodology is a collection of principles, policies, methods, procedures, practices, and definitions. Now let us expand this definition and be more specific in our description. A good place for us to start is with a review of the basic aim of a methodology.

The purpose of a DP project is to convert certain inputs into prescribed outputs within given constraints on time, resources, and quality. The purpose of a project methodology is to help explain how this conversion is to be done. This means that a methodology is involved with such matters as:

> How projects come into being (selection and authorization)
> What are the generic inputs to a project
> What are the generic outputs of a project (both intermediate and final
>   outputs)

The generic work that is required to convert inputs into outputs
How this work is to be done
How this work is to be planned and controlled
How the project should mesh with all other parts of the host
    organization

To describe all of these aspects of a project and how they interrelate is no easy task, and it is not all done in the project methodology. The project methodology does specify explicitly certain things about a project; but it also makes reference to other documents that describe aspects of a project, and it interfaces with various systems that bear on a project. There is considerable variation from organization to organization as to just where the boundaries are drawn among what is specified, what is referenced, and what is left to other systems. One reasonable division is as follows.

Items Specified

A project methodology *specifies*:

Work breakdown into phases and standard tasks
Procedures for producing the product
Policies and procedures for other selected project management tasks
Standard terminology
Data-collection procedures
Standards for documentation
Standards for project organization

As this list suggests, a project methodology specifies the most fundamental aspects of a project. Details on the procedures that are specified for producing the product and for managing the project are given in Table 4-1. Some items in this table are discussed further in the appendices.

The items specified by a methodology are by no means independent nor are they separately specified in the typical system. For instance, a discussion of project phases automatically involves standard terminology, standard documentation, and aspects of the control system. Even though they are not specified separately, it is often useful to *view* the fundamental aspects separately. This provides a technique for examining an involved system, which is what a methodology is, and it allows development of successive levels of understanding. It is much like the technique of viewing the human body in terms of its nervous system, its circulatory system, its digestive system, and so on.

Table 4-1
Some Procedures Specified in a Project Methodology

Procedures for Producing the Product	*Procedures for Managing the Project*
System development and documentation procedure	Authorization procedure
Support system procedure	Organization procedure
Site and equipment procedure	Project planning procedure
Record conversion procedure	Internal training procedure
Testing procedure	Change procedure
User training procedure	Interpretation procedure
Installation procedure	Tracking and reporting procedure
Conversion procedure	Review procedure
Acceptance procedure	Approval procedure
Operations interface procedure	Project assessment procedure
	Project documentation procedure

The most important item specified by a methodology is the work breakdown pattern. The definition of project phases and standard tasks fixes the generic work to be done and the basic way in which this work is to be done. It also fixes generic inputs and outputs for the different levels of work. This is the backbone of the methodology, and it provides a framework for planning, control, and other procedures. For this reason, the work breakdown structure is usually the most prominent feature of a formal methodology.

Items Referenced

A project methodology *references*:

Organizational policies
Standards for basic project work, such as analysis, design, coding, and testing
Standards for acceptance
Standards for operations
Standards for form design and documentation of deliverables
Standards for project management work, such as estimating, planning,

tracking, reporting, quality assurance, and business assessment (cost/benefit and risk analysis)

In general, reference is to documents that provide basic guidelines or describe how a specific task should be performed.

One of the major problems in designing a methodology is to decide what should be included and what should be put in a separate document with appropriate pointers back and forth. Often the decision is based on the use to which information will be put; information that is used to manage the project is put in the methodology, and information that is needed to do basic work is put in a separate standards manual. For instance, general statements about testing—the types of tests that will be performed, who is to perform them, who approves the results—might appear in the project methodology. Details of testing—test specification layouts, guidelines for test cases—might appear in a separate manual of testing standards.

Observe that we have not included standards for accomplishing a project in our list. This is because the project methodology *is* the standard for that task.

Interfaces

A project methodology *interfaces* with organizational systems and procedures for:

Project selection
Long-range planning
Cost accounting
Capital budgeting
Real estate
Personnel
Audit
Security
Information systems
Data administration
Legal
Management control

Systems that must be interfaced with can act as constraints on the methodology, but they can also serve to simplify it. For instance, both of these influences are exerted by the accounting system. Because this system is firmly entrenched in most organizations, the project methodology must be adjusted to its conventions. This adjustment influences the terminology used on the project, the frequency and format of certain reports, and some of the data requirements for business justification. On the other hand, data collected through the accounting system can often be used for project purposes and can thereby simplify the data-collection requirements.

One of the problems that arises in building a methodology is that some of the systems that should be interfaced with are themselves not fully specified. This problem often arises, for instance, with the systems for data administration and security. Many organizations are just now in the process of building these systems, and clear-cut policies and procedures for data and data security may not exist. In this event, the project methodology might be expanded to fill this void even though this clearly takes the methodology beyond its basic scope.

Specification of Work

We have seen above that a methodology has a lot to say about *what* work must be done on a project, but it is also useful to review *how* work is specified.

One way that work is specified in a methodology is by explicit statement of tasks. By this we mean that tasks are named, their inputs and outputs are given, and standards for performance are provided (possibly by reference to a separate standards manual). Instances of this method for describing work are: Lists of tasks, such as lists of phases and standard tasks; checklists for particular jobs, such as a checklist of the tasks required to assess risk; and procedures showing major job steps, such as a step-by-step change procedure. Explicit statement of tasks is a basic way to specify work, but it is important to realize that it is not the only way to do it.

Tasks can also be specified implicitly, that is, they can be implied by other requirements. A common way to specify tasks implicitly is by the establishment of documentation requirements. If the methodology requires that a particular form be completed, then it implicitly specifies the tasks required to collect the information and complete the form. For instance, if the Project Manager is required to complete a Work Unit Assignment Form describing a piece of work that is to be assigned to an individual (a topic discussed in Chapter 5), then it is implicit that he must break large tasks into assignable work units, estimate the duration of these work units, schedule start and stop times for them, and assign them to individuals. The methodology might not *explicitly* state that the Project Manager must do these tasks, but it is *implicitly* required if he is to fulfill the requirement of completing the form.

Recall that a methodology is a standing plan for all projects, and for each project it is necessary to produce a plan specific to that project. The task of building a project plan in accordance with the methodology is part of the work to be done on the project. A project methodology usually does not give an explicit checklist for this work of building a project plan. However, the work is often specified implicitly by the requirement that certain forms be completed for each project. You should realize that this implicit specification of planning and control tasks is one of the most important reasons for having standard project documentation.

There is still another way that tasks can be specified implicitly, and that is by providing an example. An example serves to clarify meaning, purpose, and so on, but it also serves to define the steps that must be taken to produce the required product. Frequently, of course, an example involves standard documentation; therefore it tends to reinforce the task specification implicit in the documents. Examples are rarely used to illustrate an entire project but are usually restricted to some specific task. Good examples are an effective way to specify work, and they usually add considerable clarity to a project methodology. If one were required to build a project methodology from scratch, a reasonable starting point might be simply to provide a good example of a completed project for others to use as a pattern.

While discussing how work is specified, we should observe that procedures can be specified in many different ways. They can be described in separate stand-alone sections (change procedures are frequently handled this way). But most procedures are specified simply by making certain that the required work is listed among the standard tasks and the required documents among the phase outputs. This means that the lists of standard tasks and phase outputs usually describe a large part of an organization's methodology.

4-3 ASSUMPTIONS FOR A PROJECT METHODOLOGY

The example of a formal methodology that will be presented is based on many assumptions about the organization that is to use it. Some of these assumptions are merely a convenience to establish a clear interface between the areas discussed and those not discussed; assumptions about the selection process and existing documentation fall in this class. Other assumptions, such as those relating to system size and complexity, attempt to describe the general nature of the projects we have in mind. The third class of assumptions are the most critical. These describe aspects of the project or the environment that have a significant influence on the methodology itself or even on the question of whether a formal methodology can be employed successfully. Assumptions about productivity techniques, organizational planning, and the control structure fall into this category.

Project Selection. We assume that the projects we deal with have been duly authorized and provided with initial funding and resources. We assume a project proposal and selection process similar to that described in Chapter 9.

Documentation. It is difficult to develop a formal project methodology in an atmosphere that is antagonistic to documentation. Thus, we assume a conducive atmosphere, and we assume this is evidenced by the existence of formal documents that describe the organization's identity and major policies. Examples of the types of documents we assume to exist are the following:

    Organization identity documents
        Mission
        Practices
        Procedures
        Standards
    Organization policies
        Quality
        Data
        Privacy
        Security
        Audit
    DPD identity documents
        Mission
        Policies
        Practices
        Procedures
        Standards (other than a Project Methodology)

Examples of certain policies and a DPD mission are given in Appendix C.

Complexity. We place no particular restriction on the type of DP system being developed. Although it is not a requirement, we have in mind projects that are reasonably complex and may be influenced by factors such as the following:

    Many organizational departments and functional groups are involved
        with projects. Among these groups are
        General management
        User groups
        DP management
        Project group
        DP operations
        Internal audit
        Security

Data management
Network administration

The organization has distributed data and function and it has or is heading toward data bases.

The organization has or is heading toward communication networks.

Again, factors such as these *may* influence the project, but we do not assume
them to exist. The methodology presented applies to simple, straightforward
projects as well as to more complex ones.

Project Size. We do not assume a particular system size or a particular
organization size. We shall present a methodology for a "typical" project
size, knowing that what is "typical" varies from shop to shop. Adjustment of
the methodology for system size and complexity is discussed in Chapter 6.

Modern Productivity Techniques. We assume the organization is making effective use of some of the modern DP techniques (improved programming techniques), such as HIPO design, top-down development, structured
programming, program proofing, walk-throughs, program librarian, and pro
gramming teams. These techniques "fit" with our project methodology
because they call for the systematic development of clear, readable products
and for documentation, and they stress product quality. In effect, these techniques structure the product in much the same way that the methodology
structures the project.

We do *not* assume that all of these productivity techniques are used.
We do assume that they have been examined and that appropriate ones have
been adopted. However, our methodology is predicated on a certain way of
doing development work, and variations from this will require corresponding
modification in the methodology. If, for example, top-down development is
not practiced, it will be necessary to add an integration phase to the process
we shall define. If emphasis is not placed on a complete, documented design
before coding begins, then the entire methodology will need revision.

Organization Planning. We make the important assumption that the
atmosphere of the organization is conducive to formal planning. We assume
that planning is practiced to some degree on each level of the organization.
Management is aware of the value of planning and promotes its use. We assume that the concept of a formal project methodology has the backing of
management at a level sufficiently high to ensure that adequate attention will
be paid to the concept.

Organization Control Structure. To accompany its planning efforts, the
organization has a system of control that functions at the various levels. As it
relates to DP projects, the control structure and some of the tasks for different levels might be as shown in Table 4-2.

Table 4-2
Control Levels and Project-Related Tasks

Control Level	Project-Related Tasks
General management	Select projects Establish priorities Allocate funds Authorize work Monitor progress Evaluate results
User management	Originate requests for DP services Review project plans Perform related user work Monitor progress Evaluate results
DPD management	Review authorizations Assign work Review project plans Monitor progress Transmit reports
Project management	Plan work Assign tasks Review performance Control quality Transmit results Review work process
Project worker	Plan work Perform work Review work Control quality

A very important assumption we make is that individuals control their own work effort. This means that the organization operates in a MBO (Management by Objectives) atmosphere with stress on individual responsibility and self-control. More generally, our philosophy on control is that presented in Chapter 3.

Major Business Considerations. Finally, we make the very basic assumption that the organization has a desire to improve its project-development process. We assume that the organization is striving to achieve such business goals as:

Quality products
On-time products
Cost-effective development and operations
Control of project risk
Improved accounting for project costs
Improved flexibility in resource allocation
Zero-based project budgeting

4-4 PROJECT PHASES

A project can be specified by its inputs and outputs; these are listed on an aggregated level in Figure 4-1. One of the major inputs to a project is the enabling documentation that authorizes the project and provides for its funding. Another is the baseline data. This describes the conditions and environment within which the project must function, and it can only be modified by following the change procedures that are operative. Other major inputs are the resources of people, equipment, and facilities for the project, and the methodology or procedure to be used for implementation.

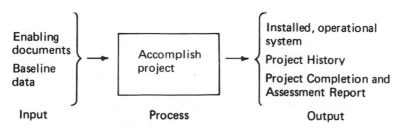

Figure 4-1. The DP project

The primary output of a project is the product or deliverable for which the project was established. This can usually be described as a system consisting of hardware, software, procedures, documentation, trained personnel, and so on. Two other important outputs of the project are the Project History and the Project Completion and Assessment Report. The Project History is a collection of the most important documents produced on the project. The Project Completion and Assessment Report is a debriefing of the project. It is used to assess the project development procedure.

In Figure 4-1 we have not attempted to show all project results. In particular, we have not shown an extremely important result that is frequently overlooked: improved people and an improved process. Continual self-improvement is an important goal of any organization. In the project area, this means finding better ways to do the project work—a better process—and ways to make project workers more productive. Productivity improvement is made possible by the knowledge and experience gained on a project, and it is made probable by the realization on the part of the project workers that their enhancement is a major project goal.

The function or work effort of a project is to Accomplish the Project. This function can be decomposed into major subfunctions, which are also described as *phases* of the project. Figure 4-2 depicts the decomposition that is the backbone of the methodology described. (The development of this decomposition is discussed in Chapter 12 and Appendix A.) The first principle for accomplishing a complex task is to subdivide it into a number of smaller, more manageable subtasks. The division of the project into phases is an instance of this general rule. In effect, each major phase can be viewed as a project in its own right. Each phase has its purpose, its inputs, and its resources. Each has its outputs that are to be delivered on time and within budget. To accomplish the project, all that is required is that the phases be accomplished in order.

To describe each phase, it is necessary to list its purpose, objectives, deliverables, and standard tasks. This information is given in Appendix A, and the reader is urged to become reasonably familiar with it. Meanwhile we shall discuss some of this material in this chapter, and we begin with a brief, informal description of each phase.

Phase 1.1 *Identify Problem.* Although DP is probably represented on the Project Selection Committee, this phase is the first opportunity that the DP Department has to examine the project from its perspective. The purpose of the phase is to make a quick assessment of the feasibility and desirability of the project. Very little resource is to be expended on this activity; some organizations place an arbitrary upper limit of, say, no more than three people for five days. The phase is a device for eliminating infeasible projects. A large number of projects, perhaps 50%, do not survive this initial DP screening.

The short time allotted to this phase suggests that there should be a standing plan for Phase 1.1 as part of the project methodology. It also suggests that the major output of the phase, the Identification Report, should be a standard form that is to be completed.

Phase 1.2 *Specify Requirements.* The object of this phase is to determine the scope of the system and to obtain a clear, detailed specification of user requirements. This phase is similar to, but much more extensive than, Phase 1.1.

The primary tasks for the phase are data collection, data analysis, and documentation. The present system must be documented in detail, which provides a useful output even if the project is not continued beyond this phase. The required system must also be documented. This means defining the goals of the system; listing the functional specifications, which state what the system must do to meet the goals; and listing the performance standards,

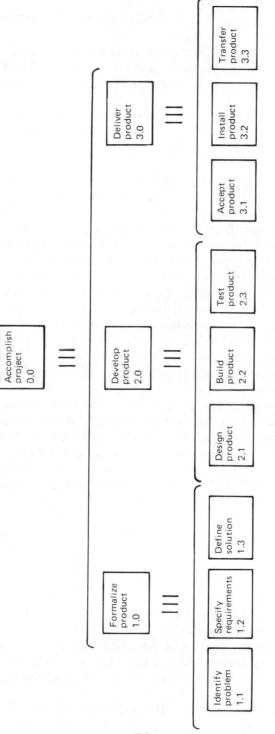

Figure 4-2. The phases of a project

73

which state criteria against which acceptance will be measured. In effect, it means producing a clear, precise statement of the problem that is to be solved. This phase is a difficult one because it is often harder to define a problem than to solve it.

Emphasis during the phase is on completeness and correctness. Errors and omissions that are caught in this phase can be corrected for a small fraction of what it would cost if they were not found until the design, build, or test phase.

The importance of this phase cannot be overstressed. Most problem projects can trace a great deal of their trouble to the fact that there was never a clear understanding between DP and the user about the project requirements and specifications. A fundamental aspect of our development procedure is that the system requirements must be stated and approved before system development starts. This means the requirements of *all* users, including DP Operations, data management, security, internal auditing, and primary users. Inevitably, of course, there will be discussion during this phase about solutions or ways to satisfy the specification requirements, but the formal determination of a solution is left to the next phase.

Phase 1.3 *Define Solution.* Phase 1.2 specifies *what* is to be done; this phase takes up the question of *how* it is to be done. The object is to define the architecture or functional design that meets the specification requirements.

The major task in this phase is design. Preferably it is done by a relatively small team because this simplifies communication and promotes understanding. Alternative design solutions are investigated, including the possibility of meeting the requirements by modifying the existing system, building a new system, buying and installing a package, or building a nonautomated system. The search for a solution might result in changing the specifications; as is done throughout the project, such change in the output of a previous phase is done only under strict change procedures (see Section 18-2).

From the various alternatives, a recommended solution is selected. This is a major checkpoint for the phase; a review is held and general concurrence obtained before going on to build a detailed system architecture or external design for the selected solution. Building the architecture involves defining the system structure or logical units that are to accomplish the required function, establishing interfaces among the logical units and other systems, and designing data structures and flows.

Approximately one-third of the total effort for the project will have been expended by the conclusion of Phase 1.3. Very little of this effort goes into Phase 1.1; most of it is divided more or less equally between Phases 1.2 and 1.3.

Phase 2.1 *Design Product.* This is the phase during which most design work takes place: design of the system, design of the test plan, design of the conversion and installation plans, and so on. The major deliverable from this phase is a system design to the level called for by the organization's standards. For some, this is to the program level; for others, it is to the level of a module that will result in about 30 lines of high-level code. Other deliverables include the design of the manual system or procedures, and plans for major functions, such as testing, conversion, and training.

On large projects, this is the phase in which a buildup in personnel often begins. The small group of designers for Phase 1.3 is augmented because there is more opportunity for parallel activity. With larger teams comes greater need for planning and controlling in a formal way and a greater need for conscious effort to maintain communications.

Phase 2.2 *Build Product.* This is often thought of as the coding phase because the major activity is the production of documented system programs. However, the phase also includes the building of a test package for systems test, the building of user procedures, and the writing of related documents.

This phase typically involves the maximum number of people and has the maximum amount of parallel activity. Therefore, it also offers the greatest potential for confusion and cost-overruns. But careful and complete work during the specification, definition, and design stages pays off at this point through reduced need for modification and change.

Phase 2.3 *Test Product.* This is the system test phase. Its purpose is to test the entire system, including hardware, software, and procedures. The test is to assure that the system is a quality product and that it meets all of the specification requirements.

Although this test is for the benefit of DP, it is often conducted by a separate test group. An independent group is used because they are more likely to spot problems than are the specialists who built the system and are extremely familiar with it.

This test involves determining if the software interacts properly with people and machines, if the system is fully documented, if procedures and programs are as described in the documentation, and so on. Errors and omissions are frequently uncovered at this point, and these must be corrected under formal change procedures.

Phase 3.1 *Accept Product.* This is the user's acceptance test. In addition to the traditional user, this should also include acceptance testing by operations, internal audit, security, and any other group that is involved with the system. The objective of the phase is to determine if the developed system meets the requirements specified for it.

Phase 3.2 *Install Product.* The purpose of this phase is to complete all activities for an operational system. This includes the conversion of data, programs, and user procedures and the training of user personnel.

Phase 3.3 *Transfer Product.* This phase completes the project by transferring the installed system to the System Group. This phase also involves an assessment of how well the project team met its objectives and how well the project methodology worked. It is a very short phase requiring a few mandays, but it is an important source of information for accomplishing future projects.

There is nothing unique or special about the phases we have selected for our methodology. We present them as an example of a useful division of a project, but with the expectation that organizations will modify our phases to meet their own requirements. Some organizations combine Phases 1.2 and 1.3 into a single phase. We have elected not to do this because we believe that the total effort involved in these phases requires that they be subdivided. But some might prefer another division. For example, it is clear that the selection of a recommended solution in Phase 1.3 is an important event, and it might well require management approval before the architecture is detailed. Thus, one might wish to subdivide Phase 1.3 into two parts consisting of a selection of a solution and a detailing of the selected solution.

Another common variation from our methodology involves Phases 3.1 and 3.2 Our methodology calls for user acceptance of the product before installation, and many organizations follow this procedure. The rationale for this is that one does not want the product near the live system until it has user approval. But many people take another approach. They want the acceptance test to take place under conditions that are as near as possible to actual operating conditions; therefore they prefer to have Accept Product after Install Product. Still others prefer to have an acceptance test, followed by installation, followed by a site test. They argue the need for a user test before having the product near live data, but also see the need for a user test after installation to verify the system under near-live conditions.

4-5 PARALLEL DEVELOPMENT

We have embedded in our phases a technique of implementation that is sometimes known as *parallel development.* This term should be explained.

In addition to the major system, it is necessary on most projects to build secondary systems for such things as user procedures, training efforts, test efforts, and conversion and installation efforts. It may also be necessary to conduct a site building effort and to have efforts to install hardware or software. Most of these efforts involve steps that amount to specification of requirements, design of a system to meet the requirements, building of required components, testing of these, and actual carrying out of the effort.

Parallel development is an approach to projects that, to the extent possible, calls for all specification to be done at the same time, all design at the same time, all building at the same time, and so on. This means, for instance, that Phase 2.2 (Build Product) is not just a coding phase but involves parallel build activities for the various secondary systems of the project. The relationship of other phases to secondary systems is depicted in Figure 4-3.

Parallel development is employed for two reasons. First, it helps to emphasize the fact that all aspects of a project require careful specification, design, building, and testing before performing the effort. This emphasis helps to prevent overlooking activities that must take place before testing, training, and so on, and it helps to assure that adequate time is scheduled for these preliminary activities. The second reason for parallel development is that it tends to shorten the project duration, but whether there are actual time savings or not obviously depends on the resources available at different times during the project.

4-6 PHASE INPUTS AND OUTPUTS

Each phase can be better understood by examining its inputs and outputs. Inputs for each phase are not listed separately because they can easily be derived from the other information. For each phase, the input is the collection of all outputs from the previous phases together with the phase authorization and the original inputs to the project. For example, the input to Phase 1.3 is the output of Phases 1.1 and 1.2, the authorization for Phase 1.3, and the original input to the project.

Outputs from the various phases can be grouped into two categories. Some outputs are *general* outputs that are due at the end of each phase. These contain management information about business aspects of the phase just completed and plans for the next phase. All other outputs will be referred to as *specific* outputs because they are unique to a particular phase.

General Outputs

The general outputs are:

Report to Management
Phase Plan
Project Plan (updated)
Project Workbook (updated)
Phase Completion and Assessment Report

	Formalize Product			Develop Product			Deliver Product		
	1.1	1.2	1.3	2.1	2.2	2.3	3.1	3.2	3.3
System									
Requirements	Identify	Specify							
Data		Specify							
Programs			Define	Design	Build				
Procedures			Define	Design	Build				
Purchased items			Specify	Plan	Buy		Receive		
Site			Specify	Plan			Construct		
Support system			Specify	Plan	Install				
Testing									
Unit			Specify	Plan	Test				
System			Specify	Plan	Build	Test			
Acceptance			Specify	Plan		Build	Test		
Conversion and Installation			Specify	Plan			Design	Execute	
Training									
Internal	Identify	Plan	Conduct						
User			Specify		Conduct				
Operations			Specify		Conduct				

Figure 4-3. Methodology summary

These outputs are required at the end of each phase (except that a Phase Plan and a Project Plan are not required at the end of Phase 3.3). The first three outputs are the *project business reports;* these are sent to upper management to inform them of project progress and plans for the future. The Project Workbook and Phase Completion and Assessment Report are resources for later use by the project team. Each of these five outputs will be described briefly; sample contents are listed in Chapter 5 and Appendix B.

The Report to Management is a brief summary of project status and an outlook for the future. It is constructed at the phase level and contains such information as:

Actual versus estimated time and cost for each completed phase
Estimated time and cost for future phases and for the total project
Updated cost/benefit analysis for the application
Updated risk analysis for the application
Significant problems that are anticipated
Recommendation to proceed, modify, or abort the project

This report is an important input to the Project Selection Committee in their decision about continuing the project and assigning it a priority. The report can also be used for other special purposes; for example, some organizations make a wide distribution of the Phase 1.1 Report to Management with the idea of alerting all potentially interested parties to the fact that a particular project is underway.

The Phase Plan is a plan at the standard task level for the next phase of the project. It contains a schedule, list of resource requirements (by categories), and a budget for the next phase. The purpose is to give a fairly accurate picture of the schedule and cost of the next phase. The Phase Plan is used by the Project Selection Committee in their decision about funding the next phase. The plan is also the basis for a detailed Work Plan that is constructed at the beginning of the next phase. A detailed discussion of the Phase Plan appears in Chapter 5.

The Project Plan is a plan at the phase level for the entire project. It contains a schedule, resource requirements, and a budget for each phase. It is first prepared in Phase 1.1 and is updated in each subsequent phase to reflect additional knowledge about the project. Often the initial Project Plan is, of necessity, very approximate. But successive revisions bring it much closer to what will actually take place, and revisions after Phase 1.3 or 2.1 are nominal.

The Project Plan provides information on the project that is summarized in the Report to Management. It is an important source for data on estimated cost, time, and project risk. More information on the Project Plan is provided in Chapter 5.

The Project Workbook is a collection of all documents that flow on the project. It is started at the very beginning of the project and is updated continually. The Project Workbook is discussed in Chapter 7.

The Phase Completion and Assessment Report is an analysis of the phase just completed; it focuses on the project, not the product. The purpose of the report is to gather information that can be used to evaluate and improve the project methodology. An important purpose of Phase 3.3 is to make such an assessment, which is then documented in a Project Completion and Assessment Report. But to complete this report, it is necessary to keep track of all problems and suggestions that arise during the course of the project; this is done through the assessment reports for individual phases.

Included in the Phase Completion and Assessment Report is data on actual versus planned time and cost for the phase, accounts of special problems encountered, suggestions for improving the methodology, and other observations that help in evaluating the project process. This report is discussed further in Chapter 5.

Specific Outputs

There are a large number of specific phase outputs. One way to classify these is as primary deliverables, special plans, implementation packages, and completion reports (see Table 4-3).

The primary deliverables are the major outputs that lead to the final delivered system. They are the results of the major project activities, such as analysis, design, and coding. Broadly speaking, the reason for doing a project is to obtain the primary deliverables.

The production of primary deliverables requires many complex subsidiary activities. For instance, it is necessary to provide support and training, and to install the system. Each of these subsidiary activities must be planned, designed, and executed; this leads to a collection of specific outputs relating to the special plans, implementation packages, and completion reports for subsidiary activities, as shown in Table 4-3. To explain these outputs, let us look at one subsidiary activity: testing the system.

A requirement on every project is that the product be subjected to a system test. This is a complex activity, and to provide for it a System Test Plan must be built. This plan addresses questions about how much time and resource will be required for the test, where the test will be conducted, who will conduct it, what are the standards for performance, how will errors and omissions be corrected, and so on. It also lays out a schedule for the work required to prepare for the test and to conduct it.

Table 4-3
Specific Phase Outputs

Primary Deliverables	*Special Plans*
Identification Report *[Project objectives]*	Training Plan
System Requirements Specification Report	Plans and Orders for Purchased Items
Documentation of Present System	Test Plans (Program, System, Acceptance)
System Architecture Report	Documentation Plan
Summary of Alternative Architectures Considered	Location and Site Plans
System Design Specifications	Conversion Plan
Integrated System	Installation Plan
Tested System	
Accepted System	
Installed System	
System File	

Implementation Packages	*Completion Reports*
Support System Specification	Unit and Program Test Reports
System Test Package	Training Completion Reports
Training Package	System Test Report
Acceptance Test Package	Acceptance Report
Conversion Package	Installation and Conversion Completion Report
Installation Package	Project History File
	Project Completion and Assessment Report

A good deal of work is involved in preparing for a test. The order of testing must be determined, data requirements ascertained, test data generated, and expected results computed. This work is tied together in a step-by-step script for conducting the test. This script, the test data, computed results, and all other material needed for the test constitute a package for conducting the test. This System Test Package provides everything that is needed to perform the test and to evaluate test results.

Successful completion of the test results is a primary deliverable: a tested system. But for management and others to know that the test *was* successful, it is necessary to record this fact in some manner; this is done in the System Test Report. This completion report contains the sign-offs or other evidence that the test is successfully completed and any other remarks that are relevant.

Special plans for subsidiary activities are an important input for phase planning. They make phase plans much more realistic and attainable. Implementation plans amount to designs for the subsidiary activities. They are part of the detailed preliminary work that makes projects run smoothly and holds costly rework to a minimum. Completion reports are the formal record that the activity is complete. Most completion reports mark the end of a subsidiary activity, but two, which deserve special mention, have to do with the completion of the project.

The Project Completion and Assessment Report was discussed above. It is completed at the end of the project and is a review of the project itself. The Project History File, as the name suggests, is a record of the most important aspects of the project. In effect, it is a synopsis of the Project Workbook and is the permanent record of the project. It is discussed in Chapter 7.

4-7 STANDARD TASKS

The standard tasks for each of our phases are given in Appendix A. To establish a methodology, an organization should build its own list of standard tasks. This can be done by using the technique of work analysis (Chapter 12) or by modifying and augmenting our list.

The standard tasks of a project are of three types: management tasks, administrative tasks, and basic tasks. By management tasks we mean the work of planning, controlling, hiring, assigning work, appraising, rewarding, and so on. The administrative tasks include such activities as office management, payroll, and typing. The basic work tasks are the activities related to the primary deliverables from the project and related subsidiary activities— the work that management and administration organize and facilitate.

The recognition that there are several types of tasks serves several purposes. First, it can be a convenient device for checking the completeness of the standard task list. It is not uncommon, for instance, to find that an organization concentrates on building a list of basic work tasks but slights the other two categories. Of the three, administrative tasks are most often omitted—some people do not even think of this as project work but assume it to be part of the environment, much like an office with proper lighting and temperature. However, for some projects administrative tasks can be critical, and failure to include them among the standard tasks and to plan for them can seriously impact the schedule and budget for the project.

A second reason for recognizing several types of tasks is that it can help in planning and control. Management and administrative tasks tend to be the same from phase to phase; there is a variation in the amount of work to be done, but the kind of work does not change very much. Also, different groups are usually responsible for these tasks; for instance, work assignments for administrative tasks are often made by someone other than the person who assigns basic work. These differences may result in procedures for management and administrative tasks that are different from those used for the bulk of the project work.

Although the above classification of standard tasks is useful, a much more important classification involves two categories: scheduled tasks and nonscheduled tasks. A *scheduled* standard task is one that ordinarily is performed at some specified point in a phase. A plan for the phase shows when the scheduled task is to be performed, and the control system monitors to determine when it is completed. By contrast, a *nonscheduled* standard task is one that may be performed continuously during the phase or whenever it is required. Most basic project work is scheduled, but so is such management work as planning and such administrative work as typing of phase reports. A good example of nonscheduled project work is tracking. This activity is not scheduled to be done at some specified point in the project, but it is a task that is performed throughout the phase. Although planning is scheduled, replanning or updating of plans is not. Typing of final reports is scheduled, but much of the administrative support effort is activity that is performed as required.

The distinction between scheduled and nonscheduled activities is important because the two are handled quite differently for purposes of planning and control. This difference has important implications for project scheduling and for estimating project time and resource requirements. This topic is discussed more fully in Chapter 5.

There is a pattern to the scheduled standard tasks from phase to phase. For each phase, there is a collection of scheduled standard tasks that have to do with initializing or opening the phase; these involve the development of action plans and the assignment of work. There is another collection that has to do with closing the phase; these involve preparing and distributing the documents that are the outputs for the phase. The remaining scheduled standard tasks of each phase have to do with the major activity of the phase. Specifics of these tasks vary from one phase to the next, but they are alike in being the primary work for their particular phase.

4-8 PHASED APPROACH

The fact that DP projects have major stages or phases has been recognized for many years. These have been used to mark project progress but generally have not been used to divide the project into separate parts. That is, the project was generally regarded as a whole for purposes of authorization, funding, and planning. Before starting the project it was traditionally necessary to estimate its entire cost and to lay out a project plan in sufficient detail to predict the completion date for the project. Generally the estimates of cost and duration were without firm foundation, and more often than not they proved to be inaccurate. It could not really be expected to be otherwise because a traditional characteristic of DP projects is that the beginning stages are used to define the purpose and to clarify the objective of the system that is to be built. To ask for firm estimates before this is done is like asking a contractor for a firm price and occupancy date on a building before he is told anything about the size, shape, and style of the proposed structure. The only way for the Project Manager or the contractor to give an early estimate that can be met is for him to pad it thoroughly. This leads to the traditional game called "fudge." In this game, the Project Manager makes an estimate, then upper management tries to guess the Project Manager's fudge factor so they know how much to slice off the estimate to bring it close to reality. In this environment, estimating is really gamesmanship with each side attempting to outbluff the other.

An alternative to the traditional way of handling a project is a style of implementation called the *phased approach*. This consists of three related concepts: phased commitment, phased planning, and phased development. The basic idea of the phased approach is to commit, plan, and develop projects one phase at a time. Each phase is treated much like a separate project. Each is to be completed in turn before the next phase is undertaken. The phased approach is adopted to do the following.

To Control Risk. From upper management's perspective, a DP project is a high-risk investment. The risk is particularly high at the beginning when very little is known about the proposed system. The phased approach gives management a means of controlling their exposure while they get a progressively better idea of the relation of risk to rewards and cost to benefits.

To Control Resources. The phased approach allows management to commit resources a step-at-a-time. This gives better control over resource allocation and enables them to react more quickly to shifting requirements.

To Enhance Quality. The phased approach requires review and approval of work at the end of each phase. This means that quality is assessed on a regular basis throughout the project. The effect is to detect errors and omissions at an early stage when the cost of correction is generally less. Also, it means that differences of intent and interpretation are uncovered and re-solved earlier.

To Simplify Project Planning and Control. It is not possible to plan an entire project at the beginning before scope, requirements, and solution are known. The phased approach gives recognition to this fact and calls for a more realistic way of planning and controlling the project.

To Ensure Management Involvement. In the past it was not uncommon for upper management to authorize a DP project and then to forget about it until around due date. As a result they were not always aware of deviations from original plans and were sometimes upset by the features of the final product. The phased approach requires regular management review and ap-proval. As a result of this involvement, there are fewer surprises for manage-ment. The added involvement also helps to maintain management interest over what is often an extended development period.

4-9 PHASED COMMITMENT

To explain the phased approach, we start by describing the concept of phased commitment. Essentially this means that management authorizes the project one phase at a time. The "snake" in Figure 4-4 depicts this approval process. Project requests flow to the Project Selection Committee where they are assessed. For an approved project, the Committee authorizes and funds Phase 1.1 of the project. This phase is then undertaken by the project team. A major output of Phase 1.1 is a Report to Management with a recommenda-tion that the project be continued or that it be aborted. This report is re-viewed by the Project Selection Committee, and they decide whether Phase 1.2 is to be authorized. If it is authorized, this phase is undertaken. One out-put of the Phase 1.2 effort is a Report to Management with a revised recom-mendation on the project. At this point the recommendation is likely to be one of three courses of action: continue with Phase 1.3, abort the project, or authorize that Phase 1.2 be redone with a modified scope (as specified in the recommendation). Based on their review of this report, the Project Selection Committee will make a new decision, and so the process continues. At each stage the recommendation from the project team can be to continue the project, stop it, or go back and redo an earlier phase in the light of current knowledge. At each stage the Project Selection Committee weighs the recom-mendation and makes its decision based on the total picture of available re-sources and competing requirements. At any point the Committee might decide to "shelve" the project in order to satisfy more pressing needs, and it might authorize continuation of the next phase at a later time when resources become available.

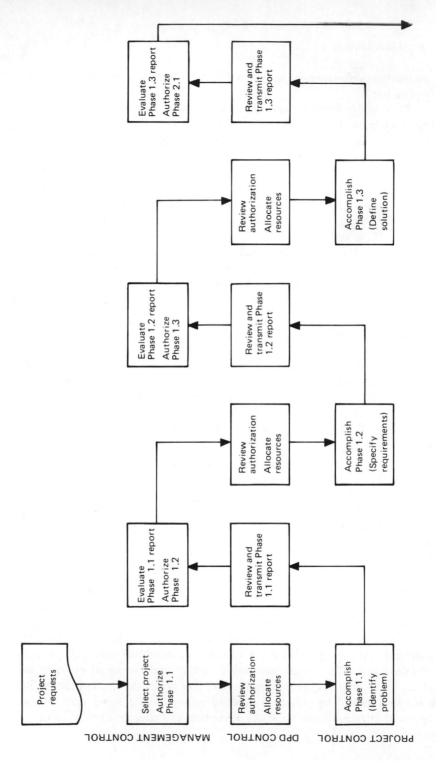

Figure 4-4. Project authorization and approval process

86

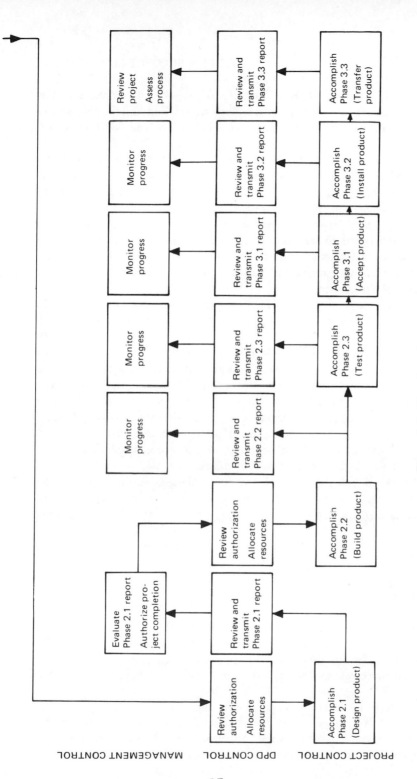

Figure 4-4. (Continued)

Phased authorization is an instance of zero-based budgeting in that funding for each phase must be justified separately. Funding for a phase does not depend on past expenditure, only on what can be justified for the next effort.

As a practical matter, once the authorization is given to build the product (Phase 2.2), it is unlikely that authorization would be withheld for later stages unless a serious problem were to develop. Therefore, in our "snake" we show that the authorization prior to Phase 2.2 is for the completion of the entire project, not just authorization for the next phase. We assume that Reports to Management for the final phases are reviewed by the Project Selection Committee and that the Committee can withdraw authorization or modify the project if they see fit. But this would be an exceptional action, not the usual one.

The lines in the "snake" of Figure 4-4 show, of course, the normal state of affairs where each phase is authorized in turn. The exceptional case where a prior phase must be redone is not shown.

The concept of phased authorization has a cost associated with it that should not be overlooked. It takes time and effort to make appropriate reports to upper management and for them to report back to the project team. This time and effort must be taken into account, particularly the time, when making estimates of project duration and cost. Also, it is necessary for project planners to alert upper management to the demands that will be made upon them for review and authorization so that these people can set aside time for these activities on their own calendars.

We have stressed the role of Reports to Management in explaining the concept of phased commitment. Let us now be more specific and look at how one part of that report, the revised analysis of costs and benefits, is used in the phased approach.

Whenever a decision is made to undertake a project or to continue an existing one, it is necessary to make an assessment of the costs and benefits of the project. When the project is first proposed to the Project Selection Committee, the cost/benefit assessment is necessarily crude because it is based on many assumptions and incomplete data. The most realistic way to state anticipated costs and benefits at this stage is to give the ranges in which these quantities are expected to lie. The analysis can be improved somewhat in Phase 1.1. In this first phase the ranges for both costs and benefits can usually be narrowed somewhat, but it is too early to have a clear idea of either.

In Phase 1.2 when the requirements and scope are specified, it is possible to get a fairly good idea of the expected benefits from the project. The range of costs can also be narrowed, but it isn't until Phase 1.3 that these are fairly well known. After the solution is selected and the external design is complete, it should be possible to assess quite closely the cost of completing the project and operating the system. Thus, the cost/benefit ratio that is computed at the end of Phase 1.3 should prove to be a fairly good indicator of what will come to pass.

To some extent, the risk of a project can be measured by the widths of the ranges for estimated costs and benefits. Before starting the project, these ranges are wide and the risk is high. Partly to control this risk, the original decision calls only for a small investment to conduct Phase 1.1. One result of this small investment is a narrowing of the ranges for costs and benefits with a resulting lowering of risk. The somewhat lower risk helps to justify the investment of the larger sum required to conduct Phase 1.2. The result of Phase 1.2 is another lowering of risk, primarily through narrowing the range of expected benefits. With lower risk, it is easier to make another fairly large investment for Phase 1.3. The result of this is a narrowing of the range of costs to match the narrow range of benefits. Altogether, the investment in Phases 1.1, 1.2, and 1.3 represents about one-third of the total cost of the project. For this investment one not only has considerable project work done but also has a much reduced risk when contemplating the expenditure of the remaining two-thirds of the cost required to complete the project.

It can be seen that the cost/benefit and risk analyses and their successive revisions are very important to the Project Selection Committee. Related to this and also important is the estimated duration of the project. Project duration is related to phased planning, which is discussed next.

4-10 PHASED PLANNING

Generally it is not possible to plan an entire project in detail at the beginning of the project. For instance, it is not possible to plan details of the build phase (Phase 2.2) before the decision has been made in Phase 1.3 to modify the existing system, to construct a new system, or to purchase and modify a package. By the same token, it is not feasible to establish a firm completion date for a project before even the scope is known. One of the most common problems faced by project managers is the fruitless attempt to meet a completion date that was set before the full requirements of the system were known. The phased approach to planning calls for planning documents that realistically can be produced.

Under phased planning, the output of each phase of a project (except the last) includes two planning documents: the Phase Plan and the Project Plan. The Phase Plan is prepared at the standard task level, and it covers the next phase of the project. This document is used in making the decision to authorize the next phase. It is also needed to plan work units and actual work assignments for the next phase. The other document, the Project Plan, is an overall, aggregated plan for the entire remaining project. This document is needed because it provides an estimate of the project completion date and of the resources needed to complete the project.

To understand the nature of phased planning, let us describe how the Phase and Project Plans might be produced on a typical project.

There was no detailed Phase Plan for Phase 1.1 when our typical project started, so the first order of business was to develop one. This was a simple task because only a few people were involved in the first phase and only five days were allotted to it. Planning for Phase 1.1 was heavily based on a Standard Phase 1.1 Plan that was part of the organization's project methodology.

One task in Phase 1.1 was to develop a Phase Plan for Phase 1.2. There was little time for this activity; therefore it was necessary to rely heavily on the general list of standard tasks in building the Phase Plan. The interviews conducted in Phase 1.2 proved to be more extensive and to take longer than had been envisioned during Phase 1.1 This resulted in somewhat more work in Phase 1.2 than had been anticipated; as a result the actual time and effort exceeded the estimates in the Phase 1.2 Plan by about 20%. However, this experience led to more realistic estimates for the remaining phases.

At the end of Phase 1.2 a Phase Plan was prepared for Phase 1.3. The estimates in this plan proved to be very close to the actual experience.

In Phase 1.3 it was possible to get a fairly clear idea of the remaining work required for the project and the resource that would be committed to it. At the end of the phase, therefore, not only was a Phase Plan prepared for Phase 2.1 (as required by the methodology), but also preliminary Phase Plans were prepared for all remaining phases. These preliminary Phase Plans provided valuable input to the Project Plan that was prepared at the end of Phase 1.3. They also simplified the planning effort in subsequent phases; for these phases all that was necessary to produce the Phase Plan for the next phase was to update the preliminary plan.

When our typical project was authorized by the Project Selection Committee, there was little that could be called an overall Project Plan. Primarily there was a range for the estimated project cost and a range for the project duration. The Project Plan produced in Phase 1.1 was almost as skimpy because there was so little time to develop it. At this point, the Project Plan called for a project with standard phases. Durations and resource requirements were given for each phase and were summarized for the project. These were stated as ranges of values to emphasize the tentative nature of the estimates.

The Project Plan developed in Phase 1.2 was given at the phase level, but it was based partly on a set of standard tasks for all DP projects. This list was not tailored to the project, but the estimated durations and resources were. Since the scope of the project was now known and some ideas had been gained of the probable solution, in reviewing the list of standard tasks it was possible to sharpen the estimate of the duration and resources for each phase. This resulted in a narrowing of the range of estimates for these quantities but left room for further improvement as more was learned about the system.

The Project Plan developed in Phase 1.3 was based on the preliminary Phase Plans that were developed for all remaining phases. This Project Plan proved to be reasonably sound and required only minor adjustments in subsequent phases.

In the example just described, we did not discuss the detailed plans that would be required for making actual work assignments. These plans are not part of the phase outputs; they are prepared at the beginning of the phase to which they apply. Detailed plans are not prepared until the phase is actually authorized because there is always the chance that some major unexpected change might hit the system or that the project might suffer some blow that would negate the detailed plans. Therefore, the rule that we follow is to build the detailed plans just ahead of the time when they are required. This rule tends to curtail replanning effort and to avoid planning work that might not be authorized. Also, spreading the planning effort over the project tends to avoid peaks and valleys in the demands placed on the planning staff. The topic of detailed work planning is discussed at length in Chapter 5.

In employing phased planning, one must be reasonable about the requirement that an output of any phase (except the last) is a Phase Plan for the next phase. If, for example, a strong recommendation is made at the end of Phase 1.2 to abort the project, it makes little sense to accompany this with a Phase Plan for Phase 1.3. If the project is continued in spite of the recommendation, this Phase Plan can always be constructed at the beginning of Phase 1.3, and a statement to this effect should accompany the Phase 1.2 output.

Some of the concepts of phased planning that have been illustrated above can be summarized as follows:

There is not one plan but a sequence of plans moving from highly aggregated to detail.

Details are introduced into the plans only when it is feasible to do so, that is, only after decisions have been made that affect the details.

A corollary to these concepts is the notion that a single, firm duration for the project is not given at the very beginning. Rather, a range is given for the completion date. As the scope of the system is defined, this range is progressively narrowed until a firm date is established. This firm date will be known by the end of Phase 1.3 for many projects, and it is known at the end of Phase 2.1 for almost all projects.

4-11 PHASED IMPLEMENTATION

The concept of phased implementation calls for each phase of the project to be developed as a separate project. This principle is almost an outcome of phased commitment since the phases are separately authorized and funded under the latter concept. But the two are separate ideas, as can be seen from the realization that phased implementation could be practiced even though the entire project were authorized and committed prior to Phase 1.1.

Under phased implementation careful attention is given to the output of each phase. This output is so well documented that a separate team could use it and go on to the next phase. This, in fact, is what often takes place on a very large project. The design team and the programming team, for example, can consist of separate people, and the phase output is the main communications link between the two. Also, with the careful documentation of a phase, a project can be "shelved" for a time if priorities change, and it can be resumed later when conditions warrant.

Even if separate teams of analysts, designers, programmers, and so on are used for separate phases, it is a good idea to have some overlapping of these groups. Having an internal designer involved in Phase 1.3 can help to avoid an architecture for which it would be difficult to build a design. Having a tester involved in Phase 2.1 can result in a design for which it is easier to construct test cases. If not part of the formal team, such "downstream" people might be brought into peer reviews and other reviews to express ideas and opinions.

An important benefit of phased implementation is the security aspect. Because each phase is treated as a stand-alone project, the documentation at the end of any phase gives a clear description of all results that have been obtained to date. If a copy of this documentation is stored off-site, it provides a convenient checkpoint and restart point for the project. If disaster strikes the project, it should be necessary at most to go back to the beginning of the then current phase to replace the material that has been destroyed. DP is accustomed to having a checkpoint and restart procedure for *products,* and phased implementation provides the same safeguards for *projects.*

In phased implementation, indeed for the entire phased approach, we have stressed that one phase is completed before management approval is given to start the next. In practice it is often the case that phases are allowed to start before formal approval has been obtained, particularly if there is a tight deadline for the project. We see no great problem with this if it is not the common practice—a formal methodology should not be a straightjacket that narrowly confines a project to a particular form. But even though the methodology is bent at times, it still serves as a standard for the way the project should be done, all other things being equal. It provides a frame of reference that gives the project form, much as a skeleton gives shape to the body.

4-12 PROCEDURES FOR PRODUCING THE PRODUCT

A project methodology should specify procedures for producing a product, such as those listed in Table 4-1. Because they are similar, these procedures will be discussed as a group rather than one at a time.

The primary means we have used to specify procedures for building a product are to require work products as part of the phase outputs and to list the required work among the standard tasks. Of course, these basic procedures are at the heart of our methodology. Our phases were designed around them, and most of our scheduled standard tasks and phase outputs relate to them.

To back up this primary way of specifying these procedures, a project methodology should provide a brief summary for each procedure. This summary should identify the procedure, key it to relevant phase outputs, and provide additional information that might be required to adjust the procedure to a particular project. This summary is also the place where relevant work performance standards can be referenced and related documentation requirements listed.

Most procedures for building the product call for a supporting plan. For instance, the Conversion Procedure calls for a Conversion Plan as an output of Phase 2.1, and preparation of this plan is part of a standard task during that phase. The purpose, content, and useful information about such a plan should be included in the project methodology. These plans for different procedures are an important foundation for Phase and Project Plans.

4-13 PROCEDURES FOR MANAGING THE PROJECT

Procedures for managing a project, such as those listed in Table 4-1, do not share too many common characteristics. Some management procedures give rise to standard tasks that can be scheduled and some to nonscheduled standard tasks. The Change Procedure falls in the latter category. It is a procedure that may or may not be invoked on a project.

Some management procedures, such as planning and review, require specific phase outputs. Others, such as approval and documentation procedures, mainly describe other project documents or how they are handled. The authorization procedure is in still another category; it describes an interfacing system and is included in the methodology largely as important background information for the project team.

Descriptions of Procedures

Because procedures for managing a project have such different characteristics, it is difficult to describe them as a group. What we shall do instead is to review each of the management procedures of Table 4-1, discuss references to it that have been embedded in the methodology so far, and point to other parts of the book that contain additional relevant information.

This treatment of management procedures is similar to the one found in actual methodologies for organizations. In part, management procedures are embedded in lists of standard tasks, required phase outputs, and prescribed project forms. In addition, however, each important management procedure is usually described in a separate section of the methodology. Sometimes this is a brief summary sheet, such as those given in Appendix C, sometimes it is a lengthy description.

Authorization Procedure. This is a procedure for selection and original authorization of the project and for subsequent authorization of project phases. These topics are discussed in Section 4-9 and Chapter 9.

Organization Procedure. There are many ways to establish and organize a project team. Some shops have fixed teams that stay together from project to project, others form a new team for each project. Some shops organize teams on a traditional hierarchical basis, some use a chief programmer arrangement, and some emphasize teamwork. Our methodology is slanted toward this last method of organization, as can be seen from our emphasis on transactional estimating (Chapter 13), self-control (Chapter 3), and peer reviews (Chapter 17). However, our methodology is not heavily dependent on the way teams are organized, and it can be molded to fit most environments.

We have done no more than touch on organizational matters in this book; to go more deeply into this topic would carry us well beyond the scope of our effort. Our omission of organizational topics parallels the practice in most methodologies. Most of the time this topic is described in a separate document and is only referenced by the project methodology.

Projects involve the authority, responsibility, and participation of all of the many functional areas that deal with the project. For that reason, projects can impact organizational and personnel procedures far beyond the confines of the project team. We touch on this impact in our discussion of responsibility grids (Chapter 18). It is clear, however, that a definitive statement of functional responsibility and authority is a subject for the organization or personnel system, not for the project methodology.

Project Planning Procedure. Time and resource planning involves laying out schedules, work assignments, machine schedules, budgets, and the like. It results in Project Plans, Phase Plans, and Action Plans. Some details of the planning process were discussed in this chapter and more are discussed in Chapter 5. Some tools that can be used in planning are function analysis (Chapter 12), estimating (Chapters 13 and 14), and networks (Chapters 15 and 16).

Internal Training Procedures. These procedures have to do with training the project team and providing the knowledge and skills required to build the project product. Internal training can be contrasted with user training, which has to do with providing the knowledge and skill needed to use the product being built.

We describe training in our methodology by listing the necessary standard tasks and phase outputs. The type, extent, and timing of training vary considerably from project to project. For that reason, an Internal Training Plan should be built for each project to detail how internal training needs will be met.

Change Procedure. This is a procedure for making changes in baseline documents, which are the original inputs to the project or documents that are produced as output of some phase. The topic of change is discussed in Chapter 18.

Interpretation Procedure. This is a procedure for resolving ambiguities in approved documents; for a discussion, see Chapter 18.

Tracking and Reporting Procedure. Tracking and reporting are part of the control process. We presented out basic control philosophy in Chapter 3. Our procedure for tracking and reporting at the project phase level was discussed in Section 4-9. Tracking and reporting within a phase will be discussed in Chapter 5.

The tracking and reporting procedure is closely linked to planning, and the two procedures might well be taken together as a planning and control procedure.

Review Procedure. There are two kinds of project reviews. *Technical* reviews are held to examine project deliverables to determine if they meet requirements. These are reviews for product quality, and they are usually held by the Project Manager or a special review group. *Business* reviews are held to determine how actual project progress compares to plan and to examine the deliverables from the point of view of the users. They are reviews of project status. Business reviews are held by the Project Manager, the DP Manager, and upper management.

Reviews are held at periodic intervals, at important checkpoints within a phase, at the end of each phase, and at special times, such as when a project is badly behind schedule. The review of phases was discussed in Section 4-9, and reviews held within a phase will be discussed in Chapter 5. A general treatment of reviews appears in Chapter 18. The topic of peer reviews (Chapter 17) is also relevant.

Approval Procedure. This describes the procedure for gaining approval of the project outputs. One way to indicate the need for approval is to show it in a responsibility grid (Chapter 18). Another approach is to indicate required approvals as part of the project documentation procedure. Still another approach is to have a more complete procedure as a separate document in the project methodology.

Project Assessment Procedure. This procedure is the assessment of the project process. We discussed this topic in Section 4-4 and will have more to say about it in Chapter 5.

Project Documentation Procedure. As is often done in a methodology, our project documentation is discussed in many places. It comes up in connection with phase inputs and outputs, and it is involved with such procedures as reviews and change control. In Chapter 5 some of the documents that are used in assigning work and in tracking and reporting progress will be discussed.

The line between project documentation and systems documentation is sometimes hard to delineate. Internal training material might be placed in the former category and user training in the latter. However, the two are similar, and it could be argued that they should be put together. A similar problem arises with reviews. They can be included under project documentation even though technical reviews are concerned mainly with systems documentation. What this illustrates is that *how* things are classified is sometimes not as important as the fact that they *are* classified.

One of the most important project documents is the Project Workbook, which contains both project and system documentation. This and the Project Handbook, which describes the project methodology, are discussed in Chapter 7.

Other Management Activities

The list of management procedures in Table 4-1 does not cover all of the management activity embedded in our methodology. In particular, the following three activities need further comment: business assessment, estimating, and quality assurance.

Business assessment means determining the worth or value of a project and its product. This assessment involves doing a cost/benefit analysis and a risk analysis. Both analyses are required in our methodology as part of the effort needed to complete the Report to Management.

In a typical methodology, procedures for doing cost/benefit analysis and risk analysis are specified by requiring that appropriate forms be completed. We have not supplied such forms here because they must be tailored to the organization that is to use them. However, in Chapter 10 (Cost/Benefit Analysis) and Chapter 11 (Risk Analysis) we discuss how such forms can be devised for an organization.

Estimating is obviously required by our methodology. In fact, many parts of our methodology relate to this activity.

The phased approach to projects is largely based on our attitude that reliable estimates cannot be made at the beginning of a project. The required accuracy of estimates for different phases might well be established as a tracking and reporting standard. The data used in estimating can be inferred from details of the planning procedure and the tracking and reporting procedure. The forms used to do detailed work planning can indicate the need to coordinate estimates derived from different sources. All of this shows that, while estimating might not be listed as a separate management procedure, it is deeply entwined with many others.

Most methodologies encountered in practice do not have a separate discussion of estimating. Many, however, have forms or formulas that are to be used in making estimates, and the estimating procedure involves completing the form or using the formula. In Chapters 13 and 14 we discuss some of the techniques that can be used to estimate. We also discuss the requirements and steps involved in building an estimating methodology for a given organization.

The last topic we will comment on is quality. Our belief is that quality is everyone's job, and our methodology reflects this by its emphasis on individual responsibility and self-control. To attain quality it is necessary to have clearly defined work objectives and relevant work performance standards. These requirements, too, are basic to our methodology.

The basis for quality is a committed worker. But many of the procedures of our methodology also have a bearing on quality. User involvement, clear documentation, realistic estimates, change procedures, adequate training, and technical reviews all help to promote a quality product. Some of these topics are discussed more fully in Chapter 18.

4-14 SUMMARY

- A project methodology specifies certain aspects of a project, it references other documents that contain project-related material, and it interfaces with other organizational systems and procedures.
- A project methodology specifies project work explicitly by listing tasks and implicitly by establishing documentation requirements.
- A project methodology must be adjusted to the organization it is to serve. We have listed our assumptions about the organization that is to use the methodology described in this book.
- The methodology described in this book is based on nine phases:

> Phase 1.1 Identify Problem
> Phase 1.2 Specify Requirements
> Phase 1.3 Define Solution
> Phase 2.1 Design Product
> Phase 2.2 Build Product
> Phase 2.3 Test Product
> Phase 3.1 Accept Product
> Phase 3.2 Install Product
> Phase 3.3 Transfer Product

- The methodology described employs parallel development and a phased approach to commitment, planning, and development.
- In our project methodology, procedures for producing the product are specified primarily by listing standard tasks and required phase outputs. Management procedures are specified in a variety of ways.

5

PROJECT PLANNING

5-1 INTRODUCTION

A project methodology is a standing plan that applies to all projects of an organization, but to accomplish a specific project it is necessary to build plans, both general and detailed, that apply to that particular project and to control against these plans. This work is the responsibility of the Project Manager.[1] The purpose of this chapter is to show how planning and control of a specific project is done consistent with the project methodology.

The project methodology does not specify completely what a Project Manager must do to plan and control a particular project, but it does indicate the major steps. This specification is usually done in two ways. First, some of the tasks to be performed are given in checklists. This is often done at the Standard Task level, but for some specific tasks more detailed lists might be provided. Second, some tasks are implied by the documentation requirements. By requiring certain reports for all projects and by specifying the content and format of these reports, many of the planning and control tasks are defined implicitly. Of course, a Project Manager is constrained not just by formal requirements, usually he must also follow certain customary practices that are "handed down" in the organization but are not formalized. However, a good methodology minimizes the amount of planning and control work done simply because "this is the way we always do it."

It is essential that the Project Manager be allowed some latitude in his planning and control function. This is necessary to accommodate differences

---

[1] The Project Manager might assign the planning and control tasks to someone else. However, we shall attribute the work to him because it is his responsibility.

from project to project in the product, people, environment, constraints, and so on. But, while recognizing the need for individual variation, it is nevertheless important to have uniformity in both documents (plans, reports, etc.) that flow from the project group to others (upper management, users, etc.) and in project data that is used outside the project (for estimating, cross-project comparisons, postinstallation reviews, etc.). These requirements impose restrictions of uniformity on such matters as:

> The size of work units
> Quality standards
> Collection and allocation of cost and time information
> Timing and content of reports to users and upper management

At the same time, it allows the Project Manager flexibility on such matters as:

> Actual work units, actual assignments
> Number of internal project reviews
> Use of specific planning tools and techniques (networks, processors, automated document handling, etc.)
> Procedures within the team for processing reports, changes, etc.
> Procedures for replanning and adjusting to minor (within phase) problems

To some extent, this flexibility can also be used by the Project Manager to adjust the methodology to his own management style.

In this chapter we shall look at the Project Manager's tasks related to detailed planning at the beginning of a phase, tracking progress during a phase, and planning at the end of a phase for the next phase and for the remainder of the project. The Project Manager has many other duties, including communication, motivation, hiring, evaluation, and enhancement of people. Most of these duties will be ignored to keep within the scope of this book.

Although it might be logical to start at the beginning of a phase and trace activities in sequence, we find it more instructive to begin with the third activity (planning at the end of a phase) because that will provide us with information needed to discuss planning at the beginning of a phase.

5-2 BUILDING THE PHASE PLAN

Near the end of each phase (except Phase 3.3), the Project Manager

must build a Phase Plan for the next phase.[2]   The Phase Plan is used by the
Project Selection Committee in making their decision to authorize the next
phase, it is used in the beginning of the next phase to construct the action
plan, and it provides one basis for assessing the performance of the next
phase. It is *not* used for making actual work assignments; therefore it is not
used in conjunction with tracking and control at the project level.

The Phase Plan is built at the standard task level. It is not a detailed
plan, but it should provide a good idea of the weekly requirements for the
next phase. The time and cost estimates in the Phase Plan should correspond
reasonably well to what will actually be observed. How close actuals should
be to estimates will depend on the organization, but they might be, say, within 10% for the first three phases and within 5% for the rest. Typical contents
of a Phase Plan are listed in Table 5-1.

No plan is ever prepared in a straight-line, step-by-step manner. Everything affects everything else, so the decisions made at one stage may well
impact the work that was done earlier. Plans are usually made in an iterative
manner—a rough plan is made, then it is gone through again to adjust for
problems and discrepancies, then again, and so on until a feasible solution is
found. This is the reality of planning. However, in discussing how to plan,
there is little choice but to describe the process one step at a time. Therefore,
this is what we shall do in discussing the process of preparing the Phase Plan.

Steps in Preparing the Phase Plan

Step 1. List the standard tasks for the next phase. A good place to
start is with the list of standard tasks from the project methodology. Some
of these might not apply to the present project (for instance, Perform Training Tasks); these should be dropped. On the other hand, if the project is at
all unusual, there may be required tasks that are not in the project
methodology list. These should be added and appropriate accounting numbers should be secured for them. (Be certain to report such additions in the
Phase Completion and Assessment Report. Such information is useful for
assessing and revising the project methodology.)

Step 2. Determine responsibility for each standard task. The standard
tasks for the project may involve many functional areas. A responsibility grid

---

[2] The Phase Plan for Phase 1.1 must be constructed at the beginning of the phase.
Because Phase 1.1 is usually limited in duration, the project methodology might provide
a standing plan for this phase. Further, the short time allowed for Phase 1.1 suggests
that the Identification Report should be a standard form for the project team
to complete.

Table 5-1
Typical Contents of a Phase Plan

Identification of phase and project
Purpose, scope, and objective for the phase
Summary information:
      Completion date for the phase
      Total man-hours for the phase
      Total machine-hours for the phase
      Cost for the phase
Detailed information:
      Schedule by standard tasks
      Schedule of personnel required by skill categories
         (weekly basis or more aggregated)
      Schedule of machine requirements
         (weekly basis or more aggregated)
      Budget
Other information:
      Service requirements (administrative, clerical, support, . . .)
      Other special requirements
      Potential problems
Preparation and authorization information (dates, signatures, . . .)

should be prepared showing the responsibility and involvement of the various areas. A standard responsibility grid from the project methodology should provide much of the information required for this step.

Step 3. Estimate the duration and resource requirements for each standard task. Use the planning data base to estimate machine requirements and total effort (man-days) by skill category for each standard task. Since these elements are based on "typical" past projects, they must be adjusted up or down based on your assessment of the work involved in this particular project. Once the total effort is estimated, a decision should be made as to the duration and number of people (by skill category) required for each standard task.

Step 4. Decide on the ordering (network) for the scheduled standard tasks. The definitions of the standard tasks provide information on precedence requirements, and an ordering can be built from this. Alternatively, an ordering might be established by making appropriate adjustments in another network, for instance, a standard network from the project methodology or a network from the history of a similar project.

*Step 5.   Build a schedule for the scheduled standard tasks and deter-
mine the completion date for the phase.*   This can be done by using formal
networking techniques or by building a bar chart directly from the standard
tasks. In any event, it is a good idea to display the schedule on a bar chart as
an aid in communicating the plan to others. Also, a bar chart will be useful in
taking the next step.

*Step 6.   Determine the resource requirements by categories for the
phase.*   Resource requirements for scheduled activities can be derived from
the schedule and the resource requirements for the individual standard tasks.
To this must be added resource requirements for nonscheduled activities,
such as certain management and administrative tasks.

Step 7.   Prepare a budget for the phase. Expenses for personnel and
equipment usage can be derived by applying standard costs to the resource
requirements. To this must be added special budget items, such as travel and
living, hardware or software products charged to the project, consulting fees,
etc.

Step 8.   Adjust the plan to meet known constraints. Constraints can be
imposed on people, equipment availability, completion date or other deadlines, and funding. We have placed this step near the end of the sequence
because it is not until this point that all parts of the plan can be checked for
constraints. In practice, of course, constraints are taken into account as one
goes along. For instance, constraints on time would be considered when the
schedule is being built; if adjustments are necessary, they will be made at
that point.

Step 9.   Make an independent assessment of the plan. By using the
planning data base or some other means, such as the Delphi technique, make
an independent estimate of the total effort and duration for the phase. This
should be made by treating the phase as a whole in contrast to the above approach of looking at individual pieces. Compare the independent estimate
with the plan that was developed from an analysis of standard tasks; reconcile
any major differences between the two.

Step 10.   Examine the plan for potential problems. Is the project
scheduled at full capacity during a heavy vacation period? Is the schedule
tight because of imposed constraints? Are there potential personnel changes
that might impact the project? Will the project depend on a new and largely
untried software package? Some potential problems might have been overlooked in building the schedule; adjustments should be made to correct for
this oversight. Other potential problems will have been recognized all along;
these should be noted in the plan to keep attention focused on them.

Step 11.   Hold a review of the plan. Before submitting a plan, every
effort should be made to see that it is complete and reasonable. A peer
review is one of the best ways to accomplish this. If a group of peers cannot

be assembled, an alternative is to have a review of the plan by the project team or by a selected group of experienced team members. In lieu of a peer review, some organizations have the plan reviewed by a Systems Assurance Group.

   Step 12. Prepare the final copy and submit the plan.

Partial Resources

   As the details of planning are worked out, two questions usually arise about personnel: How do you handle vacations, sick time, and other non-productive activities?   How do you handle the situation where a person is assigned only part time to a project?   Clearly it is necessary to establish a policy for recording time that answers both questions. It is also clear that the policy must be applied uniformly to all projects, which means that it must be part of the project methodology, not just part of the plan for a particular project.

   One policy for recording time spent is to recognize three general categories: (1) time spent on a work unit that is part of a standard task; (2) time spent on a project activity that is not part of a standard task; and (3) time spent on nonproject activities. The first and third categories should be reasonably clear.   The second category refers to any activity that is to be charged against the project but does not fall in the first category; this would include vacation time, sick time, waiting time, and so on.   Although it is a slight distortion, the first category will be referred to as *productive* project time and the second as *nonproductive* project time. Each of these three categories would have many subcategories, and each subcategory would have its own distinctive account number for reporting purposes.

   Questions arise even when there are well-defined categories for recording time.   Is the time spent saying hello in the morning and discussing last night's football game to be charged to the subsequent work unit, therefore productive time, or is it nonproductive time?   Is the time spent waiting for a test result idle time or part of the testing activity?   How should the time spent on a peer review of a colleague's work be charged?   For each question that arises, there are usually at least two reasonable answers. Most of the time it is not too important which answer is selected. What *does* matter is that the selected answer be used uniformly throughout all projects. If time spent is always recorded in the same way and if this way is at all sensible, then there is a firm basis for estimating and making other cross-project comparisons.

   On the assumption that the above general categories are used for recording time, let us make a few additional remarks about estimating personnel requirements and meeting constraints (Steps 3 and 8). For convenience, we shall assume there is only one skill category. If there are several categories, the procedure described should be followed for each category.

First, let us see how resource requirements are adjusted to reflect nonproductive effort. As an examination will show, the estimate of required man-hours developed above in Step 8 refers only to productive project work. An allowance must be made for nonproductive work; a simple way to do this is to make an appropriate adjustment when man-hours are converted into man-days. From data on past projects it is possible to determine what percent of a typical working day is productive. By applying this percent to the number of working hours in a day, the number of productive hours in a day can be determined. If this number is divided into the number of productive man-hours required to do a task, the result is the number of required man-days. This is the total number of man-days or total *effort* to do the task, and it takes into account the fact that part of each day will be productive and part nonproductive.

An example will help to illustrate this. Assume that data from past projects shows that about 60% of the typical working day is productive. This means that $8 \times 0.60 = 4.8$ or about 5 hours of an 8-hour day are productive. If a certain standard task requires 65 man-hours of productive work, then it will require $65 \div 5 = 13$ man-days of effort. As a check, we see that in these 13 man-days there are $13 \times 8 = 104$ total man-hours. This consists of $13 \times 5 = 65$ productive hours and $13 \times 3 = 39$ nonproductive hours.

Next, let us see how to adjust for part-time workers. We shall handle this by adjusting the resource constraint on the project.

A phase is constrained by the number of people assigned to it and by the amount of time each person is to spend on the project. If the fractions representing the time each person is to spend are added together, one obtains the number of full-time equivalent (FTE) persons assigned to the phase. For instance, suppose that five people are assigned to a certain phase of a project. If one person is assigned full time and the others are assigned half time, then the phase has the equivalent of $1 + (4) (0.5) = 3$ FTE people assigned to it. That is, three people working full time would contribute the same effort as the people actually assigned. For planning purposes at this stage, we can proceed as if there were really three people assigned full time.

A plan for a phase is feasible as far as personnel restrictions are concerned if it does not require more people at any time than the number of FTE people assigned to it. A less stringent test for feasibility is that the total number of hours required (productive and nonproductive) must not exceed the number of FTE people assigned multiplied by the total number of hours one full-time person will work on the project. This second test does not consider the timing of resource utilization, but it does show that the total required effort is available.

There are two places where the procedure of this section can be adjusted to advantage. First, in calculating the number of FTE people on a project, we tacitly assumed no loss of effort from splitting a person between two jobs. But in fact if one is switched back and forth between jobs, it is often necessary to spend time after each switch in getting reoriented. An adjustment might be made to reflect this loss of effectiveness from the use of part-time people. For instance, if a person is assigned half time to each of two projects, it might be reasonable to count him as, say, 0.4 FTE persons on each project.

The second adjustment relates to the estimate of productive work generated in Step 3. As described there, we assumed that the man-hours required for a standard task could be estimated without first fixing the duration of the standard task. This is not an unreasonable assumption to make for scheduled standard tasks, but nonscheduled standard tasks, which include many of the management and administrative tasks, are often performed throughout the phase. This means that the man-hours required for them depends on the duration of the phase, and this is not known until the schedule is constructed. This problem can be adjusted for as follows. In Step 3, estimates can be made for scheduled standard tasks as described in that step. With this information, it is possible to build a schedule as described in Step 5. After this is done, an estimate can be made of the resource required for nonscheduled standard tasks prior to determining the total resource requirement in Step 6.

5-3 EXAMPLE OF PHASE PLANNING

An example will illustrate some of the steps that a Project Manager takes in building a Phase Plan. In our example we deal with only a single resource—people—and make other assumptions to simplify the discussion.

Assume the plan is for Phase X. This phase has four standard tasks, all requiring the same skill. Three of these standard tasks (numbers 1, 2, and 3) are scheduled, and one (number 4) is not. Some information about the average experience for Phase X on past projects is given in Table 5-2. This information is taken from the planning data base.

From work to date on the present project, the Project Manager estimated that Phase X would be about average size. Thus he anticipated a plan with around 800 man-hours of total effort. He was told to base his plan on the assumption that two full-time and three half-time people would be assigned to Phase X.

The data on past projects showed the Project Manager that about 60% of the effort on Phase X is productive ($470 \div 800 = 0.59$). Therefore he decided to base his plan on the estimate that 5 hours out of each 8-hour day would be productive $(8 \times 0.60 = 4.8)$.

Table 5-2
Average Effort and Duration for Phase X

	Average Man-hours
Standard Task 1	100
Standard Task 2	150
Standard Task 3	150
Standard Task 4	70
Total productive effort	470
Nonproductive effort	330
Total effort	800

Average duration of Phase X = 25 work-days

As another preliminary step, the Project Manager made a rough estimate of phase duration. He observed that a total of 800 man-hours would amount to $800 \div 8 = 100$ man-days. Since the project was to have $(2)(1) + (3)(0.5) = 3.5$ FTE people assigned to it, the duration should be about 29 days $(100 \div 3.5 = 28.6)$. This, of course, is slightly longer than the average length of Phase X on past projects. However, the histories of several past projects revealed that they were shorter on average because they typically had more people assigned to them.

The Project Manager next made an assessment of the effort required for each scheduled standard task. This assessment was based partly on the data in Table 5-2 and partly on the special circumstances and requirements of the present project. He first estimated productive man-hours, then converted these into man-days by dividing by 5, the estimated number of productive hours in a day. The results are shown in Table 5-3.

Table 5-3
Effort for the Scheduled Standard Tasks of Phase X

	Man-hours	Man-days
Standard Task 1	90	18
Standard Task 2	165	33
Standard Task 3	170	34
Total	425	85

Next the Project Manager decided on the order of the work. He found that Tasks 1 and 2 could be done in parallel, but that both should be completed before Task 3 was started. This ordering is shown in Figure 5-1.

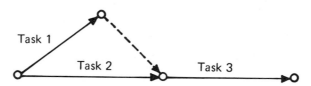

Figure 5-1. Network for the scheduled standard tasks of Phase X

On a typical project, Standard Task 4 requires 70 man-hours of productive effort over a 25-day period (Table 5-2). This amounts to $70 \div 25 = 2.8$ productive hours per day, which is the effort per day of about 0.5 FTE persons. On observing this, the Project Manager decided to build a plan for the present project by allocating 3 FTE people to the scheduled standard tasks and 0.5 FTE people to Standard Task 4.

On his first attempt to build a plan, the Project Manager decided to allocate people among scheduled standard tasks as indicated in Table 5-4. This allocation results in task durations as shown in that table and a schedule as indicated in Figure 5-2. (That schedule is based on starting each task as soon as possible.)

Table 5-4
The First Allocation of FTE People to Standard Tasks

	Man-days	FTE People	Days Duration
Standard Task 1	18	2	9
Standard Task 2	33	1	33
Standard Task 3	34	3	12

Figure 5-2. Bar chart for the schedule associated with Table 5-4

The allocation of resources indicated in Table 5-4 resulted in a 45-day duration for the phase. The effort of the three FTE people allocated to the scheduled standard tasks is expended as follows:

Total man-hours	$= 45 \times 3 \times 8 = 1080$
Productive (scheduled) man-hours (Table 5-3)	$= \underline{425}$
Nonproductive man-hours	$= 655$

Thus about 40% of the effort of the three FTE people is productive (425 ÷ 1080 = 0.394).

There are two obvious problems with this schedule: The duration is too long, and not enough effort is productive. Both problems might be corrected if more people were assigned work during the middle of the phase (days 10 through 33).

On observing these points, the Project Manager decided to try another approach. This time he decided to allocate people as indicated in Table 5-5. This results in the schedule in Figure 5-3.

Table 5-5
The Second Allocation of FTE People to Standard Tasks

	Man-days	FTE People	Days Duration
Standard Task 1	18	1	18
Standard Task 2	33	2	17
Standard Task 3	34	3	12

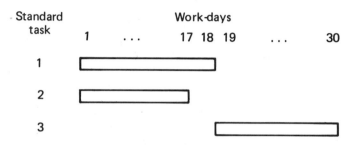

Figure 5-3. Bar chart for the schedule associated with Table 5-5

The allocation in Table 5-5 results in a 30-day duration and the following expenditure of effort:

Total man-hours	$= 30 \times 3 \times 8 = 720$
Productive (scheduled) man-hours (Table 5-3)	$= \underline{425}$
Nonproductive man-hours	$= 295$

Thus about 60% of the effort of the three FTE people is productive (425 ÷
720 = 0.59).

This second schedule looked reasonable to the Project Manager. The
duration is in line with the rough estimate of 29 days made earlier, the total
effort is in line with the amount usually expended on scheduled standard
tasks, and the percent of effort that is productive is right at the traditional
level. Observing this, the Project Manager decided to go on with this plan and
to add the unscheduled standard task. Because Task 4 will be required for
the entire phase, it meant adding a 30-day task for 0.5 FTE people. The total
effort for this is therefore $30 \times 0.5 \times 8 = 120$ man-hours. Assuming typical
productivity, the productive effort is $30 \times 0.5 \times 5 = 75$ man-hours.

Table 5-6
A Summary of the Effort for Phase X Using the Schedule
Associated with Table 5-5

	Man-hours
Total Effort	3.5 × 8 × 30 = 840
Productive Effort	
Standard Task 1	90
Standard Task 2	165
Standard Task 3	170
Standard Task 4	75
Total Productive Effort	500

A summary of the effort required for the second plan is given in Table 5-6. This shows that the total effort exceeds the traditional Phase X effort by 5% (40 ÷ 800 = 0.05). Partly this is because the scheduled standard tasks require extra effort, and partly it is because the nonscheduled standard task is to be performed for five more days than usual. (In turn, these extra days are required largely because less resource than usual is being allocated to the phase.) Table 5-6 also shows that the traditional percent of total effort is being spent on productive work (500 ÷ 840 = 0.60). Thus the plan appears to be reasonable by historical standards.

The Project Manager now had a good start on a Phase Plan, but his job was not yet complete. He had to build the other parts of the plan, check it for potential problems, and review it with peers or other appropriate people. We shall not, however, extend our example to these activities.

5-4 BUILDING THE PROJECT PLAN

At the end of each phase (except Phase 3.3) the Project Manager prepares a Project Plan in addition to the Phase Plan just discussed. More precisely, he updates the Project Plan so that it will include the actual data on the phases completed (including the phase just closing) and a revised estimate for future phases. Typical contents of a Project Plan are given in Table 5-7.

Because it provides a summary of the project to date and an outlook to the future, the Project Plan is a primary input to the Project Selection Committee for their decision on authorization and continued funding of the project. The Project Plan is also used for the after-the-fact assessment of a project; it provides the estimates against which actuals can be compared.

Table 5-7
Typical Contents of a Project Plan

Identification of project and phase being completed
Purpose, scope, and objective of the project
Summary information:
      Completion date for the project
      Project cost
            Phases completed (actual)
            Phases to come (estimated)
            Total
      Major changes from the previous Project Plan for this
         project
Detailed information (by phases; actuals for phases completed
   and estimates for future phases):
      Completion date
      Man-hours by skill categories
      Machine time
      Cost
Other information:
      Significant service requirements (by phase)
      Other special requirements (by phase)
      Potential problems
Preparation and authorization information (dates, signatures, . . .)

A Project Plan is highly aggregated and is usually built at the phase level. This is not to say that additional detail is never considered in developing the plan, but once developed it is presented at the phase level. In fact, the part of the Project Plan that deals with the next phase is obviously based on a detailed analysis because it is a summary of the Phase Plan discussed in Section 5-2. For phases beyond the next one, the Project Manager might also look at the standard task level in building the Project Plan. How much of this detailed examination is done depends to some extent on the stage the project is in. If the Project Manager is building a Project Plan near the end of Phase 1.2, he might not explore details beyond the next phase because too much is still unknown about the system being built and an "accurate" Project Plan is not required. On the other hand, a Project Plan prepared near the end of Phase 2.1 should be reasonably close to what will actually transpire, and it may be that the only way the Project Manager can achieve this accuracy is to plan all subsequent phases at the standard task level.

The Project Plan is usually built near the end of a phase. It requires information from the Phase Plan, so it must be built after that; and it requires information on the actual cost and duration of the current phase, which is known only at the very end of the phase. The steps in building the Project Plan are listed below. We shall not comment on those that are similar to steps in preparing a Phase Plan.

Steps in Building the Project Plan

Step 1. Record information on actual durations, resources used, and costs. For prior phases, this information can be obtained from the Project Plan prepared at the end of the previous phase. All that must be added is information on the current phase.

Step 2. Record estimates for the next phase. This information can be obtained from the Phase Plan for the next phase.

Step 3. Estimate durations and resource requirements for phases after the next one. The planning data base and actual figures to date (Step 1) provide some of the information needed for this. Estimates can be made at the phase level or can be made at a standard task level by following the Phase Plan steps (Section 5-2).

Step 4. Estimate costs for phases after the next one. In addition to required resources, the estimated costs should include costs of hardware, site preparation, fees, software, and so on.

Step 5. Adjust plans for known constraints.

Step 6. Examine for potential problems.

Step 7. Compare the plan with the previous Phase Plan and note any major differences. If there is a major difference in duration or cost, discover the reason for it.

Step 8. Hold a peer review of the plan.

Step 9. Prepare final copy and submit the plan.

5-5 THE PHASE ASSESSMENT

The assessment of a phase is not part of the planning process. However, it is a task that the Project Manager performs at the end of a phase, and for that reason we believe it is appropriate to comment on it briefly at this point.

The purpose of a phase assessment is to provide input to Phase 3.3, Transfer Product. The phase assessment is a device for capturing information about the project process while it is still fresh in the minds of the people. This assessment is used to evaluate and improve the project methodology,

Table 5-8
Typical Contents of a Phase Completion and Assessment Report

Identification of project and phase being completed
Comparison of Phase Plan and Work Plan:
      Phase duration comparison
      Phase man-hours comparison
      Phase machine time comparison
      Phase cost comparison
      Significant deviations, reasons for them
Comparison of Work Plan and Actuals:
      Phase duration comparison
      Phase man-hours comparison
      Phase machine time comparison
      Phase cost comparison
      Significant deviations, reasons for them
Other observations:
      Significant deviations from standard Project Methodology
      Additions to standard task list
      Valuable new techniques
      Problems
      Suggestions
Preparation information (dates, signatures, . . .)

estimating techniques, and the like. Typical contents of a Phase Completion and Assessment Report are shown in Table 5-8.

The assessment of a phase calls for certain routine data, but it also calls for observations about problems or new techniques, reasons for deviation from plans, suggestions for improvements, and so on. This is not routine data; it requires thought and analysis to provide useful information and observations about the project process. The time to develop information of this sort is *not* at the end of the project while the formal assessment report is being prepared. A good idea can occur to anyone associated with the project and it can arise at any time; the time to capture the idea is when it arises. The Project Manager should maintain a file throughout the phase into which he puts comments and ideas as they occur to him, and other team members should be encouraged to do likewise. Alternatively, some member of the team can be appointed as the recording secretary and all ideas and observations that might be suitable for the phase assessment can be funneled to that person. If good ideas are captured as they occur, the task of completing the phase assessment is very simple. Moreover, the assessment will probably be much more useful than it would be if it were simply the product of a last-minute brainstorming session.

5-6 ACTION PLANNING

We have described some of the project planning that is done at the end of a phase; now we turn to the planning that is done at the beginning of a phase. In essence the Project Manager converts the Phase Plan into a collection of action plans that spell out the details of the work to be done during the phase. How this is done will depend to some extent on the way the project is organized; therefore we begin by reviewing this topic.

At the present time most shops organize their teams in one of two ways: as fixed teams or as *ad hoc* teams. A fixed team is a group of people who stays together (barring normal attrition and additions) from project to project. They are formed as a unit and work flows to them. With this form of organization, skills are well known to the Project Manager, but they are relatively inflexible and work must be carefully tailored to them. The other method of organization has no generally accepted name, but we refer to it as an *ad hoc* team because it is put together for one particular phase or project. Usually people are drawn from a "pool," and they are selected because their particular skills match the requirements of the job. In effect, the people flow to the work. At the end of the assignment, people return to the "pool" and await their next assignment. With the *ad hoc* method of organization, the Project Manager may actually recruit the team members, and he does this on the basis of the manpower requirements of the project.

Ad hoc teams are often formed for extremely large projects or for projects of a special nature. They are frequently used by software contract houses and other shops that handle large numbers of diverse projects. The more common method of organization, on the other hand, appears to be fixed teams. They are used by both small and large shops and are almost a standard in some industries, notably banking, insurance, and government.

To be definite, in our discussion of action planning we shall assume the fixed team method of organization. Thus we assume that a team of people has been assigned the task of completing the phase. A team leader, whom we call the Project Manager, has been appointed and given responsibility for coordinating the team effort. After action planning in this environment has been discussed, we shall comment on the minor differences for *ad hoc* teams.

Degree of Formality

There are many kinds of plans that should be made at the beginning of a phase. Some of these are always laid out as formal, written plans; others are sometimes handled informally. The degree of formality in action planning depends on many factors, including:

The size and complexity of the project. Planning is more formal for a 20-person effort than for a 2-person effort.

The actual phase. Phase 1.1 usually requires less formal planning than Phase 2.2, which typically involves a high degree of parallel effort.

The completeness of the project methodology. If, for instance, the project methodology spells out review procedures, then it is only necessary to fix frequency and other details; otherwise it is necessary to specify all aspects of the review procedures in the action plans.

Experience of the team. If a team is experienced and is accustomed to working together, there is less need to detail all aspects of plans than if the group is newly formed and cannot reply on past practice.

Management philosophy. An organization that is heavily involved with formal planning will usually carry this philosophy into the project area.

As action planning is discussed, keep in mind that the procedure actually used by an organization will vary with the above factors. Action planning, as with other aspects of a project methodology, must be adapted to the requirements of individual organizations.

5-7 THE WORK PLAN

At the beginning of a phase, the Project Manager has available:

Enabling documents, which provide funding, resources, and authorization to start work
The Phase Plan, which gives aggregate guidelines for detailed planning
The project methodology, which provides guidelines for conducting the phase
Baseline data, including
    Specific outputs from previous phases
    Data specific to the current project
    The Project Workbook, which contains all project documentation
Personnel Register, which describes the skill, experience, and other relevant information for each person assigned to the phase

The Project Manager must study these input documents, construct appropriate plans, organize and orient the team, and get the project under way. Of all his activities, we shall focus only on the planning that must be done.

The foundation for all action plans is the Work Plan. This document shows the work to be done, a schedule for doing it, and the individuals assigned to do it. Following are the steps that are taken in building the Work Plan. As you read these steps, keep two things in mind. First, although we discuss the steps sequentially, the building of a Work Plan is an iterative process with many loops and much back-tracking. Second, although we speak as if the Project Manager were building the plan by himself, there is a continual exchange of thought between the planner and the workers while the plan is being built.

Steps in Building the Work Plan

Step 1. Classify standard tasks into those that are to be scheduled and those that are not. Usually this classification will follow the pattern laid down in the Phase Plan. Most standard tasks will be scheduled; the exceptions typically relate to management and support activities.

Step 2. Allocate personnel between scheduled and nonscheduled activities. Specific individuals are assigned the nonscheduled tasks. Although time spent on these tasks will appear in final resource summaries, it is not covered by the schedule and is not followed by the project tracking system (Section 5-10).

Step 3. Determine work units. Each scheduled standard task is analyzed and work units are defined to accomplish it. In defining work units, the Project Manager may use function analysis, the history file for a similar project, or personal experience.

Work units are defined in keeping with the standards laid down in the project methodology. In general, these specify that each work unit:[3] (1) must be clearly described in writing; (2) must have a clearly defined output, an indication of the skill levels required to accomplish it, and an estimate of the effort required in each skill category; and (3) must be assigned an identification that relates to the specific project and the accounting number of the corresponding standard task.

The total effort required for all work units must be reconciled with that estimated in the Phase Plan. It is not necessary that the efforts match for

---

[3] Additional characteristics of work units are listed in Section 5-10.

each standard task, but the total effort for all work units should be in line with the total in the Phase Plan. If it is not, the discrepancy should be investigated and understood.

Step 4. Estimate duration and manpower for each work unit. Given the effort required for each task, it is necessary to fix the duration and required number of people in each skill category. This is done on the basis of experience, the history of similar projects, and planning data, such as the number of productive hours of work in the typical day. Work units are usually sized so that each represents a three- to six-day task for one person. But they may be larger, (say, four days for two people), or smaller (say, five days for one-half person). When more than one person is scheduled for a task, sufficient time for communication should be allowed.

The manpower assigned to work units should be reconciled with the manpower estimate in the Phase Plan, and major discrepancies should be explored.

Step 5. Estimate other resource requirements for each work unit. An estimate is made of the machine time and special administrative support (typing, keypunch, clerical) required for each work unit. The total requirement for these resources is then reconciled with the Phase Plan.

(It has been convenient for us to list Steps 3, 4, and 5 separately, but obviously they are closely related. In practice they are often combined into one effort.)

Step 6. Build a dependency table. For each work unit, a list is made of the work units that must be completed just before it (immediate predecessors). This is done by looking at each input to a work unit and matching these with the outputs of other work units; matching outputs belong to work units that must be completed prior to the work unit in question.

Step 7. Schedule the work units. This means establishing a start date and a due date for each work unit. The schedule must be consistent with the constraints (deadlines, due dates, and given start dates) in the Phase Plan and with the dependencies listed in Step 6.

A schedule can be constructed by building a bar chart directly; this is a practical approach if there are few work units involved. For larger efforts, it is easier to use network techniques, and a network processor can be useful. However built, the final schedule is most easily communicated to others if it is displayed in a bar chart.

Step 8. Determine (scheduled) manpower requirements for the phase. At this step manpower requirements have been stated for each work unit, and each work unit has been scheduled for a specific time period. This information is combined to produce a statement of the day-by-day manpower requirements for each skill category.

Step 9. Level the schedule to meet the manpower constraints. At this point it is necessary to match the manpower requirements (Step 6) with the manpower assigned to the phase. This means adjusting the schedule so that for each skill category the number of people required on any day does not exceed the number available. To attain such a feasible schedule it may be necessary to adjust start and due dates on some tasks, to adjust the duration and resource requirements on others, or even to revise the entire network.

Although we are primarily concerned with a single project, we should note that the influence of other projects makes itself felt at this point because resource constraints reflect the other work going on in an installation. If a feasible schedule cannot be attained in any other way, it might be necessary at this point to reallocate resources among projects. This, of course, is not a decision for the Project Manager.

Step 10. Determine (scheduled) other resource requirements for the phase. This is similar to Step 8 except that it involves finding the machine and special support requirements.

Step 11. Adjust the schedule to other resource constraints. This is similar to Step 9 except that it involves constraints on machine time and support services.

(Because of similarities, manpower and other resources could be taken together for purposes of finding requirements and leveling to constraints. We have taken them separately, however, because manpower is usually a critical factor and the other resources are less critical.)

Step 12. Reconcile the tentative Work Plan with the Phase Plan. Although some reconciliation has been done previously (Steps 3, 4, and 5), at this point the evolving Work Plan and the Phase Plan are compared. This is done for the following reason.

For each phase, there are two estimates of the duration and resources. The first estimate, which is part of the Phase Plan, was obtained by judging the overall project size, comparing this to historical records for similar projects, and then estimating how much time and resource each phase should take. This might be considered an estimate "from without" the phase—it is based largely on comparable past projects and an overall judgment of size. The second estimate of phase duration and resources is the one obtained by following the steps listed above. This involved estimating durations and resources for individual work units, scheduling these, and modifying the results in light of constraints. The estimates obtained in this way were built up "from within" the phase by examining the individual pieces of work and their interrelations.

In most cases, these two estimates will be in substantial agreement; when they are not, it is necessary to resolve the difference. It might be discovered, for instance, that the present project is not comparable to those done in the past, or that the resource constraints are not typical, or that the development technology or project organization is different. Any of these facts would suggest that the estimate developed "from within" is the more reliable guide to phase performance. On the other hand, a difference in the estimates might be caused by overlooking tasks that must be performed, or by inaccurate estimates of work unit durations, or by an unusually bad arrangement of the work units into a network. Problems such as these suggest that the estimate "from within" is faulty and that it would be wise to recheck the entire Work Plan and make necessary modifications. In those situations where the difference in the two estimates cannot be explained satisfactorily, it is advisable to monitor phase progress very closely.

(At this point adjustments have been made to meet known constraints. The aim is to have a reasonably good plan prior to making work assignments so as to minimize confusion and inconvenience to people.)

Step 13. Make work assignments. At this point the "supply" of people is matched to the "demand" for their services and individual work assignments are made.

The requirements for people are fixed in a general way by the responsibility grid of the Phase Plan and in a specific way by the descriptions and skill requirements of the individual work units. To match people to these requirements, it is necessary to have information on the availability of people (vacations, meetings, nonproject assignments, etc.) and on their skills and experience (languages, past training, past projects, etc.). This information should be available in writing; we assume it is in a document we call the Personnel Register. The need for formality is stressed because personnel information is frequently in oral form unless the project is very large or there is considerable turnover. The Project Manager frequently has all of this information in his head and believes there is no need to reduce it to writing—because, of course, nothing will ever happen to *him.*

In making individual assignments, it is necessary to allow some slack to cover contingencies such as illness, accidents, promotions, and resignations. Slack can be measured on an aggregate basis by comparing the personnel available at any time with the personnel required. The desired level of slack for a project can best be determined by examining the history of the organization. One point to watch for, however: Don't build slack in twice! If estimated durations for individual work units take slack into account, it is not necessary to make a second provision by holding overall resources significantly above the resource requirements.

The outputs of this step are individual work assignments. These should be written statements telling who is to do what and when it is due. The assignments should also indicate responsibility if more than one person is assigned to a work unit.

Step 14. Validate individual work assignments. A smart Project

Manager involves his team in the planning process as much and as early as he can. He touches base with them on such matters as the work units involved, the efforts required for them, and the potential schedule for the phase. In spite of this, the Work Plan may not look sensible to some members of the team. To learn if this is so, the Project Manager checks with each individual to determine if each work assignment is reasonable.

Each worker reviews his assigned tasks for clarity and completeness. He verifies that skill requirements are appropriate and that all prerequisite tasks have been identified. By using transactional estimating (Chapter 13) or some other technique, the worker and Project Manager reach mutual agreement that task durations are reasonable.

In the process of validating work assignments, problems are likely to be uncovered. Correction of these will generally require some replanning, and in extreme cases it can lead to substantial changes in the schedule. Troublesome as this may be, rescheduling the phase is preferable to ignoring the problem and having it surface at a later point in the form of missed deadlines or unsatisfactory quality.

Step 15. Build plan summaries. The Work Plan is almost complete at this point; all that remains is to summarize material and add financial information. Summaries are made to meet specific requirements of the Project Manager and others who interface with the project. They usually cover such aspects as manpower plans, machine requirements, and administrative support.

Summary information can be displayed in many ways, and the choice depends to some extent on the size of the team. For instance, manpower assignments might be shown on an individual basis for a small team and by skill categories for a large one. Or assignments might be summarized into such categories as productive work, training time, vacation time, and idle time. The format of the report should be dictated by the use to which it will be put.

Summary reports should include all resources of the phase. Specifically, they should include the resources assigned to nonscheduled standard tasks as well as to the scheduled ones.

Step 16. Build budget. Next a budget or financial plan is built to show the expected pattern of expenditure for the phase. Usually the most important element of this plan is the cost of manpower and equipment. These costs are found by applying standard cost factors, which typically include fringe benefits, to the estimated requirements for the resources. Other elements of the budget might be special charges, such as the cost of hardware, software, supplies, and contract services, and an allowance to cover general overhead.

The budget should be validated against the Phase Plan and the funding provided for the phase. Discrepancies should be analyzed and dealt with.

Step 17. Review the Work Plan. Before submitting the plan, it should be reviewed and checked for bugs. This can be accomplished in many ways: a peer review, a less formal review with colleagues, a review with selected team members, or a review by a Systems Assurance Group.

Step 18. Prepare final copy and implement the plan.

Ad Hoc Teams

These steps complete the Work Plan; they provide specific assignments for the people and specific requirements for equipment and other resources needed for the phase. The major focus of the Work Plan is on time and resources. There is need to supplement this plan with other action plans, which focus more on the quality aspects of the phase. These will be discussed in Section 5-9. Before we conclude the present section, however, let us see how the above work planning steps would be modified if *ad hoc* teams were used.

For *ad hoc* teams, the major change in the above procedure has to do with the use made of the statement of manpower requirements prepared in Step 8. This document becomes the basis for recruiting members to the team. It is sometimes referred to as a *Manpower Plan* because it is viewed as a blueprint for a staffing activity. To some extent, this staffing activity does away with the need for leveling in Step 9; people are added or dropped according to the demands spelled out in the statement of requirements rather than adjusting demand to fit the available resource. Recruiting a staff requires considerably more time than it takes to adjust a plan to a given group. This means that with *ad hoc* teams there may not be too much difference in the planning steps, but there is a very big difference in the time required to execute the steps. To keep this added time from delaying the project, some of the detailed work planning is frequently done at the end of the previous phase—in effect the phase plan is built at the work unit level and goes up to the point of making individual assignments. The recruiting of a team then becomes one of the first activities of a phase, and action planning starts at Step 13 in the above list.

5-8 EXAMPLE OF WORK PLANNING

To illustrate work planning, let us continue the example of Section 5-3. In that section we developed a Phase Plan for Phase X. Some of the steps that might be taken to convert this plan into a Work Plan will be described now.

From the Phase Plan it can be seen that Standard Task 4 is not scheduled. We assume that this is the task of managing the project and that it has been assigned to the Project Manager. He is to work on this and another project simultaneously and is to charge half of his time to each project.

A careful analysis of the work required for this project suggested that the other three standard tasks could be divided into work units as shown in Table 5-9. (In that table and throughout this example, the names of the work units have been abbreviated; a full name would have a prefix to identify the project and phase.) Table 5-10 compares the effort required by this work

Table 5-9
Work Units for the Scheduled Standard Tasks

Standard Task 1		Standard Task 2		Standard Task 3	
Work Unit	Effort	Work Unit	Effort	Work Unit	Effort
1-1	25	2-1	23	3-1	20
1-2	16	2-2	25	3-2	20
1-3	20	2-3	23	3-3	25
1-4	15	2-4	26	3-4	30
1-5	19	2-5	25	3-5	20
		2-6	24	3-6	24
		2-7	23	3-7	25

Table 5-10
Effort for Scheduled Standard Tasks

Standard Task	Total Effort for Standard Task	
	Table 5-9	Phase Plan
1	95	90
2	169	165
3	164	170
Total	428	425

breakdown with the effort estimated in the Phase Plan. The close agreement between these two suggested that the work breakdown was reasonable.[4] The Project Manager was a little troubled by the size of Work Unit 3-4; however, he decided not to subdivide it because doing so would involve adding considerable extra effort for communication.

The estimation of duration and resource requirements for each work unit was made simple by the decision that each work unit would be assigned to a single person. This decision automatically fixed responsibility for work units with the individuals assigned to the tasks, so it simplified this aspect of planning, too. Because five productive hours is the average for a day, the durations (Table 5-11) follow quite automatically from the estimate of effort in Table 5-9. The only durations that the Project Manager was uneasy about were those of Work Units 1-2 and 2-4. Both could use slightly more time judging from the effort required. However, the Project Manager did not want to deal with fractional days, and a full extra day for each work unit seemed too much. Therefore the Project Manager left the durations as shown in Table 5-11, but he noted that these two work units would bear watching.

Table 5-11
Durations for Work Units
(Each Work Unit Requires One Person)

Standard Task 1		Standard Task 2		Standard Task 3	
Work Unit	Duration	Work Unit	Duration	Work Unit	Duration
1-1	5	2-1	5	3-1	4
1-2	3	2-2	5	3-2	4
1-3	4	2-3	5	3-3	5
1-4	3	2-4	5	3-4	6
1-5	4	2-5	5	3-5	4
		2-6	5	3-6	5
		2-7	5	3-7	5

---

[4] A quicker but less detailed check is as follows. The Phase Plan calls for 3 FTE people to be assigned to the scheduled standard tasks for 6 weeks. This amounts to 18 man-weeks of effort; hence there should be about 18 work units if each is to be assigned to 1 person and is to take almost a week. Table 5-9 lists 19 work units, which is in the right neighborhood.

The durations assigned in Table 5-11 compare with the estimates in the Phase Plan as shown in Table 5-12. The close agreement between the two suggested that there was no major problem up to this point in preparing the Work Plan.

Table 5-12
Durations for Scheduled Standard Tasks

	Duration for Standard Task	
Standard Task	Table 5-11	Phase Plan
1	19	18
2	35	33
3	33	34
Total	87	85

The Project Manager decided to schedule the project by following the pattern in the Phase Plan. That is, he decided to perform Standard Task 1 and 2 in parallel, and to start Standard Task 3 when these two were completed. Within the standard tasks themselves, he observed the precedence requirements shown in Table 5-13. These gave rise to the phase network shown in Figure 5-4.

Table 5-13
Precedence Requirements for Work Units

Work Unit	Prior Work Unit	Work Unit	Prior Work Unit	Work Unit	Prior Work Unit
1-2	1-1	2-2	2-1	3-2	3-1
1-3	1-2	2-3	2-2	3-3	3-1
1-4	1-1	2-4	2-2	3-4	3-2
1-5	1-4	2-5	2-4	3-5	3-4
		2-6	2-2	3-6	3-4
		2-7	2-6	3-7	3-3

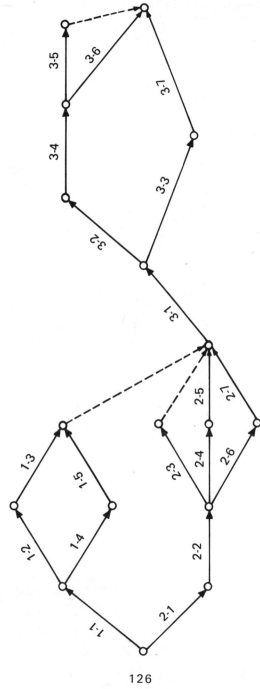

Figure 5-4. Network #1 for scheduled work units

In line with the Phase Plan, four people had been assigned to the project for Phase X in addition to the Project Manager. Frankie and Johnny had been assigned full time, and Jack and Jill were assigned half time (their remaining time was to be spent on a concurrent resource acquisition program). The Project Manager decided to schedule the phase by allocating tasks to the four workers—in this way he could schedule, check resource constraints, and make preliminary task assignments simultaneously. The schedule he constructed and the assignments for the four workers are given by the bar chart in Figure 5-5.

It was easy for the Project Manager to see that his schedule was not practical. It allowed too many days (39) for the phase, and it did not make sufficient use of the part-time people. Without making a formal calculation, it was easy for him to see that this schedule did not allow people to work in a productive manner.

The Project Manager examined his schedule carefully to discover what might be done to improve it. He observed that some work units might be shortened by assigning more than one person to them. More basically, however, he realized that his network could be revised. At the standard task level (as in the Phase Plan) it was necessary to show Standard Task 3 starting after the other two standard tasks were completed, but at the detailed work unit level it was possible to have some overlap of these activities. A careful analysis of the work associated with Standard Task 3 revealed that the only necessary constraints among standard tasks were those given in Table 5-14.

Table 5-14
Additional Precedence Requirements for Work Units

Work Unit	Prior Work Unit
3-1	1-5, 2-4
3-2	1-3, 2-3, 2-5, 2-7, 3-1

As a result of his analysis, the Project Manager listed several specific things that he might do to improve the schedule:

Shorten the durations of Work Units 1-1, 2-2, and 3-2 by assigning multiple people to them. (He wanted to do the same thing with Work Units 2-1 and 3-1 but decided against this after examining the nature of the tasks.)

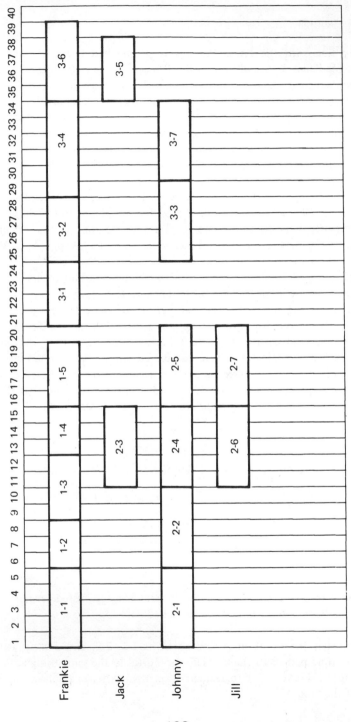

Figure 5-5. Schedule #1 for scheduled work units

128

Subdivide Work Unit 3-4 even though this required extra effort for communication

Start Work Unit 3-1 after Work Units 1-5 and 2-4

Start Work Unit 3-2 after Work Unit 3-1 and after all work units of Standard Tasks 1 and 2

Using these ideas, the Project Manager constructed a revised network (Figure 5-6) and a revised schedule (Figure 5-7).

The revised schedule assigns two people to Work Units 1-1, 2-2, and 3-2, and it reduces each to a three-day activity. Work Unit 3-4 is subdivided into concurrent Work Units 3-4A and 3-4B, each dependent on Work Unit 3-2 and each requiring four days. All of these changes add six man-days of effort to the phase, bringing the total effort to 93 man-days. The distribution of effort among the four workers is shown in Table 5-15.

Table 5-15
Days Assigned to Workers in the Schedule of Figure 5-7

Worker	Days Assigned
Frankie	29
Jack	19
Johnny	28
Jill	17
Total	93

In reviewing the plan up to this point, the Project Manager made the following observations:

The duration (30 days) matches the estimate in the Phase Plan.

Responsibility must be assigned to Work Units having multiple people assigned to them. He decided to ask Frankie to be responsible for 1-1 and 3-2, and to ask Johnny to be responsible for 2-2.

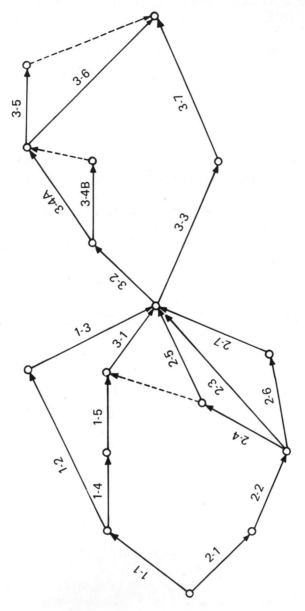

Figure 5-6. Network #2 for scheduled work units

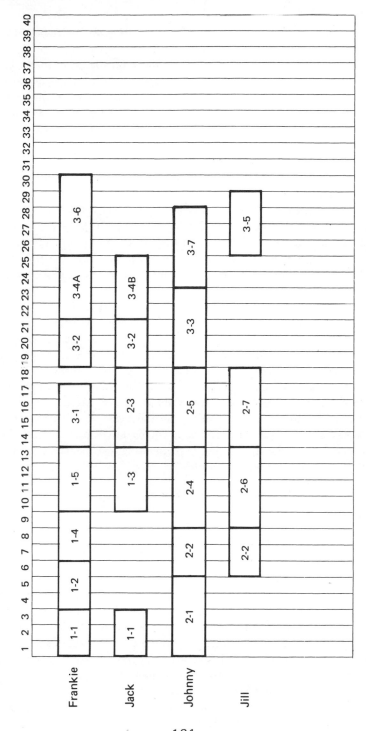

Figure 5-7. Schedule #2 for scheduled work units

131

Both Jack and Jill have slightly more than a one-half time load. Activities could be exchanged between them if required by the demands of their other assignment (for instance, Jill could do Work Unit 3-4B in exchange for Jack doing Work Unit 3-5). But the total load for the two might be too great; it would be necessary to review this point with them and the manager of their other project.

Because Work Units 1-2 and 2-4 were slighted on their durations, the Project Manager checked to see what would happen if they slipped behind schedule. He found that Work Unit 1-2 could slip a day with no problem. But Work Unit 2-4 was critical; if it were delayed a day it would delay Work Unit 3-2 and hence the project. This presented a potential problem, but it was lessened somewhat by the observation that Work Unit 3-2 seemed to have ample resource, therefore it might absorb a delay.

In reviewing the schedule, the Project Manager observed that it was "tight." The phase would require careful monitoring because any delay would be difficult to overcome. Nevertheless, the plan up to this point looked reasonable enough for the Project Manager to go further with it. It was still necessary for him to review the plan with the four workers and to verify that his work units looked reasonable to them. After making necessary adjustments to reflect their views and the slight overload for the part-time workers, it would be necessary to review the plan with other experienced project managers before implementing it. However, our example will not be extended to these activities.

5-9 OTHER ACTION PLANS

A Work Plan is always built for each phase of a project. It is the primary plan for a phase because it sets the schedule and resource usage. Frequently, however, there are planning requirements that are not covered by the Work Plan. To meet these, it is necessary to supplement the Work Plan with other special action plans. Just which other plans are required will depend on factors such as the project size, the extent and flexibility of the formal methodology, and the experience of the project team. In this section, some other action plans that are built for phases will be described.

Organization Plan. This plan shows how the project team is to be organized and fixes major responsibilities; it adds organization structure to the personnel requirements given in the Work Plan. A formal Organization Plan is generally required only for very large teams or for *ad hoc* teams. For smaller teams, particularly if they are fixed teams, the organization is usually established outside the project.

Facilities Plan. This plan relates to the facilities needed by the project team to do its work. It covers the space for accomplishing work assignments, conference rooms, facilities for testing, clerical facilities, and so on. The Facilities Plan does *not* relate to site preparation, installation of software and hardware, and other facility matters that are part of building the product.

The Facilities Plan is most necessary when the project team is to work in a location they are not accustomed to. For instance, such a plan might be needed if a team is to work in a remote location or if the location is to be supplied by another organization (as is the case for many software shops).

Clearly the Facilities Plan has financial implications for the project; if a Facilities Plan is required, it should be prepared before the Budget is completed.

Internal Training Plan. This is the plan for training project personnel (team members and users) in order that they have the knowledge and skills required to accomplish the project. It covers training for such skills as design, coding, testing, and project management. The Internal Training Plan does *not* include the user and operations training required to use the system being built; that training is covered by a plan that is one of the project deliverables.

The Internal Training Plan must be coordinated with the manpower requirements in the Work Plan. For that reason the Internal Training Plan is usually prepared before the Work Plan is completed.

Change Plan. The project methodology should specify a change procedure that is to be used on all projects (see Chapter 18). However, the Project Manager must detail this procedure and state how change will be administered on the current project. This is done in a Change Plan, which covers such matters as:

> How change requests are submitted; by whom; to whom.
> How change requests are processed; how they are classified as major
>   or minor; who approves requests.
> How approved requests are processed.
> The mechanism for distributing information on changes that are made.

The Change Plan is independent of other action plans.

Tracking and Reporting Plan. The project methodology should specify general procedures for tracking and reporting, but it is up to the Project Manager to detail these for the current project. This is done in a Tracking and Reporting Plan, which covers such matters as:

> The procedures for reporting time

    Procedures for processing Work Unit Completion reports
    The frequency and content of periodic reports
    The content, preparation, and distribution of management summaries
    Procedures for exception reports

Tracking and reporting will be discussed in Section 5-10.

    Review Plan. This plan specifies the review procedures to be used on the current project. These procedures must be consistent with the general standards given in the project methodology, and they must be coordinated with the requirements of the Tracking and Reporting Plan. Among the matters covered by the Review Plan are:

    Policies on peer reviews
    Key points within the phase at which to hold checkpoint reviews
    Responsibility for each review

    The Review Plan must be prepared in conjunction with the Work Plan because the phase schedule must include time for reviews and selection of review points depends on the schedule.

    Approval Plan. This plan is a schedule of the various approvals that must be obtained for the products of the phase. The purpose of the plan is to assure that appropriate time is allocated for approvals and to assure that those who must give approval are given adequate notice of the demands that will be made on them by the project. A formal Approval Plan is required only for phases involving a large number of sign-offs; otherwise the information in the Approval Plan is incorporated directly into the Work Plan.

    Documentation Plan. This is a plan detailing the procedures and schedule for preparing, editing, proofreading, and publishing phase documents. The purpose is to assure that adequate time and resource are planned for these activities and to provide required information to support organizations. A formal Documentation Plan is required only if the phase involves a heavy amount of documentation. The Documentation Plan is prepared in conjunction with the Work Plan.

    From the above descriptions it can be seen that most of the other action plans discussed are supplements to the Work Plan. In general they are built to detail an area that is particularly important or complicated. The building of a special plan for such an area allows a division of the planning effort and it also assures that the area gets proper attention. Of course, what is important or complicated can vary from phase to phase and from project to project. If an area covered by one of the other action plans does not present problems, then that plan can be omitted and its contents can be incorporated directly into the Work Plan. For example, if some phase of the current project requires only a few routine sign-offs, then it is not necessary to construct a separate Approval Plan because the sign-off details can be incorporated directly into the Work Plan. The decision to build a particular plan or not is made by the Project Manager within the guidelines specified in the project methodology.

Flexibility in using other action plans also extends to organizations. Some organizations prefer to build most of the action plans discussed, others prefer to build very few and to incorporate much of the planning data into the Work Plan. Whether or not an organization specifies the particular action plans described above, it is important to realize that provision must be made in some way for all of the planning data that these plans detail.

5-10 PROJECT TRACKING AND REPORTING

In previous sections we discussed the detailed plans that a Project Manager builds for time and resources and the reviews that are planned for monitoring quality. In addition to this planning effort, the Project Manager has the responsibility for tracking actual work and for reporting on the progress of the phase compared to plan. In this section the information that must be gathered and the reports that must be generated to accomplish this will be discussed.

During a phase, the Project Manager deals with two classes of reports: those he receives and those he sends. He uses the first class of reports to monitor progress and usually considers that these are part of the tracking activity. He uses the second class of reports to convey information about project progress to others. When a Project Manager talks about reporting, he is usually talking about this second class of reports—those that he sends to others.

Tracking Progress

Some of the reports that are used to track progress include the weekly time report, work unit completion report, computer usage report, special expenditure report, and exception report.

Weekly Time Report. This report is completed each week by each member of the project team, and it indicates weekly time spent on each work unit, time spent on other project activities (training, meetings, etc.), time spent on miscellaneous activities (illness, vacation, etc.), and time charged to nonproject accounts.

This report is the source of information on the actual effort used on the project. It is the basic document for monitoring cost and manpower usage. The information is also used for payroll and personnel purposes; therefore the report must be designed so as to coordinate with those systems. The report should be signed and dated because it is the legal justification for deducting salary expenses for the purpose of tax reporting.

Work Unit Completion Report. This report is filed upon the completion of a work unit (or on the next reporting date after completion) by the person responsible for that unit. The report contains the identification of the work unit, the identification of the responsible person, and the date the work unit was completed. The report might also contain the total effort spent on the work unit, but this information can be computed from the Weekly Time Reports and other documents, and it is better obtained that way.

In filing the Work Unit Completion Report, the responsible person is attesting to the fact that the work unit was completed according to all applicable quality measures (specifications, standards, and so forth). The report is the basic document for quality assurance.

This report is used to track the time aspect of the project. Also, it is used to monitor the project for unusual or recurring problems.

To simplify project documentation, the Work Unit Completion Report can be combined with the Work Unit Description and the Work Unit Assignment Form into a single document. Successive sections of this document can be filled in as work is defined, assigned, and completed.

Computer Usage Report. This report is generated by Operations from machine logs, and it shows the equipment usage per work unit. It is used to monitor cost and equipment usage. It is also used to monitor performance to discover recurring problems with meeting estimates for machine time.

Special Expenditure Report. This report covers all expenditures that are charged to the project other than those that relate to people and equipment. It covers charges for such items as hardware, software, contract services, and training. The report is completed by the Project Manager; it is used to track project costs.

Exception Report. This report is used to highlight trouble or unusual situations that might impact the project. It can be filed by any person connected with the project and should be submitted as soon as the exception is spotted. The report describes the problem and a proposed solution if one can be suggested.

Note that there are no special reports for quality; that is, there are no tracking reports that focus exclusively on product quality. Quality is monitored through appropriate reviews that are built into the work schedule; these range from peer reviews of work units to a review of the entire phase. Work is not complete until quality standards are met; therefore the monitoring of quality is automatically included as part of monitoring work completion. (Of course, some organizations have a separate Systems Assurance Group whose job it is to monitor product quality, and the reports of such a group do focus on quality.)

The content and format of tracking reports are usually specified by the project methodology. This is done to standardize data collection, which is necessary to make project-to-project comparison and to serve other systems (accounting, personnel, etc.) that use the data. The Project Manager is usually required to use the existing reporting mechanisms, but he does have some leeway on the procedures for collecting and processing the reports.

The Project Manager may have more leeway in the way he presents tracking information to others. The project methodology usually specifies an outline for reports and may specify the content and format for summary information, but detailed information can often be presented as the Project Manager sees fit. What will be discussed here is one of the many ways that information can be presented.

Data for Monitoring Progress

Many control systems are based on estimates of the percent of work completed, and it is common knowledge that such systems are notoriously unreliable. An alternative is to base control on estimates of the percent of work remaining to be done or the number of days required to complete a task. While this is logically no different from percent completed, it does seem to have a different psychological impact and it does lead to somewhat better results. But it too requires estimates that at best necessitate some time and thought to obtain and at worst are unreliable. Instead of a control system relying on subjective judgment, we shall present one that is based entirely on completed work. This might be viewed as a system based on fact, not fiction.

Because detailed project control is to be based entirely on work units completed, it is important that work units are:

Based on visible results
Approximately equal in size
Of relatively short duration

The first of these attributes is obviously desirable in order that the completion of a work unit be easily identified. To see that the second is important, suppose that we have a phase consisting of 100 activities, and our reports

show that 50% of the activities are completed. If the work units are of unequal size, this figure tells us nothing about the amount of effort required to
complete the phase. But for work units of about the same size, we can infer
that about one-half of the phase work is accomplished.

In asking only for a report of work completed, we lose ability to
monitor the project within the individual work units. If, for example, a work
unit with an estimated 30-day duration were seriously behind schedule, we
would not know there is trouble until we failed to receive a report of its completion. If, for instance, Work Unit Completion Reports are filed on a weekly
basis, this could mean that the activity would be almost a month behind
schedule before we first learned there is a problem. Obviously this would be
an unsatisfactory situation, and to prevent it we require that all activities be
of short duration. One rule of thumb is that each work unit should take from
three to six man-days. Moreover, if more than one person is assigned to the
work unit, then the duration should be close to the minimum.

This system of control based on work completed has many advantages.
It requires very little effort on the part of the people doing the reporting. In
particular, it eliminates the need to make estimates, which require considerable effort if done regularly and conscientiously. Another advantage is
that it results in more accurate reports because it removes subjectivity.

How practical is this system? Is it possible to satisfy the requirement
that the phase be divided into work units of uniformly short duration? It
must be admitted that it might be hard to do this in some phases of a project.
For instance, it might be difficult to subdivide Phases 1.2 and 1.3 in this
manner. But during these early phases there are generally only a few people
involved with the project and there is not very much parallel activity taking
place; therefore it is not quite so necessary to control by the use of formal
techniques. What about the possibility of using this control system when it
is really needed, for instance, in Phase 2.2 when, traditionally, the greatest
number of people are on the project and the most parallel activity is involved? How easy is it to divide the Build Phase into uniform, small tasks?

The answer to this is dependent on the development technology used
on the project. If traditional methods are employed for design and coding, it
might be quite difficult to divide the Build Phase into work units of the
requisite size; but if modern productivity techniques are employed, it is
another matter. If the design is expressed in HIPOs and follows the approved
standards, then each module in the HIPO chart will represent about one page
of structured high-level code. Thus, if a work unit is taken to be the coding of
a module and the integration of that module into the evolving system, then
the work units are automatically small, uniform, and identified by a visible
result. It follows that the control system we have outlined can be used quite
readily.

It should be acknowledged that a control system based on completed work requires more extensive planning than does the more traditional system. But, as indicated earlier, the traditional system of managing projects has not worked, and more planning and control are required if project objectives are to be met.

Reporting Progress

It is customary for the Project Manager to prepare periodic reports on the progress of the project. Since we propose to control each phase of the project on the basis of work units completed, these reports should contain a comparison of the scheduled with actual work units completed to date. A convenient way to present this information graphically is illustrated in Figure 5-8. That diagram shows two curves for the cumulative number of work units completed to date plotted against time measured in weeks from the project start date. One curve shows the work units scheduled to be completed at any point in time, and it is obtained from information in the network schedule. For example, if the schedule shows that seven work units are to be completed by the end of the fourth week, then this curve has a height of 7 opposite the fourth week. The second curve shows the total number of work units actually completed up to any point in time. Information for this curve is obtained from the Completion Reports. Since both curves are cumulative, it is clear they can never decrease, and the maximum height for both curves is equal to the total number of work units in the phase. The difference between the two curves shows the number of work units the project is ahead or behind schedule at any point in time. For instance, in Figure 5-8 at the end of 10 weeks there are 12 work units scheduled to be completed but only 7 have been completed. Therefore the project is 5 work units behind schedule.

Some reflection will reveal that the information presented in Figure 5-8 is incomplete. For example, it is quite possible that many work units have been completed ahead of schedule and others are badly behind schedule, and still the total number completed might match the number scheduled. In this event the project could still be in serious trouble, particularly if the late tasks are on critical paths.

To overcome this deficiency, we add one more curve to the diagram, as shown in Figure 5-9. This curve represents the number of work units that are both scheduled to be completed and are actually completed by the corresponding date. Stated another way, it is the number of activities completed less the number that are actually completed but are not scheduled to be finished until after the date for which the report is being made. This third curve can never exceed either of the other two.

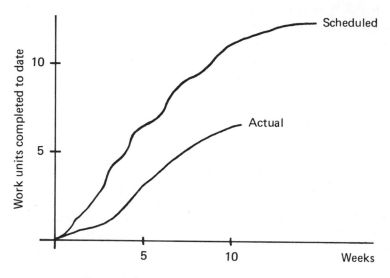

Figure 5-8. Report of completed activities

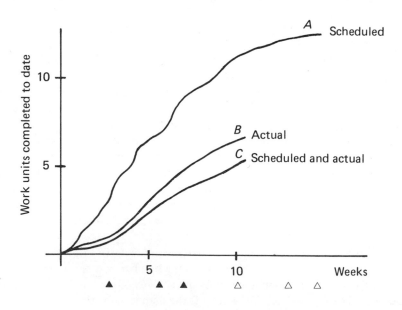

Figure 5-9. Augmented report of completed activities

For convenience the curves of Figure 5-9 have been labeled *A, B,* and *C.* The difference between *A* and *C* shows the number of work units that are behind schedule. The difference between *B* and *C* is the number of work units completed ahead of schedule. The difference between *A* and *B* is the *net* number of work units the project is behind schedule. (Of course, curve *B* could exceed curve *A*, and then the difference would be the *net* number of work units the project is ahead of schedule.)

(The triangular symbols below the time axis of Figure 5-9 are explained in Section 5-11.)

In lieu of or in addition to the charts of Figure 5-9, similar charts displaying information on work units started can be supplied. Some people prefer this because they believe that it gives a slightly earlier warning of potential trouble than does the chart we have shown. Another possible variation is to display the percent of scheduled work units that are actually completed, but if this number is desired it could also be appended as a line of numbers at the bottom of the chart in Figure 5-9.

If the project is on schedule, the information in the charts is probably all that is required. For a project that is in trouble, it is necessary to provide information as to where the problem is. This information can be obtained by rescheduling the network using actual completion dates for finished tasks in lieu of estimated dates. This rescheduling will provide a revised slack for each activity. A list, sorted by slack, of unfinished activities will help to pinpoint the problem area and, in particular, will highlight the late activities that are on critical paths.

The charts just discussed help to report on the time aspect of a project; similar charts can be prepared for reporting each category of resource that is being controlled. For instance, a comparison of actual to scheduled personnel involvement with the project might be presented for each category along the lines of the chart in Figure 5-10.

If a project is ahead of schedule in terms of tasks completed, it would be reasonable to expect that it is also ahead of schedule in resources expended on the project. More generally, it is of interest to compare the percent of work units completed with the percent of resources expended. One way to present this is shown in Figure 5-11. For each week a point is plotted to show the percent of total personnel time expended compared to the percent of work completed (curve *A* in Figure 5-11). If the resulting curve follows the straight line *B* in Figure 5-11, the project is on target. However, if the curve climbs above *B*, it indicates that resources are being expended without the expected output of work, and it shows that a problem exists.

If the summary charts suggest there is a problem, it is necessary to have back-up information showing for each task the scheduled resource on the task, the actual resource used, and the variance. This list should be

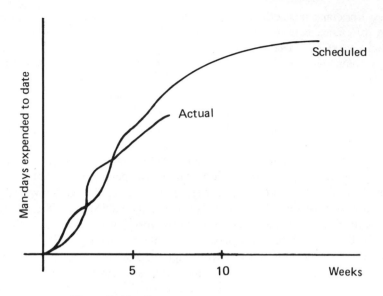

Figure 5-10. Report of man-days expended

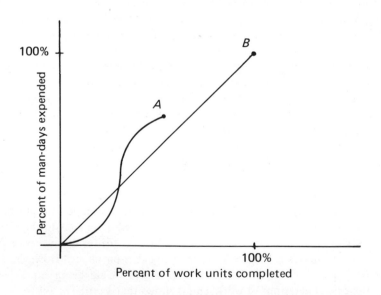

Figure 5-11. Comparison of completed work units and man-days expended

sorted by variance to show at once the type of task on which overruns are being experienced.

Generally it is a good idea to display publicly the charts used to track time and resource utilization. This is an easy way to inform personnel about project progress, and it will generally help to enlist their support in meeting project deadlines.

The charts discussed are used to report on overall phase progress. Some organizations also build summary reports for each individual. They record information such as the actual versus estimated time spent on all work units assigned to date and the actual versus estimated machine time to date. Or they may track the number of test shots used for a particular segment of code. The mechanics of building reports for individuals are similar to those for building reports on the entire project team. But the impact on motivation and morale can be quite different. Records on individuals are required for appraisal and other personnel uses; whether or not they serve a useful purpose in controlling a project is a topic that can be hotly debated. We take no stand on this issue to avoid taking us far beyond the scope of this book, but we do caution that an organization should explore this question carefully before designing their reporting procedures.

To a large extent, the financial reports for a project can be derived in a fairly automatic way from the information about personnel and equipment. A slight problem arises in that most of this information is oriented toward work units, whereas the financial statements usually relate to accounting periods. This can be overcome simply by distributing data for work units on a pro rata basis to the relevant accounting periods. A second problem that arises is that the forms and procedures for financial management are usually prescribed by the organization's accounting department. This may make it difficult to interface financial management as smoothly as one would like with the other aspects of project control, and it may prevent the design of an optimal system for collecting control information. But these problems can usually be classified as minor irritations rather than serious headaches.

For reporting purposes, the most important financial information has to do with actual expenditure for personnel and equipment because these are under the control of the Project Manager. These expenditures are obtained by applying standard costs to the man-days expended and equipment utilized, respectively. The other expenses are generally fairly automatic. Actual expenditures for supplies and contract services can be ascertained from expense accounts, inventory changes, and invoices. Actual project overhead is usually computed from a formula.

Reports comparing budget to actual expenditures may be prepared by the project control group or by the accounting department. Often they are prepared monthly; weekly amounts can be estimated fairly accurately from the reports of resource utilization. The usual format for reports lists the pertinent line items with three columns for each reporting period. These columns are for budget amounts, actual amounts, and the variance (budget minus actual). A report might also have a set of three columns to show the year-to-date figures for budget, actual, and variance.

From the preceding discussion, it can be seen that a comprehensive project reporting system involves a large amount of paperwork. There are a number of software packages that are designed to facilitate the handling of the data and preparation of reports. Many of these systems have facilities for doing network scheduling, computing resource requirements, leveling to constraints, preparing the resource schedules and budgets and the reports of actual progress. In addition, there are various packages for report writing and for budgeting that can simplify the mechanics of project reporting.

5-11 CHECKPOINTS

Thus far we have examined project control at two levels. The planning and tracking discussed in this chapter are at the detailed work level, the most fundamental level of formal control, and are used by the Project Manager, who is responsible for detailed monitoring of the project. The authorization and reporting discussed in Chapter 4 are at the phase level. That level of aggregation is appropriate for upper management, who require only a synopsis of the project. However, neither of these levels of control might be satisfactory for some people associated with the project. For instance, the DP Manager may not want to follow the project at the detailed work unit level, but he may want more than an indication that the major phases have been completed. Some users may have similar requirements. Checkpoints provide an in-between level of control that can meet such needs.

A *checkpoint* is an event or a point in time within a phase when a significant set of work units is completed. It should be identified by visible results, such as the integration of specific modules into the evolving system, or the typing of a certain document, or the end of a test stage. Such ambiguous "events" as "coding 50% completed" should be avoided. Some people like to correlate checkpoints with standard tasks; that is, they select checkpoints that mark the completion of all work units associated with a particular standard task. Some use the rule of thumb that there should be at least one checkpoint for every 15 man-days or one per month, whichever is sooner. However, if the project is behind schedule, more frequent checkpoints might be in order.

A project is monitored at the checkpoint level by comparing the actual time that checkpoints are reached with the scheduled time. A checkpoint is reached when all associated work units are completed according to all quality measures. This means that checkpoints bear on the quality aspect of work as well as the more obvious time aspect.

If checkpoints are used to monitor progress, the Project Manager must build them into the Work Plan. It is necessary to select checkpoints, schedule them, and assign responsibility to individuals for reporting when checkpoints are reached. All of this should be done after work assignments have been made and validated because the checkpoint schedule follows quite automatically from the work unit schedule.

To track progress, a Checkpoint Report is completed by the responsible individual whenever a checkpoint is reached. This report should indicate the date the checkpoint is reached, attest to the quality of the work, and indicate any problems that have arisen or are anticipated. It is not necessary to indicate the resource used on associated work units because this information is available from other sources. The Checkpoint Report is filed with the Project Manager, who might include it with reports to higher levels of management as background information.

Summary information on checkpoints can be added to reporting charts in a simple way. Symbols can be appended at the appropriate points below the time axis of a chart to indicate the checkpoint schedule and checkpoints actually reached. For instance, one method is to use the following symbols:

△ Scheduled checkpoint
▲ Completed checkpoint

Figure 5-9 shows how these symbols would be used to indicate that three out of six scheduled checkpoints have been met.

5-12 SUMMARY

- It is necessary to build general and detailed plans to accomplish a specific project. Although there is some flexibility, these plans must be consistent with standards established in the project methodology.
- Among other things, the Project Manager is responsible for:

  Detailed planning at the beginning of a phase (Work Plan)
  Tracking progress during a phase
  Planning at the end of a phase for the next phase (Phase Plan) and
      for the remainder of the project (Project Plan)

- A Phase Plan is a schedule and budget for the next phase; it is constructed at the standard task level.

- A Project Plan is a schedule and budget for the project; it is constructed at the phase level, although analysis for the plan is frequently made at the standard task level.

- At the end of each phase, an assessment is made of the project to provide input to Phase 3.3, Transfer Product.

- At the beginning of a phase it is necessary to build a detailed Work Plan for the purpose of assigning and tracking work. This plan is a detailed schedule and budget for the current phase; it can be viewed as a detailing of the Phase Plan.

- In addition to a Work Plan, a phase may require such action plans as:

> Organization Plan
> Facilities Plan
> Internal Training Plan
> Change Plan
> Tracking and Reporting Plan
> Review Plan
> Approval Plan
> Documentation Plan

- Project tracking is done by means of:

> Weekly Time Reports
> Work Unit Completion Reports
> Computer Usage Reports
> Special Expenditure Reports
> Exception Reports

- Project tracking and reporting are based on completed work. Within a phase, it is done at the level of work units and checkpoints.

6

ADJUSTING FOR SIZE

6-1 INTRODUCTION

A project methodology must be tailored or customized to the needs and realities of the particular organization that is to use it. One of the realities is that the need for formality and documentation differs with the size of the project. In this chapter some of the adjustments that must be made to fit a project methodology to projects of various sizes will be explored. Also, some of the other realities that could impact a project methodology will be examined.

For purposes of discussion, four project sizes will be assumed: mini projects, small projects, typical projects, and large projects. By a *mini* project we mean one that takes less than a man-week of effort. Typically these arise as small patches or enhancements to existing software. Definitions for the other three size categories are dependent on the organization, and part of the job of adjusting a methodology is to establish these categories. In Section 13-4 we discuss how size categories might be established.

The project methodology discussed up until now was aimed at projects of a typical size. What we shall do here is to show how that methodology can be adjusted for projects in the other three size categories.

In this chapter two other realities that could impact a project methodology are discussed. One of these is the situation of a small shop, which presents problems of a special sort. The other is the impact that could result from individuals being involved with several different projects at the same time.

6-2 SMALL PROJECTS

The methodology discussed has many phases, a fairly involved authorization procedure, and generates many documents. For a small project this level of documentation might not be cost effective. The benefit derived from applying the methodology might be outweighted on a small project by the time and cost of documentation and other formal procedures, and the close upper management control might be totally inappropriate if a lower level of resource is involved.

But on small projects, it is important not to let procedures go to the other extreme. Because one methodology is too extensive, it does not mean that small projects can be undertaken with no formal procedures. It is still advisable to define phases for a small project and to use a phased approach to authorization, planning, and implementation. And every project, even the smallest, must be documented. This documentation is necessary for various purposes, including:

> The need to supply users with information regarding their request, how
> it was complied with, and the cost of doing so
> The need to audit the project to confirm authorization and effective
> use of project resources
> The need to collect information for the planning data base, which will
> be used for estimating future projects

Just what documents should be required for all projects can be determined from a study of the organization's requirements. One standard is to require that every project document at least:

> Project request
> Project authorization
> Project aim, consisting of objective, estimated time, and estimated
> resources
> Project deliverables
> Actual time and resources used
> Product acceptance

It is important that the methodology designed for small projects be consistent with the standard methodology for typical projects. The consistency will make it easier to use the two methodologies. If small projects and typical projects are run in essentially the same way, have similar authorization and control systems, and call for similar reports, then project workers will find it much less work to follow the rules than if there were two completely different systems. Ease of use promotes compliance and leads to more accurate reports. Another reason to keep the two methodologies similar is to generate more useful planning data. If data from projects of different sizes is compatible, it is easier to make project-to-project comparisons and this, in turn, leads to better project estimates.

One way to keep them consistent is to build the methodology for small projects by abridging and "subsetting" the methodology for typical projects. To show how this might be done, we shall discuss what might be required in the way of phases, authorization, documentation, and standard tasks for a small project.

Phases for Small Projects

In Chapter 4 nine phases for the typical project were defined. To obtain these, the function Accomplish Project was decomposed two levels. For small projects, the function is decomposed only one level, thereby obtaining the three phases shown in Figure 6-1. In effect, the first three phases of a typical project are collapsed into a single phase for a small project —all of the work leading to the architecture of the system is regarded as one phase. In the same way, the typical phases of design, build, and test are collapsed into the second phase for the small project. And the typical phases of install, accept, and assess become the third phase for a small project.

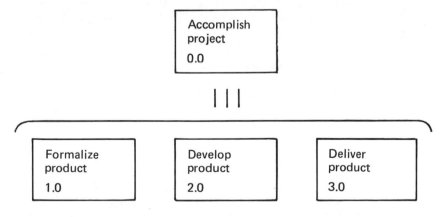

Figure 6-1. Phases of a small project

Once the phases are established for small projects, the phased approach to projects can be applied in much the same way that it is applied to typical projects. For example, let us consider the matter of authorization. Initial authorization, which is an outcome of the project selection process, is for the first phase only. In the case of small projects, this means the authorization of 1.0 Formalize Product. When this phase is completed and the system architecture is designed, a management review is held. If a decision is made to proceed with the project, authorization would generally be given for the completion of the project. It would be understood, however, that a report to management would be made at the conclusion of Phase 2.0 and that the project could be stopped or altered at that point if conditions warrant such measures.

Documentation for Small Projects

The documentation required at the end of each phase of a small project can be defined by subsetting the documentation for a typical project. As a general rule, all documentation that has to do with the project product must still be required: specifications, architecture, design, code, program documentation, test plans, and so on. But some of the documentation that has to do with the project process can be reduced. For the most part, this reduction is made by consolidating reports and reducing the amount of detail rather than by doing away with the reports altogether.

Figure 6-2 illustrates the subsetting of documentation for Phase 1.0, and the other phases are treated in a similar manner. The required documents at the end of Phase 1.0 can be established by condensing the requirements for Phases 1.1, 1.2, and 1.3 of a typical project. For example, the Identification

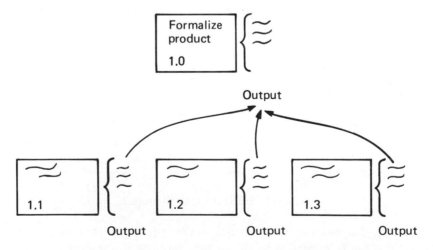

Figure 6-2. Source of required documents for Phase 1.0

Report, System Requirements Specification Report, and System Architecture Report, which are outputs of Phases 1.1, 1.2, and 1.3, respectively, would most likely be consolidated into a single Systems Formalization Report that would describe the scope of the system, the user requirements, and the solution adopted. Of course, there would be only one phase to review (Phase 1.0), and the plan for the next phase would cover all of Phase 2.0.

Except for reducing some of the control and documentation requirements, the generic output of a small project is the same as for a typical project. This means that the generic work or standard tasks for a small project are not much different than for a large project. Some of the standard tasks, such as Determine Support System Specifications, are less likely to be required on a specific small project, but they must be left in the list to be ready for the unusual project to which they do apply.

Having different methodologies for projects of different sizes brings the need for some procedure for classifying projects by size. This classification might be done as part of the selection process, or it might be done by the DP manager when the project is started. It might be done automatically based, for example, on the estimated cost of the project, or it might be done judgmentally. But one fact of life must be faced: If small projects require less documentation, authorization, and control than do large projects, then every project will be small unless very careful control is maintained. For this control, it is necessary to have a clear definition of size and a means of assuring that the definition is carefully followed. A procedure for reclassifying the size of a project if its scope is changed is also required.

6-3 MINI PROJECTS

Mini projects are very common. It is also very common to find that for mini projects there are no records of any kind. Often there is no record of authorization or of the resources used and no documentation of the project product except for the actual change in code that was made in some program. Because there is no documentation, organizations frequently do not have any idea what these projects cost them.

One organization decided to keep records on mini projects. They discovered that the cost of mini projects was being charged by workers to the primary project to which they were assigned—they simply charged all of their time to the primary project and made no allowance for the time spent on other work. Upon analysis it was discovered that these hidden mini projects accounted for 40% of the cost charged to the average project. Incidentally, they also learned that people actually preferred working on the minis and were quite willing to do them because they got quick reward and satisfaction for effort expended.

Mini Project Methodology

An organization should establish a methodology for mini projects, but obviously it should be kept very simple. This simple methodology can be conceptualized as an abridgment and subsetting of the methodology for small projects. For instance, a mini project is conducted in a single phase, Accomplish Project; this can be thought of as having been obtained by collapsing the three phases for a small project into one. This way of conceptualizing the methodology for mini projects provides a framework for deciding what should and should not be required in the way of formal procedures. Also, it helps to keep the methodology for mini projects consistent with that of other projects.

In Section 6-2 the type of documentation that should be required for every project was listed. A mini project is no exception. It should be possible, however, to record this required documentation on a single page for mini projects.

One part of the required documentation for any project is its authorization. For mini projects, the authorization procedure is very simple—the entire project is authorized at the beginning. Thus all that need be recorded is the date and name of the person or group that approves the expenditure of resources on the mini project.

A list of standard tasks is usually not compiled for mini projects. Tasks that have to do with the project product are usually well known to project workers. On the other hand, control and documentation tasks that are sometimes overlooked are implicit in the documentation requirements for the project. The best way to ensure that these tasks are done is to be certain that required documents are completed on all projects.

A mini project is no different from any other project in that it needs to be planned and controlled. But the total effort of a mini project is comparable to a single work assignment of a small or typical project. For tasks of this size, the planning and control effort is part of the job. It is done by the worker as part of his standard procedure, and it is usually done informally; therefore the planning and control effort of a mini project is not documented. However, this does not mean that upper management, say at the DP level, does not have to keep formal control over mini projects. But for their purposes all that is necessary from an individual project is a record of estimated and actual time and resources spent on the project.

Mini Project Problems

There are two problems that are peculiar to mini projects. One of these is that, due to the small resource involved on any one project, they are frequently implemented without formal authorization and control. Thus an important part of the methodology for handling mini projects is to make certain that they are conducted within the organization's guidelines. As indicated earlier, one reason for this control is that the total resource involved in mini projects can be very large. A more important reason is the need to make certain that all program changes are reflected in the program documentation. But the most important reason to control mini projects is for system security. It is impossible to maintain security without maintaining control on every change that is made to a system. Since mini projects usually result in changes to code, these must be authorized and controlled with the same attention that is given to larger projects.

One organization with an on-line order entry system requires at least a dozen pages of documentation before authorizing *any* change to the system, even a one-liner. This documentation must be presented to a review board and approval must be obtained before the change can be made. On some mini projects, the justification and approval process can take several times the effort required to make the change in programs and program documentation. But the organization believes that this situation cannot be avoided if they are to maintain a secure system. (If this level of documentation is required, of course the definition of a mini project must be adjusted upward to allow for this planning and control effort.)

A second problem that is peculiar to mini projects is that they are frequently done by a single person. It is not uncommon for a change to be designed, coded, and tested by one individual, and often this change is installed into the system by this same person. Many problems can arise from such a situation. In the rush to get the job done, standards for coding might be bypassed, or changes might be made in the code but not in program documentation, or testing might not be as thorough as prudence would demand. But beyond these concerns about quality there is another basic problem, and that has to do with audit considerations.

For an auditor, one of the fundamental principles of control is the separation of duties. As applied to a sensitive system, that is, a system that deals with the organization's assets, this principle means that duties should be assigned in such a way that no one individual can modify the system by himself. Thus, if an attempt were made to change the system in an unauthorized manner, it could be accomplished only through the collusion of two or more people. This has some obvious implications for mini projects. Most mini projects involve changing some system, and most systems deal with organizational assets in some way. Therefore the separation of duties requires that at least two persons be involved with every mini project. For instance, one person might make the required change and another might review and install it; or a change might be subjected to a peer review prior to installation. However achieved, separation of duties must be designed into the project procedures. Also, the project documentation should show that the procedure has been complied with, for example, by recording the names of the two or more individuals who were involved with the project.

6-4 LARGE PROJECTS

An organization usually becomes reasonably proficient in doing projects that are typical in size for them. Serious problems do not arise until a big project comes along—one that is five or ten times their usual effort, or even larger—then they find they cannot cope. Most project failures can be classified as very large projects for the organizations conducting them. Part of this, of course, is a case of the bigger they are, the harder they fall and the greater the splash they make. A more fundamental fact is that what works well in one situation might not work at all in another; a methodology that works well for a typical project might not be at all appropriate for a large project. In this section, two ways to cope with this problem will be explored.

One possible solution to the problem of a large project is to expand the methodology for a typical project. Except for Phases 1.1 and 3.3, which are quite short, each of the standard phases can be decomposed into, say, three new phases. This leads to a methodology for large projects involving 23 phases. Deliverables and standard tasks can be defined for each phase following the pattern established for a typical project. Phased authorization, planning, and implementation can be used in a fairly obvious manner. In short, all of the procedures for a typical project can be applied to the large project—the only real difference is that there are many more phases.

There are several problems with this approach. Some phases, such as Phase 1.3, have fairly natural points for division into subphases, but others do not. For instance, Phase 2.2 might more naturally be subdivided along lines of responsibility; but this subdivision would lead to subnetworks that are implemented in parallel rather than to phases that are implemented sequentially. Another problem with introducing over 20 phases is the time it would take to do the project. In theory at least, the phases would be implemented sequentially, and this would prevent taking maximum advantage of opportunities for parallel activity. Under this scheme, the increase in project size is accommodated largely by increasing the length of the project rather than by increasing the resources employed. The approval process would also add considerable time to the project. If one extrapolates from the methodology for a typical project, approximately half of the 23 phases for a large project would be approved on a phase-at-a-time basis. This means that the project would face perhaps 10 points where work must be held up while management is making a "go/no-go" decision. All in all, the time to produce a product under a 20-some phase methodology would probably be so great that the change in technology could obsolete the project product before it was completed. But the major problem with this expanded set of phases is the documentation requirements. Any large project has a sea of paperwork, but with 20-some phases to contend with it is likely that the project team would drown in paper.

Fracture the Large Project

There is a second solution to the problem of large projects. It is a practical, workable solution that has been implemented successfully by many organizations, and we recommend it. This solution is to fracture or subdivide the large project into a number of projects of a typical size. This amounts to reducing the difficult problem of a large project to a number of smaller problems that one knows how to solve. In effect, it is just another application of the basic rule for handling any complex work activity: breaking it into a number of smaller activities. Only instead of breaking the large problem into successive phases as was described above, it is a matter of breaking it into separate projects.

The subprojects into which the large project is split should be stand-alone projects, each of a typical size. Each should have a clear purpose, clear deliverables, and a clear target date. Each of the subprojects should be such that it can be accomplished by itself without impacting or being impacted by the others. This means that each subproject can be conducted by using the methodology for typical projects—in effect, no new project methodology is required.

Of course, the problem of finding a way to fracture a large project into a number of typical projects is not an easy one. Clearly some spadework must be done before the subdivision can be made. In particular, the large system's purpose and objectives must be firmly established, the specifications must be established at least in gross terms, and the overall architecture must be devised. Beyond this, it is necessary to determine the subprojects and to establish clear interfaces among them. All of this will undoubtedly take enough time and effort to be classed as a project in its own right.

One insurance company was faced with a three and one-half year, $7.5 million project, which was definitely a large project for them. To accomplish this, they broke the large project into 10 subprojects. A small team was assigned to each of the 10 subprojects, and each was given the task of constructing an overall plan for its subproject. Major attention was to be given to those points that required interfacing with one of the other nine subprojects.

After these subproject plans were made, the 10 subproject leaders and the overall project leader held several lengthy sessions in which the 10 separate plans were meshed together. Disputes about dependencies and interfaces were settled, and an overall schedule was established. From this overall schedule, separate schedules were derived for the 10 subprojects.

Next, the 10 subproject teams determined the resources that would be required to meet the established schedules. By combining these 10 sets of requirements, the resource requirements for the total project were established.

As a result of this advanced planning, the company was able to conduct 11 projects—10 subprojects and an eleventh project that handled overall coordination. All 11 projects were successfully accomplished by using the standard project methodology for the company.

This example shows an effective way to subdivide a large project, but there are others. For instance, one very successful custom contract organization often subdivides large projects into a stand-alone design project and a project to implement the design. This is done not so much because of problems in employing the project methodology, but as a means of controlling risk.

Subdividing large projects has proved to be an effective technique, but it rests on the fundamental assumption that the organization knows how to accomplish typical projects. This means that the typical project must be mastered before going on to the large project. However, it also means that once the typical project *is* mastered, the large project can be mastered too.

6-5 THE SMALL SHOP

Next, let us consider some of the problems of the small shop. By a small shop, we mean one with only a few people in the DP department. A small shop can exist in a large organization, and it can even have a sizable budget. For instance, we know of one large mutual fund with a sizable DP budget that employs only one person in DP! All of their development and operations are handled by a service bureau, and the DP manager's job (he is also the DP flunky) is to interface with the service bureau.

A basic problem of the small shop in the project area is that all of the work tasks associated with a project are the same as they are for a large shop, but there are not enough people around to do all the work. One person is forced to be the Project Manager, architect, designer, programmer, tester— just about everything but the user of the system. And sometimes he has to do the user's work as well. In this situation, scheduling and establishing priorities become major problems. Also, it is traditional that not all of the work can be done, so documentation and paperwork usually suffer very badly.

A more serious problem for a small shop is one that is only now emerging: the problem of satisfying the requirements of the auditors. In recent years the auditing profession has been under increasing pressure to prevent fraud in organizations. Many in the profession believe that this is not and should not be their function. Nevertheless, threats from legislators and various cases that have found their way into court compel them to look more closely at this problem. In many organizations, this has resulted in a reexamination of internal controls. What is often discovered is that the traditional separation of duties that was built into manual systems tended to be eroded in the process of automating these systems. A transaction that was handled by several people in a manual system might be handled by a single person in an automated one. Moreover, procedures in manual systems were designed with audit considerations in mind whereas DP and automated procedures often were not.

There is a general attempt by auditors to reestablish the separation of duties in organizations. In large organizations this is being done by the internal auditors, and in small ones by the external auditors. This move to separation of duties will have its impact on tasks that traditionally have been done by a single individual. We already mentioned this in discussing mini projects, but it also has obvious implications for the small shop. How do you satisfy the audit requirements for separation of duties if there is only one person in DP? In a somewhat larger shop, how do you control design work if there is a single analyst-designer? Clearly there are no easy answers. It may mean adding additional people. It may mean that more reliance must be placed on buying packages from outside vendors or using a service bureau. Perhaps it means that the traditional barrier between users and DP must be dissolved. But whatever the solution, it is clear that the small shop must find some way to accomplish projects in conformance with audit requirements.

6-6 MULTIPLE PROJECTS

Project workers can be organized in many ways. The traditional approach is to assign a project to a team that works under the direction of a Project Manager and reports to him. This one team-one project organization is what we have tacitly been considering as we have discussed our project methodology. A variation of the team approach is increasingly common, one that is sometimes referred to as a task force. In this arrangement a project is assigned to a team that works under a Project Manager, but the team members are on special assignment and actually report to other individuals for purposes of evaluation and pay. Although the task force approach presents new and interesting problems concerning the management of people, it presents nothing new in terms of managing work. Thus the methodology discussed applies to this organization as well.

Still another way to organize is to have workers reporting to and working for a Project Manager and to assign the team several projects to work on at the same time. In this section we will examine the impact, if any, these multiple projects have on our project methodology. (In theory one could have a task force with multiple projects. We ignore this case because it is not commonly found. Besides, it does not really present any new problems concerning the management of work over those presented by teams with multiple projects.)

As multiple projects are discussed, keep in mind that we mean multiple projects for a single team. A DP department can have many projects under development simultaneously and still have only a single project assigned to each team. This means, for example, that if a large project is fractured into several subprojects, it might or might not result in multiple projects for any team.

The assignment of multiple projects to a team is standard practice in many shops. This is done because it can be an efficient way to use resources, and it can lead to increased productivity. It does, however, require additional overhead for planning and control and for the time required by workers to shift from one project to another. Also, the assignment of multiple projects to a team increases the risk element for all of the team's projects because one late project can impact others and cause them to be late. To contain this risk, there is a need for careful planning and clear communication. Thus, multiple projects multiply the need for a standard project methodology that everyone understands.

What additional project work, if any, is entailed if a project is one of many that a team is working on? Let us examine this question. The phases of the project are the same whether it stands alone or is one of many. The authorization process is the same, and so are the phase deliverables. This means that the standard tasks are the same; that is, there is exactly the same work to be done if the project stands by itself or is one of many. From this we conclude that the standard methodology for projects need not be altered to account for multiple projects. Of course, multiple projects do present additional problems at the level of project coordination. This coordination might still be the job of the Project Manager, but he should recognize that the special problems do not relate to how an individual project is conducted (which is what the project methodology addresses) but rather to the way several projects are coordinated. In effect, a Project Manager for multiple projects has problems of coordination that are similar to the problems faced by a DP manager in a shop in which each project team is assigned to a single project. This is an important observation—it helps to give a clear understanding of the nature of multiple projects.

The problems of coordinating multiple projects are, broadly speaking, problems of scheduling. A plan must be devised to assign the right skill at the right time so as to meet all project deadlines. The duration for a project, which is the time usually estimated, might be quite different from the calendar time, which must reflect the amount of interference from other projects.

From a formal view, the problem of coordinating multiple projects is not difficult. In the terminology of Section 15-11, several projects can be viewed as several interrelated subnetworks; the total task is simply a combination of these subnetworks. Total resource requirements can be obtained by summing the requirements of the subnetworks. The task of finding a feasible schedule is simply the task of leveling the total network to the constraints imposed by resource availability.

If one is dealing on an aggregated level, this view of multiple projects is useful and practical. However, it may bog down in paperwork if it is applied at the detailed level. As a result, a compromise is usually necessary. For example, blocks of test time might be allocated to individual projects by examining the project requirements on an aggregated level. Division of the blocks into separate tests, however, might be done within the individual projects. From the view of the individual projects, this is simply a problem of scheduling within a resource constraint.

Obviously the meshing of plans for multiple projects is much more complex than these brief comments suggest. However, even this view shows the need for standard, well-understood procedures for accomplishing the individual projects.

6-7 SUMMARY

- A project methodology must be adjusted for project size. A useful approach is to recognize four project sizes: mini, small, typical, and large.

- Every project of any size should document at least:

    Project request
    Project authorization
    Project aim, consisting of objectives, estimated time, and
        estimated resources
    Project deliverables
    Actual time and resources used
    Product acceptance

- A methodology for a small project can be obtained by collapsing the standard project methodology into three phases; the methodology for a mini project can be obtained by further collapsing this to a single phase.
- Large projects can best be handled by splitting them into a collection of typical projects.
- Assigning multiple projects to a team adds to the scheduling and tracking work, but it does not require any basic change in the project methodology.

EFFECTIVE
PROJECT COMMUNICATION

7-1 INTRODUCTION

Communication is a huge topic. It includes formal or written communication and informal communication, such as undocumented speeches, phone conversations, and meetings in the hall. If communication is verbal, it involves language, tone of voice, and timing of phrases. If communication is nonverbal, it involves body language and expression. In any event, communication is intertwined in a complex way with organization, status, culture, involvement, perception, motivation, and similar attributes of ourselves and our environment.

Being such a broad subject, it is not surprising to find that scores of books have been written about communication. And, being such a complex subject, it is not surprising that in all of this vast literature there is no simple prescription for effective communication. There are, however, certain statements that most of us can accept: Free and open communication is essential to the success of a DP project, and good communication is difficult to achieve. Successful projects require more than a good methodology and able workers—they also require good management. And an important part of good management is the fostering of effective communication.

If we look at a DP project, we can see that some of its communication problems are no different from those of any other group in an organization. For any group there can be problems associated with intragroup communication, with communication between the group and its manager, and between the group and upper management or with other groups. These general problems of organizational communication are widely discussed in the literature, so we shall not comment on them here. What we do want to focus on in this chapter are some topics of communication that are more specially related to DP projects. The first of these is communication between the project team and the users. This communication involves one group learning in detail certain aspects of another group's activities (or proposed activities), and it is central to successful projects. Although not extensive in an organization, problems with this type of communication are not unique to DP; for example, the legal department has similar problems when it steps in to defend a department in a lawsuit. However, it is not a usual communication problem in an organization, although it is central to successful projects. The second topic is the formal (written) communication associated with the project. This topic covers the Project Handbook, which describes the project methodology, and the Project Workbook, which contains the documentation for a particular project.

7-2 USER-DP COMMUNICATION

No matter how good it is, communication in an organization can always be improved. The first step toward improvement is to make an assessment of the current situation. In reviewing user-DP communication there are several questions that should be asked. These questions and related discussion will be phrased as if they were directed toward people from DP; but, with appropriate modification, these questions obviously apply to users and should be asked of them too.

Do people understand? Does DP understand the user's area, the user's problems, the user's point of view? Should some DP people spend time on assignment in a user area to become better acquainted with their operation? Obviously, there is so much to learn about DP that a person can never know it all, but perhaps some people would be better off learning less new technical DP material and learning more user material. DP understanding of user areas has improved greatly in the last several years. Many organizations establish teams that concentrate on specific user areas, and these teams get to know their areas extremely well. Some organizations have even established DP groups in the user areas to provide better user-DP liaison.

Do people explain? Does DP explain to the user what DP is trying to do? What it cannot do? What the proposed system will not include? What is required of the user during the project and during operation? Do people explain, or do they rattle off incomprehensible DP jargon that intimidates and infuriates the user? With their jargon, do they force the user to agree to things he doesn't understand simply because the alternative is to be forced to admit he isn't up to date with all this modern stuff? Of course, the problem is not one-sided. Users have their jargon too, and it is just as baffling as DP-speak (as George Orwell might have called it). Sometimes the specification of a DP system by a user and a DP representative is like a conversation between a German and a Turk with each speaking his native language. To improve the situation, we suggest DP and the user resort to a neutral language, say, English.

Do people ask? Does DP really ask the user to be involved? For instance, is the user asked to be in charge of the project for Phase 1.2? Or for Phase 3.1? Do people ask the user for input? Or do they assume that the user doesn't want to get involved so they supply a lot of input for him? One would like to think that the days are past when DP designed a system and then "threw it over the fence" for the user to use. But just recently we heard of a case where the DP shop in a very large organization completed a system, took it to the user, and said, "Here's your system." And the user said, "What system?" Obviously the user hadn't been asked for much of anything during the building of that particular product.

Do people listen? If asked, most people would probably answer, "Yes, of course," because we all think of ourselves as good listeners. But the truth is that most of us would rather hear ourselves talk than listen to someone else. Moreover, even if we try to listen we have problems because we tend to hear what we expect to hear; and we hear only what we are capable of hearing. We once tried to explain some concepts of DP project management to a group of college undergraduates; it was like explaining sex education to a group of second graders—they understood all the words, but they didn't understand the ideas because it was outside their realm of experience. Because listening is very difficult, we often take a short cut and simply assume we know what is being said. One way for a person to improve his ability to listen (and to improve communication generally) is to explain what he has just heard back to the original sender. This forth and back transmission gives both parties a chance to check on the other's understanding.

Do people document? Explaining, asking, and listening are fine, but do people write it down? Do they write it while it is fresh in their minds, or do they wait until they have more time? Putting things in writing serves several purposes. It provides a permanent record of what the writer understood to be the case. It will probably force the organization of material into a more coherent form than it originally had. The organization of the material will usually reveal shortcomings and inconsistencies, which can then be explored and clarified. And a written record can be used to clear up misunderstandings, which brings us to our last question.

Do people review? Does DP review completed work with users? With peers? With special groups, such as Systems Assurance? When we say completed work, of course we do not mean just the final project output, but any significant piece of work produced during the project. An interviewee should be asked to review the written report of an interview to reveal misunderstandings (as suggested in the previous paragraph). Obviously all phase deliverables should be reviewed, but so should the important intermediate products developed during the phases. Reviews can be formal or informal—even a matter of asking someone to read and approve a one-page document. The objection to reviews is that they take time and resource. Clearly this is so; but if an error or omission can be caught, particularly if it is caught at an early stage in the project, it can save much agony and expense later on.

Once communication problems are identified, solutions usually suggest themselves. If you need special assistance on a topic, scan the communication literature. There are books on a wide range of topics, including how to conduct a meeting, how to write effectively, how to recognize and overcome communication barriers, and how to select the right communication media for a given situation. Although most communication literature is not directed specifically at the project area, you will generally find it is very useful.

7-3 THE PROJECT HANDBOOK

The *Project Handbook* (sometimes known as the *Project Guidebook* or *Systems Development Methodology*) is a document that describes the methods and procedures for conducting DP projects in an organization. It is a written description of the project methodology. The Project Handbook does not attempt to cover all aspects of a project; instead it concentrates on *how* projects are to be accomplished. The Project Handbook must be used in conjunction with other documents describing related project matters, such as the Manager's Manual, standards manuals, and various statements of procedures. (See Section 4-2 for a list of documents referenced by a project methodology and a list of interfacing systems and procedures.)

Stating that the Project Handbook describes the project methodology still leaves considerable latitude as to the book's actual content, and there is wide variation in practice. Some of this variation stems from the need to match project methodologies to the widely different backgrounds for DP projects in different organizations. Some variation in the content stems from a lack of guidelines and examples in this area. And some variation stems simply from differences of opinion as to the importance of different topics and where they should be located. In this section our ideas about the characteristics of a useful project handbook will be discussed, and in the next section a representative table of contents will be described.

Characteristics of a Useful Project Handbook

Physical Size. A project handbook is a document that should be used to guide all DP projects. This means that it should be human engineered for ease of use. An important aspect of human engineering is the size of the document. A handbook, as the term suggests, should be small enough to be held comfortably in one's hand. A big, heavy manual of standards is certainly more encompassing, but usually such a book just gathers dust at the far reaches of some bookcase. A project handbook is not a textbook on project methodology. This means that a handbook should concentrate on *how* projects are to be done and should leave much of the *why* to other sources. Another way to keep the size down is to make abundant use of pointers to other documents. A DP project obviously involves personnel, but personnel matters should not be described in a handbook. If the need arises, appropriate references can be made to other documents that deal with personnel matters, such as the Manager's Manual, policies of the Personnel Department, and descriptions of employee benefits. In much the same way, the Project Handbook should not contain standards for such project work as design, coding, program documentation, and testing. These should be placed in a separate standards manual(s) and referenced as required.

Clarity. Another aspect of human engineering is clarity. A handbook should be well written, clear, and concise. This is easy to say, of course, but it is not easy to achieve. One point that should be kept in mind to promote clarity is that the Project Handbook is to be used by *all* people involved with the project, not just DP people. Jargon and technical DP terms should be avoided. On the other hand, concepts that are obvious and well known to DP people should not be slighted if they are not equally obvious to the other people who will use the Project Handbook. A related point is that one must guard against the temptation to concentrate on the DP and automated aspects of the project and to slight user and manual aspects. Clarity of a handbook also requires that it be compatible with the many organizational policies, practices, procedures, methods, and standards with which it must interface.

User Convenience. A third aspect of human engineering is convenience of use. Two points can be mentioned here. First, a handbook should be designed so that topics can be located easily. It should contain an index or else the table of contents should be expanded and organized to serve the same function. Also, sections of a handbook should be numbered to facilitate cross referencing. A second way to promote convenience is to publish an abstract or a subset of the Project Handbook containing the most essential features. This abstract should consist of only a few pages and should be small enough to fit in a shirt pocket or a handbag. Many organizations print their abstracted Project Handbook on sheets that fold accordian-style into the size of a punched card, which makes it easy and convenient to carry.

Management Considerations. No matter how good it is, a project methodology must be altered over time to reflect changing views and requirements. Thus, procedures should be established for initiating, evaluating, and installing changes in the methodology, and a person should be appointed with responsibility for maintaining and improving it. (See Section 8-7 for a discussion of this topic.) To evaluate change proposals, it is necessary to establish standards against which a project methodology can be judged. (An example of such standards is given in Section 8-6). Changes in the methodology involve changes in the Project Handbook, and this means that it is necessary to establish a mechanism for updating a handbook. Because copies of the Project Handbook will be widely distributed, updating requires a mechanism for distributing changes to all copyholders. If updates are made frequently, it might be advisable to use an automated text editing system to assist with this activity. In any event, the need to change requires that handbook pages be dated or marked in some other way to identify different versions of the material and that the handbook contain information indicating the current version of each section. Also, the need to change suggests that the Project Handbook be published in a loose-leaf binder rather than in a bound volume.

Having a good Project Handbook and a good project methodology is a big step in the direction of project success, but it is not a guarantee of success. A good methodology is not a substitute for good management. Success requires good procedures *and* good management to see that the procedures are applied effectively and sensibly. This point is extremely important and must be stressed because it is frequently overlooked. Good procedures by themselves will accomplish little. Good procedures combined with good management and the commitment of the entire organization to the procedures will accomplish a great deal.

7-4 CONTENTS OF A PROJECT HANDBOOK

In this section we shall comment on the major parts of a project handbook. Particular emphasis will be given to topics that are not covered more fully in other sections of this book.

As stated earlier, there is great variation in the contents of handbooks from organization to organization. In practice many handbooks do not include all of the parts that will be described. In some cases, most parts are included, but they are arranged differently or are grouped into fewer major sections. Many handbooks contain topics that we have omitted; our omission of such topics is based on our opinion that the material more properly belongs in another organizational document or in a text on methodology rather than in a handbook. Obviously, considerable judgment has entered into the discussion that follows, and we recognize that not everyone will judge matters as we have. For this reason we want to emphasize that the descriptions in this section are not intended as a guide that can be accepted without change by any organization; instead they are intended as comments that can be studied for ideas.

1. *Preface.* A handbook should have a preface that concerns the Project Handbook itself rather than the project methodology the Project Handbook describes. The preface concerns the mechanics of a handbook: How it comes into existence, who is to receive it, and the update procedure.

2. *Table of Contents.* The table of contents can serve a dual purpose. In addition to being a straight list of contents, it can serve as an index if a formal index is not included. To fulfill the index function, the table of contents should be expanded and presented in both a sequential and an alphabetical order.

3. *Foreword.* The purpose of the foreword is to show upper management commitment to the project methodology. The foreword should be a letter signed by someone in the organization with wide authority—the higher the person in the organization, the better. The letter should indicate that the project methodology is part of the organization's overall planning and control structure and that compliance with the methodology is expected and required. The letter should convey the signer's strong support for the methodology. Experience shows that a supporting letter from an important sponsor has a significant impact on the acceptance and success of a project methodology. Such a letter should be part of every handbook.

4. *Introduction.* The introduction marks the real substantive beginning of a handbook. It introduces the concept of a project methodology and a project handbook. It states what these are, why they are needed, their benefits, and how they relate to other organizational systems.

5. *Organizational Overview.* The purpose of the overview is to provide basic organizational data that might reasonably be required by people connected with projects. The overview includes only the most important aspects of the organization and provides references to other documents containing more detail.

6. *The Project.* The purpose of this part is to introduce basic terms about projects and to show the relation of projects to the overall organizational activity and objectives. In particular, this part of a handbook describes how projects come into being.

7. *Project Phases.* Much of the information up to this point can be described as general background information. This part of a handbook presents the backbone of the methodology: the project phases and the standard tasks.

8. *Planning Work.* The purpose of this part is to show how the project methodology, which applies to all projects, can be applied to a specific project. This part discusses the activities that a Project Manager must perform to build a plan for a specific project.

9. *Doing Work.* The part on doing work has two purposes. It provides a brief description of and appropriate references to work procedures and standards that are described elsewhere. These might include procedures for design, coding, testing, and so on. Also, this part provides a detailed description of project work procedures that are not described elsewhere. These might include some of the tasks of the Project Manager.

10. *Controlling Work.* Procedures for controlling project work are described in this part. It is closely related to Parts 11 and 12.

11. *Reviewing Work.* The need for reviews, the different types of reviews, and the procedures for each type of review are described in this part.

12. *Reporting Completed Work.* This part of a handbook explains the types of project reports and the purpose and procedures for each type.

13. *Change Procedure.* This part of a handbook deals with the control of baseline documents. It discusses the problem of change, the need for worthwhile change, and presents a change procedure. It also discusses the interpretation of baseline documents.

14. *Accounting and Administrative Procedures.* The purpose of this part of a handbook is to explain those accounting and administrative procedures that have the greatest impact on projects, and to provide references to other documents for more detail. This part also explains the need for uniform practices and procedures in this area, and it relates these to project requirements such as budget control, planning data, and expense reporting.

15. *Approval Procedure.* The procedure for obtaining approval of completed work is described here.

16. *Project Workbook.* This part describes the Project Workbook. It establishes the Project Workbook table of contents and describes the distribution guidelines.

17. *Adjusting Procedures to Project Size.* The basic methodology described up to this point is for any typical project. The purpose of this part of a handbook is to establish project-size categories and to establish allowable adjustments of the methodology to various project sizes.

18. *Methodology Management Procedure.* The purpose of this part is to describe the procedure for changing and updating the project methodology.

19. *Glossary.* An optional feature of a handbook is a glossary of terms used in describing the project methodology.

20. *Appendix.* The appendix contains sample forms, examples, and similar material that should be part of a handbook but is not included else-

where. The appendix often contains the glossary, too.

21. *Index.* A handbook definitely should have an index unless the table of contents is designed to fulfill this function.

Appendix B contains an outline of the contents of a Project Handbook following the format just described.

7-5 THE PROJECT WORKBOOK

Projects generate paper. The amount generated goes up nonlinearly with project size, and large projects sometimes appear to be nothing more than paper mills. Even small projects generate enough paper to warrant thought about how it should be filed to facilitate ready reference.

All documents that flow on a particular project are collected in a file called the *Project Workbook* (sometimes also called the *Project File*). The Project Workbook is established at the beginning of a project, and at this point it is nothing more than a structure or classification system for project documents. As documents are generated on the project, they (or copies) are filed in the appropriate section of the Project Workbook. Once filed, a document is not removed. If a corrected version of a document is generated or if a change is made, then this is added to the file, but the original document is not destroyed. Thus, at the end of the project the Project Workbook is a complete, structured file of all documents that have been generated on the project. Clearly, there is a separate Project Workbook for each project.

Characteristics of a Useful Project Workbook

Some aspects of a workbook are independent of project size, and these are discussed next. After that, adjustments for project size are considered.

Standardization. The filing system for project documents should be standardized so that all projects of an organization use the same system. One reason for this is easy to see. It is obvious that the design of a good filing system is not a trivial job; having a standard system saves inventing a new filing system for each project. A more important reason is to save the time needed for all people to learn a new filing system as they go from project to project. A standard filing system is just one more step toward a uniform process for producing applications.

To provide standardization, the Project Handbook must establish guidelines for the filing procedure to be used on projects. The Project Handbook should specify at least the following information:

Who has responsibility for the Project Workbook
Filing structure for the Project Workbook
Procedures for creating a Project Workbook and for adding documents
Procedures for distributing copies of documents
Final disposition of the Project Workbook

Note that the improvement of the Project Workbook, that is, recommendations for change, modification of the file structure, and so on, is part of the process of improving the project methodology. This control function is handled as part of the general assessment of the project methodology.

Availability and Security. There is one Project Workbook per project, but many people must have access to some of the documents contained in it. This means that considerable attention must be given to procedures for making the documents available as required. In general, the documents in a workbook should be viewed as "public" data, that is, data that is readily available to anyone in the organization who has a need to know. However, it must be recognized that some data must be regarded as confidential and must be secured. Among such confidential data might be some that relates to individuals and is subject to rules and laws relating to an individual's privacy. To secure certain data, it might be necessary to extract a portion of the Project Workbook and keep it in a separate physical location. Of course, notice to that effect with an appropriate pointer should be filed in the Project Workbook itself.

Documents that are not subject to special security measures can be described loosely as those that relate to the project (plans, reports, correspondence, and so on) and those that relate to the product (designs, coding, program documentation, test results, and so on). Generally the procedure for filing and distributing project documentation is not the same as it is for product documentation.

Distribution. Distribution of project documents to those with a need to know is usually accomplished by sending the document to an appropriate distribution list. For example, a copy of a letter is sent by its author to all those who would reasonably be concerned with its contents; a report of a project review is distributed to a specified list of recipients. (In all cases, of course, a copy will be sent to the person maintaining the Project Workbook.) This procedure takes care of most needs for information, and exceptions can be accommodated by requesting and receiving a copy of the document from the Project Workbook.

Documents relating to the product are usually handled differently. Although the Project Workbook contains *all* documents that flow on a project, it is sometimes convenient to extract some of the documents for products and handle them in a separate file. (This separate file, however, can still be viewed conceptually as a part of the Workbook.) If a programmer requires several runs before obtaining a clean compile, it is probably not effective to file successive computer outputs directly in the Project Workbook. Instead these are maintained in a separate file (by the programmer or by a librarian) until an appropriate product level has been obtained. At that point, the documents for this product become part of the Project Workbook. Organizational standards should clearly specify at what point the product documents are added to the Project Workbook—on an evolving document by document basis, at important checkpoints within the phase, or at the completion of a phase—and this point might depend on project size. At a minimum, all product documents should be added to the Project Workbook at the end of each phase, and all subsequent modifications should be documented by filing appropriate change reports in the Project Workbook.

Whether they are part of the Project Workbook or in a separate file, distribution of product documents is often handled differently from project documents. Usually the person responsible for product documents (Project Manager or librarian) maintains an updated version of the evolving product and makes this readily available to all concerned people, often by reproducing it and distributing it in some way.

Document Identification. Another point that applies to projects of any size is that *every* document should be dated. This includes designs, flowcharts, versions of program documentation, compiles, as well as memos and notices. Dating documents (and putting a time on them if there are several similar versions in the same day) is an effective way to prevent effort being lost by working on a document that has since been superseded. This idea of dating documents is a simple one—so simple that it can easily be overlooked. But in terms of cost (which is trivial) to benefit, it is a rewarding idea.

All documents that are entered in the Project Workbook should be time-stamped. This establishes a date for the document if it did not already have one, and it helps to establish a time sequence for documents. All documents should also be assigned a number to help in identifying them in the Workbook.

Adjustment for Project Size

Let us consider how the Project Workbook varies with project size. Obviously there is no single industry standard, so our comments must be tailored to the requirements of a particular organization. For our discussion, we assume the size classifications of mini, small, typical, and large projects as discussed in Chapter 6.

A workbook structure for a typical project is given in Appendix B.

With such a structure, documents are dated on receipt and are filed by date within the proper classification. In establishing a workbook for a typical project, the major point to clarify is the standard for entering product documents into the workbook. For instance, it might be established that product documents (such as coding sheets, machine runs, and so on) generated while working on a work unit are not entered in the Project Workbook; what is entered are the product documents submitted on completion of a work unit together with any subsequent changes to these documents.

Large Projects. In Chapter 6 we suggested that large projects be fractured or subdivided into a number of typical projects for ease of management. If this can be done effectively, then there would be a Project Workbook for each subproject and a Project Workbook for the umbrella project that involves subproject coordination. Each of these workbooks can be structured in the standard way. However, there is still a special problem that arises for such a collection of related projects: There can be many and complicated interfaces that require considerable exchange of data among the projects. This means that the number of documents that flow will be considerably larger than if each were a stand-alone project. This special problem often leads to adoption of automated procedures for handling documents, such as the use of text-editing systems and the use of microfiche or terminals. With a large project it is also likely that the product documentation within a phase will be extracted from the Project Workbook and handled by a separate librarian system. This system would be used to record day-to-day product documentation and, if volume warranted, would summarize the daily modifications. The Project Workbook would then contain major product documents, such as phase deliverables, together with subsequent changes to these documents.

Small Projects. Small projects, too, have special documentation requirements. Here the problem is that the volume of documentation is small and it does not justify an elaborate procedure for handling it. For small projects the most reasonable filing system might simply be to insert all documents in a single file by date of receipt.

Mini Projects. Mini projects can be handled by the technique suggested for small projects. The major problem with mini projects is not how to handle documents, but to make certain that documents are generated (as discussed in Chapter 6).

Final Disposition

What happens to the Project Workbook at the end of a project? One school of thought is that it should become the Project History File and should be preserved in the project archives. It can be preserved as it is, or it can be simplified. Documents relating to products can be delivered to appropriate groups. Operating procedures can be collected into a Run Book, and this together with the automated system can be sent to Operations. User procedures can be collected in a User's Manual and sent to user departments. System documentation can be collected into System and Technical Manuals and sent to those with responsibility for maintaining the system. The remaining project information can be culled to eliminate unnecessary and trivial documents. The point of stripping the Project Workbook is to produce a History File that can be referenced readily.

We suggest an alternative disposition of the Project Workbook. Elsewhere in this book we have stated our opinion that every system should be assigned to an "owner" who is responsible for use, maintenance, and final disposition of the system. Generally the owner would be the major user of the system or a specially appointed person if there are several major owners. We suggest that the Project Workbook be turned over to the owner of the system and that it become the basis for a document called the *System File*. If this is done, product information should not be removed from the Workbook but should be duplicated and sent to the appropriate groups. Whether or not unnecessary and trivial documents are culled from the Project Workbook is something to be decided by each organization.

The purpose of the System File is to have a document that provides a complete record of the system from project selection through final retirement of the system from use. In addition to the project information, the System File would have sections for documents relating to operating and maintenance experience. For instance, it might have sections covering such topics as:

Operations reports
Trouble reports
Maintenance changes (repairs)
Maintenance changes (enhancements)
Postinstallation reviews
Final system audit

These sections would be appended to the Project Workbook, and documents would be filed in these sections throughout the operation and maintenance cycle.

Whether the Project Workbook is converted into a Project History File or a System File, the importance of preserving its contents at the completion of the project must be stressed. Data on completed projects is essential to:

Document agreements on the completed project, such as project authorization and user acceptance

Assess the completed project for matters such as project selection, project planning, and the suitability of the project methodology

Assist in planning future projects by adding to the planning data base and by pointing to improvements in methodology and practice

7-6 SUMMARY

- User-DP communication can be assessed by asking of both users and DP:

  Do people understand?
  Do people explain?
  Do people ask?
  Do people listen?
  Do people document?
  Do people review?

- The topic of formal (written) communication involves the Project Handbook, which describes the methodology for all projects, and the Project Workbook, which contains the documentation for a particular project.
- The Project Handbook, as a guide for conducting all DP projects, should be human engineered to be concise, clear, and convenient to use.
- Good project procedures by themselves are not sufficient to assure project success. For success, it is necessary to have good procedures, good management, and commitment of the entire organization to the procedures.
- The Project Workbook is established at the beginning of a project as a structure or classification system for all project documents. As documents are generated they are filed in the Workbook, and at the end of the project the Workbook is a complete, structured file of all project documents.
- On completion of a project, the Project Workbook becomes the Project History File or the basis for the System File. In either event, the data in the Project Workbook is preserved to:

  Document agreements on the completed project
  Assess the completed project
  Assist in planning future projects

8

INTRODUCING CHANGE

8-1 INTRODUCTION

The act of installing or improving a project methodology is a project. It is not an application development project such as we have been discussing, but it is a project—one that significantly affects DP and has ramifications throughout the organization. As with any project, to conduct it a methodology is needed. The question naturally arises: To what extent can the methodology we have been discussing in this book be used for the project of installing or improving a methodology? The answer is that the broad outlines of our methodology apply to this or any other project, but the details need modification.

In this chapter we shall show how the methodology of this book can be adapted and adjusted to cover the project of installing or improving a methodology. Our primary purpose in doing so is to provide a guide that can be used for such projects. A secondary purpose is to suggest the generality of the ideas we have been discussing and to show that the methodology can be adapted to a wide range of projects. Finally, this adjustment will serve as a review of some of the planning and methodology concepts we have been discussing.

The subject of this chapter is not one but two closely related projects: the project of establishing a methodology where one did not exist before (or where the existing methodology is not a significant factor) and the project of improving an existing methodology. The differences between the two projects are described in Figures 8-1 and 8-2. As these figures show, formally there is not a great deal to distinguish between these two situations. Of course, there could be a difference between the two in terms of total work effort and of the acceptance by various people of the project output. There is a difference in that the establishment of a methodology is viewed by most organizations as a one-time effort, whereas improvement is usually done on a regular basis, but the basic methodologies for the two projects are so similar that they will be discussed together. To accomplish this we shall discuss a project to *change* a methodology. Our comments can be easily modified to fit either the project of installing a methodology or the project of improving one, whichever is of more interest to you.

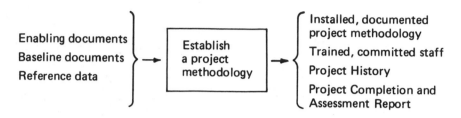

Figure 8-1. Project to establish a methodology

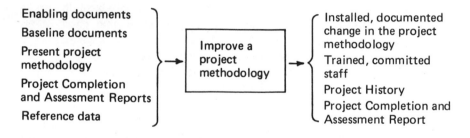

Figure 8-2. Project to improve a methodology

8-2 INITIATION OF THE PROJECT

The suggestion for changing a methodology can come from many sources. It might arise from DP's recognition of the need for a standard procedure for accomplishing projects, or from a user department's dissatisfaction with the existing procedure, or from a recommendation from an audit. Increasingly the suggestion arises from a session on information systems planning. These sessions pinpoint the need for new systems and, quite naturally, lead to a review of the procedure for developing these systems. Deficiencies that surface are brought to the attention of the high-level people who attend these planning sessions, and this can result in what amounts to a mandate for changing a methodology.

Although we recognize all of these potential sources, in practice the main emphasis for changing a methodology comes from DP. It is usually the project managers in an organization who are most intimately involved with the project process and who suffer the greatest frustration from deficiencies in procedures. These people are frequently the first to recognize the need for changing a methodology, but they cannot do it alone because it has ramifications outside their range of authority. A common reaction of project managers is, "I'm sold, but how do I sell my manager?"

Convincing Management

To sell a manager at any level, there are about four major steps.

Facts. First, it is necessary to study the problem so that you can talk from facts, not just opinion. Historical data should be obtained on projects to determine actual past performance. Specific problems in the project process should be uncovered and documented with examples. Some preliminary calculations should be made of the cost of not having a good project process and the benefits from having one. At this stage these costs and benefits will probably be qualitative, but if a quantitative dimension can be added so much the better.

Plan of Action. The next major step in selling management is to develop a basic plan of action. Not a plan at the level of schedules and details, but the major approach that should be taken and the basic objectives to be achieved.

There are two basic approaches to changing a methodology: top-down and bottom-up. A top-down approach starts with a high-level committee. This committee would be given the charter to change the methodology and would have representation from major areas that are involved with projects. It would be headed by an executive with authority across these major areas. The committee would set the purpose and objectives of the project and would resolve major issues, but the bulk of the "nuts and bolts" work would probably be done by a subcommittee or a project team that would include specialists.

With a top-down approach, the project to change a methodology is likely to be a large effort and would involve sweeping changes. The effort would focus on major questions of responsibility and could involve questions of organizational change. The effort may be costly and lengthy, but the benefits are likely to be high in the long run.

A bottom-up approach to changing a methodology is likely to start in DP with cooperation of major users. It would require the sanction of upper management, but not much active involvement. A bottom-up approach starts with a project team consisting of operational level people from DP and participating users. The project team would handle the entire project from initiation through installation of the product.

With a bottom-up approach, the project would be a more modest effort and would involve incremental change in existing procedures. The effort is likely to focus on clarifying and fixing responsibility rather than attempting to reassign it; it is more a matter of "getting our house in order" than an attempt to strive for an ideal solution. A bottom-up approach can vary in cost and length from a small effort to a large one. Benefits can be considerable and are likely to be realized at once.

In a sense, the top-down approach is revolutionary and the bottom-up approach evolutionary. The top-down approach probably will result in a big change in methodology all at once, but with only minor adjustments for a period following that. The bottom-up project probably will be repeated at regular intervals and result in smaller, incremental changes.

Which approach should an organization take? Obviously it depends on the organization and its needs. Generally our preference is for the bottom-up approach. We believe that large change is hard to digest and may cause more disruption than its proponents expect, particularly change that threatens to disturb an existing power structure. We also believe that many organizations have working methodologies now, and much benefit can be achieved by modifying these rather than starting fresh. Our main reason for preferring the bottom-up approach has to do with worker involvement and worker acceptance. Too often the top-down approach carries with it the implication that upper management knows best; they will tell the project workers what to do and then the workers will do it. Too often the top-down approach proceeds on the assumption that project workers haven't been working on this problem, so we had better do it for them. Admittedly these attitudes are *not* a necessary part of the top-down approach, but they accompany it too frequently to be ignored. In Section 8-8 we discuss resistance to change; that section should be read before deciding on a top-down or a bottom-up approach.

Education. A third step in selling management on the project to change the methodology is education. It is necessary to tell management what a methodology is, why it is needed, and why their support is required to change one. This education must be directed at whatever level of management you are aiming at and some levels below that.

Commitment. The fourth step in selling management is to ask for the order. You must submit a proposal for action and ask for their endorsement. This step might be made through an existing selection process, a topic discussed next.

8-3 SELECTION AND AUTHORIZATION OF THE PROJECT

The suggestion to change a methodology will probably be directed to the organization's Methods and Procedures Group. If there is no such group, the suggestion will probably be directed to the Project Selection Committee that authorizes application development projects. Although this is a different type of project, its relation to DP is so strong that this seems a logical route for authorization. Just who authorizes the project is not important as long as they have authority to promote the use of the methodology that is developed.

Authorization is needed on any project for at least two reasons: (1) to provide the funding and permission to commit resources and (2) to provide the project team with the authority needed to carry out their assignment. For most application development projects, the key reason is the funding; authority usually is not an issue. A request for a project by a user carries an inference that the user will cooperate in the project and will use the product if it meets specifications. But a project to change a methodology is different. A user may not be at all interested in changing a methodology; he might even be hostile to the idea. However, his cooperation will be required in building the methodology, and he must use it if it is to be successful. Thus it is important that the project carry with it the ability to promote interdepartment cooperation in the development and use of the product.

In addition to giving authorization, the authorizing group must assign the project a priority, allocate resources, and coordinate the project with other DP efforts. They must also indicate how they plan to control the work at their level.

The authorizing group sets the overall purpose and objective of the project. For example, they should specify the type of projects the methodology should cover and the groups that will be using it. They should also delimit the bounds of the methodology; for instance, they might specifically exclude project selection on the one hand and maintenance and operations on the other.

Cost/Benefit Analysis

As with any project, the authorization decision rests in part on a cost/benefit analysis. The cost can be considered in two parts. One part is the cost of the project itself—the cost of developing and installing changes. This cost can vary considerably. If the project consists of building a full methodology including an automated control system, the project can easily run 1 to 2 years and involve 10 to 20 man-years of effort. If the project is small, starting with a fairly good idea of what is wanted and involving little customization, it can involve less than one man-year of effort expended over several months. The other part of the project cost is the cost of using the methodology once it is installed as compared with the cost of the current development procedure. We call this difference a cost, but it frequently is a benefit. That is, the cost of using the new methodology is often less than the cost of current procedures. A problem in assessing the worth of the project is that these costs are usually very hard to obtain. About the best one can do is to compare the total cost of a project using the new methodology with the total cost of a comparable project using the current procedures.

Benefits of the project to change a methodology are also difficult to assess. Among them might be:

Development of correct products
Improved product quality
Better control of risk
Improved ability to audit projects
Improved people
Increased productivity
Reduced development time

It is difficult to quantify such benefits, but sometimes a way can be found to do so. For instance, improvement in product quality might be measured by estimating the savings from reduced maintenance; the reduction in development time might be measured by estimating the value of an earlier realization of benefits from systems being built. One particularly difficult problem in measuring benefits is to fix the cause of improved performance. For instance, if a marked improvement in product quality is discovered after making changes, should this be attributed to better workmanship, better standards for programming, design, etc., better project management, or a better project methodology? Problems in measuring costs and benefits for any project are discussed in Chapter 10, so we shall not dwell on them here.

8-4 THE PROJECT TEAM

The project to change a methodology requires considerable knowledge, so it is best undertaken by a team of people rather than by an individual. It need not be a large team; somewhere between two and six people should suffice unless substantial software products must be built. Here are some of the qualifications that should be found among the team members:

Ability to manage a project. The changing of a methodology is a project, and it is important that it be managed successfully. The Project Manager should have the ability to complete the project on time, within budget, and with a quality product.

Knowledge of DP project methodology. Since the team is to design a methodology, it is important that they understand what are some successful ways to run DP projects. The Project Manager need not be an expert in this area, but more than one project member should have up-to-date knowledge on the subject.

Knowledge of DP project technical work. The development of a methodology can best be done by a group having familiarity with the work done during a typical project. This includes the work of DP, such as specifying, designing, coding, and testing, and the work in other areas, such as designing procedures, conversion, and training.

Understanding of human factors in DP projects. This qualification should be noted particularly because a common fault in designing project methodologies is to overemphasize the technical aspect of the methodology at the expense of the human aspect. An important qualification of the project team is a recognition of the need to design a methodology with people in mind.

Ability to deal with various functional areas. It is important that the methodology be designed by a team that can work effectively with the many functional areas that will be using the methodology. They should be able to work with the people and to understand their requirements and concerns.

Ability to deal with resistance to change. The introduction of a methodology involves changing the work patterns of many individuals. Resistance to such change is not uncommon, and in extreme cases it can frustrate the entire effort. It is vital that the project team understand the ramifications of changing work procedures, and that they be able to avert serious problems.

Experience and competence. The changing of a project methodology is an important project because it will have a pronounced impact on all application developments on which the methodology is used. For this reason, the team that develops the changes should have some capable, highly experienced members. This is a project for senior people, not for greenhorns or misfits.

The DP development area is the primary user of the methodology being designed, and for this reason it is most likely that DP development will house the project and will supply the Project Manager. The analysis and design skills needed by the project team will also most likely come from DP, although Internal Consulting and a Methods and Procedures Group are alternate sources in some organizations. It is very important, however, that the entire team *not* be from DP. The team should include some members of the more important user groups. It is not enough simply to "touch base" with users; the team needs someone from these areas to exert a continual influence on the details of the methodology as it is being formed. To give the team clout, it would also be desirable to have representation from a level to which DP and all important users report. Because the project deals largely with procedures rather than policy, it is likely that such a high-level representative would be an appropriate staff person rather than a high-level manager.

Of course it is not possible for the team to have a representative from each affected area and still be small enough to be productive. For that reason it is important to establish liaison or contact points in each area that is not represented on the team but is affected by the methodology—Operations, Internal Audit, Security, Data Management, Systems Assurance, and so on. Such a contact helps to fix responsibility in the affected area; it becomes one person's job to see that the methodology will be acceptable in that area. Also, it provides the affected area with a channel for real participation in shaping the methodology, not just a sense of participation.

8-5 THE GENERAL PROJECT METHODOLOGY

A methodology for a project of changing a methodology will be described; such a project comes one step before the material discussed in previous chapters. Of course, for a specific project it would be necessary to produce specific phase plans, action plans, and so on; but we shall not get into this level of detail. What we describe in this chapter is comparable to Chapter 4 for an application development project. To detail this chapter for a specific project, it would be necessary to produce detailed plans comparable to those discussed in Chapter 5.

Phases

Following the usual pattern, our first step in planning for a project is to subdivide it into a number of separate phases. Since the nine phases we have used on a typical development project are a good way to view *any* project, it will save much trouble and reinvention if we simply start with those nine phases and make whatever modifications are required for this new type of project. As we shall see, the nine phases might be collapsed for the present project if it is small, but they might be left intact if it is large. If the methodology being established calls for the building of an automated system for planning and control, this large subactivity might be split off as a separate project after the specifications for the system are complete. We leave it to you to incorporate this and other modifications as required.

Authorization and Approval

For a typical application development project, we advocated an approval process with upper management intervention at the end of each major phase (see Figure 4-4). That approval process might be used on the present project, but more than likely it will be used in a modified form. The project to change a methodology has major implications for an organization. Because of this, the project might be mandated; this is particularly true if the suggestion for the project originates at a high level in the organization. In this case the initial authorization is for the entire project, and the project team will merely have to send upper management progress reports at the end of each phase. Of course, the project can be aborted or modified if problems arise, but in the absence of problems it will continue through all of its phases.

Authorization might also be made for a cluster of phases. One likely scheme is for the initial authorization to cover Phases 1.1 through 1.3, and for a subsequent authorization to cover the remaining phases.

Deliverables

Each phase of the project has deliverables, and to a remarkable extent these resemble the deliverables from a typical application development project. In the next section the phases and major phase deliverables will be described. In addition to these, the following output is produced for each phase:

Report to Management
Phase Plan
Project Plan (updated)
Project Workbook (updated)
Phase Completion and Assessment Report

Further reference will not be made to these routine outputs when the individual phases are discussed, but it is understood that these must be delivered and the necessary work done to produce them.

To produce these outputs and the major phase deliverables, it is necessary to perform certain tasks. A list of these tasks can be compiled fairly easily by using the standard task list for the typical application development project as a guideline. A larger number of those standard tasks apply to the present project; among these are tasks of planning, controlling, training, documentation, designing and ordering of forms, and completing reports. Other standard tasks apply but with altered interpretation. For example, it is necessary to design a test, but in this project it is a test of the methodology, not a test of a program or a computer system. Still other standard application development tasks are probably not applicable to the present project. For instance, in changing a methodology it is probably not necessary to do any site preparation and it may not be necessary to do any coding.

We shall not attempt to produce a list of standard tasks for each phase of the project to change a methodology. To undertake such a project it would be necessary to build such a list. It would also be necessary to establish a responsibility grid and to build networks to synthesize the tasks into a work process. The grids and networks for application development projects can serve as examples and help to simplify this effort.

The work that is performed on the project to change a methodology must be checked for quality. The best way to do this is to use peer reviews just as is done on application development projects.

8-6 THE PROJECT PHASES

The nine phases of a project to change a methodology will be discussed next. This discussion will be informal and general because by now we can assume that you have a knowledge of project planning. Because of this knowledge, a step-by-step approach is not necessary to convey our thoughts. Also, by now you will recognize that a wide range of plans can be established, and the details selected depend heavily on the particular organization and situation.

Phase 1.1 Identify Problem

The purpose of Phase 1.1 is to determine if the project is feasible from the perspective of the project team.

A major activity of this phase is to refine the statement of project purpose and objectives. This entails determining such matters as:

The types of projects to be covered by the methodology

Which activities of user departments are to be covered by the
methodology

Who has responsibility for establishing user procedures related to the
methodology

Interfaces between the project methodology and other management
systems (preliminary)

Manner in which the methodology will be introduced (evolutionary or
revolutionary)

Whether user training is part of the project

This phase is intended as a "first look" at the project by the project
team and should ordinarily take only a few days. This phase might well be
combined with Phase 1.2 because the project is usually relatively small. The
combining of the first two phases is particularly likely if authorization is for
the entire project, not just a phase at a time.

Phase 1.2 Specify Requirements

The first objective of Phase 1.2 is to produce the specifications for a methodology, including a detailed list of the requirements of DP
and all functional areas that interface with development projects. As with
most projects, this is probably the most important part of the effort. If done
well, the project is likely to be successful; if done badly, it may be difficult
and expensive to recover.

This phase has a second objective, the importance of which depends on
the organization, and that is to proselytize. Not everyone will understand
what a methodology is and why it is needed. Many will be on guard when approached with a request for their requirements; they will be afraid that, whatever it is you have in mind, it will probably do them more harm than good.
Thus, it is important to explain the purpose of the project to each person
who is interviewed and to show how the project product will help him to do
his job better. It is important to convert people to the goals of the project
because its success depends on general acceptance of the project product.

One activity of this phase is the documentation of the current
methodology and current practice. Also to be documented are the cost of
developing projects with the current methodology and other performance
measures. These activities amount to an audit of the current situation, as
discussed in Chapter 19.

To obtain the requirements for the methodology to be built, it is necessary to study the organization, its environment, and its performance. A large part of the information comes through interviewing many people: project workers, project managers, operations, DP management, users, auditors, security, legal, data management, and upper management. In most cases it is also useful to talk with vendors, consultants, and other outside people. These interviews should cover such questions as:

What are your requirements for DP projects?
What does project success mean to you?
What do you require to achieve success on a project?
What problems do you have with projects?
What do you think a good methodology should provide?

Answers to these and similar questions give a guide to the requirements for a methodology. Usually it is necessary, however, to analyze the answers and to probe for basic needs—to probe beneath the symptoms for basic causes. For example, in response to a question, it might be stated that the problem with DP projects is that they are always late. In probing for the cause of the lateness, you might be told that the last project was late because it was necessary during coding to go back and add a function that had been overlooked before. This information might point to the need for a procedure to assure that user requirements are fully known and documented prior to design and build.

The major deliverable from this phase is a set of specifications for the methodology. This is generated from the comments of all those concerned with projects, and it must be checked by the project team to see if it is consistent enough to be met. The team must also judge the impact of meeting the specifications.

Another deliverable from this phase is a set of criteria that can be used to judge a project methodology. These criteria are needed for evaluating the existing project methodology and the methodology being developed, and for the continual assessment of the organization's project procedures. Criteria probably do not exist in the organization, so it will be necessary for the project team to devise them. These criteria can be qualitative or quantitative.

What are some qualitative characteristics of a good project methodology? This is hard to answer because a reply can be given on various levels; an answer can be given on a broad "motherhood" level that gives no useful guidance for judging a methodology, or at a "bits and bytes" level that relates more to technique than purpose. In giving our answer to the question, we shall attempt to strike a balance between these two extremes.

We believe that a good project methodology provides a means for doing the following:

Assuring continual user and management involvement in the project

Determining the requirements of all those involved with the system

Providing useful estimates of project cost, effort, and duration

Assuring comparison of costs and benefits

Assessing and controlling risk

Promoting only those projects that are consistent with organizational policies and goals

Assigning clear, unambiguous responsibility for project work

Fixing system requirements before attempting to design and build the system

Evaluating and implementing worthwhile changes

Providing accurate reports of project progress

Assuring appropriate reviews on completion of major steps

Assuring quality at each step, including assurance that system requirements are met

Providing for smooth installation of the system

Documenting the project and the product

Making interproject comparisons of duration, cost, quality, and so on

Providing interfaces with other systems, such as project selection, accounting, security, personnel, operations, and maintenance

Developing and improving techniques for estimating

Providing for continual reassessment and improvement of the project methodology

This list is intended as a guideline, not as a definitive checklist. You should examine it and modify it to reflect your own notion of a good methodology.

In describing aspects of a good methodology, we listed some of the function that should be provided. We did not, however, go into the question of *how* this function is provided, and this is often what makes the difference between a successful and an unsuccessful methodology. A methodology can be too rigid or too flexible. The amount of planning, reporting, and approvals required can be excessive or insufficient. The administration of the methodology can be too authoritarian or too permissive. The attitude of project personnel can be hostile—their aim is to defeat the system; or it can be defensive—their aim is to use the system to play CYA (Cover Your Arrear). In short, there are extremes in both directions that must be avoided. As with any management tool, the establishment and maintenance of a good project methodology requires human engineering and concern for the individuals who are to use the system.

Some examples of quantitative measures of a methodology are:

The ratio of actual project cost to estimated project cost
The ratio of actual project duration to estimated project duration
The size of the application development backlog
User attitude (as measured by a survey, for example)
Cost of a project per thousand lines of delivered code
Bugs discovered in operations per thousand lines of delivered code
Mean time to failure of the system during operation

Fault can be found with any of these criteria, and certainly none by itself would be a good measure of a methodology. However, at the present time no one seems to have a measure that is significantly better than those we have listed. This is unfortunate because the choice of criteria for measuring a methodology is extremely important. The choice tends to direct future effort; emphasis on the wrong criteria means misdirected effort and bad methodologies. We can only hope that as our industry matures, we improve our ability to measure the effectiveness of the tools we employ.

The end of Phase 1.2 is a key point for management and user approval of the project. The output of this phase sets the direction for the rest of the project, and it is important to obtain concurrence on the specifications from all parties before proceeding. It is also important at this point to review the project scope and make any necessary adjustments before moving into the design stage.

Phase 1.3 Define Solution

The objective of Phase 1.3 is to examine alternatives and to select an external design for a methodology that meets the requirements of Phase 1.2

The project team begins by gathering all the information they can on alternative project methodologies. Some of this information comes from examining their own current practice and the practice of other organizations with which they are familiar. Some comes from the literature on projects, including books such as this one. Trade associations, user groups, and other professional organizations are also sources of ideas on project methodologies. Finally, the team should examine the project management systems supplied by various vendors.

At present there are at least 50 commercially available project management systems. These vary considerably in scope, function, and style. Some are basically network processors, some are fairly complete management systems. Some are manual, some have automated features. Some embody a rigid methodology, some are flexible. Some are modular and allow phased installation, some do not. Some installations of such systems have been highly successful, and some have been failures. Prices for such systems vary from under $10,000 to over $100,000 (exclusive of costs of adapting to an organization) and tend to correlate with the features offered and education required.

Based on all of this information, the team will devise alternative methodologies and examine those for the most suitable one. In this examination, they will use the output of Phase 1.2 to verify that specific requirements for a methodology are satisfied and that performance criteria are likely to be met. They will also verify that the methodology has clean interfaces with other management systems, particularly project selection, accounting, personnel, security, maintenance, and operations.

In arriving at a selected methodology, the project team must make some basic decisions. They must decide if the methodology is to be a modification of existing practice, if it is to be freshly designed and built in-house, or if it is to be based on outside support. In the last case, they must decide if the methodology will be centered on a package management system, if it is to be tailored for them by an outside vendor, or if they should take the middle ground of building it themselves with heavy support from an outside consultant.

These are some of the questions you should answer if you are evaluating the suitability of a packaged management system for your organization:

Does the system meet the specifications established in Phase 1.2?

Is documentation clear and complete?

Is the system easy to understand? To use?

Can it be adapted to your organization?

Does it fit in with the management style of your organization?

Is it modular? Can it be installed in phases?

What help does the vendor provide in installing the system? Tailoring it to your requirements? Maintaining and updating it?

What does the vendor supply in the way of training?

What is the vendor's reputation?

What experience have other organizations had with the system? How many other users are there?

What is the price of the system? What will be the total cost, including the cost of adapting it to your organization?

Subsequent project activity depends on the "build or buy" decision. We shall discuss the project on the assumption that the decision is to build a methodology. If the decision were to install a package, it would be necessary to modify our discussion and to provide for the specification, design, and building of required modifications to the package.

Having selected a methodology, it must be documented. This documentation should include such matters as:

Content of the methodology
External design of automated procedures
External design of manual procedures
Standards that are referenced by the methodology
Interfaces with other systems
Versions to be introduced
Requirements for maintenance and improvement of the methodology

The end of Phase 1.3 is another important point for management and user approval. It is also a good place to clear up any lingering questions about use of the methodology once it is built and about procedures for evaluating and maintaining it.

Phase 2.1 Design Product

The objective of Phase 2.1 is to develop a complete design for the selected project methodology.

The major deliverable from this phase is a complete design for the methodology, including the design of all manual procedures, all automated procedures, the planning data base, and all forms. This design should cover all procedures listed in Table 4-1.

A good sequence for designing some of the major components of a methodology is: phases (purpose, objectives, outputs, inputs), authorization procedure, standard tasks, and planning and control procedures. Other procedures can then be designed around this basic framework.

In this phase it is also necessary to plan subsequent project activity. The plans of Section 5-9 that are appropriate to the size of the project should be evolved. We stress that each of these plans applies to the present project and its product. For instance, the test plan is the procedure whereby the methodology that is being developed is to be tested before it is installed as a standard for the organization.

Phase 2.2 Build Product

The objective of Phase 2.2 is to build a working methodology complete with all documentation.

The major task in this phase is to build procedures and all automated systems that are required. Documentation for these must also be built, including text for the Project Handbook. It is necessary to build materials for training and for test and installation of the methodology. This is also the phase in which the planning data base is constructed. To do this will require gleaning data from past projects and organizing it in a manner appropriate to the new methodology.

If the project involves building an automated planning and control system, this phase can be quite extensive. On the other hand, for a small project it might be difficult and unnecessary to draw a careful line between Phases 2.1 and 2.2; and it might be reasonable to collapse the two into a single design/build phase.

Phase 2.3 Test Product

The objective of Phase 2.3 is to test the methodology that has been built.

Although the Phase 2.3 test "belongs" to the project team and is for their benefit, the test is best conducted by outside testers. That is, the test should be conducted by people who were not involved in designing or building the methodology. For best results, the test group should include people who can examine the methodology from the viewpoint of those who must use it.

We shall propose that the product be tested in the next phase by applying it on a small project or a test case. It is *not* likely that two such practice tests will be held, which means that some other testing procedure is likely to be used in the present phase. If a live test is to be conducted in Phase 3.1, the principal tool for testing in Phase 2.3 is most likely the review process. A review might consist of simulating a project to determine how the methodology would apply step by step. This test should look at all aspects of the methodology, including all documentation, forms, and user procedures.

In addition to examining the methodology, the test should review plans for installing the methodology. Particular attention should be paid to the team's concern for human factors and their plans to minimize resistance to the change that will be brought about by the methodology.

During Phase 2.3, training should be conducted for the people who will be involved with the acceptance test of Phase 3.1. In addition to providing these people with skills, this training serves as a test of the training package that will be used later to acquaint all people with the methodology.

Phase 3.1 Accept Product

The objective of Phase 3.1 is to make certain that all who are involved with development projects find the methodology acceptable.

The acceptance test "belongs" to the users of the project methodology, which is everyone who will be involved with development projects. The best way to gain acceptance is to try the methodology on an actual project. For best results, the selected project should not be too critical, too large, or subject to great time pressure.

The test consists of accomplishing the project by following the methodology. Results should be compared with the requirements and performance standards generated in Phase 1.2. Errors and omissions should be noted and corrections made where appropriate. If a careful job has been done in previous phases, the acceptance test should present no real surprises.

Phase 3.2 Install Product

The objective of Phase 3.2 is to install the methodology as part of the working process.

Following plans, installation of the methodology will be either parallel or replacement. Also, it might be for all projects or for only a selected class. The principal tasks in this phase are to publish and distribute descriptions of the methodology and to complete required training.

A great deal of attention should be paid to the way in which a methodology is installed. We know of one organization where a methodology was installed and immediately required on all projects, even ongoing ones. This meant replanning and modifying implanted control systems to conform to the new procedures, and it resulted in much resentment and disapproval of the new system. That organization would have fared much better simply by requiring the new methodology on all new projects.

Phase 3.3 Transfer Product

The objective of Phase 3.3 is to complete the project, to transfer responsibility for the methodology, and to assess the project itself.

This project assessment is similar to that of an application development project. Its purpose is to record the experience of the project team, actual versus estimated time and cost, and suggestions for improvement. The output of this phase is important to those who must maintain the methodology and have responsibility for improvement.

8-7 MAINTAINING A METHODOLOGY

Every organization should establish who has the responsibility for maintaining the project methodology. It should establish who receives the assessment reports from all projects (including the project to install a methodology), who makes periodic evaluations of the methodology, and who tunes it, updates it, and eventually replaces it. There are several candidates for the position, including the DP Manager, Systems Assurance, the project team that develops and installs the methodology, Methods and Procedures, and the Project Selection Committee. We have no advice about who should have the responsibility; it depends on the organization. We *do* advise, however, that the responsibility be clearly established.

8-8 RESISTANCE TO CHANGE

Our primary emphasis in this book is on project methodology or the technical aspects of project management. We have dealt very little with the "people" side of projects—that is a huge subject in itself and beyond the scope of our effort. In the same spirit, our concern with the project to change a methodology has been with the technical side—the tasks to be performed and the phase deliverables. But this project, as with so many DP projects, is really a project to introduce change into an organization; and change cannot be introduced successfully without paying careful attention to the needs of people. Any attempt to bring about change is very likely to meet resistance; therefore, we shall conclude this chapter with a brief comment on this important topic.

Many people underestimate the difficulty of producing lasting, beneficial change in an organization. It is hard to design a useful change, but it is even harder to have it accepted. "Build a better mousetrap and the world will beat a path to your door" has got to be one of the most inaccurate statements ever made, yet some people act as if it were literally true. They believe that a new, well-designed process will automatically be acceptable to those who are supposed to use it. Or if there is any reluctance, it will disappear as soon as the workers are shown that the new process is "logical" and "rational" and superior to the one it replaces. Still other people view change in another way. They believe that it is management's job to design procedures and the worker's job to accept them. Thus they believe that a rational process can be imposed by management decree.

We all know from personal experience that these attitudes about change are not realistic. We can all think of instances within our experience where management installed a change that they believed to be rational and they carefully explained the logic of the change to the workers, but still it did not work. And the reason it did not work was that the workers resisted the change, and they made certain that it did not work. This experience points out that a person who is attempting to produce change, a *change agent,* must understand something about the process of organizational change, what causes resistance to change, and what can be done to lessen this resistance. We shall only touch on these topics here, but there is a large and growing literature that the interested reader should pursue.

Organizational change has two aspects: technical and social. The technical aspect is the change in procedures and practices; that is, the change in the physical routines of the job. This is the aspect of change that the change agent usually concentrates on. It is generally the result of a great deal of discussion and thought, and it is carefully documented before it is put into place. The social aspect of change has to do with the changes in established relationships within the organization. Usually social change is not planned, but it is a consequence of technical change. In fact, quite often the social consequence of technical change is not even considered in designing new procedures. Because social relationships in the organization are usually not formally recorded, neither are the social changes unless they result in problems for the organization.

Studies show that resistance to change in an organization is usually resistance to social, not technical, change. Most people do not object to changes in their mechanical routines if they are given time to learn the new procedures and if they are not required to make vastly greater effort. They may even welcome a technical change to break the tedium of their job. What disturbs people and causes them to react adversely is change or the threat of change in their human relationships. Changes that disturb the way people interact, the relative position of people in the social order, or an individual's own view of himself can be a cause of great disturbance.

People are usually not in a position to rebel openly and refuse to accept the change that disturbs them. They think, rightly or wrongly, that such actions might cost them their job or their next raise or call for some other form of management retaliation. Instead, their reaction is to resist the change and attempt to make it fail. Their resistance is generally not overt, but manifests itself in subtle actions for which they cannot be blamed. User conflicts are harder to resolve under the new system. Design and coding under new procedures seem to take longer and be more error prone. Other work suddenly gets in the way of projects, or sickness strikes the work force. New reports take inordinate amounts of time to complete, and reported data is distorted. In extreme cases, resistance can turn to sabotage of hardware or software, and the project product might emerge with the equivalent of a wrench welded under the fender.

A change agent needs to be well aware that if a promising new procedure does not work, it very likely means that the procedure has disrupted established social patterns and the people doing the work have succeeded in discrediting the procedure. And a change agent should be aware that this resistance to change can take place at any level in an organization. A manager can feel threatened by social change just as easily as the lowest person on the totem pole. A manager's resistance can be just as subtle as that of the lowest project worker. Resistance by management can often be detected by those who work for him, but it is generally not in their interest to do much about it. Thus the resistance of management can defeat a change as surely as that of anyone else.

Since resistance to change is quite common, what can a change agent do to contain it? Here are some suggestions that might help:

Explain the need for change. If people have adequate warning of impending change and if they understand why change is necessary, they are less frightened by it. They are less likely to view change as a personal attack if they understand the situation that brought it about. But in explaining reasons for change, be sure to avoid technical jargon and theoretical concepts. If the explanation is too complex, it will only confuse and create the fright you are trying to avoid.

Attempt to gain the participation of all groups to be affected by a change. People are much less likely to resist change if they have had a hand in shaping it. We are all aware of the NIH (not invented here) complex. It can't be any good if we didn't invent it. However, remember that for participation to be effective, it must be *real* participation. If participation is used as a device to secure acceptance, it is very likely to backfire. If people believe they are being conned, they can easily frustrate your efforts.

Take advantage of the experience and know-how of workers. Too often people overlook the fact that the troops in the trenches know some of the basic problems better than so-called experts. Those close to the work can often suggest sollutions to problems or spot flaws in proposed changes that are missed by those who view the situation from another perspective.

Avoid preoccupation with the purely technnical aspects of change. Don't overlook the social and human aspects. Don't be so involved with technical matters that you fail to observe what is bothering people.

Allow sufficient time for change to be accomplished. It takes time to learn new practices and procedures. Impatience with those who are learning the new ways can foster insecurity and resentment, which leads to resistance.

Realize that *you* are resistant to change as much as anyone else. We all have our own way of doing things, and it is hard for us to change. If we like technical matters, we find it hard to consider human factors. We like to perform in a manner that impresses our peers even though we realize that another style might accomplish the organization's objectives more effectively. To some extent every professional knows the NIH complex first hand. But if we are to be successful change agents, we must be prepared to change our own mode of behavior if it gets in the way of obtaining results.

If resistance to change does develop in spite of your best efforts, look on this as a symptom of a problem. It may be a technical problem—your proposed change may require too much effort or it may require skills that the people do not possess. Or it may be that the resistance is a symptom of a threat to established social arrangements—it may pose a threat to an individual's self-esteem or it might disrupt established work relationships. Whatever the problem, if resistance develops, use this as an indicator that there is likely to be trouble if you try to go ahead blindly.

8-9 SUMMARY

- The act of changing a methodology is a project; as with any project, it must be planned and managed.
- There are two basic approaches to changing a methodology: top-down and bottom-up. The top-down approach is likely to result in a large initial change followed by minor adjustments. The bottom-up approach is likely to result in a series of small, incremental changes.
- To promote the cooperation of the various affected areas, the project to change a methodology should be authorized at a high level.
- Change of a methodology is best accomplished by a team with the following qualifications:

Ability to manage a project
Knowledge of DP project methodology
Knowledge of DP project technical work
Understanding of human factors in DP projects
Ability to deal with various functional areas
Ability to deal with resistance to change
Experience and competence

- With modifications the project methodology of this book applies to the project of changing a methodology.
- An organization should establish what it regards to be the attributes of a good project methodology; the list of these attributes is used to assess the existing methodology and the proposed one.
- A number of vendors supply systems for project management; these should be investigated along with other proposals for supplying the methodology required.
- An organization should fix the responsibility for maintaining the project methodology.
- The modification of a methodology amounts to the introduction of change in the organization; attempts to bring about this change are very likely to meet with resistance.
- Organizational change has two aspects: technical and social. Most resistance is usually directed at social change.
- Some suggestions for reducing the resistance to change are:

Explain the need for change
Attempt to gain the participation of all groups affected by a change
Take advantage of the experience and know-how of workers
Avoid preoccupation with the purely technical aspects of change
Allow sufficient time for change to be accomplished
Realize that *you* are resistant to change as much as anyone else

9

PROJECT SELECTION AND REVIEW

9-1 INTRODUCTION

Before a project is born, it must be conceived. Since the conception or initiation comes before the project itself, it is not covered by the project methodology presented earlier. Nonetheless, the close relationship between project selection and project development compels us to say something about the former process.

There are two other activities that are closely related to a project but are not actually part of it. One of these is the periodic review of an ongoing project by upper management for the purpose of deciding whether the project should be continued or aborted. The other related activity is the postinstallation review of the final project product that takes place well after the project is completed. In this chapter we shall comment on all three activities: project selection, review of an ongoing project, and postinstallation review. (A general discussion of reviews is given in Chapter 18.)

9-2 GENERATION OF PROJECTS

It is convenient to classify DP projects as originating in three places: user departments, the organization's Opportunity Analysis Group, and the DP department itself.

The impetus for user requests can come from many sources—the user's problem, a top management concern, audit department requirements, the government through changed laws and regulations, the user's user's. problem (namely, the customer's problem), and so on. Whatever the impetus, it generates a request for a project to install or modify some system. Such a request can originate in any user department, and increasingly it is likely to involve several departments. For instance, a request from the sales department for an automated on-line order entry system will also heavily involve accounting, manufacturing, auditing, and possibly several other departments.

User requests are often generated by lower-level personnel who are close to operating conditions and see the need or opportunity. This means that the procedures for the initiation of project proposals should be designed so as to encourage suggestions from personnel on all levels.

Many organizations have an Opportunity Analysis Group or Systems Analysis Group whose purpose it is to generate requests for projects. This group reviews performance in key areas and makes suggestions for systems improvements. It may also be their function to decide if the recommendation calls for an automated solution; alternatively, this decision might be made by the group that reviews all project requests.

In the past and even today in many organizations, the opportunity analysis function is performed by the DP department. This has been the case because the DP department is the home of a group of trained systems analysts. The trend, however, is toward having a separate group, and there are several good reasons for this. A separate group with a clear-cut responsibility for reviewing performance is more likely to make continual and systematic searches for opportunities to improve systems. Also, by having a separate group outside the DP department, attention is more likely to be paid to opportunities that do not involve automation. Finally, having a separate group eliminates the possibility that DP might have a self-interest in the projects being proposed.

Systematic study of business opportunity by a group that can concentrate on this function proves to be worthwhile. Organizations that do not have a separate group for this activity should think seriously about forming one.

Internal auditors frown on having project proposals originate in the DP department. They view this as a lack of separation of duties and are concerned about the fact that the requests might be self-serving. But it is inevitable that a certain number of project proposals will be generated by DP. A proposal for installing a new computer or a new operating system is one that properly is generated by the DP department. In fact, any request for a change that should be transparent to the users, such as the installation of a data base, is one that would most likely originate in the DP department; to us this seems to be entirely proper.

In many organizations it has been traditional for the DP department to originate proposals of another kind, namely, proposals for improvements in user areas. The reason usually given for this is that the user doesn't know about the potential of the computer and has no knowledge of hardware and software developments. To save the organization money, the argument goes, it is necessary for DP to take the initiative and to drag the user kicking and screaming into the twentieth century. It is open to debate whether this view was ever valid, but the concensus is that it certainly is not valid today. DP may still be the first to recognize an opportunity and may make suggestions to user departments, but actual proposals for improvements in user areas should be initiated by the user department. Audit concerns for separation of duties requires this, but such a procedure also helps to assure that only necessary and cost-effective projects are proposed. Moreover, the way to promote active user participation in projects is to start by having him understand his need well enough to make the project proposal.

9-3 PROJECT SELECTION COMMITTEE

Proposals for projects should be forwarded to a committee whose function it is to select those that are to be implemented. The committee might also have the duty of encouraging the initiation of project proposals. In this book this group is referred to as the Project Selection Committee, but it might also be called the Management Committee, the Automation Committee, or the Applications Committee.

In the past the functions of the Project Selection Committee often have been performed by the DP department. It is, however, preferable to have a separate group because this encourages wider organizational support for the group's work. And, of course, it is another way to provide separation of duties, which is such an important cornerstone of internal control. But whether DP or a separate group is used, the function must be performed by somebody; and to be definite this topic will be discussed as if it were performed by a separate group.

Project Selection Committee members typically are from DP, finance, user departments and other functional areas. The specific departments represented is not as important as ensuring that committee members represent different areas whose interests must be considered, understand the role of DP as a change agent, and carry clout in the organization. The Committee must cooperate closely with the DP department, and it must also have close ties to the financial area and others with sign-off authority over projects.

It is the function of the Project Selection Committee to receive all project proposals. These then must be reviewed to assess feasibility, risk, impact, the suitability of automation, and potential cost relative to potential benefit. Much of the data for this assessment should be supplied by the proposer, but the Committee must be convinced that the supplied data is reasonable. The Committee's review is not made in great depth, but only to the degree necessary to determine if further study is warranted. Investigation and decision on a proposal should take no more than a few man-days of effort.

The approval of a proposal by the Project Selection Committee marks the initial authorization and funding of a project. Based on the same information used in the selection process and on resource availability, the Committee assigns the project a priority to indicate the urgency for accomplishing the project. Based on the authorization and priority, the DP department will then start the project as soon as it is feasible to do so. From this point on, the project is subject to the methodology discussed in this book. The initial approval of the project by no means indicates that the project will go all the way through to final completion. As was indicated in Section 4-9, the project is reviewed at the end of each phase to reassess its worth and priority.

Ordinarily the Project Selection Committee will review many proposals for each one that is approved. If a proposal is not approved, it may be rejected outright or it may be returned to the proposer for modification and resubmittal. In any event, the Committee should notify the proposer as to the disposition of the proposal. The Committee should also maintain a log of all proposals and indicate in the log the disposition of each.

There are many variations on the approval process just described. One organization has a dual system. A Selection Committee first reviews all proposals for technical feasibility and technical benefit. If they approve a proposal, it then goes to the Finance Committee where it is judged along with all other proposals for the expenditure of funds. A project is authorized only if the proposal gains the approval of the Finance Committee as well as the Selection Committee.

As indicated above, the Project Selection Committee may also have the duty of soliciting and encouraging proposals for projects. This activity could require missionary work and active salesmanship. The Committee may also have the duty of maintaining a long-range plan regarding DP projects, requirements, and the like. Such a plan would be helpful to the Committee in deciding how many projects to authorize and in assigning priorities among projects.

To do its job, the Project Selection Committee needs to establish an organization and to adopt a set of practices and procedures for performing its function. One of the key requirements is to design a formal input document to be used in making proposals. In addition to a descriptive name for the proposal and information concerning the proposer, this key document should contain (1) the objective to be achieved by the proposed project, (2) justification based on stated criteria, and (3) a preliminary plan for accomplishing the project. For an example of such a document, see Appendix D.

The criteria on which justification is to be based relate to financial, qualitative, and institutional considerations. These criteria should be widely known and generally acceptable. Because they are so important, we shall take a closer look at them.

9-4 CRITERIA FOR PROJECT SELECTION

Project selection is an extremely important function and one that calls for considerable judgment. First, the Project Selection Committee is required to select from all proposals submitted to them those that they consider most appropriate for the organization. Then, for the selected projects, they must decide whether or not automation is called for and must recommend automation only if it is the best alternative.

Unfortunately, there is no simple criterion by which these judgments can be made. Nor is there one set of criteria that is valid for all organizations. Judgment must be based in part on quantitative factors, such as measurable objectives for cost savings, benefits, improved productivity, and speed. In part judgment must be based on qualitative factors, such as improvements in the organization's image, information, or customer service. Moreover, judgment is required in several dimensions, including economic, technical, and operational feasibility, as well as management attitudes.

The economic feasibility of a proposal is determined by making two studies: a cost/benefit analysis and a risk analysis. The first of these studies relates the anticipated cash outflows to anticipated cash returns and is aimed at learning whether or not the project meets required financial objectives. The second study is an attempt to assess the risk of the project and to ascertain means of controlling it. Both studies are important, and both are repeated at various stages within the project itself. For these reasons each study will be described in a separate chapter (see Chapters 10 and 11).

A study of technical feasibility has to do with the ability of the organization to accomplish the project in view of other present and planned systems and the capability of the people. This study looks into such factors as the technical ability of the personnel who must build and operate the proposed system and the compatibility of the proposed system with the general technical state of the organization. It also explores the likely future technical impact of the proposal. For instance, a proposal to install a distributed system in lieu of a centralized system would have profound and lasting effects throughout an organization, as would the installation of an on-line order entry system. Either could be economically justifiable without being technically feasible or desirable in a given situation.

Operational feasibility has to do with the impact of the proposed system on the organization and its operations. It would include, for example, the impact on facilities and personnel, the problems involved with introducing the system (cut-over), and the impact on various procedures. It would include an assessment of the impact of and impact on control constraints, such as organizational, administrative, procedural, and financial controls. It would examine the impact on various checks and balances that are part of the internal control system. And it would examine such basic issues as the impact of organizational policies in the areas of quality, data, security, privacy, and audit.

It is not always the case that management concerns and aspirations are reflected in the statement of mission and the goals, objectives, and plans of the organization. In addition to their explicit statements, management has certain ideas about the types of systems that the organization should be installing, and these ideas must be taken into account by the Project Selection Committee. A proposal can be economically, technically, and operationally feasible, yet be unsuitable because it is not in synchronization with the pulse of management. There is no point in proposing a system that management will not support. Conversely, at times the Project Selection Committee may need to authorize a project that is marginal on other grounds simply because it has strong management backing. In such a situation the decision might be described as a political one; but let's face it, politics is a fact of life in any organization and it cannot be ignored by the Committee. It is worth observing, however, that the more formal the Committee's procedures and the more they call for written proposal justification, the less likely it is that strictly political factors will dominate their decisions.

The criteria for judging proposals are influenced by one other important factor: the resources available for projects. Typically the resource availability does not alter the type of criteria used in judgment, but it does affect the standards or hurdles that are set. And resources must always be viewed along a time dimension—a lengthy project started today might still be in development a year from now and thereby preclude some new project being undertaken at that time. Stated another way, the Committee has the task of balancing the needs and resources of today against those of tomorrow, and this is not an easy job.

From the brief account just given, it should be apparent that project selection is not a mechanical task but is a matter of judgment. It is a difficult job and one that has a profound effect on the future of the organization. Because of this, it pays for an organization to staff the Project Selection Committee with extreme care.

9-5 REVIEW OF ONGOING PROJECTS

The project methodology of Chapter 4 calls for reviews of ongoing projects by upper management at the end of each phase. The purpose of these phase reviews is to determine if the outlook for the project is such as to justify its continuation. The review group receives as input a phase report from the project team. They are required to examine this report and to pass judgment as to whether the project should be continued as planned, whether certain work should be redone and resubmitted for review, or whether the project should be aborted.

It is easy to see that the process of judging on the continuation of a project bears a close resemblance to the project selection process. Both call for judgment based largely on input from others and on the criteria described in the previous section. Both call for the commitment of resources in the DP area, and obviously they must be directed to the same objectives. Because the process of initial selection of projects is so closely related to ongoing review, we have assumed throughout this book that they are done by the same group—the Project Selection Committee. In practice, there could be separate groups for these two functions; this might be done as a means of dividing a heavy work load. But if separate groups are established, it is important to have extremely close cooperation between them because they are making judgments that involve the same resources. Also, if there are separate groups, one should be designated as the dominant one; and it should be assigned clear responsibility for coordination of efforts. It should also be the group that is given responsibility for long-range planning of projects.

Section 18-4 contains a general discussion of reviews, and many of the comments of that section apply to phase reviews. Also, Appendix D contains a description of the purpose, scope, and other information on phase reviews; it also contains a guide for conducting such a review.

In reviewing ongoing projects, the Project Selection Committee can find itself in the role of a tie breaker. Disputes can arise on a project between DP and users or among various user groups. When this happens, it is often necessary to appeal to higher authority to resolve the issue, that is, to break the tie. As a representative of upper management, the Committee might officially be given responsibility for mediating disputes. In any event, the Committee will perform this function implicitly as it passes judgment on the output and recommendations from the project phases.

One important point to remember about phase reviews is that time and resources must be provided for them. It is easy to overlook this when making project plans because a phase review, strictly speaking, is not part of any phase; moreover, it is not a task under the direction of the Project Manager. But phase reviews do consume time and resource, and the Project Manager must allow for this.

9-6 POSTINSTALLATION REVIEW

The postinstallation review of a product is quite different in character from project selection or an ongoing project review. It is not a review that culminates in the commitment of resources; rather, it is an audit to determine if a past commitment of resources fulfilled its expectations. Because it is different in nature, the postinstallation review need not be conducted by the group responsible for selection and ongoing review. Sometimes postinstallation reviews are conducted by the DP department or by user groups. Sometimes a review is conducted by an *ad hoc* committee formed to assess a single product rather than by a standing review committee. If the organization has a Systems Assurance Group (which is discussed in Section 18-7), it would be natural to assign them the responsibility for postinstallation reviews of all products. If no special group has the assigned responsibility, then it usually falls by default to the DP manager.

(As an aside, it should be noted that during the development period the emerging or "infant" product has a clear-cut "parent" in the shape of the Project Manager. In many organizations, once the project is completed and the product is installed, it becomes an "orphan." The installed product is held by the librarian, run by operations, used by the user, and "belongs" to no one. By this we mean that it is often the case that no one individual is assigned the responsibility for monitoring, maintaining, enhancing, and eventually removing the product. These tasks usually fall by default on some hapless individual who was associated with the project and who is unfortunate enough still to be within hailing distance. Where some specific individual has been assigned responsibility for the product, he is also likely to have the responsibility for postinstallation review. Interestingly, some of the privacy legislation may speed the emerging trend toward assigning responsibility for products to specific individuals. This is because such legislation is tending to require that some specific person can be named as the responsible party who is to be charged in case the law is violated.)

The postinstallation review is conducted to assess the product. It covers such questions as:

Is it a quality product? How does actual performance compare with projected performance? Does the product meet specifications? Standards? Satisfy professional opinion? (See Chapter 20 for a discussion of quality.)

Are business projections being realized? Are product use and transaction volumes as anticipated? Are benefits as anticipated? Operating costs?

Is the product successful? Is it the right product? Should it have been built? Built differently?

Any other important comments? Special problems? Special or un-anticipated benefits?

Answers to these questions should be obtained from all the functional areas that are involved with using the product.

The postinstallation review can be used in two ways. It can be used to appraise the people connected with selecting and building the product under review and, to some extent, those who operate it. But, in our opinion, a more important use of the postinstallation review is to appraise the project process with the aim of improving it. Most organizations spend a lot of resource on building computer systems, and any improvement that can be made in the project process will yield significant benefits. The Phase 3.3 assessment of projects is an attempt to measure the process, but the real test is the effectiveness of the new systems after they are in operation. The review of a system in operation can lead to improvements anywhere in the project process, including improvements in:

Project initiation and proposal process
Project selection process
Project methodology
Standards and work procedures
Work environment
Performance of people

It is not a simple matter to determine the true cause of a problem un-covered by a review and what should be done to improve the situation. For example, if a review discloses that maintenance costs are high, this might indi-cate a faulty process, poor standards, a badly conceived product, poor worker performance, or all of these. Sometimes it takes reviews from several in-stalled systems to locate the cause of the trouble.

Because a postinstallation review can point out problems in so many different areas, the review report should be given wide distribution. Among those who could make good use of it are upper management, the Project Selection Committee, users, DP management, the guardian of the project methodology (see Section 8-7), and the project team if in existence.

9-7 SUMMARY

- Some DP project proposals originate with users; some originate with the Opportunity Analysis Group, whose function it is to review performance in key areas and to search for opportunities to improve systems; and some proposals originate with DP, particularly in connection with the need for system changes that are transparent to the users.

- The Project Selection Committee reviews all project proposals and selects those that are to be implemented. The Committee might also be charged with encouraging the initiation of project proposals.
- Project selection is based on

    Economic feasibility
    Technical feasibility
    Operational feasibility
    Management attitudes

- Ongoing projects are reviewed at the end of each phase to determine if they should be continued, modified, or aborted. These phase reviews are conducted by the Project Selection Committee or by another closely associated group.
- A postinstallation review is made to assess the installed product; it covers such questions as:

    Is it a quality product?
    Are business projections being realized?
    Is the product successful?
    Any other important comments?

- The most important use of a postinstallation review is to assess the project process with the aim of improving it.

10

COST/BENEFIT ANALYSIS

10-1 INTRODUCTION

All organizations—government or private, profit or nonprofit—are faced with the problem of allocating their resources as effectively as possible in keeping with organizational goals. And in all cases, a basic rule applies: The goals to be achieved and the benefits to be derived are boundless, whereas the resources that can be brought to bear are strictly limited. Thus the allocation problem is one of weighing benefits and comparing them with the resources required.

Among the benefits to be achieved by an organization might be such items as more timely reports, better health care, higher levels of production, fewer customer complaints, and greater employee productivity. The resources to be allocated might include the use of personnel and equipment, productive facilities, and raw materials. Clearly if such disparate entities are to be compared, it is necessary to find some common denominator that can be used to assess the value of each. The most widely used common denominator, of course, is money—say, dollars. But whether dollars, or units of satisfaction, or hours of labor, or whatever is used is of no consequence. What is necessary is to find a common denominator for comparing apples and oranges so that it can be stated how much of one item should be expended in order to obtain the other. This common denominator then becomes the monetary unit for purposes of analyzing resource allocation.

There are three steps in deciding whether or not a particular commitment of resources should be made:

Determining the required resources and benefits, and setting a value on them

Measuring the relationship between the cost of resources and value
of benefits

Using this measure to decide whether or not to commit the resources

Before discussing these three steps, let us briefly examine the role that
such a cost/benefit analysis plays in the typical DP project.

10-2 ANALYSIS AND PROJECT AUTHORIZATION

Ideally, a project is authorized by a group that we call the Project Selection Committee. In practice, the project might be initiated in a less formal manner. In any event, before a project can be started, some individual or group must make the decision that the project is beneficial. This decision involves the judgment, either explicit or implicit, that the benefits to be derived bear a suitable relationship to the costs involved. Since this first cost/benefit analysis takes place prior to authorization, not too much is known about the proposed project. Admittedly, this means that the estimates of benefits and costs are sketchy and the values assigned to them are only "ballpark" figures. Nevertheless, an analysis is necessary at this stage to make certain that the organization's resources are guided in the right direction.

As the project moves through its phases, and particularly during Phases 1.1 through 1.3, the costs and benefits come more closely into focus. Therefore, it is necessary in each phase, especially in the first three, to reassess the costs and benefits and to make a revised estimate of the project's worth to the organization. This sequence of revised cost/benefit analyses provides management with an ever-improving basis for making informed decisions concerning resource allocation. The *analysis* of costs and benefits is usually done by the project team (with input from users and other groups), and they may also make a recommendation to management. But the actual *decision* based on the cost/benefit analysis is the responsibility of upper management, not the project team.

What we have just sketched is the procedure to be followed under a reasonable project methodology. But what takes place in practice? In fact, such a careful analysis of costs and benefits for DP projects is more the exception than the rule. From an informal survey, we estimate that fewer than one-third of all DP organizations require an honest cost justification of their projects. The remaining two-thirds either require no cost justification, or they require an "after-the-fact" justification as a formal ritual to vindicate a previously selected project.

When asked why cost/benefit analyses are not made, typical

responses are:

> "Our projects are mandated by top management."
> "It's the policy in our organization to keep up with the state of the art—that becomes our criteria for project selection."
> "We can't estimate the benefits because so many are intangible."
> "We don't know how to allocate costs in an equitable manner because one project benefits another."

Some of these responses are excuses, but it should be acknowledged that others reflect genuine problems that arise in assessing projects. For many of these problems there is no solution that will satisfy everyone; the best that can be achieved is a reasonable compromise. However, the fact that the problem is difficult does not mean that it can be avoided. Regardless of whether a formal cost/benefit *analysis* is made, a cost/benefit *judgment* is always made. Whenever a project is authorized there is a judgment, perhaps implicit, that the benefits to the organization sufficiently outweigh the costs; whenever a project is rejected, there is a judgment that the costs are too great for the benefits to be derived. In making such judgments, management must always weigh imponderables and grapple with the nonquantifiable. The task of the project team is to clear away as much fog as they can and to provide the best possible estimates as a basis for sound judgment.

It is important that the Project Manager have a clear awareness of the concept of cost/benefit analysis and the crucial role it plays in project selection and phase approval. The calculational details are of secondary importance. When the basic need and framework of the analysis are recognized and accepted, reasonable accommodations can be made to the practical problems that arise in dealing with specific projects.

10-3 EVALUATING BENEFITS

The hardest part of cost/benefit analysis is the first step: the identification and evaluation of benefits and costs. Of the two, benefits are usually the harder to assess. Nevertheless, justification of a project should start here—this puts the analysis on a positive footing by emphasizing the reasons for considering the project in the first place.

Identifying Benefits

Traditionally, data processing projects have been justified on the basis of measurable cost avoidance. Evidence of this can be found by examining the forms used to record cost/benefit data. One such form, typical of many, requires evaluation of the cost reduction from repair and maintenance, stationery and supplies, machine rentals, and staff expense (including fringe). Other benefits that are frequently listed are savings resulting from reduced space requirements or from replaced equipment.

Savings and avoided costs are certainly factors to be considered in justifying a project, and they must be taken into account. But in today's environment, these benefits are usually of secondary importance. The primary reason for most of today's projects is not to "save money" but to achieve some specific business improvement. The primary benefit of the project is this business improvement, and the formal analysis should acknowledge this fact. For example, today many systems are installed to achieve such improvements as increased sales, faster delivery, reduced inventory, faster, more reliable information, and better customer service. An analysis of benefits should start with the dollars to be saved or earned from the expected improvement.

Assessing Benefits

Unlike cost reductions, many business improvements appear to be "intangible," and serious questions arise in attempting to assess their worth. How is a value put on "faster delivery" or "improved service"? There is no easy answer, but several suggestions can be made.

First, the need to quantify benefits points to the need to establish measurable objectives for DP projects. Instead of an objective of "reduced inventories," the objective of "reducing inventories by $750,000 before January 1, 19xx" might be specified. Instead of a variable system life, a "death date" can be established for retiring the system from use; this fixes a definite cut-off point for calculating benefits. Quantifying objectives for projects not only helps to establish benefits, but it also establishes a clear standard for judging performance once the system is installed and running.

A second suggestion is that benefits can sometimes best be estimated by incremental analysis. To assess the value of "increased sales," an attempt might be made to assess the percentage increase that can be expected. By applying this percentage to the present level of sales and by taking into account the gross margin on sales, an estimate of the benefit can be obtained. Similarly, the benefit from "reduced inventory" might best be estimated in terms of a percent of the current inventory that can be reduced and the value of this reduction.

Finally, the problem of establishing the value of benefits (or costs, for that matter) is a problem in estimating. As with any estimating problem, if there is insufficient data to make a projection, then a Delphi experiment might be conducted (see Chapter 14) to take advantage of informed opinion. For example, various users might be asked, "If we have to buy the proposed system from an outside vendor, what is the maximum we should be prepared to pay?" A Delphi experiment on this question could elicit a consensus figure for the benefit of the project, and might also generate an interesting discussion of the real benefits the users expect from the system. And don't be surprised if these benefits are quite different from the ones listed in the original project proposal. Don't even be surprised if the benefits expected by the user cannot be delivered by the proposed system!

All of this raises an important point: In assessing the benefits of a project, look at the entire organization and at the proposed system from various views. Frequently there are real benefits (and costs) that are overlooked in the first analysis. For example, a large on-line order entry system was justified primarily on the basis of the 30% reduction in personnel that the system would make possible. After the system was installed, it was discovered that there was another significant benefit that had been overlooked in the original justification. The system handled customer payments as well as orders, and the instant knowledge provided by the system made it possible to deposit those payments in a bank drawing interest two days sooner. It turned out that this additional interest paid for two-thirds of the line costs of the system!

Another point to remember is this: DP is a service department in most organizations, so there is no way that they can cause business improvements to take place. DP can provide a system that has the potential of bringing improvements, but only the user can make it happen. Since the primary benefits of the system are in the user's hands, it is really up to him to identify and assess those benefits. DP can provide assistance and direction, but in the final analysis the user is responsible for evaluating benefits that are to be derived in his area.

10-4 EVALUATING COSTS

The most important point to keep in mind in evaluating the cost of a project is that *all* costs should be considered. In addition to those in the DP area, take into account the costs in the user area and such other departments as auditing, security, legal, and data management. Moreover, "absorbed" costs should be considered as well as the direct costs that are charged to the project. Always remember that the attempt is to assess the cost/benefit to the organization as a whole, not to some artificial subunit such as DP.

Costs can be divided into the two general categories of initial or de-velopment costs and recurring or ongoing costs. Some of the charges that fall within these categories are the following:

Initial or development costs
    Direct project costs
        Personnel (including fringe)
        Equipment usage
        Material and supplies
    Conversion of records and procedures
    Restructuring the data base
    Hardware and software packages
    Training
Recurring or ongoing costs
    Operations
        Personnel (including fringe)
        Equipment usage
        Material and supplies
    Data preparation
    Control
    Maintenance (repairs, not enhancements)

Various problems arise in estimating costs. One of the most frequent is the tendency to trim estimated costs in order to promote a popular applica-tion. Review of estimates by independent sources should help to highlight such a gross underestimation; if not, it should become apparent no later than the end of Phase 1.3. One organization attempts to solve the problem by having independent estimates of costs and benefits. Costs are estimated by DP and benefits by the user, each without knowledge of the other's results. Another problem is the difficulty in assessing costs when there is no com-parable project to be used as a basis for comparison. In this event, it might be useful to resort to a Delphi estimate, and it might be a good idea to have some outside experts join the estimating team.

Recurring costs are often underestimated through a failure to recognize the number of exceptions that cannot be handled by the system. Another common mistake is to make a cost estimate based on static volume and to ignore the growth that can be expected over the system's life. This mistake, however, might not be too serious because growth usually affects the benefits as well as the costs. Thus the net effect of ignoring growth might not be too large.

In estimating costs, problems can arise for which there is no entirely satisfactory solution. For example, suppose that a project requires a new piece of expensive hardware, but the hardware will have excess capacity that can be used for some subsequent projects. Should the first project be charged the cost of the new hardware and subsequent projects be charged only an incremental amount? Or should the cost be prorated on the basis of the capacity to be used? Obviously, the first approach penalizes the first project and under-costs the subsequent ones. But the second approach fails to account for the cost of unused capacity and thereby understates the actual expense of the first project to the organization. A compromise between these two extremes is probably the most satisfactory approach to this particular problem. The main point of this example, however, is that estimates and compromises must be made in assessing costs just as they must be made in assessing benefits.

10-5 INVESTMENT EVALUATION

Having evaluated benefits and costs, it is necessary to relate the two and to assess the value of the project to the organization. Viewed from the DP department, the way in which this assessment is made depends on whether or not the organization has a charge-back procedure for DP services—that is, a procedure for charging the cost of DP services back to the requesting user department.

If a charge-back procedure is in operation, DP's responsibility is to make a reliable estimate of the cost of the system to be built and to provide it within this estimate. It is up to the user to relate the cost to anticipated benefits and to assess the value of the system to the organization. DP might be called on to assist in estimating user costs and benefits, but the responsibility for evaluation lies with the user. If the user "buys" or approves the system, the decision is that the benefits relate favorably to the costs. From DP's perspective, this is a simple situation, and we estimate that about one-third of the organizations operate in this mode. Charge-back procedures are not without their disadvantages, but they do make for an easy cost/benefit analysis as far as DP is concerned.

If an organization does not have a charge-back procedure, then the cost/benefit analysis for the project must explicitly relate costs and benefits and must provide information for management assessment of the value of the project. There are three basic methods for relating costs and benefits: the pay-back method and two interest-based methods. For each method a measure is obtained, and this measure can be used in one of two ways. It can be used to make a selection, that is, a "yes-no" decision about whether the project should be undertaken. This selection is made by comparing the measure of the project to a preestablished standard. Alternatively, the measure can be used to rank all contending projects (non-DP as well as DP projects) so that the most attractive projects can be undertaken within the constraint of available resources.

The assessment of projects falls under the general heading of *investment evaluation.* Much has been written on this topic, and it will not be covered in any detail here. Instead only a brief outline of the principal techniques used will be presented and the reader will be referred to the literature on finance for a detailed account. The project team often is not required to make the actual investment evaluation, so they need not be experts in this area. But they are called on to supply data for the process, and to do this intelligently they should be acquainted with how this data is used.

The three methods of investment analysis will be illustrated by considering a DP application development project. To simplify matters, certain assumptions will be made. First, the various federal, state, and local taxes, which can add considerable detail to the calculations but do not alter the basic principles, will be ignored. Second, some simplifying assumptions about the timing of cash flows will be made. The development costs are all assumed to be encountered at one point at the beginning of the project, and the yearly benefits and yearly ongoing costs are assumed to be experienced at the end of the year. In an actual project the development costs may be spread over several years, and the benefits and ongoing costs are usually experienced throughout the respective years. Although we could have done so, we elected not to build this additional realism into our illustration because it would tend to obscure the basic principles we are attempting to illustrate.

For our project, assume that the cost of development (in dollars) is C. In its first year of operation, the application results in a benefit and an ongoing cost; let R_1 be the value of the benefit less the ongoing cost. (Note that R_1 is positive if the benefit exceeds the ongoing cost; otherwise it is negative.) Similarly, for each year t that the project is in operation, let R_t be the benefit in year t less the ongoing cost in year t. Assume that the application has a life of n years. We can summarize these statements as follows:

n = life of the application (in years)
C = development cost at time 0
R_t = benefit in year t less ongoing cost in year t for $t = 1, \ldots n$

From the financial point of view, the project we are considering calls for an investment or an outflow of C dollars at time 0 and a return or inflow over a period of n years. It is convenient to depict this graphically as in Figure 10-1.

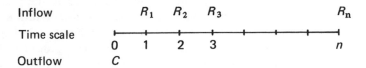

Figure 10-1. Cash flows from a typical project

In evaluating the investment, the basic problem is that the outflows and inflows of cash do not occur at the same point in time. The three methods of investment analysis to be discussed are designed primarily to adjust for this difference in timing.

Each method of investment analysis has certain pros and cons, and these will be summarized. The choice of which method to apply in evaluating a project is usually not made by DP; it is usually prescribed by organizational policy. Approximately one-third of all organizations that make a formal analysis base their investment decisions on the first method discussed, the pay-back method. Approximately one-third use an interest method, either the internal rate of return method of Section 10-8 or the net present value method of Section 10-9. The remaining one-third of all organizations use both the pay-back method and an interest method.

10-6 PAY-BACK METHOD

The *pay-back* or *pay-out* method of investment evaluation is based on the time it takes to recover the initial investment in the project. Specifically, the *pay-back period* is the smallest value of k such that $R_1 + R_2 + \ldots + R_k \geq C$. The following principles show how the pay-back period is used in making investment decisions.

Selection Principle: Select the investment if the pay-back period is less than some prescribed standard, say, n_0 years.

Ranking Principle: Rank all investments in order of increasing pay-back periods—that is, the shorter the pay-back period, the better the investment.

Example 1. It is expected that a certain application development project will cost $100,000 and will return a net benefit (benefit less ongoing costs) of $20,000 for each of the first two years of operation and $30,000 per year for the next four years. It is anticipated that the application will be withdrawn at the end of six years.

This project has a pay-back period of four years because the total return in the first four years equals $100,000, whereas the total return in the
first three years does not. If the organization has a policy of selecting all
projects that pay-back in, say, five years or less, then this project will be
selected. If the required pay-back is, say, three years or less, then the project
will not be selected.

If the organization has a policy of ranking investments, the project will
be considered together with all other investment opportunities. The project
will be undertaken if the available funds are sufficient to accept it and all
other investments that rank above it (that is, have pay-back periods of less
than four years).

The advantages of the pay-back method of investment analysis are:

It is easy to compute, sanctioned by use
It gives some insight into risk and liquidity of an investment
It recognizes the need for early returns
It is useful as a screening device

The disadvantages of the pay-back method are:

It fails to consider cash flow after the pay-back period, thus it is not
    a measure of profitability
It fails to account for the timing of returns within the pay-back period
The acceptance criterion for investments is completely subjective

10-7 INTEREST

Money has a time value. This statement is a shortened way of saying
that a dollar received today is worth more than a dollar received a year from
today. This difference in value stems from the fact that today's dollar can be
invested at interest so it is really equivalent to the dollar plus a year's interest
at the end of the one year.[1]

This can be illustrated with a specific example. If the prevailing
interest rate is 10%, then today's dollar will earn $0.10 interest in a year;
hence a dollar today is equivalent to $1.00 + $0.10 = $1.10 at the end of one
year, which is ($1.00)(1.10). And if this $1.10 is invested a second year, it

---

[1] Of course, inflation also plays a role in determining the future worth of today's dollar.
A complete analysis of an investment opportunity should take inflation into account,
but such a discussion is beyond the scope of this book.

will earn $(\$1.10)(0.10) = \$0.11$ interest during the second year. Thus $1.00 today is equivalent to \$1.21 at the end of two years, which is equal to $(\$1.00)(1.10)(1.10) = (\$1.00)(1.10)^2$

The reasoning of the previous paragraph can be generalized. Assume that an amount A is invested at interest for n years at rate i, and let B be the value at the end of the n years. Then

$$B = A(1 + i)^n.$$

To see this, observe that in the first year the interest on A is Ai; hence the value at the end of the first year is $A + Ai = A(1 + i)$. If this is now invested a second year, it will earn $A(1 + i)i$ in interest; hence the value at the end of the second year is $A(1 + i) + A(1 + i)i = A(1 + i)^2$. The relationship given above is arrived at by repeating this argument n times.

As has just been illustrated, if the rate of interest is known, the future value of a present amount can be calculated. On the other hand, the above formula can be rewritten to obtain

$$A = \frac{B}{(1 + i)^n}.$$

This expression allows the determination of the present value A at rate i of an amount B to be received in n years.

The preceding ideas can be summarized by saying that if the interest rate is given, it is possible to find the equivalent value at any point in time of an amount received at some other point in time. This observation is very important because it provides a financial means of adjusting for cash flows that occur at different points in time. It is the underlying rationale for the investment evaluation methods taken up in Sections 10-8 and 10-9.

Up to this point, we have assumed a known interest rate and have calculated either the present value or future value of a given amount. This is essentially the idea used in the *net present value* method of investment evaluation, which will be discussed in Section 10-9. However, the *internal rate of return* method of investment evaluation, which will be discussed in Section 10-8, is based on calculating an interest rate from the investment. Some simple examples will illustrate this concept.

If both the present value and the future value of an amount are given, it is possible to compute the rate of interest that relates the two. For example, if an amount $A = \$1.00$ grows to $B = \$1.07$ in one year's time, the rate of interest must be 7%. This is obtained from the fact that $A(1 + i) = B$ implies that $(1.00)(1 + i) = 1.07$, from which $i = 0.07$ or 7%. If an amount $A = \$20.00$ grows to $B = \$30.00$ in two years, then the interest rate i is determined by

$$20 (1 + i)^2 = 30.$$

This is a more complicated expression for i than in the first example, but it is possible to show that i is approximately 22.5%. More generally, for a given sequence of outflows and inflows, it is possible to determine an interest rate that relates them. Actual calculation of the numerical value of the rate may be complex and may require resorting to approximating techniques, but in principle the rate can be inferred from a knowledge of the cash flows.

10-8 INTERNAL RATE OF RETURN

The *internal rate of return* method or, simply, the *rate of return* method of investment evaluation is based on the rate of interest earned by the investment. This is the rate that makes the cash outflows from the investment equivalent to the cash inflows. For the application development project introduced in Section 10-5, this rate of return is the value of i that satisfies the equation

$$C = \frac{R_1}{(1 + i)} + \frac{R_2}{(1 + i)^2} + \cdots + \frac{R_n}{(1 + i)^n}$$

This equation is arrived at by setting the present value at rate i of the cash outflows (the left member of the equation) equal to the present value at rate i of the cash inflows (the right member).

The following principles show how the rate of return is used in making investment decisions.

Selection Principle: Select the investment if and only if the rate of return exceeds some prescribed *cut-off rate,* say, i_0.

Ranking Principle: Rank all investments in order of decreasing rates of return.

Example 2. Let us reconsider the application development project of Example 1 that has a cost of $100,000 and is expected to return a net benefit of $20,000 for each of the first two years and $30,000 in each of the next four. This project has a rate of return i given by the equation

$$100,000 = \frac{20,000}{1 + i} + \frac{20,000}{(1 + i)^2} + \frac{30,000}{(1 + i)^3} + \frac{30,000}{(1 + i)^4} + \frac{30,000}{(1 + i)^5} + \frac{30,000}{(1 + i)^6}$$

By successive approximation, one finds that i is about 14%.

If the organization has a policy of selecting projects with a rate of return of at least, say, 10%, then this project will be selected. If the required rate is, say, 15%, this project will not be selected.

If the organization uses a ranking principle, then this project will be undertaken if the available funds are sufficient to accept it and all other projects (DP or not) that rank above it (that is, have rates of return exceeding 14%).

The advantages of the internal rate of return method of investment analysis are:

The rate of return is directly related to profitability
The method is conceptually simple

The disadvantages of internal rate of return are:

Calculation of the rate of return is not trivial
The rate of return concept can be misunderstood
The method does not distinguish well among investments of unequal size
An investment can have multiple rates of return

10-9 NET PRESENT VALUE

An alternative to calculating the rate of return for an investment is to assume a rate of interest and to determine if the investment yields at least this rate. Essentially this is the idea behind the net present value method of investment analysis.

Let j be a given rate of interest; this should be the rate desired on investments and is possibly the cost of capital for the organization. The *net present value* of an investment is the present value of the inflows from the investment less the present value of the outflows. For the applications development project of Section 10-5, this net present value is given by

$$NPV = \text{(Present value of inflows)} - \text{(Present value of outflows)}$$

$$= \left(\frac{R_1}{1+j} + \frac{R_2}{(1+j)^2} + \cdots + \frac{R_n}{(1+j)^n} \right) - C.$$

Investment decisions based on the net present value are made according to the following principles.

Selection Principle: Select the investment if and only if the net present value is positive.

Ranking Principle: Rank in order of decreasing net present value if investments are substantially of the same size. Otherwise, rank in order of the *profitability index (PI)* given by

$$PI = \frac{\text{Present value of inflows}}{\text{Present value of outflows}}.$$

For most investments, it can be shown that there is a simple relationship between the internal rate of return and the net present value: The net present value is positive if and only if the internal rate of return on the investment exceeds j. Thus if j is taken to be the cut-off rate i_0 of Section 10-8, an investment will be selected under the selection principle of Section 10-8 if and only if it is selected under the selection principle of Section 10-9.

Example 3. Assume that j is 10%, and consider the project with cost $100,000 and net benefit of $20,000 for the first two years and $30,000 for the next four. The net present value of this investment is

$$NPV = \frac{20,000}{1.10} + \frac{20,000}{(1.10)^2} + \frac{30,000}{(1.10)^3} + \frac{30,000}{(1.10)^4}$$
$$+ \frac{30,000}{(1.10)^5} + \frac{30,000}{(1.10)^6} - 100,000$$

$$= 113,302 - 100,000 = 13,302.$$

Since this is positive, the project would be undertaken if an organization were deciding on the basis of the selection principle.

For this investment, the profitability index is

$$PI = \frac{113,302}{100,000} = 1.13.$$

If the ranking principle is used to make commitments, this investment would be undertaken if funds were sufficient to engage in this project and all others with higher indices.

The advantages of the net present value method of investment analysis are:

Net present value is easy to calculate

There is no problem of multiple values as in the case of rate of return

The disadvantages of this method are:

In practice, j is difficult to obtain and may be confidential

For very large investments, the rate j might not be constant, but might depend on whether the investment under consideration is made or not

10-10 SUMMARY

- Cost/benefit analysis is an attempt to measure the relationship between the cost of resources and the value of benefits, and to use this measure to decide if an investment is worthwhile.
- Estimates of costs and benefits are difficult to make, and they must be revised and improved as the project progresses.
- The primary benefit of most projects is not to save money but to achieve some specific business improvement.
- In evaluating a project, all costs should be considered, not just those that are charged to the project.
- The three basic methods for relating costs to benefits are pay-back, rate of return, and net present value. Each has its pros and cons.

RISK ANALYSIS

11-1 INTRODUCTION

We all recognize that some projects are more risky than others. An organization's first communications-based system carries more risk than a customary batch system. But what exactly do we mean by risk? How is it measured? How can it be reduced? And what can be done to control it? These are the questions that will be explored in this chapter.

Although risk is generally acknowledged, very little is done in most organizations to cope with it directly. Most do not have procedures for measuring risk, and such procedures as do exist are usually based more on intuition than on sound analysis. While the use of intuition is better than doing nothing, a more formal approach to risk needs to be taken in most shops. The analysis of risk and the search for means of coping with it should be ongoing efforts in any organization that is striving to improve its project process. The comments of this chapter are intended as an aid to those efforts.

11-2 DEFINITION OF RISK

To gain a better understanding of the nature of risk, let us look at one dimension of a project: project duration. Along this dimension, let us consider the risk that the project will not be completed by due date. Whenever we speak about such a risk, two things can be assumed. One is that we are speaking about a future event, something that has not yet taken place. If due date had come and passed, we would know whether or not the project was late and would not be talking about the risk of this event. A second point is that when we speak of risk, we are talking about a situation where the outcome is in doubt. If we were in the midst of a project and knew for certain that the due date could not be met, we would not be talking about a risk of being late but the fact that the project *will* be late. Thus, when we speak of risk, we are talking about some future event that may or may not take place. We are recognizing that there are various chance factors and unforeseen events that may impact the project and cause it to be late. The greater the chance of these adverse factors, the greater the risk associated with the project. Another way to put this is to say that the risk associated with late project duration is related to the *probability* that the project will not meet its due date.

However, risk is not simply the probability of being late—the *loss* associated with being late is also important. If a project is not critical, if it can be late without great loss to the organization, then it does not carry a great risk. But if a project is critical, if lateness entails large additional costs or a delay in realizing significant benefits, then the project carries a great risk. Thus, the risk associated with late project duration is a measure of the loss to the organization of missing the date weighted by the probability of missing the due date.

Of course, risk is entailed with all objectives of a development effort, not just with project duration. This observation and the foregoing analysis leads us to the following definition: The *risk* of a development effort is the loss associated with missing any of the objectives weighted by the probability of missing these objectives.

This definition of risk is somewhat informal, but it is sufficiently precise for most purposes. However, a more formal definition can be presented, and it is included for those readers who are familiar with statistical concepts. Those who do not have such familiarity can simply skip the next few paragraphs and go on to Section 11-3 with no real loss of continuity.

Statistical Model

To gain additional understanding of risk, let us once more restrict attention to a project duration. The duration or length of a project can be viewed as a random variable; that is, project length can be viewed as taking different values with different probabilities. The risk associated with late project duration is related to the event that this random variable assumes a late value. It also is related to the loss associated with being late; that is, we assume that there is a loss function defined for each late date and risk is related to this. A formal way to define risk associated with late duration is to state that it is the sum (integral) over all late dates of the loss from being late multiplied by the probability of being late. In other words, risk is the expected loss from being late.

Of course, the loss from a late project depends on the nature of the project, but it also is a function of *how* late the project is. If there is a high probability that a one-year project will be late by a few days, it is usually not as serious as a high probability of missing the due date by a few months. This means that the loss function is usually an increasing function of the amount late. It follows that risk is not too different from the variance of the random project length. In fact, since a project can be viewed as an investment, it is worth observing that many studies on investment analysis simply define risk as the variance of the random return from an investment.

In planning a project, two assessments can be made concerning the distribution of project length. One of these is an estimate of the value that length will take; this is related to estimating the expected value of the random variable. The other assessment is the risk associated with length; this is related to the variability of the random variable or the deviation of the variable from its expected value. Stated another way, the problem of estimating project duration and risk is similar to the traditional statistical problem of estimating the mean and variance of a random variable. Just as traditional estimators of mean and variance may be dependent, so it is that the estimators of duration and risk may be interrelated. This interrelationship complicates the problem of assessing risk and suggests that risk assessment should be done in conjunction with the estimation of duration.

The statistical model used here for discussing project length is a useful conceptual tool for viewing risk. It helps us to gain insight into the concept and, by analogy, to anticipate some of the complications that arise in measuring risk. But our statistical model is usually not a practical tool for making actual calculations of risk. One reason for this is that most organizations do not have enough data to carry out statistical analyses; but a more fundamental reason is that risk is associated with many aspects of a project, and not all of these can be easily quantified. The quality aspects of a project are the best examples of these. If an aspect of a project cannot be quantified, it is difficult to see how it can be represented as a random variable except in a broad conceptual manner. Some day a way might be found around this difficulty, but for the present our statistical model for risk should be viewed as a guide to our intuition rather than a formal computational tool.

11-3 PRODUCT RISK AND PROJECT RISK

Duration, which was used to illustrate the meaning of risk, is only one of several dimensions of a project that relate to risk. A project can also be classified as a high risk because there is a danger that it will not keep within its budget or it will not result in a quality product.

But there are many other risks that an organization faces when it undertakes a new application. Even if a quality product is delivered on time and within budget, there are still potential risks such as the following:

> The product will meet the specifications but it will solve the wrong problem because the user provides the wrong input
>
> The product will be prematurely obsoleted by new technological developments
>
> The product will be prematurely obsoleted by changes in laws or regulations
>
> Demand for the product will not materialize as expected
>
> Cost of operating the product will exceed projections

Events such as these contribute to the risk attached to any application, but these are risks associated with the *product,* not the application development *project.* They are factors that may lead to heavy maintenance work, costly operations, or a product that sits on the shelf. All of these affect the product during its operations and maintenance life cycle, but they are not factors that relate directly to the project development life cycle.

The total risk associated with an application can be divided into the risks associated with the product, such as those listed above, and the risks associated with the project. The two classes of risks are not independent; for instance, a badly overdue project can result in a cut in scope, and this in turn can lead to a product that is not satisfactory. But in spite of this dependence, the division into product risk and project risk is a useful conceptual view because it helps us to see the full dimension of risk. It is useful for management purposes, too, as the next discussion shows.

Product risk is primarily the concern of the Project Selection Committee. It is their responsibility to evaluate applications for risk prior to selection and to reevaluate them at the end of each major project phase. The project team probably will be involved with this evaluation only to the extent of supplying information concerning what the product will do, when it is likely to be obsolete, the cost of operation and enhancement, and so on. For the most part, this information has to do with the "supply" side—what services will be supplied and at what cost. Information on the "demand" side or the benefits to be derived from the product will probably be obtained from the user. It is the Project Selection Committee, however, that must put the information together and rank the product as one of high, medium, or low risk.

Project risk, on the other hand, is primarily the concern of the project team. It is their responsibility to evaluate the risk associated with project length, resources, and quality, and to reevaluate it at the end of each phase.

It is up to them to evaluate the project as one of high, medium, or low risk. This evaluation will be reviewed by the Project Selection Committee, but the responsibility for making the assessment rests within the project team.

The analysis of risk should be made in conjunction with the cost/benefit analysis because the two involve many of the same factors. For instance, both involve the cost of building the system and the potential level of usage. The analyses differ, however, in that they look at different aspects of these factors. A cost/benefit analysis deals with reasonable estimates for the various factors—estimates that are believed to be close to what will actually take place. Risk analysis deals with the question of variability from these reasonable estimates. It asks how likely it is that the expected values will not be realized, how likely is a significant deviation from what is expected. Thus, cost/benefit analysis deals with the typical or expected, whereas risk analysis deals with the extreme.

11-4 MEASURING RISK

There are some inherent problems in making a careful statistical study of risk. One of these is that risk relates to the probability of an adverse event. If this event does not take place, we don't know if we were lucky or simply misjudged the risk. Consider an example. Assume that a project is rated as risky because it deals with an inexperienced user. If the lack of experience does not hamper things and the project meets all of its targets, does this mean that the risk assessment gave a false signal or that the project was very lucky? On the other hand, suppose that a project is late because an unexpected shipping strike delays a key piece of hardware. Did we simply observe a rare phenomenon, or should we have placed the project in the high-risk category? These questions cannot be answered by looking at only a few projects. The number of observations must be large enough for chance factors to counter one another and for underlying relationships to stand out. Another way to state this is that the study of risk requires data on a large number of projects, and it requires that this data be collected in a consistent manner.

Another problem in studying risk is a variation of the old problem in measurement: The act of measuring distorts the quantity that is to be measured. If a project is rated as a high risk, then generally provisions are taken to counter and control the risk. If the project later turns out to be successful, there is no way of knowing if the countermeasures were successful or if the original assessment of risk was in error. It is difficult to study risk without such an element of contamination because, naturally, no one wants to leave an identified risk uncontrolled. One approach that can be tried is to base the study on completed projects. A group of past projects can be classified by degree of success, and an attempt can be made to find predictive factors that correlate with success. A real problem here, of course, is that most organizations have incomplete data on past projects. Moreover, the predictors that one would like to use before the project starts are almost certainly not recorded for past projects.

Because of problems such as these, most organizations at present cannot identify indicators for risk by means of a statistical study. Instead, they rely on the informed opinion of professionals. What professionals need to help them make informed judgments are some guidelines and a standard procedure for assessing risk. Some shops supply this assistance by providing professionals with a questionnaire that can be used to assess risk. By completing the questionnaire and scoring the response, it is possible to classify the project as one of high, medium, or low risk. Because such questionnaires have proved to be useful tools, let us explore how they are constructed and used.

11-5 RISK ASSESSMENT QUESTIONNAIRES

Before building a questionnaire, its purpose and use should be decided upon. Is it to be used to assess product risk, project risk, or both? Is it to be used by the Project Selection Committee, the project team, or some other group? In present practice it seems that most questionnaires are used by project teams to assess project risk, and this is what we shall assume for our discussion. If the questionnaire were to be used by the Project Selection Committee to assess product risk, the only major change from what we shall say would be in the questions to be asked.

Constructing a Questionnaire

There are three steps in constructing a questionnaire for assessing risk: (1) determining the questions and the answers that will be accepted for each, (2) determining the weights to be assigned to questions and acceptable answers, and (3) determining the rules for classifying a response as one of high, medium, or low risk.

Formulating Questions. The first step in constructing a questionnaire for assessing risk is to identify specific attributes that are related to risk and to formulate questions about these attributes. For example, one attribute that relates to risk is the critical nature of the project. A question about this is: Does the project have a mandated due date? Questions should be formulated about all aspects of a project and especially those that traditionally involve risk. Some of the attributes that might be considered are listed in Table 11-1; along with them are shortened versions of the type of questions that might be formulated.

A questionnaire should be tailored to the requirements of the specific organization that plans to use it. Table 11-1 might serve as a useful guide for formulating relevant questions. Another fruitful approach is to hold a brainstorming session—an open discussion with a group of informed individuals for the purpose of finding a list of questions related to risk. Whatever approach is taken, the list of questions that is developed will almost certainly be too long to be used in its entirety, and it will be necessary to trim it. A questionnaire with more than about 25 questions appears complex to those who must use it, so the size should be kept within this rough bound. What is sought are the most probing questions, the ones most closely correlated with risk. This requires evaluating each question for its importance, and it should be done in conjunction with the second step in building a questionnaire.

Assigning Weights. The second step in constructing a questionnaire is to assign weights to questions in proportion to their importance as predictors of risk. As just stated, this step is really an extension of the process of culling the total list of questions to arrive at those that will actually be used. Once the relative weight of each question is assigned, it is necessary to determine the answers that will be accepted for each question and to assign weights to each of these possible answers. For example, assume that one question to be asked is as listed below and that there are three accepted answers to the question, as follows:

How experienced is the Project Manager?
___ A. Highly experienced; has lead many successful projects.
___ B. Average experience.
___ C. Little or no experience

Suppose it was decided that this question should carry a weight of 5. Then weights might be assigned to the answers as follows:

Answer	Weight
A	0
B	2
C	5

Note that weights are assigned in keeping with the weight assigned to the question, so that the greater the risk, the higher the weight.

The question naturally arises: How does one actually select the ques-

Table 11-1
Attributes and Questions Related to Risk

Project Attributes	*Questions*
Project and product:	
Scope	Too broad?
Size	Requires long project? Large team?
Length	Over two years?
Specifications	Complete? Subject only to minor change?
Complexity	Simple? Involved? Replace existing system? New system?
Uniqueness	First-time effort? Leading edge? New procedures?
Critical nature	Time constraint? Other constraint?
Deliverables	Number? Complexity?
Completion criteria	Complete? Clear-cut?
Personnel:	
Organization	Team reports directly to one person?
Availability	Need to recruit? Personnel full time on project?
Team members	Ability? Experience? Knowledge about product area?
Project Manager	Ability? Experience? Style of management?
User	Ability? Experience with DP? Knowledge of product area?
Enthusiasm for project	Team? Users? Management?
Project process:	
Selection	Careful assessment of cost/benefit? Risk? Complex approval procedure?
Project methodology	Established? Understood? What procedures for planning? Controlling? Reviewing?
Work standards	Established? Complete?
Environment:	
Hardware/software	Not yet ordered? Delivered? Installed? New product?
Physical facilities	Established? Conducive to work?
Test environment	Established? Adequate?
Other:	
	Multiple departments involved?
	Multiple installations?
	Tasks outside project control?
	Schedule appears tight at outset?
	Management committed?

tions that will be used on the questionnaire and how does one determine what weights to assign to questions and answers? Theoretically this is a statistical question to be determined by some sort of regression study. For reasons discussed earlier, this is not the approach that can be taken typically. Initially, at least, a questionnaire is usually based entirely on opinion and intuition. For best results this opinion should be sought in a systematic manner, and an ideal way to do this is by using the Delphi technique (see Chapter 14). This technique can be used to select the questions for the questionnaire, to select the appropriate answers, and to fix weights to questions and answers. Also, use of the Delphi technique might reveal ambiguities and potential misinterpretations of questions or answers, and it might suggest ways to rephrase or reformulate defective statements.

The weighting scheme just outlined above suggests that each question be viewed independently, but a more complex scheme can be employed. Certain questions are related, and a system of weights can be devised to show this relationship. For example, it might be decided that a weight of 5 should be given if a Project Manager is inexperienced and a similar weight if there is no established project methodology. But if the Project Manager is inexperienced *and* there is no established methodology, the risk of failure is much greater than the sum of the individual risk factors. It might be decided that the two together should be assigned a weight of 5 X 5 rather than 5 + 5. This brings realism to the weighting scheme, but it also makes the construction of the questionnaire much more complex, so it should be done sparingly if at all.

A closely related problem in devising a weighting scheme is that of highlighting certain totally unacceptable risk situations. These are situations that arise from a combination of factors where the total impact exceeds the sum of the individual impacts. For example, suppose a questionnaire has 10 questions with answers weighted from 0 to 10 on each question. A risk score of 40 obtained by a score of 4 on each of 10 questions might not be as serious as a risk score of 40 obtained by scoring 10 on each of 4 questions. That is, total risk in 4 areas might be unacceptable whereas a risk of 4 in each area might be manageable. It is difficult to design a weighting scheme that reflects all of these possibilities. Instead of attempting to do so, it might be better to state separate rules for totally unacceptable risks. For example, it might be stated that a maximum score on more than, say, 5 questions makes the project unacceptable, or a maximum score on more than 3 of a certain selected set of questions makes the project unacceptable. Again, rules such as these complicate the use of the questionnaire and should be used sparingly if at all.

Determining Classification Rules. When a questionnaire is actually used to evaluate a project, each question is answered and a total score is calculated by adding the weights assigned to the answers. The third step in constructing a questionnaire is to decide how this total score is to be used to classify the project into a high-, medium-, or low-risk category. Again, an effective way to do this initially is to use the Delphi technique; but as data is accumulated it is possible to replace this by a more refined analysis. We shall return to this point shortly.

For scoring answers to a questionnaire, there will be two dividing points: one between high- and medium-risk classifications, and another between medium- and low-risk classifications. These two points can, of course, fall anywhere between the minimum and maximum scores for the questionnaire (the first dividing point, obviously, being above the second). However, once these dividing points are determined, it is a good idea to go back and revise the weights for answers so as to make the dividing points fall at easily remembered numbers. For example, one scheme is to adjust weights so that the total score (worst possible risk) is 100 and so that a project is classified as high risk if it scores 50 or more, medium risk if it scores 25 to 49, and low risk if it scores under 25. It will take a little juggling and compromising to adjust weights to this scale, but in the long run it is worth the effort. Remember that a risk questionnaire will go through several versions before questions, answers, and weights are found that work well for the organization that is building the questionnaire. Even then minor adjustments will be required over time to reflect the changing environment. To avoid confusing those who will use the questionnaire and to facilitate project-to-project comparisons, it is best to adjust the weights to some standard yardstick such as the one suggested above.

Initially a questionnaire might be based on opinion, but as data is accumulated it is possible to replace this by a more refined analysis. As history of completed projects is accumulated, it is possible to compare scores for projects with actual project experience. The first thing to check is the overall value of the questionnaire—do high-risk scores match with high-risk projects? It might be found, for instance, that some projects classified as high risk did not actually prove to be problems. If this is due to the fact that effective countermeasures contained the risk, then there is no reason to believe that the questionnaire is defective. But if there were no extenuating circumstances, it would be an indication of a false signal—a signal of a problem where none actually existed. This type of false signal can be lived with. A much more serious problem would be to discover projects classified as low risk that did, in fact, prove to be problems. Examples of this type indicate that the questionnaire is not discriminating as it should.

Once there is general agreement that the questionnaire measures what it is intended to measure, attention can be turned to individual questions. On the basis of experience, the weights assigned to questions can be adjusted, and unsatisfactory questions can be replaced. By continual reevaluation, the questionnaire can be tuned to the point where it is a reasonable indicator of project risk.

Using a Questionnaire

Even with a well-tuned questionnaire, there is a problem as to how it is used. Many of the questions on a typical questionnaire call for judgment on the part of the respondent, but the respondent is often involved with the project in some way and is likely to have a positive attitude toward the project. This can easily be reflected in optimistic responses to the questions and can result in an incorrect assessment of risk. One way to guard against this is to accompany the questionnaire with a detailed guide for completing it. Another safeguard is to require that all completed questionnaires be reviewed carefully by an impartial authority, by the leader of another project, say, or by a systems assurance group. But however it is handled, the problem of overly optimistic responses cannot be ignored.

A risk questionnaire is devised for all projects of an organization and is part of the standard project methodology. For each project, a questionnaire is completed, scored, and used to help rate the project according to potential risk. Responsibility for completing the questionnaire is usually given to the Project Manager. There are two schools of thought, however, as to who should grade the answers and determine the total score for the completed questionnaire. One approach is to prevent the Project Manager from knowing the weights for the answers and to have all questionnaires scored by some impartial body, such as a systems assurance group. The argument for this approach is that knowledge of the weights will influence the Project Manager and might prejudice his answers to the questions; it is felt that a less biased assessment will result if he does not know how the answers are to be used.

We strongly believe that this is *not* the right way to score a questionnaire. The Project Manager should be given the weights for the answers and should score his own responses for several reasons. First of all, if the Project Manager can't be entrusted with the task of scoring the questionnaire, then perhaps a different Project Manager is needed. Or a different manager for the Project Manager. If the Project Manager is mature enough to be given project responsibility, then he should be given the authority and should not be second-guessed.

A second reason for giving the Project Manager the weights is that any half-way enterprising person will soon know them anyway. Management is just kdding themselves if they think that project managers cannot figure out the scoring system—at least in rough outline. By changing a response or two and observing the resulting change in total score, it is easy enough to sort out the key questions and answers. Figuring out the weights is, of course, an interesting game, and this naturally leads to another interesting game called Beat the System. Attempts to keep the Project Manager in the dark may lead to the playing of both games, which is certainly not productive.

Aside from these reasons, which fundamentally have to do with assumptions about people and how they are motivated, there is another important reason why the Project Manager should score the completed questionnaire; this relates to the way that the questionnaire is used. The reason for assessing the risk of a project is to attempt to reduce risk and to control it. By knowing which answers contribute heavily to the risk score, the Project Manager can judge where efforts should be made to contain risk. Knowing that the project has a high-risk score is not enough; what the Project Manager needs to know is that there is a high risk because of certain specific factors. Attention to these factors will help to reduce the risk, or at least assure that adequate controls are in place to monitor critical developments. After all, this is the objective, not a mechanically derived risk score.

The primary reason for having a risk questionnaire is to *help* the DP professional make an assessment of potential risk. As with any tool, a risk questionnaire should not be used mechanically. It is easy to be overawed by a questionnaire, particularly if it is well formatted and packaged; but questionnaires are usually based on informed opinion and common sense, and they should be used with common sense.

Responsibility for rating the project risk is given, say, to the Project Manager. He probably will use the questionnaire to help him make his rating, but there are times when his judgment might overrule the classification mechanically derived from the questionnaire. Notice we are *not* saying that use of the questionnaire should be optional. We believe that it should be completed and scored for each project. But the Project Manager is ultimately responsible and should have the authority to give the project a risk rating that differs from the one derived from the questionnaire. For instance, the Project Manager may realize that there is a high risk of failure because of an unusual factor that is not covered by the questionnaire. He should be able to rate the project as one of high risk even if this conflicts with the result of the questionnaire. Any rating by the Project Manager, naturally, should be supported with reasons and may be subject to challenge by reviewing authorities, but it should be his own informed judgment. Instances where the Project Manager's rating differs from that of the questionnaire should be reviewed and analyzed with an eye toward improving the questionnaire if possible.

11-6 REDUCING AND CONTROLLING RISK

Most of the discussion of risk up to this point has involved assessing risk. It should be remembered, however, that we assess risk not only to know what we are getting into, but also to suggest means of reducing risk and to plan means for controlling risk. The remainder of this chapter is given to the topic of reducing and controlling risk after it has been identified.

Standard Project Methodology

The first and most important means of reducing and controlling risk is to have an effective standard project methodology. The reason this is so important is that most of the features of a project methodology are designed precisely to contain risk. For instance:

Work breakdown into standard phases and standard tasks reduces the risk of omitting necessary activities

Phased authorization allows controlled committment of resources and reduces financial exposure

Standards for documentation and output of phases reduce the risk of incomplete specification before design and incomplete design before coding

Short-interval scheduling and transactional estimating provide realistic, attainable time goals

These are but a few of the provisions of a project methodology that have an impact on risk. A worthwhile exercise is to review all of the features of a project methodology, such as those described in Chapter 4, and ask yourself what impact each has on reducing or controlling risk. What you should learn is that most of the major, traditional sources of risk are reduced or controlled by various features of an effective project methodology.

Of course, the risk-containing features of a project methodology are basic techniques that apply to all projects. In the previous sections, however, the assessment of risk on specific projects was discussed. We tacitly assumed the existence of a standard methodology that was constructed with risk in mind. To match our earlier discussion, we should now ask: What special measures to reduce risk might be taken beyond those that are built into a standard project methodology? What should a Project Manager do on a specific project to reduce risk?

Specific Steps

One of the first steps that should be taken when a special risk is identified is to inform management of this fact. They need this information to do their job. Because of the risk, management may decide to change the priority of the project, change the resources, or change the project time table. In any event, they will probably decide to give more attention to the project and to monitor progress more closely.

Existence of special risk is a signal to increase project control. More frequent checkpoints might be established and exceptional reviews might be instituted. The level of management involvement in reviews might be increased, particularly for those reviews that cover the high-risk factors. But this increased level of control will require additional resources, and allowance must be made for it.

A common reaction to risk is to try to increase the time and resources committed to the project. In theory this is an easy action to take; in practice it is often very difficult. Time and resource constraints are facts of life, and it is usually difficult to change them significantly. Even if an adjustment could be made in these factors, there is a danger that doing so would amount to an overreaction to the situation. This can be illustrated by an example. Suppose that a project is rated as a high risk because the project team is inexperienced, and suppose that an adjustment is made in the estimated length of the project to compensate for this risk. Assume, also, that the team inexperience was taken into account in making the original judgment about project length. Then obviously the adjustment for risk was not necessary, and it resulted in an unnecessarily high estimate. It is not easy to avoid this problem of double counting, particularly if "formulas" are used to estimate duration and risk. But being aware of the problem is the first step in taking effective measures to avoid it.

There is another way that duration is sometimes adjusted to account for risk. Suppose that a high-risk project should take 12 months. To be on the safe side, the DP manager tells the Project Manager that the project must be completed in 11 months. And to give himself some protection, the Project Manager lays out the time for project phases on the assumption that the total job will take 10 months. Within the phases the time allotted to individual tasks is further shaved until the final plan down at the work level calls for the entire job to be done in 9 months. What actually happens on the project is that most work activities come in late because the schedules are unrealistic. Every major deadline is missed, and yet the project comes in on time! That is, it is completed within the original 12-month deadline. This game may work the first time it is tried, but after that people will be on to it. Deadlines will not be taken seriously because it will be assumed that they contain built-in fat. Work estimates will be bloated to be prepared for the expected management cut. In place of a meaningful estimating procedure, there will develop elaborate schemes for outguessing the other guy. Meanwhile, how does management appraise and motivate workers who bring in projects on time but who are late with individual work efforts?

Instead of attempting to squeeze resources, a better approach to risk is the attempt to reduce it. Once major risk elements are identified and brought clearly into focus, it is usually possible to take steps that will reduce or contain the risk. Training and education can be undertaken to help overcome shortcomings in this area. The use of consultants or other advisors might compensate for a lack of experience or critical skill. Testing problems can sometimes be eased by securing more machine time or by revising test requirements and schedules. Holes in specifications can be plugged. If a project is too ambitious, the scope can be revised or thought can be given to splitting the project into several small projects. Whatever the risk, there is usually something that can be done to reduce it.

The responsibility for finding means of reducing risk is usually assigned to the Project Manager. One way for him to do this is to make a written list of the specific factors that carry high risk for the project. Then for each high-risk factor, he should list specific steps that can be taken to reduce or control the risk. This list of high-risk factors and specific countermeasures should then be subjected to a peer review or some other impartial review. It should then become part of the risk analysis report filed as a phase deliverable and the basis for an action plan to contain risk.

11-7 SUMMARY

- Risk is the loss associated with missing objectives weighted by the probability of missing them.
- The total risk that an organization faces when it undertakes a new application can be divided into the risk associated with the product and the risk associated with the project.
- Risk is difficult to analyze statistically, but its assessment can often be made by using a questionnaire designed for this purpose.
- The assessment of risk is used to suggest means of reducing risk and to help plan means for controlling risk.
- The most important tool for reducing and controlling risk is an effective standard project methodology; this will contain risk-reducing and controlling features that apply to all projects.
- To deal with risk for an individual project, a list should be made of the particular factors that create a high risk for that project and then specific countermeasures should be listed to reduce or control each high-risk factor.

12

FUNCTION ANALYSIS

12-1 INTRODUCTION

One mark of our society is the number of complex projects that have been undertaken successfully. Although landing a man on the moon captures headlines, also demanding are the tasks of constructing complex computer systems and of coordinating huge multinational corporations. To accomplish such complex tasks, it is necessary to identify and specify carefully the function to be accomplished and to break the complex tasks into a number of simple activities that can be handled individually. *Function analysis* is the name given to the systematic identification and specification of functions and to the breakdown of identified functions into subfunctions in such a way as to facilitate the achievement of goals. It is a basic skill that should be mastered by all knowledge workers, including managers on all levels, designers, and architects of complex systems.

The concepts of function analysis are not strikingly new nor are they rigorously derived. Rather they are an orderly arrangement of ideas, unifying concepts, and tools for the systematic treatment of the problems inherent in identifying the basic tasks required to accomplish a complex activity. Table 12-1 lists some typical areas in which function analysis is applied. That table indicates the two basic components of function analysis: function definition and subfunction identification. It also indicates the usual names in various areas for equivalence structures, which are charts of subfunctions. (Equivalence structures are discussed in Section 12-3). Our aim in this book is to apply function analysis to the study of work, and because of this the terms function and work are frequently used interchangeably. However, function analysis applies to many more areas than just the study of work.

241

Table 12-1
Applications of Function Analysis

Function Analysis	Work Analysis	Systems Analysis	Organization Analysis	Corporate Planning
Function definition	Work definition	Function definition	Unit definition	Aims definition
Subfunction identification	Work breakdown	Function refinement	Unit identification	Identification of aims
Equivalence structure	Work structure	Hierarchy chart	Organization chart	Network of aims

In data processing, concepts of function analysis were first systematically explored as a design tool; they were used to help determine basic tasks to be performed by a computer in accomplishing a complex job. Our interest in function analysis, however, is in the design of a development process, not a computer system.

As with many basic tools, the concepts of function analysis are so simple and clear that on first reading there is an inclination to think it is the pattern of analysis that has always been followed. Observation of actual work practice discredits this contention. Often when attempting to analyze complex tasks, work is confused with worker, and both with the activity of working. What emerges is often a mixture of tasks, products, and procedures; more often than not important elements of work are omitted and must be added as an afterthought. Function analysis is an attempt to avoid these difficulties by installing order into the process of work analysis.

12-2 FUNCTION DEFINITION

There are many ways to describe work: by describing the process of doing the work, the skills required to do it, the person or group assigned to do it, the organization assigned to oversee it, the system used to monitor it, and so on. All of these aspects of work are important; all must be described before a complete picture is given. However, if a complex work activity is to be analyzed, the place to start is with the basic question: What does work do?

Work is an activity that results in some tangible or intangible product or output. To produce this output, work requires certain resources, called inputs. What work does is to convert or transform the inputs into outputs. Because of its use in mathematics, such a transformation is referred to as a function. Thus, work is a *function* that transforms certain *inputs* into *outputs.*

To define a specific piece of work, all that is required is to specify its inputs and outputs. This tells what the work does. Of course, to accomplish the work it is necessary to describe how it is to be done, who is to do it, and all of the other aspects mentioned above. But these aspects of work can be added after the basic definition is given in terms of inputs and outputs.

A view of work in terms of inputs and outputs amounts to a description of a system from a vantage point outside the system. From outside a system, one can observe the inputs that flow into the system from the environment and the outputs that are returned to the environment. But one cannot see inside the system to learn how inputs are converted into outputs. These comments about systems are important because they help to suggest the generality of some of the ideas discussed here. For example, our "outside" view of work is similar to the approach an engineer takes when he views a circuit as a "black box." He is concerned only with the inputs and outputs of the "black box," not with how the transformation is made from one to the other. Our view is also similar to the approach a designer takes when he views a computer function in terms of inputs and outputs.

Usually work can be given a "verb-object" description in which the verb is the action and the object is the thing acted on. For example, "compute payroll," "wash dishes," and "sell product" are examples of verb-object descriptions of work. Use of such standard descriptions helps to systematize the discussion of the work process. In itself this convention promotes an orderly approach to work analysis.

Some examples of work are given in Table 12-2. A complex work activity may have many inputs and outputs, and then the simple format of Table 12-2 is not suitable for describing the function. Instead, it is convenient to use an IFO diagram to list the inputs, function, and outputs. These are also known as IPO diagrams standing for input, process, and output, which is how these three components are known in the related area of system design. Figure 12-1 shows such a chart for the function "compute payroll."

To define a function, it is best to start by specifying the required outputs because these usually are environmentally determined. Then one can find the inputs that are necessary and sufficient to produce the required outputs. Usually discretion is possible as to the detail of input and/or output that is explicitly indicated in an IFO diagram. For instance, the inputs for the function "wash dishes" in Table 12-2 are those that we chose to make

Table 12-2
Examples of Functions

Input	Function	Output
Dirty dishes, soap, water, laborer	Wash dishes	Clean dishes
Salesman, product line, customer population	Sell product	Sales
Plans, materials, plot of land, workers	Build house	House

explicit for illustrative purposes. In order to "wash dishes" one also requires such inputs as a suitable environment for carrying out the activity, a dishpan or other equipment, requisite skill and motivation on the part of the laborer, and so on. Also, the outputs would include dirty dishwater, a more highly experienced laborer, statistical information on the activity, and the like. In attempting to strike a useful balance between specifying too much detail and not enough, the guiding principle should be that the IFO diagram is a tool for helping to solve a problem, not for creating one. Too much detail can create needless confusion; on the other hand, the omission of an important input or output can cause serious problems. For instance, many industrial functions produce pollutants as outputs and only recently have these been explicitly acknowledged; omission of this output has resulted in the design of many poor processes for accomplishing the work. In the project area, failure to recognize that a suitable working environment is an important input to the

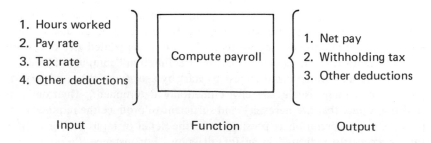

Figure 12-1. Example of an IFO diagram

work of producing an application can result in failure of the project. In analyzing work, the underlying assumptions and purpose of the analysis must be visible; if this has not been achieved by other means, then it should be done by including appropriate inputs and outputs in the definition of work.

12-3 FUNCTION SUBDIVISION

The definition of work in terms of inputs and outputs can be used for any activity, simple or complex. But a complex activity by its nature is such that one cannot grasp its complete significance; one cannot conceive of a detailed procedure for converting inputs into outputs. It is natural to seek some way to reduce a complex function to a sequence of simpler steps; that is, to seek a collection of simpler functions, called *subfunctions,* that will accomplish the original function if performed in an appropriate sequence. The process of establishing such a division of a function is called *subfunction identification, function decomposition,* or *function breakdown.* As applied to work, it is known as *work breakdown.*

(The reference to performing subfunctions in sequence is less restrictive than it may sound at first. This point will be discussed in 12-6.)

Figure 12-2 shows a possible decomposition for the work involved in writing a report. The diagram indicates that to accomplish the function "write report" it is necessary and sufficient to accomplish the subfunctions "gather information," "compose text," and "type report." If these three subfunctions are accomplished in order from left to right as shown in the diagram, then the basic function will be accomplished. A diagram, such as Figure 12-2, that identifies subfunctions is called an *equivalence structure* or a *work structure.* The diagram indicates that the work depicted in the top box is equivalent to the collection of work depicted by the lower boxes. The three short lines in the diagram are the traditional equivalence sign joining the top box and the three bottom boxes as bracketed by the horizontal line. In depicting a decomposition, it is often convenient to represent only the functions and to omit the inputs and outputs; this is what was done in Figure 12-2. However, it is important to realize that each of the four functions shown in that figure must be specified by listing appropriate inputs and outputs. This is ordinarily done on separate IFO diagrams.

Guidelines for Breakdowns

A function can be broken into subfunctions in several ways. There is no such thing as the best breakdown, but some breakdowns are more useful

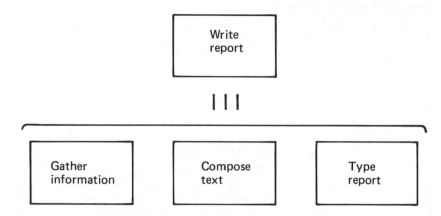

Figure 12-2. Example of an equivalence structure

than others. In Section 12-4 we shall list some of the considerations that should be used as guides in choosing one breakdown over another, but before that we want to discuss some of the mechanics of the process.

Experience shows that for most functions a useful breakdown can be obtained by specifying three subfunctions that have to do with receiving the inputs and putting them into an appropriate form, transforming the inputs into the required outputs, and preparing outputs in the form required for delivery. A breakdown with these three subfunctions is shown in Figure 12-3. For any work function, you should consider if this format can be applied successfully.

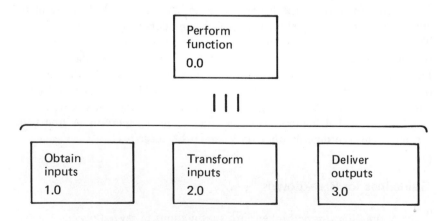

Figure 12-3. A standard breakdown into three subfunctions

Note that in Figure 12-3 we have adopted a decimal numbering scheme for the subfunctions in the breakdown. We recommend that you establish this or some other simple, standardized way of numbering your function boxes because this will facilitate cross-referencing.

Figure 12-3 shows one level of breakdown (and two levels of function), but in most practical problems it will be necessary to carry the breakdown to a second or deeper level. This is done in an iterative fashion; that is, the procedure used to break the top box into subfunctions is applied to each bottom box that requires further subdivision. As before, it is a good idea to explore the possibility of dividing each bottom box into three subfunctions dealing respectively, with input, transformation, and output. All legs of an equivalence structure need not be broken down to the same level. A box is not subdivided unless there is a good reason to do so; when you have a clear, implementable subfunction you should not decompose it further.

Figure 12-4 shows the work "accomplish project" broken down two levels; it also illustrates how the numbering scheme is extended to further levels of breakdown. An alternative way to display the breakdown of Figure 12-4 is by the use of *structured English,* as depicted in Table 12-3. Obviously this breakdown consists of the phases we have been using for an applications development project, but with minor modification in the names of the subfunctions the breakdown would apply to any project, such as constructing a building, producing a movie, writing a term paper, or moving a data center.

Table 12-3
An Example of Structured English

0.0 Accomplish project
    1.0 Formalize product
        1.1 Identify problem
        1.2 Specify requirements
        1.3 Define solution
    2.0 Develop product
        2.1 Design product
        2.2 Build product
        2.3 Test product
    3.0 Deliver product
        3.1 Accept product
        3.2 Install product
        3.3 Transfer product

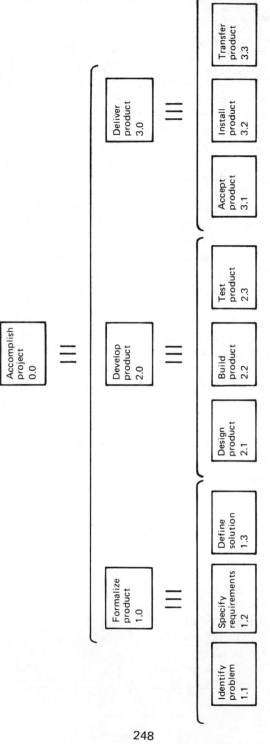

Figure 12–4. Work structure for accomplish project

248

Recall that in our project methodology the work of accomplishing a project was broken down into three major levels: phases, standard tasks, and work units. For a large project, it was suggested that an additional level be obtained by breaking the project into subprojects. These are the formal levels in the methodology, but the work breakdown concept can and should be used by the individual workers in laying out their own work efforts.

For a complex work activity, considerable care should be given to the definition of the top box. Experience indicates that this is *the* problem in establishing a useful definition of work. The identity of the top box has a profound influence on the entire breakdown structure because implicitly it contains answers to such questions as: What are we trying to do, and what is the purpose of this activity? The specification of the top box delineates the boundaries of the function and helps to spell out what should not be done as well as what should be done. The name given to the top box is important because it has an impact on everyone's point of view. Remember, though, that the function is really specified by listing its inputs and outputs. Because of its great influence, it is generally worthwhile to postulate several versions of the top box before proceeding to a decomposition.

An equivalence chart with more than two or three levels of breakdown is difficult to read. If more detail is required, each of the lowest level subfunctions on a chart can be exploded into separate equivalence charts. Alternatively, a decomposition can be displayed in structured English as was done in Table 12-3. Still another way to display a breakdown is to give a list of subfunctions, as illustrated in Figure 12-5.

12-4 SELECTING A BREAKDOWN

Function breakdown is a basic tool for analyzing work. Having a tool is one thing, and using it successfully is another. Let us now explore the difficult question of how work is divided effectively into pieces.

At the outset it should be recognized that the effective subdivision of work is a creative act. It can be looked upon as the essence of the design process. As with most creative acts, it can be guided by certain principles and examples, but there is no mechanical procedure for producing an effective breakdown. Skill comes with practice, so the more you apply the tool the better you will be at using it. What is offered in this section, then, is not a cookbook for producing effective decompositions, but comments on some considerations that can guide the process.

Basic Purpose. In breaking work into smaller pieces, it is necessary to keep in mind the basic reasons for the decomposition. Among these are: to make work assignments, to facilitate scheduling and control, for financial

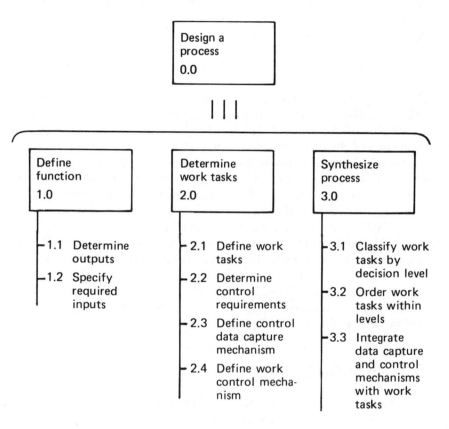

Figure 12-5. A display of subfunctions by listing

accounting, to improve estimates, and to reduce risk. The reader is also referred to the discussion on reducing complexity and short-interval scheduling
in Section 3-7.

Clear Deliverables. We have stated that control is based on completed
work; therefore pieces of work should be structured so that each has a clearly
defined deliverable. This is an important consideration, but one that is sometimes difficult to observe. Nevertheless, every reasonable effort should be
made to specify task output clearly and unambiguously.

Feasible Tasks. In defining a subfunction, it is necessary that there
exist a process for converting the inputs into outputs. The task "create
wealth" can be defined with an input of base metal and an output of gold,
but it is not a useful definition because as far as we know there is no process
for accomplishing it, although alchemists spent years searching for one! In
defining a task, there must be reasonable assurance that a process can be devised for accomplishing it. In fact, the problem is even more complicated
than this. In describing work, an attempt is made to separate inputs and outputs from the process of transformation; but it must be admitted that the inputs and outputs can be influenced by the choice of the transformation
process. If we wash dishes mechanically, we probably need electricity; if we
wash by hand, we probably don't. At a high level of abstraction, the influence
of process on inputs and outputs is usually not great; but as one drops down
the levels of an equivalence chart, the interplay between the two tends to increase. At the level of work units, it must definitely be taken into account.

Minimum Interface. Division of work is best made so as to minimize
the interfaces among pieces of work. Construction of a house could be
divided into the tasks of constructing the kitchen, the dining room, and so
on. Such a choice would probably be bad because there would be many complex interfaces among these separate tasks. A better choice is the more usual
division into stages of construction.

Related Skills. It is usually a good plan to try to divide work on the
basis of related skills. This simplifies problems of staffing and communication.

Levels of Control. Control is usually achieved through various levels,
and it is best to keep this in mind when subdividing work. The responsibility
and range of response for each control level helps to define successive levels
of work division. Each level of control has its limit for authorization of
funds, its tolerance to risk, its time for reaction, and its quality requirements.
These considerations help to determine the general size and duration of work
pieces. They also tend to determine whether work pieces should be done
sequentially or in parallel.

Relation to Other Management Systems. Division of project work into
pieces is governed in part by requirements imposed by other management

systems. The accounting system may impose requirements for financial reports on a weekly or quarterly basis. The personnel system may impose
resource constraints on projects. The security system may impose checkpoint and restart procedures for the project. Considerations of this type must
be taken into account.

Traditional Tasks. A work breakdown structure is usually not designed
from scratch, but must fit into existing practices. And even if a completely
new structure is being constructed, there are traditional divisions of work that
professionals know and are comfortable with. These existing practices and
traditional definitions should be kept in mind as project work is divided into
small units.

Employee Satisfaction. Employee reaction to a work breakdown pattern is an important consideration in its design. Several of the above factors
(clear deliverables, feasible tasks, related skills, traditional tasks) have an important bearing on this reaction. But it is not just the content of a breakdown pattern that is important, it is also the method used to arrive at it and
to introduce it to those who must use it. Installation of a work breakdown
pattern will introduce change in an organization, and it is important to avoid
resistance to this change. The comments of Section 8-8 should be kept in
mind when subdividing work.

Considerations such as the above interact in a complex way to influence
the breakdown of work. This can be seen by reviewing some of the things we
considered in designing the methodology of this book. First of all, we
studied the breakdown patterns of many organizations to learn about accepted practice. Our decision to break down a project into the levels of
phases, standard tasks, and work units was based largely on the requirements
of different control levels. The decision to have nine phases was based partly
on upper management control requirements, including their needs regarding
authorization, risk control, and response time. This decision was also based
on the natural division of a project into three major portions and each of
these into three phases. The actual work to be done in the phases was based
on this natural division and on such requirements as the need for clear deliverables, for grouping of related skills, and for minimum communication.
Standard tasks were selected to tie in with accounting requirements and to
build a base for better estimates. Work units were fashioned to assign work
and were sized to facilitate control. The need for clear deliverables led us
to specify outputs for each phase and to emphasize the need for clear outputs of work units. The entire work breakdown structure was predicated
on the need to make work productive and workers achieving.

12-5 PROOFING

Up until now our discussion of function breakdown has concentrated on the discovery of subfunctions. We now take up the question of proving that a collection of subfunctions *is* equivalent to a given function. In our discussion it will be assumed that subfunctions 1.0, 2.0, and 3.0 are defined, and we shall show that these subfunctions in the given order are equivalent to a function 0.0. It should be clear that our restriction to the case of three subfunctions is simply a convenience and that the discussion can easily be extended to any number of subfunctions.

The inputs available to the process we are considering are those listed in the specification of function 0.0. Thus, the only inputs that can be available to subfunctions 1.0, 2.0, and 3.0 are those that are supplied to 0.0 or those that are developed as output of a preceding subfunction. For instance, the only inputs that can be available to subfunction 2.0 are the inputs to 0.0 and the outputs of subfunction 1.0. Similarly, the outputs of function 0.0 must be produced by subfunctions 1.0, 2.0, and 3.0, and must therefore be among the outputs of those subfunctions. *Proofing* is the process of verifying two things. First, for each subfunction of the breakdown, the inputs are among the inputs of the box above it in the breakdown structure or are among the outputs of a previously executed subfunction. Second, the outputs of a function are among the outputs of the subfunctions into which it has been decomposed. Proofing establishes that the collection of subfunctions provides the same transformation of inputs into outputs as does the function it breaks down; proofing therefore establishes the equivalence of the given function and the sequence of subfunctions.

In breaking down a function, it is obvious that a collection of subfunctions for the given function must be discovered. It is not so obvious that each level of decomposition must be proved before declaring it complete, but this step is necessary to validate the decomposition. If a function is broken down into successive levels, then each level should be proofed before going on to build the next level.

The purpose of proofing is to show that all inputs are available where required and that all required outputs are actually produced. What proofing does is to establish that subfunctions interact only through interfaces comprised of their inputs and outputs. The effect of proofing is to establish that each subfunction is an independent entity that can be further analyzed and accomplished without regard to other subfunctions. This is an important point; it states that proofing amounts to the modularization of the function.

The careful application of proofing will reveal unnecessary inputs and intermediate outputs, and it will uncover failures to provide for required output. But most important, it will establish clean interfaces among subfunctions, thereby eliminating one of the most troublesome problems in the subdivision of work.

12-6 PROCESS SYNTHESIS

To accomplish a job, one begins by breaking the required function into appropriate subfunctions. Next, these subfunctions must be synthesized into a process that will produce the desired outputs. Process synthesis involves estimating requirements for the subfunctions, determining an appropriate order for doing them, scheduling them, structuring them into jobs, assigning jobs to people, and building a control structure. In this section we shall discuss how work analysis is involved with two steps of this activity: the determination of an appropriate order for doing work and the structuring of jobs.

Ordering Tasks

Recall that the definition of work breakdown involves finding a collection of subfunctions that, if performed *sequentially,* would accomplish the given function. The emphasis on sequential performance of subfunctions is less restrictive than it may seem at first. This is because the definition of function breakdown does *not* say that the subfunctions will accomplish the given function *only if* performed sequentially. In other words, the definition of work breakdown assures only that there is some order for the subfunctions (the sequential one) that will accomplish the function, but it leaves open the question of whether or not some other order will also be satisfactory. Usually it is possible to find another ordering; an example will illustrate how this comes about.

Let us consider a task T and subtasks T_1, T_2, ..., T_5 with inputs and outputs as listed in Table 12-4. It should be easy for you to prove that the sequence of subtasks is equivalent to T. This means that task T can be accomplished by the sequence of work shown in Figure 12-6. (This and Figure 12-7 are examples of networks, which are discussed in Chapter 15.) However, by examining the inputs and outputs of the subtasks, it can be seen that there is no reason to delay T_4 until T_3 is completed. Subtask T_4 only requires the output of T_1; therefore it could be performed while T_2 and T_3 are being performed. This means that the pattern of work shown in Figure 12-7 will also accomplish task T.

Table 12-4
A Task and a Collection of Subtasks

Work Function	Input	Output
Task T	A	B
Subtask T_1	A	W
Subtask T_2	W	X
Subtask T_3	X	Y
Subtask T_4	W	Z
Subtask T_5	Y,Z	B

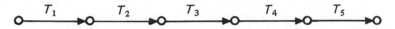

Figure 12-6. A sequential ordering for the subtasks of Table 12-4

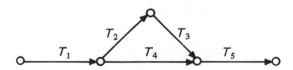

Figure 12-7. A nonsequential ordering for the subtasks of Table 12-4

This example illustrates that in structuring a work process, the tool of work analysis is used primarily to identify and define subtasks (that is, to list their inputs and outputs) and to ensure that the subtasks will produce all required outputs. A separate step is required to determine an appropriate arrangement or ordering of the subtasks into a work process. This step can be described as the design of a network of activities, a topic that is discussed in Chapter 15. Work analysis, therefore, provides input to the step of network design.

(We would like to make an aside to those who are familiar with networks and who are interested in theoretical points. The example above shows that *some* networks can be obtained from a sequence of tasks. It is also worth observing that *any* network can be obtained in this way. A formal proof of this can be given, but it can also be established informally. Consider an arbitrary network. This could be accomplished by a single person who worked on only one task at a time, and the order in which he did his work would define a sequence of tasks; clearly the given network could be obtained from this sequence. As an alternative argument, consider the work done in scheduling a network. The scheduling algorithm requires assigning dates to activities in a sequential fashion; the given network could be obtained from the sequence for scheduling. By showing that any network can be obtained from an appropriate sequence, we have established that the restriction to sequential performance of subtasks in the definition of work breakdown does not impose a real restriction—it does not eliminate any potential work pattern.)

Job Structuring

The other step of process synthesis that work analysis is involved with is job structuring. A job is a collection or package of work units. In forming jobs it is necessary to consider skill requirements, schedule restrictions, and human requirements, such as the need for growth, variety, and challenge. Work units must be defined so that these various requirements can be met. Thus, work breakdown provides the basic building blocks for job structuring; but job structuring shapes work breakdown, particularly in the final stage when assignable work units are formed.

12-7 FUNCTION ANALYSIS AND HIPO

Many readers are familiar with the design tool known as HIPO. They will recognize many similarities between this and function analysis and, indeed, might make the mistake of thinking that the two concepts are identical. We shall not explain HIPO in this book, but would like to make a few comments for those who are familiar with it.

HIPO involves two ideas: function definition and function refinement. The letter H stands for "hierarchy," which is a display of a function refinement, and the letters IPO stand for "input, process, output," which relate to function definition.

The definition of a function in HIPO and in function analysis is the same. In both, a function is regarded as a transformation that converts inputs into outputs. There is some difference in the level of detail that is explicitly given for the inputs and outputs of a function because computer systems require greater precision than do work processes, but this difference is unimportant.

There is, however, a significant difference between the concept of subfunction identification that we have been discussing and function refinement of HIPO. In subfunction identification we subdivide the original function into parts with the idea of replacing the function by its parts. However, in function refinement we do *not* do away with the top function; we refine it, which means we look for lower-level functions that the top function can invoke. The lower-level functions are appended to the top function and are used by the top function to accomplish its purpose.

The distinction between subfunction identification and function refinement is reflected in the diagrams used to represent the two concepts. In subfunction identification diagrams such as Figure 12-2 are used to show that the top function is equivalent to a collection of subfunctions. These diagrams indicate that the top function can, in fact, be replaced by the subfunctions below it. However, in the typical hierarchy diagram for function refinement, the top function is joined by lines to the functions below it, as depicted in Figure 12-8. The lines are intended to show the relative relationship of functions in a hierarchy; the lower functions are subordinate to the upper function. But the lines also depict a control structure. In a hierarchy diagram, control is originally lodged with the top function. Control can be passed down to a subfunction (for example, by a call); but on completion of the subfunction, control is returned to the top function. The existence of the control structure in itself shows that the top function retains some processing ability (the control process at least), which means that the collection of lower functions is not equivalent to the top function—taken by themselves they do not do all the things that are done by the top function.

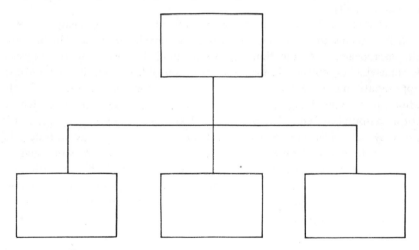

Figure 12-8. A typical HIPO diagram

The above comments can be summarized as follows. Function analysis involves dividing a function into a sequence of subfunctions; the subfunctions can replace the function. HIPO involves parceling out portions of a function to subordinate subfunctions; the subfunctions accomplish part of the processing required of the original function and do it under control of that function.

The function analysis view can be likened to splitting a company into separate but interfacing divisions, whereas the HIPO view can be likened to splitting a company into a collection of departments that are hierarchically controlled through a chain of command.

The distinction between function analysis and HIPO has many interesting ramifications that we shall not attempt to explore because it would take us too far afield. The distinction does imply, however, that the concept of proofing discussed in Section 12-5 must be modified when it is applied to hierarchies.

12-8 CONCLUSION

Sometimes an important invention can seem very obvious in retrospect—the wheel is one of the best examples of this. We do not claim that function analysis is another wheel, but we do see it as an important tool. In the shape of HIPO, it is being used increasingly as a tool for the construction of computer systems. But function analysis has not been applied to work as consistently as it deserves to be, although this situation seems to be changing rapidly.

One reason function analysis is overlooked as a tool for analyzing work is that it seems to be so obvious that it is considered trivial. In fact, the simple appearance of function analysis as applied to work—work analysis— is somewhat deceptive. The careful definition of work and its division into appropriate pieces requires a combination of analysis and ingenuity. In effect, it requires doing for work what product specification and design do for a computer system. The problem in learning to analyze work is that it is not easy to concentrate on what work does and to downplay who does it, how it is done, who oversees it, and so on. It is easy to confuse work analysis with organizational analysis and with planning and control. But, as with most tools, skill in using work analysis comes with practice; and with a little practice you will soon realize that this is a natural and effective starting point for the design of work processes.

12-9 SUMMARY

- Function analysis is a tool for the systematic identification and specification of functions and for breaking them down into subfunctions in such a way as to facilitate the achievement of goals.
- A function transforms inputs into outputs, and it is defined by specifying these.

- Subfunction identification is the process of dividing a function into a collection of subfunctions that will accomplish the original function. A diagram that depicts the function and equivalent subfunctions is an equivalence structure.
- Subfunction identification is guided by many needs and considerations, including:

  The basic purpose of the function breakdown
  The need for clear deliverables
  The design of feasible tasks
  Minimum interface
  Combination of related skills
  Levels of control
  Relation to other management systems
  Traditional tasks and work patterns
  Employee satisfaction

- Proofing a function breakdown verifies that the inputs for each subfunction will be available as required and that all required outputs of the function will be produced by the subfunctions.
- Work breakdown analysis provides input to the design of a network for a process, and it provides basic building blocks for structuring jobs.
- Function analysis and HIPO are related but not identical concepts. Function analysis involves dividing a function into equivalent subfunctions; HIPO involves finding subordinate subfunctions that can be invoked by a function.

13

ESTIMATING— PRINCIPLES AND METHODS

13-1 FACT AND FICTION

Data processing projects require estimates for aspects of the production process and of the product. The purpose of this chapter is to describe procedures for estimating project variables, such as duration, cost, and resources. We are not directly concerned with estimating aspects of a product, such as usage, operating cost, or useful life, but some of our comments will have obvious application to this problem too.

Estimating is a topic that is surrounded by a number of misconceptions. For instance, the fiction is widespread that it is not possible to do a good job of estimating, and the well-known history of failures is cited as supporting evidence. The fact is that not all organizations do a bad job. Some consistently produce estimates that are within 5% of the actuals; some do even better.

Another prevalent fiction is that there is an easy way to estimate. There is a belief that all one needs to be initiated into the group of knowledgeable people is to meet the right expert or attend the right seminar. The fact is, estimating is hard work. It is a complex process; probably it will always remain so because project development is influenced by dozens of variables, many of which are subjective and nonquantifiable.

Closely related to the previous fiction is the thought that there is some universal estimating model or formula that can be used by all organizations. The fact is that general principles hold for all organizations, but the specific implementation needs to be tailored to the organization. Each organization has its unique people, procedures, and history; and it is necessary to adjust the estimating procedure to these unique factors. Moreover, as the factors change, so must the estimating techniques.

From the realization that estimating techniques must be adjusted to the idiosyncrasies of individual organizations, an important conclusion can be drawn: If effective estimating procedures are to be developed and maintained, it is essential to gain understanding of the estimating process, not just to gain skill in applying some specific technique.

Still another common fiction has to do with the nature of an estimate. Some people look upon an estimate as a prediction of what will be. The estimate is either right or wrong, and obviously it must be right to be of any use.

The fact is that if anyone *could* predict the future, he would never use this skill to determine the cost of a DP project. Las Vegas, Wall Street, or the nearest race track would offer far greater reward for such a priceless gift. We estimate precisely because we cannot predict the future. We do not expect the estimate to be right on target, nor is this important. It is only important that the estimate be close enough so that the user of the estimate finds it helpful. We seek *useful* estimates, not accurate estimates; and the meaning of useful is determined by the application and the needs of the person who uses the estimate.

There are many people involved with a DP project who need estimates. To some extent their requirements overlap, but they certainly are not all the same.   Upper management needs estimates for making business decisions about authorizing and continuing the project.   DP and user managements need estimates to make recommendations to upper management and for obtaining and deploying resources. The Project Manager usually needs more detailed estimates than most others. These are required for detailed planning, for assigning individual work, and for controlling the project. The project worker, too, needs estimates for planning and controlling his own work. It is only by analyzing each requirement that you can decide how close an estimate must come to actual to be useful for any particular purpose.

The usefulness of an estimate also depends on the stage of the project at which it is required. In the beginning of a project, generally only approximate costs and completion dates are needed. As the project matures, the need is for more accuracy. Thus an estimate that is useful at the beginning of a project may not be later on.

One of the reasons people have trouble making useful estimates is that they do not know some of the specific techniques used in estimating. But there are more basic shortcomings—shortcomings that stem from a failure to understand the nature of an estimate and the fundamental requirements for obtaining good estimates. Among the problems are:

A lack of understanding about the purpose of an estimate and, more fundamentally, about the development process itself

A view that each project is unique, which inhibits project-to-project comparisons

A lack of planning data, which stems from questions about what data to collect, how it should be formatted, and whether it is worth the effort to collect it

Some specific estimating techniques will be discussed in this chapter and the next. Before discussing these techniques, however, we want to comment on these problems. We shall begin by examining the characteristics of an estimate.

13-2 CHARACTERISTICS OF AN ESTIMATE

In estimating aspects of a DP project, an attempt is made to answer questions that are similar to many that arise in other fields: What will be the reaction of an individual to a specific drug? What will be the unemployment rate next year? What will be the sales next year for a specific organization? Who will win next Sunday's ball game? All of these questions ask for an estimate; all involve making an inference based on incomplete data. A framework for addressing questions of this type is provided by the notion of random variation from the field of probability and statistics. To gain a better understanding of estimating, let us look at this concept.

First, consider a non-DP example. Suppose you are asked to estimate the weight of a person. (This information might be required, for example, to design an auditorium or an airplane.) You would realize that the weight of an individual can vary considerably. You might expect that most people would weigh somewhere between, say, 10 pounds (infants) and 300 pounds; and you would expect it to be more likely that an individual's weight would fall somewhere in the middle of this range rather than near the extremes. If you are pressed to give a single estimate for weight, you might give a number such as 140 pounds. You would realize that the chance of any one person selected at random being 140 pounds is extremely small, but you might feel that this number isn't a bad estimate since you have so little information to base it on.

Next, suppose the question is modified and you are told only to consider adult females. You would now expect that the weight would fall in a narrower band, perhaps from 90 to 175 pounds, and you would probably adjust your estimate to, say, 120 pounds. Also, you would expect that this estimate is better than the previous one because it should be closer to the actual weight. If we continued to modify the question by providing additional data on such factors as age, occupation, and height, you would continue to improve your estimate and would feel increasing confidence in it.

Data Processing Project Estimates

Let us draw an analogy with a DP project for which we are to estimate some quantity, say, project cost. At the beginning of a project we have very little data on which to base an estimate of cost. We recognize that, given our limited knowledge, the cost could fall anywhere in a fairly wide range, and it is more likely to be in some parts of this range than others. If pressed for a single number, which is what often happens, we would give an estimate that is somehow central to the various possible outcomes—the cost we think is average or the one that is most likely. But it is important that both we and the person receiving the estimate understand that our estimate is only one of many that could be given. We believe it is "reasonable" in the same way the above estimates of weight were reasonable, but we certainly do *not* expect that the actual cost will equal the estimate. We do expect, however, that the actual cost will be in some likely range,[1] as depicted in Figure 13-1.

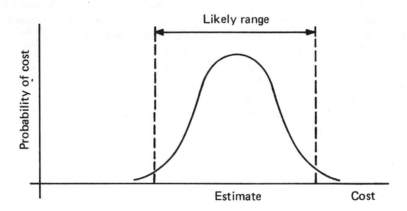

Figure 13-1. Distribution of the cost of a project

Another way to state this is as follows. The cost of a project depends on many factors. At any given point in the project, only certain of these factors are known. This known data will not, by itself, uniquely determine the cost. Two projects could be identical up to a given point in the projects

---

[1] We are using the term "likely range" to avoid a formal technical discussion of this topic. If you are interested in more information, read under the topic *confidence interval* in any book on statistics.

and still end up with different actual costs. Therefore, the data that is available at any point can only provide us with a likely range for the project cost. We can assert that some numbers in this range are more probable than others, but we cannot predict with certainty what the actual cost will be.

As a project unfolds, we gather more data about the product and the project itself. If we estimate project cost at the end of successive phases, we would expect our estimate to shift. More importantly, we would expect the likely range for cost would narrow because of our additional data. This narrowing of the likely range would lead us to have increased confidence in our estimate—the chance of our estimate differing from the actual cost is decreasing. This shift in our estimate and the likely range with time (which brings additional data) is depicted in Figure 13-2.

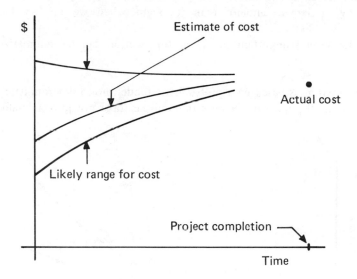

Figure 13-2. Change in estimate of cost over project life

Another important point about estimating is that our confidence in an estimate is related to the relevance of past experience. All estimates are based on past experience, and the closer the experience is to the situation for which the estimate is required, the more confidence we have in our estimate. This can be explained with an example.

Suppose that we have examined our past projects and have discovered a relationship between system size (measured, say, by lines of delivered code) and system documentation (measured, say, in pages) as shown in Figure 13-3. Our past experience has been with systems of a certain size, as indicated by the solid lines in that figure.

Now suppose we must estimate documentation requirements for a system of a size Q that is larger than any with which we have had experience. This means we must project or extrapolate outside our field of experience to obtain the estimate P. But when we project outside our field of experience, we should expect that the likely range for our variable will widen, as shown in the diagram. This widening of the likely range can be established statistically. But it is also clear intuitively because when we project outside our field of experience we are making an estimate based on data not closely related to the new project—we are estimating with less information because we have never been involved with a project of the new size. With less information, we have less confidence in our estimate. From this observation it follows that when we make an estimate outside the field of our past experience, we should anticipate that our estimate can vary from the actual value by a larger amount than it might when we are on familiar grounds.

The several important points in this section can be summarized as follows:

Estimating is based on a probabilistic model, not a deterministic one—that is, the quantity being estimated can take not just one value but

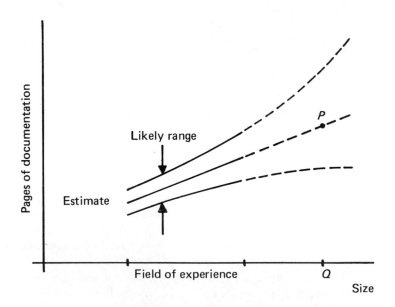

Figure 13-3. Extrapolation beyond the field of experience

several values with some more likely than others.

An estimate is a number in the likely range of the quantity being estimated. An estimate is a measure of central tendency, such as an average, median, mode, or midrange value.

Our confidence in an estimate depends on the size of the likely range of the quantity being estimated. If the likely range is small, we have confidence in the estimate; we believe that the actual value will be close to the estimate.

The more information we have on which to base an estimate, the smaller the likely range and the greater the confidence we have in the estimate. More information is usually obtained with the passage of time and the completion of project phases.

The more relevant the information on which we base our estimate, the smaller the likely range. We have less confidence in estimates if we have little or no experience that is comparable to the situation for which the estimate is made.

13-3 THE PROJECT PROCESS

The first step toward improved estimates is to standardize the project process. If this is not done, it is difficult to make project-to-project comparisons. The cost of one project may include much maintenance on unrelated systems, another project may include none of this. One project may have started with reasonably clear specs, another may have had the specs formalized during coding or testing. Unless projects are similar in broad outline, comparing one to another is like comparing apples to oranges. Standardization is required to reduce this problem.

Three statements can be made about any estimate:

To the extent that it is not an out-and-out guess, an estimate must be based on past experience.

The closer one's past experience resembles the situation for which the estimate is required, the more likely one is to produce a useful estimate.

Past and present experiences are likely to resemble each other if both arise as instances of the same general process.

If these three general statements are accepted and applied to the DP project process, one conclusion is inescapable: The way to improve project estimates is to regularize the development process and to view application development as a repetitive process. As long as each project is viewed as a unique event, a base for relevant past experience cannot be established and it is extremely difficult to make project-to-project comparisons.

At one time the attitude of most people was that DP projects were all unique and there was no way they could be fit into a standard mold. Today it is generally agreed that there are unique project *products,* but the project *process* is basically the same for all. The establishment of a standard, formal project methodology is possible, and it is a necessary first step toward obtaining better estimates.

However, the mere existence of a formal methodology is no guarantee that good estimates will be forthcoming. With a formal methodology it is still possible to commit a standard error of estimating,[2] which is to overlook activities that must be performed. Usually people do a fairly reasonable job of estimating the time and cost for specific tasks, but when it comes to making an estimate for a project, they frequently get into trouble because they forget to consider all of the activities that are required. They estimate for the major functions, such as design, coding, and testing, but they omit other activities, such as planning and control, documentation, and training. On a large project, there is also a tendency to overlook the effort required for interaction and communication.

The way to make certain that tasks are not overlooked is to develop the tasks for a specific project from a list of standard tasks that describe the work for any project. A good project methodology calls for such a list of standard tasks and establishes a procedure for updating and revising it. Even though the list might not be all-inclusive when first drawn up, as it is augmented and revised it will become more and more complete. This means that the problem of overlooked tasks can gradually be reduced to insignificance.

In addition to a list of standard tasks, a good project methodology should provide for standard terminology, standard project phases, standard ways to collect data, standard reports, and standards for the various tasks to be performed. With all of this in place, it is possible to establish a standard procedure for estimating and to begin to assemble the data on which the estimates are to be based.

_____

[2] No relation to the standard error of estimate.

Estimating and the Phased Approach

An organization's formal project methodology may or may not call for a phased approach to projects. This choice has important implications for the estimating procedure that is used.

The phased approach to projects is based in part on the recognition that initial project estimates are neither precise nor reliable. To adjust for this fact, two actions are required. First, the risk that is inherent in imprecise estimates must be controlled. This is accomplished by committing resources for only one phase at a time and by requiring upper management approval for continuation of the project from one phase to the next. The second action that must be taken is to obtain improved estimates. This is accomplished by requiring reestimation of the project at the end of each phase. The phased approach thus provides the time required to collect data needed for improved estimates and provides an opportunity for this data to be taken into account in a formal way.

The two parts of the phased approach that have the closest connection with estimating are risk control and progressive reestimation. But the most important contribution the phased approach makes to the estimating procedure is to bring out into the open and to recognize explicitly the fact that initial project estimates, while useful, are not very precise. This may not be stated formally in the methodology, but it is a clear and obvious principle on which the phased approach is based. Because of this, the acceptance of the phased approach helps to overcome one of the problems that everyone recognizes but very few want to face: The fact that upper management often refuses to understand that "there is no free lunch"—one cannot have precise estimates before a project is fully specified. Or maybe the problem is really that DP people *believe* that upper mangement thinks this way. In either event, by bringing this problem into the open as the phased approach requires, satisfactory project results are more likely to be obtained.

13-4 CLASSIFICATION OF PROJECTS

After stabilizing the development process, the next step in establishing an estimating procedure is to decide on the class of projects for which the estimating procedure is to be constructed. Are all projects to be treated the same way? Or are projects to be classified into different types with separate estimating procedures for each type? Before we attempt to answer this question, let us look at some of the ways that projects are classified.

Lines-of-Delivered Code. One way that projects are classified is by size, and to do this it is necessary to decide how size is to be measured. A common measure is the number of lines of delivered code—that is, the number of lines of code in the final project deliverable. This measure has been used for a number of years, and at one time it was much in favor. It has the advantage of being visible and easily calculated. For projects that are relatively similar, it gives an easy-to-use method of grading for size. Lines-of-delivered code does have some drawbacks, however, which have cut into its popularity in recent years. One drawback in using this measure is that not all projects result in delivered code. For instance, we know of one project that was to document all of the programs in the production library—and we doubt that the hero who took on this assignment would agree that he had no measurable output since there was no delivered code!

Another drawback relates to the fact that the delivered code is only a fraction of the total code that is written on the typical project. So-called support code is required on the project, but it does not get delivered to the end user. Support code is written to provide "scaffolding" for modules as they are constructed—to provide a simulated environment for the module. Support code may also be required for building a simulator or a test generator or a trace routine, none of which will be included in the final package. Often there is more support code on a project than delivered code, and in extreme cases the ratio can go as high as eight to one. Because of this and the variability of support code from project to project, many people find that delivered code is not a reliable measure of project size. But in spite of these and other problems, lines of delivered code is one of the most used measures of project size.

Aspects of Product. Another way to measure project size is to look at several aspects of the project product. Those selected are usually aspects that are highly visible and fairly easy to quantify—for example, the number of inputs and outputs, the number of files to be created, the number of functional areas to be served by the system, the number of locations to use the system, and so on. This measure of size is highly adaptable and has been used successfully by many organizations. It has some problems, however, and among these is the question of what weight to give the various aspects in order to arrive at a single measure of size. Generally this problem is solved in an *ad hoc* manner, and the weights that are used would not bear up under close examination. As with lines of delivered code, this measure is applicable only to projects that produce software systems.

Total Cost. Still another measure of project size is total cost. One organization divides projects into size categories by classifying a project as "small" if the total cost is under $10,000, and "typical" if the total cost is between $10,000 and $250,000. This particular organization does not have a "large" classification—if a project appears to exceed $250,000, then it is subdivided into two or more projects of "typical" size.

Total cost is a universal measure in that it can be applied to projects of any kind. It also has the advantage of being unambiguous and relatively easy to measure. However, many organizations find they cannot base an estimating procedure on a cost classification for one important reason: cost is one of the major elements they are trying to estimate—they regard it as an output of the process, not an input!

Complexity. Because there is no simple, universally accepted way to measure size, some organizations classify projects according to complexity. One classification recognizes three categories based on the type of product produced:

Control programs
Communications-based programs
Other applications programs

The most complex projects are those to construct control programs or operating systems. Next in complexity are programs that are communications based. All other programs tend to fall in the third or least complex category. Since most organizations do not build operating systems, their projects can be classified into just two categories.

Type. Still another way to classify projects is by type. Categories that might be considered are:

Application development projects
Mini projects
Purchase and modify packages
Maintenance projects
Conversion projects
Performance enhancement projects
Other projects

Additional categories can be proposed, but this list is already too long for most organizations.

Classification by type has much to recommend it. Different types of projects tend to have different deliverables; therefore different aspects on which to base an estimating procedure. Also, even if the same type of output is delivered, the effort to produce it might differ from one type of project to another. For example, both application development projects and maintenance projects produce delivered code, but the effort per thousand lines might be significantly different for the two. Another advantage of classification by type is that many organizations have grown accustomed to thinking of projects in this way, and this makes it a natural classification upon which to base an estimating procedure.

With so many different ways to classify projects, how many categories should an organization actually establish for estimating purposes? There is no simple answer to this question, and only a few general guidelines to help. If projects differ greatly, it may be that one estimating procedure will not give good results for all and then classification is necessary. On the other hand, if too many categories are established there will not be enough experience (data) in some categories to provide the information required for estimating. As a rule, it is better to err on the side of having too few categories rather than too many. Except for large shops with many projects, it is probably best not to establish more than two or three categories—there generally is not enough experience to support more than this.

13-5 ESTABLISHING AN ESTIMATING PROCEDURE

Procedures for producing useful estimates vary from organization to organization. Better procedures, however, usually have the following characteristics:

The procedure is formal. Rules for making estimates are stated in writing, and the rules themselves call for documentation of assumptions and resulting estimates.

The procedure is simple and easy to use. Input requirements are kept to a minimum, and output is provided in a usable form. Simplicity of use does not mean, however, that the procedure is easy to develop.

The procedure is stable in that it yields consistent and reproducible output.

To help produce stability, the procedure minimizes the human factor. As much as possible, estimates are based on objective rather than subjective criteria.

The procedure treats estimating as a sequential process. It provides for improving estimates progressively as the project matures.

The estimating procedure itself is dynamic and self-correcting. Provision is made for evaluating estimates and adjusting the procedure over time so as to improve the estimates that are produced.

An estimating procedure should be simple to use, but setting up the procedure is another matter. This can require considerable skill and insight; and it can take quite a bit of time, particularly if there is little past data with which to work.

Once the project methodology has been standardized and a class of projects has been specified, there are five major steps in establishing an estimating procedure for this class.

Step 1. Determine the estimates required. Estimating can be regarded as a function with inputs, processing, and outputs. As with most functions, the place to start careful specification is with the output, in this case with the estimates required. It is necessary to learn answers to such questions as:

Who needs estimates?
What do they need?
What use will be made of the estimates?
How frequently are they required?
In what form are estimates required?
For time estimates, do they require
    Total time?
    Elapsed time?
For cost estimates,
    Are non-DP costs included?
    Any accounting restrictions to consider?

Step 2. Select the estimating technique. Next, it must be decided which technique will be used to generate each estimate. There are many different estimating techniques; each is suitable in certain situations and not in others. Four estimating techniques will be discussed in the next section.

Step 3. Determine the data requirements. Data requirements depend on the estimating technique to be used. Some techniques require very little data, some require considerable. Required data is of two types: (1) historical data, that is, data on completed projects (this is needed to structure the estimating procedure) and (2) prospective data, that is, data on the prospective project for which an estimate is to be made (this is needed to make an estimate).

Two rules should be observed in reviewing data requirements. First, make certain that the data to be required can actually be captured. For example, one might wish to estimate project duration based on the number of modules in the completed system. Historical data can be gathered on the number of modules in completed projects, but is it reasonable to know this number for a prospective project at the point in time that the estimate is to be made? Second, keep the data requirements to a minimum; collect only what is absolutely required. If it is specified that data must be collected on a specific task in a specific phase of a project of a specified type and size, then this determines a data element to be collected. Unless a person is careful, he can drown in such data elements.

In addition to identifying the required data, decide how the data should be arranged or structured when it is captured. That is, format the *planning data base,* which consists of the data required for the estimating procedure. A well-conceived arrangement of planning data does much to ease the use of any estimating procedure.

Step 4. Capture historical data. Next, build the planning data base. Some of the data required for the estimating procedure can be captured from past projects, but this is usually not an easy task. Most of the data will be captured as projects are undertaken, and it is necessary to build a mechanism into the work process for doing this. The estimating procedure should be compared with the control procedure and the accounting system in order to coordinate the data-capture mechanisms of the three.

If no data has been captured in the past, it will take time to build an estimating procedure that works well. To speed the process, "seed" the planning data base by estimating the behavior of past projects, perhaps by using the Delphi technique of estimating (Chapter 14). In any event, start slowly and do the best job possible with what is available. As projects are completed and new data is added to the planning data base, the estimating procedure and the results can gradually be improved.

Step 5. Structure the estimating procedure. The next step is to structure the selected estimating procedure—that is, to build the equations, graphs, tables, or other devices that are required. Some procedures require little structure, others require that variables be specified and that parameters be assigned values. These values are determined from the historical data. For example, if project cost is to be computed, it is necessary to specify that it will be done in terms of, say, size; and it is necessary to establish a relationship between cost and size. The details of this step will be discussed in Section 13-10.

These five steps for building an estimating procedure are taken prior to any project for which estimates are to be made. Although these steps can be costly and time consuming, they result in a procedure that can be applied to all subsequent projects of the class of projects being considered.

Most of the work of estimating goes into building the estimating procedure; using the procedure for a project is a relatively simple matter. Although details vary with the estimating technique, to make an estimate all that is usually required is to obtain input data for a prospective project and to derive an estimate from this by using a mathematical formula. In later sections we shall illustrate how this is done for specific estimating techniques.

Once an estimating procedure is in use, it must be monitored to determine how well it is performing and to make adjustments to improve it. Judgment about a procedure is usually based on the difference between estimated and actual values expressed as a percent of the actual value. A quantifiable target should be established against which performance can be measured, and adjustments should be made to the procedure until this target is met consistently. Responsibility for monitoring and improving the estimating procedure should be clearly assigned to some individual, usually the person who has responsibility for monitoring other aspects of the project methodology.

13-6 SOME ESTIMATING TECHNIQUES

A number of techniques are used to produce estimates for DP projects. Some organizations use only one technique, some use several. Some organizations use the same technique throughout a project, some vary the technique with the maturity of the project.

In this chapter and the next, four estimating techniques will be discussed:

1. Scenarios   (Section 13-7)
2. Transactional estimating   (Section 13-8)
3. Projective estimating   (Sections 13-9, 10, 11)
4. Delphi technique   (Chapter 14)

A scenario is an outline or description of a scene or situation. A scenario might be constructed, for example, to describe the environment for a certain computer system four years after its installation. Scenarios are used to establish broad parameters of a system, such as utilization, cost of operation, benefits, alternatives, and so on. Scenarios are useful in defining the scope of a system and in system justification.

Transactional estimating is a means of obtaining estimates through negotiation. It is used to estimate time for individual work assignments.

The most commonly used formal estimating technique for DP projects is the projective technique. This is a statistical procedure that produces estimates through use of a mathematical formula or a graph. It is used to estimate cost and duration, either for a project, a phase, or a standard task.

The Delphi technique is a method of estimating through use of group opinion. Its chief advantage is that it does not require formally structured data on previous projects as do some other techniques. The Delphi technique might be used to estimate project cost and duration if these cannot be estimated in another way. The technique can also be used to estimate in areas where there is no applicable data, for example, the rate of inflation over the next decade.

As these brief sketches suggest, the four techniques are used in different ways and for different purposes. Several might be used on a single project. Before a project begins, you might construct a scenario to depict the general environment within which the system will operate. Specific parameters of this environment—say, inflation rates and utilization rates—might be estimated by using the Delphi technique. When a project starts, its cost and elapsed time might be estimated by a projective technique and confirmed by using the Delphi technique. As the project unfolds, estimates for the time of individual work units might be arrived at through a transactional process. These can be summarized to arrive at a time estimate for the phase, and this estimate might be confirmed by using a projective estimate. It can be seen from this discussion that estimates and revisions are continually produced on a project, and they are produced by whatever is the most suitable technique.

Classification of Techniques

An estimating technique can be described in many ways. It is a *qualitative* technique if it is largely verbal, and a *quantitative* technique if it is numerical. It is used to produce a *micro* estimate if the estimate for the whole is assembled from estimates for the parts. On the other hand, it is a *macro* estimate if it is arrived at for the whole without examining the constituent parts. As generally used on DP projects, the four techniques can be classified as follows:

Technique	*Characteristics*
Scenario	Qualitative; macro
Transactional	Quantitative; micro
Projective	Quantitative; micro/macro
Delphi	Quantitative; macro

Estimating techniques can also be classified by the degree to which they require continuity from the past to the future. The seeds of the future are always produced in the past, and it is true that every estimate is based in some way on past experience. But some techniques, such as scenarios and the Delphi technique, do not depend on the future being a steady continuation of the past. Abrupt changes in the environment or discontinuities in trends can be accommodated by such techniques. What would happen to system's cost and utilization if wage rates were to double? If the government passed a severe privacy law? If a state were to tax computer software? If a new generation of computers were announced? Questions of this type can be addressed by scenarios and the Delphi technique.

On the other hand, projective estimates are based on past history and the expectation that the past will be a reasonable predictor of the future. Transactional estimates fall somewhere in the middle. To some extent they depend on past history, but the dependence is not mechanical and can be adapted to changes without too much trouble.

13-7 SCENARIOS

Scenarios are generally used as a tool for long-range planning. They can be used by the Data Processing Department to form a picture of the environment that is likely to exist for the organization in, say, five or ten years. Such a conception is necessary if intelligent plans are to be made about the likely demands for DP services and the cost of providing these services. Of course, other areas of the organization have need for a long-term view for similar reasons. Because of this, scenarios are generally provided to the entire organization by a long-range planning group. If such a group does not exist, however, the DP Department might be forced to fill the void, at least as far as its own needs are concerned.

Scenarios might be used to estimate aspects of the development process, particularly for very long projects. But a more usual role is to provide a means of estimating some of the parameters for the project product. Most products are systems that will be in operation for many years, and it is necessary to consider the environment in which they will operate during that period. What hardware and software systems will the system interface with in the future? What enhancements are likely to be proposed in five years' time? What is likely to be the utilization of the system over its life span? Are there any legal, political, or social attitudes or changes that might impact the system? For example, what is likely to be the customer acceptance of a supermarket point-of-sale system? These questions have a bearing on the cost and benefit of the system being constructed and might help to determine its scope. They cannot be answered by simple projection of the present into the future because they are influenced by changes in trends.

One experienced Project Manager told us that three of his recent projects had to be modified drastically in midstream because users had failed to anticipate future events that would have a large impact on the systems. He believed that these future events would have been reasonably easy to forecast if a more systematic study had been made of the potential environment in which the systems would operate. In his opinion, if users had constructed scenarios before specifying their requirements and if they had thereby been forced to focus on the future, significant savings in the time and effort would have resulted on all three projects. He now strongly urges users to construct scenarios during Phase 1.2 if they have not already done so.

Of course, we all speculate on the future quite regularly. A scenario differs from the usual speculation in that it is a formal, written statement. Also, it is arrived at more purposefully and more systematically than is the usual speculation. Following are some topics that a scenario generally covers.

Demographic Factors. A scenario for the environment, say, five or ten years in the future should take population statistics into account. Changes in age distribution, educational level, and major shifts of population, say from rural to urban or vice versa, can have a significant effect on system's usage, availability of staff, the number of locations using a system, and so on. For instance, the downward trend of the college-age population will influence the supply of entry-level DP professionals through the early 1980s. More generally, population trends affect attitudes. The trend toward an older population with more retired people is one that will influence many facets of American life. Demographic factors are generally fairly easy to project, and many studies by the U.S. Government are readily available. For this reason, a good place to start building a scenario is with these factors.

Technological Factors. It is relatively easy to project the technology that will be available in five or ten years. Things that will be available for commercial use in a few years are probably out of the research stage and into development at the present time. For a scenario affecting projects, the most important technological factors are those involving computer hardware, software, development tools, and project methodology.

Political Factors. In a relatively stable society such as the United States, political factors are not too difficult to project. By the same token, the relative stability means that these factors will probably not have a major influence on most systems. Major political trends are largely influenced by demographic factors, which means that political factors should be projected after the demographic ones.

Economic Factors. These are extremely important for most systems, but very difficult to anticipate. Key questions relate to such topics as inflation, unemployment, government control and interference with the market mechanism, resource availability, taxes, interest rates, and credit.

Other Social Factors. A scenario should not be restricted to a narrow range of subjects but should encompass any issue, trend, or attitude that has a bearing on the environment being discussed.

Because many factors, such as the economic ones, are very difficult to project, it is often a good idea to construct several scenarios. One scenario might be built of the most likely situation, one for a pessimistic situation, and one for an optimistic situation. For these three, you could set parameters for the system and describe the range in which the parameters are likely to fall.

Generally, a scenario is largely verbal or qualitative. Numerical or quantitative aspects are introduced to the extent that this is possible and useful. To assist with quantification of some of the projections, it might be helpful to use the Delphi technique in building a scenario.

13-8 TRANSACTIONAL ESTIMATING

Most estimates are impersonal. They are based on overall performance of past projects and, by their nature, depend on the average performance of project workers. But work is not performed by average people, it is performed by individuals. Some are more productive than others. This means that the estimate of the time required to perform a given task will to some extent depend on who does it—one person's four-day task may take another person anywhere from three to five days. A typical estimate for the duration of a task does not take this individual variation into account, and this omission can lead to problems ranging from worker frustration and dissatisfaction to missed deadlines.

There are other variations in tasks that typical estimates do not consider. The current project might involve a complex control structure, which means that more time should be allowed for design and coding than usual. Or it might be that the system to be replaced was well documented, which means some time can be saved in Phase 1.2. Since estimates are usually based on average past performance, they do not allow for these typical random variations around past norms.

The worker who is assigned to a specific task can usually spot a bad estimate. If the task is well defined with clear inputs and required outputs, the worker can usually tell before starting whether he can take it easy or can expect to put in a lot of overtime. If someone were to ask him, he could give a reasonably good estimate of the time required to do the task—but usually he is not asked. Or he is asked for an opinion in such a way that it is understood by him and the requestor that he is expected to concur with the estimate handed to him.

There is a method of estimating that takes the knowledge and experience of workers into account; we call this method *transactional estimating*. It is based on the notion that the person who is to do the work has a good idea of how much time and resource it will take, and this information should be used in making the estimate. Transactional estimating produces useful estimates, and it also promotes motivation and commitment to meet these estimates.

Transactional estimating is frequently used to adjust estimates made by other techniques. It is used to spot bad estimates and make adjustments in advance rather than after a problem has arisen. An estimate for an aggregated level of work—a project, a phase, or a standard task—is usually made by using a projective technique. To obtain a transactional estimate for this same effort, the first step is to break the work into units that can be assigned to specific individuals or groups. (Characteristics of such work units are described in Chapter 5.)

Estimating Procedure

The procedure for obtaining a transactional estimate for a work unit can vary from organization to organization, but a common method is as follows. The Project Manager makes an estimate of the time required for a given work unit. He bases his estimate on past experience and his assessment of the work unit and the worker to whom it is assigned. This estimate is then given to the worker who is responsible for doing the work. The worker reviews the estimate and compares it with his own estimate of the time he thinks it will take him to do the work. If his estimate and the Project Manager's are in substantial agreement, the worker concurs with the Project Manager's estimate and this becomes the recognized estimate for the work unit. If the two estimates differ, the worker and the Project Manager confer and negotiate a new estimate that both think is reasonable and workable. This negotiated estimate then becomes the recognized work unit estimate.

The final estimates for work units may differ considerably from the original estimates of the Project Manager. Some final estimates may be higher, some lower. Generally, however, there is a constraint on the total time available for all work units, and this constraint must be kept in mind while adjusting individual estimates. Usually adjustments must be made in such a way that the total time of all final estimates is about the same as the total of all original estimates. As a final step in applying transactional estimating, it is usually necessary to reconcile the transactional estimates with any projective estimates that might have been made for the collection of work.

As a result of the transactional estimating process and the reconciliation of transactional and projective estimates, it might be that substantial changes must be made in the original plan and schedule for a phase. It might even be necessary to reassign certain work units, which in turn calls for a new transactional estimate with the person having the new responsibility. Of course, this can amount to a large planning effort. But recognizing a missed task or a bad estimate early in a phase and adjusting for it is better than being forced to make a lot of midphase corrections as planning errors surface.

The better the original plan, the fewer plan and schedule changes, and the smoother and less costly the project. As an organization gains experience in using transactional estimating, the whole process becomes more regular. As a result, projective estimates and transactional estimates tend to be closer, and major planning changes become less and less frequent.

Although the transactional estimating procedure has been described in terms of the duration of work, it is clear that the technique can also be used to estimate resource requirements. The important point is not the quantity being estimated, but the fact that the individual responsible for the work helps to make the final estimate.

A variation on the above procedure can also be employed. The original estimate for the work unit can be made by the worker and presented to the Project Manager; he then concurs or initiates negotiations to reach an estimate on which both can agree. We do not recommend this variation because it is difficult to manage. One reason for this is that a single person, the Project Manager, who makes estimates for many work units soon becomes more expert at estimating than the typical project worker, who makes relatively few estimates. This means that an estimate by the Project Manager is usually a more reasonable starting point for negotiation than the estimate of the typical worker. The second and more important reason for the variation being difficult to manage is that estimates are usually required before a schedule and work assignments are made; hence they are required before transactional estimating is possible. In effect, the Project Manager makes what he considers to be a reasonable schedule, assigns the work, and then asks the workers to point out adjustments that are necessary.

Benefits of Transactional Estimating

Why should you do transactional estimating? Because experience shows that transactional estimates are more likely to be correct than are estimates obtained by other techniques. The reason for getting better results is that workers feel committed to estimates that they have had a hand in shaping. It becomes a point of honor to meet estimates that they have agreed to, and they will adjust their effort to make certain that this happens. Thus, *transactional estimates become self-fulfilling prophecies.* With transactional estimating the entire focus of planning shifts from one of trying to outguess what will happen on a project to one of making realistic plans that can and do come to pass.

Many people are skeptical when they first hear about transactional estimating. A common reaction is, "I'm sure workers let you know if they think your estimate is too low, but I can just see them coming back and saying they can do their work in less time than you have estimated." In fact, most organizations find that this is not a problem. Most workers welcome the chance to manage their own work, and they frankly identify high estimates as well as low ones. If anything, many shops find they have just the opposite problem. Workers usually are overly optimistic and expect they can complete tasks much sooner than they actually can. When transactional estimating is first introduced, it is often necessary to talk people out of these optimistic estimates. After people gain more experience, their estimating ability improves and this bias toward low estimates disappears. Of course, some workers are optimists and always make low estimates; others are cautious and always give themselves plenty of cushion. A good Project Manager soon spots these tendencies. But these are still honest, open estimates, not an attempt to use the transactional process as a means of beating the system.

People realize that there is only so much resource for doing all the required project work. Transactional estimating is a procedure for making a fair allocation of resources to the various tasks. If one worker holds out for more time than he really needs for his task, then someone else on the project team will probably have to get by with less. The need to balance resource and to share the load equitably with teammates is a strong motivation for making transactional estimating work.

Transactional estimating can have beneficial side effects, such as in the following two cases.

> One Project Manager reported that when transactional estimating was introduced in his organization, workers started to take much more interest in the entire planning process. Not only did they become more committed to their own deadlines, but they were more concerned about meeting all project goals.

> Another Project Manager reported that transactional estimating sometimes averted unnecessary work, particularly on the part of less experienced workers. She found that if she estimated a task to take, say, five days and a worker thought it should be 15, the discrepancy often stemmed from a difference in their approaches to the problem. On understanding her approach, the worker might agree that it was better and that, in fact, the job could be done in the shorter time. Without transactional estimating, the longer approach of the worker might not have been discovered until he was well into the effort.

Transactional estimating cannot be practiced in every work environment. If the worker believes that the organization is out to get him, if he thinks that his estimates are a scaffold on which he is to be hung, if he feels that he is being pitted against his coworkers, then it is not too likely that the beneficial effects of transactional estimating will be realized. But if the worker is motivated to be achieving, if he looks upon himself as a member of a productive team, if he believes the goal is a quality product and not a disciplined worker, then transactional estimating can be a useful tool. As with so many concepts discussed in this book, the effective implementation of transactional estimating depends on the philosophy of management and their attitude toward and treatment of workers—topics that are far beyond the scope of this book.

13-9 PROJECTIVE ESTIMATES

Projective estimates are based on a statistical analysis of completed projects. From this analysis, a mathematical equation or formula is derived. Estimates are made by assigning values to the variables in this equation and carrying out the required calculations. We refer to these as projective estimates because the formulas summarize the past experience and are used to extrapolate from past projects to the present one.

The chief advantage of projective estimates is the ease with which they can be made. Given the proper equation, it is a simple matter to make estimates and to revise them as warranted. However, deriving the equation is sometimes another matter. It need not be a complex undertaking if only a crude equation is required—one that meets the test of being "better than nothing." But it is a complex project if a more refined equation is wanted or if there is an interest in the statistical significance of the equation. It is very easy for the uninitiated to include the wrong variables or to make statements about equations that the underlying data will not support. The derivation of sophisticated equations is best left to those with a knowledge of statistics.

Two conditions must hold if projective estimating is to be possible. First, it is necessary to have continuity in the project process. This means continuity in the people who are involved with the process, continuity in the hardware and software environment, and continuity in the project methodology and development techniques that are employed. Continuity does not mean that none of these factors can be changed, rather that changes should not be large in comparison with the total picture. If a new group is brought in to develop a project using a new operating system and if they are going to introduce structured programming and top-down development, then don't be surprised if projections of costs based on past projects are far from actual values.

A second requirement for projective estimating is a knowledge base.

A planning data base from completed projects is needed to structure estimating equations. Data about the current project is needed to produce estimates from these equations.

Continuity in the project process and a knowledge base are necessary for projective estimating, and they are also sufficient. If these two conditions are met, it is possible to devise formulas that can be used to make projective estimates. This has been demonstrated by many organizations that have developed such equations, and the process for doing it will be described in Section 13-11.

We tend to think of the projective method as being used to estimate the time and resource of a project, a phase, or even a standard task. But it can also be used to establish special relationships or "rules of thumb" among aspects of a project. For instance, it might be used to relate the amount of test time to the number of lines of code, or the number of lines of code to the number of program modules, or the amount of program documentation to the effort expended in Phase 2.1. In the next section, a few examples of projective estimates will be given; these should suggest many other examples to you.

13-10 SOME SIMPLE PROJECTIVE MODELS

Some examples will show how the projective technique can be used to make estimates. *All examples in this chapter are for illustrative purposes only;* the data in the examples is hypothetical, and the given equations should *not* be used on real projects.

Example 1. For the first example, the problem is to estimate the effort (man-hours) required for the Phase 2.2 standard task Build Modules. We would like the estimate at the end of Phase 2.1 as part of the input to the Phase Plan for Phase 2.2. This means that we must estimate in terms of some quantity that is known at that time.

We reason that the effort for Build Modules is related to the number of modules to be built. This number can be obtained for each project, but it is not presently collected in an automatic way by the project tracking system. We realize, however, that the number of modules, in turn, is related to the effort spent in designing modules; and this information *is* automatically captured. Therefore we decide to explore the relationship between Build Modules and the standard task Design Modules of Phase 2.1.

In our planning data base we have statistics on ten projects that were completed recently enough to be relevant. Data for these ten projects is displayed in Figure 13-4. Each point in that figure represents one project; the point relates the effort (man-days) actually expended on Build Modules to the effort (man-days) actually expended on Design Modules.

From Figure 13-4 it can be seen that there is a general linear relationship between the two quantities we are interested in. Therefore, we draw the line through this data (the solid line of Figure 13-5) that we feel best describes this relationship. We draw parallel lines (the broken lines of Figure 13-5) to encompass the observed points; these parallel lines form a band that gives us a likely range in which new observations should fall.

We use our model to make an estimate as follows. The effort charged to Design Modules for a project is marked on the horizontal axis (point D of Figure 13-6). The related point on the vertical axis (point B) is then our estimate of the effort that will be required to Build Modules. The actual effort might not equal this estimate, but it is likely to fall in the range between points A and C of Figure 13-6.

(Note: We fit our line in Figure 13-5 "by eye." We could have applied formal curve-fitting techniques but felt that this added refinement was not required. From past experience we find that someone with a good eye comes quite close to the curve derived by formal techniques. But our real reason for an informal approach is that there is so little data to work with that we plan to use our line with caution; a more careful drawing of the line would make little difference in the estimate we use. The parallel lines of Figure 13-5 were drawn so as to encompass all of the observed points. We did this because

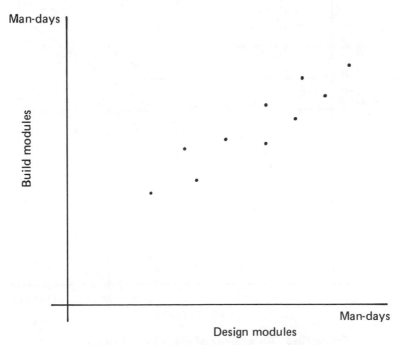

Figure 13-4. Historical data on ten projects

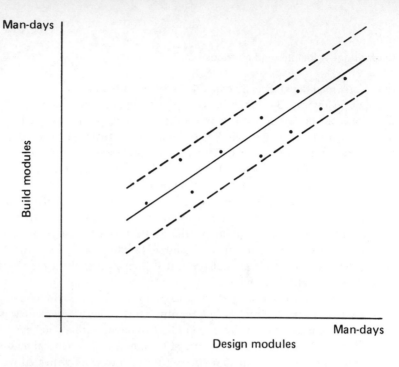

Figure 13-5. Best-fitting line and likely range of observations

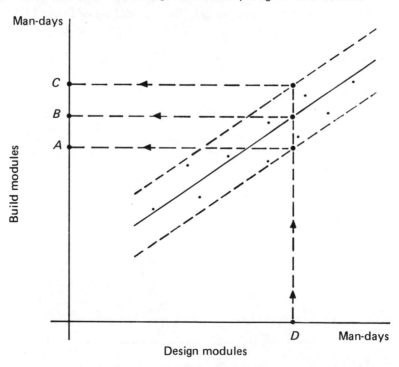

Figure 13-6. An estimate of effort to build modules

286

there were few points and all fell fairly near the best fitting line. If there were more observations, there would be a greater chance that some observations would be "outliers," and the likely zone need not include all of these. A reasonable rule of thumb is that the likely zone should include 90% to 95% of the observations.)

Example 2. As a second example of a projective estimate, let us suppose that total cost of a project has been determined in some way, and the problem is to use this to estimate the cost of each phase.

The first step is to determine from the data for all completed projects the fraction of the total cost that was incurred in each phase. Let these fractions be denoted by $f_{1.1}, f_{1.2}, f_{1.3}, f_{2.1}, \ldots, f_{3.3}$, respectively. This means, for instance, that $f_{2.1}$ is the fraction of the total cost of all past projects that was expended in Phase 2.1; if, say, $f_{2.1} = 0.20$, then 20% of project cost was expended on average in Phase 2.1. Next, these fractions are applied to the total cost for the project to obtain the estimated cost of each phase. That is, if C is the total cost of the project, the estimated cost of the phases is $Cf_{1.1}, Cf_{1.2}, \ldots, Cf_{3.3}$. For instance, suppose that a project has a total cost of \$200,000. If the fractions for the cost of phases are as indicated in Table 13-1, then the expected cost by phases is given in Table 13-2.

In this example we are concerned with the cost of a project, but the same technique can be used to divide total time or total resource into requirements for the different phases. Also, the technique can be used to split, say, the cost of a phase into the cost of the various standard tasks.

(Note: For an actual organization, fractions such as those in Table 13-1 generally depend on project complexity. To apply the technique of the example, projects should be classified as batch systems or on-line systems and separate tables determined for each category. As a further refinement, projects can be classified into size categories.)

Example 3. As a third example of the projective technique, let us consider a useful procedure for estimating the total cost of a project based on the cost of beginning phases. The advantage of this procedure is that it requires little effort to devise or use and little information from completed projects. It is a technique that can be employed to advantage at the end of Phase 1.2 or later, and it can be used as a simple check on estimates found by other methods.

We illustrate this technique by assuming that a project has been underway and that Phase 1.3 has just been completed. An estimate of the cost to complete the project is desired.

Assume that the fractions $f_{1.1}, \ldots, f_{3.3}$ and the constant C have the meanings previously assigned. Let $C_{1.1}, C_{1.2}, \ldots, C_{3.3}$ signify the costs for the various phases. At this stage in the project, $C_{1.1}, C_{1.2}$, and $C_{1.3}$ are known. It is reasonable to assume that the cost of the first three phases of

Table 13-1
Fraction of Total Cost of Past Projects Incurred in Each Phase

Phase	1.1	1.2	1.3	2.1	2.2	2.3	3.1	3.2	3.3
Fraction	$f_{1.1}$	$f_{1.2}$	$f_{1.3}$	$f_{2.1}$	$f_{2.2}$	$f_{2.3}$	$f_{3.1}$	$f_{3.2}$	$f_{3.3}$
Value	0.01	0.14	0.15	0.20	0.25	0.10	0.07	0.07	0.01

Table 13-2
Estimated Cost for Each Phase Based on a Given Total Cost

Phase	1.1	1.2	1.3	2.1	2.2	2.3	3.1	3.2	3.3
Estimated cost	2,000	28,000	30,000	40,000	50,000	20,000	14,000	14,000	2,000

the present project represent the same fraction of the total cost as has been observed in the past, from which it follows that

$$C(f_{1.1} + f_{1.2} + f_{1.3}) = C_{1.1} + C_{1.2} + C_{1.3}.$$

From this, the total cost of the project is estimated to be

$$C = \frac{C_{1.1} + C_{1.2} + C_{1.3}}{f_{1.1} + f_{1.2} + f_{1.3}}.$$

The remaining cost is therefore estimated to be

$$C - (C_{1.1} + C_{1.2} + C_{1.3}).$$

Of course, costs for remaining phases can also be estimated from C as in the previous example.

As an illustration, assume that the first three phases of a project cost a total of \$84,000. With the same fractions as in Table 13-1, the total cost of the project is then estimated to be

$$C = \frac{\$84,000}{0.30} = \$280,000.$$

The remaining cost is estimated to be \$196, 000.

13-11 BUILDING ESTIMATING EQUATIONS

It is necessary to make estimates on any well-run project—building a computer system, constructing a building, writing a book. You might be interested to see how this can be done in one other field.

An article in a business publication[3] reported that just as construction on a building was completed the owner saw an advertisement stating that an estimate of construction cost could be obtained from a certain construction management company for a fee of \$20. For fun the owner decided to get an estimate and see how it compared with the actual construction cost of \$6,600,000. After a phone call and a three-hour wait for processing, he was startled to receive an estimate of \$6,087,468. The comparison of estimate to actual is even more striking

---

[3] *Business Week,* January 19, 1976.

when it is realized that the actual cost included a charge of $500,000 for special equipment, which was not included in the estimate.

Obviously the estimate in this story was obtained by using an appropriate model or equation. Many DP organizations have developed comparable models for estimating aspects of DP projects. Our purpose in this section is to learn how such models are built. However, instead of turning directly to DP projects, we want to take a closer look at estimating models for the construction industry. If we understand how models are built in that industry, it will help us to understand how to do the same for DP projects.

Construction Industry Example

To understand estimating models for the construction industry, imagine that you are a DP professional working for a construction firm and the boss has just told you that he wants an estimating model. As analyst/designer, what assumptions would you make, what information would you require, and how would you satisfy your boss? We believe that the answers to these questions are as follows (as you read these, check to see if you agree).

Assumptions. A model rests on basic assumptions about the process and the product. These two assumptions are important.

1. A Stable Production Process. You would need some assurance that the production process is essentially the same from project to project. There is no point in trying to estimate if one project is well planned and the next is done by trial and error.

2. A Known Class of Projects. Your job will be difficult if your model is to cover every type of project: a single-family dwelling, plant sites, high-rise office buildings, chicken coops. Before getting down to details, you would need an indication of the class of projects to be covered. The more nearly homogeneous the class, the easier your task and the better your product. For our purposes, let us assume we are to estimate for single-family dwellings.

Development of Model. To develop the model, you would require the following facts.

1. A Clear Statement of What Is to be Estimated. Does the boss want to estimate cost? Does cost include the land? Does he want to estimate time for construction? Size of construction crew? The quantities that are to be estimated are sometimes called the *dependent variables.* For our purposes, let us assume we are to estimate the cost of the project, that is, the cost of building a single-family dwelling (exclusive of the land cost).

2. A Clear Statement of Information that Will Be Available at the Time an Estimate Is to be Made. This is getting to the heart of the problem because

to estimate, say, cost we must know something about the project. We must be given certain information on which to base the estimate. In particular, this means we must know at what point in the project the estimate is to be made because this tells us something about the information available. For our purposes, let us assume that the estimate of cost is to be made after the architectural design is completed but before construction starts. Thus we can probably assume we have information on such things as number of stories in the structure, number of rooms, number of bathrooms, square footage, attached or detached garage, and exterior material. Items such as these on which the estimate is to be based are sometimes referred to as *independent variables*. These are quantities whose values are given before we make our estimate of the dependent variables.

3. Data on Past Projects. To build an estimating equation we must have data for past projects on the dependent and independent variables. Moreover, this data must be relevant—it must be from projects that are fairly recent (so that costs, types of materials, etc., have not changed drastically) and were undertaken in the same general way as the projects we will be estimating.

4. Relationships Among the Variables. Next we must analyze past data to see, for example, how the number of bathrooms influences the cost of a dwelling. This involves a statistical analysis of data—a technical job that we shall assume we can do or can get help in doing.

Equations for Data Processing

These assumptions and steps for building and using an estimating model seem quite reasonable when we apply them to a field most of us are not directly involved with. But they also apply to data processing. The needs for a stable production process (Section 13-3) and a well-defined class of projects (Section 13-4) have already been discussed. Next, let us comment on the facts needed to build a model for estimating DP projects.

Dependent Variables. A quantity to be estimated is called a *dependent variable*. Examples of dependent variables are total project cost, project cost by phases, cost by standard tasks, total project effort, and effort by phases or by standard tasks. Elapsed time is usually not a good choice for a dependent variable because it depends in an important way on factors that are outside the project.

In establishing the dependent variables, it is helpful to begin by asking: What quantity would I like to have an estimate for if I had my choice? After deciding what one would like ideally, it is then possible to temper this in the light of what is possible.

To simplify the estimating process, the number of dependent variables should be held to a minimum. Also, alternate estimating procedures should be explored and weighed. For example, separate formulas can be established for estimating the cost of each phase of a project. Alternatively, the total cost can be estimated and then this allocated to the various phases by applying the ratios that have held historically between the cost of each phase and total project cost. Each method has its pros and cons, and each its proponents. Both methods might be tried to learn which is more effective for a given organization.

Independent Variables. Dependent variables are estimated by establishing their relationship to other variables, called *independent variables* or *explanatory variables.* Independent variables are quantities that can be measured, projected, or easily estimated, and that relate to the dependent variables.

Bob Burns, the bazooka-playing comedian of a few years ago, used to tell how people in Arkansas would weigh a pig. First, a log was balanced on a stump. Then the pig was placed on one end of the log and rocks were piled on the other end until the pig and the rocks balanced. Then the rocks were weighed, and this was taken as the weight of the pig. The moral obviously is that the independent variable (rocks) should be more easily measured than the dependent variable (pig's weight) unless, of course, you have a statistician you wish to keep employed.

A great deal of judgment goes into the selection of independent variables, and to some extent the selection depends on the philosophy of the person making the study. People with training in econometrics are inclined to restrict attention to variables that can be measured with some precision; people with a background in systems dynamics are inclined to augment these with variables whose values depend largely on judgment. The first group prefers to base estimates on sound statistical principles and demonstrable relationships; the second group argues that intuitively important variables should not be omitted simply because sufficient data is not available to establish formally what "everyone" knows. Whatever your propensity, it is important to select independent variables that have a big impact on the dependent variable. For example, if the ability of project personnel is relatively constant from project to project, then ability is not likely to be a good predictor for project cost and probably should not be included among the independent variables.

Care should be taken to restrict the number of independent variables because the more there are, the more data that is needed to obtain meaningful estimating equations. We shall return to this point later.

A quantity should be selected as an independent variable only if its value can be determined at the point in time that an estimate is required. For instance, suppose that we want to develop an estimate during Phase 1.1

of the total project cost. We might try to base this estimate on the number of lines of delivered code in the final product. However, this is not a good independent variable to choose because its value is not known at the point when the estimate is required. If we were to use it, we would end up estimating cost based on an *estimate* of the number of lines of delivered code. A better choice of an independent variable would be some variable whose value is known at the time the estimate is to be made. There aren't many such variables in Phase 1.1, which is one reason why it is so hard to estimate total cost at this early stage.

Most useful independent variables for estimating project cost or effort can be grouped into three categories: variables relating to the product or system being produced, variables relating to the project personnel, and variables relating to the environment. Within these categories there are some variables that are known fairly early in the project and some known fairly late. This suggests that several equations might be built for estimating a quantity; each equation would be based on the variables that can be evaluated at the point in time when the estimate is required.

Variables relating to the project product are usually the most important for predicting cost or time for the project. That is, product variables usually change considerably from project to project, and time and cost are closely related to this variation. The number of product variables incorporated in the estimating equation will depend on how much data is available and on how many other variables appear to be significant. For many situations, three to five product variables will provide useful results. Examples of product-related variables are:

System size (number of inputs, outputs, files, subfunctions, . . .)

Scope (functional areas served, locations served, number of user groups involved, . . .)

Complexity (batch or on-line, first of a kind, novelty, sophistication, status of current system, special hardware, software packages, exception handling, . . .)

Requirements (status of specifications, completion criteria, mandated deadline or not, . . .)

Other variables can be added to this list, and these four can obviously be subdivided into finer categories. For instance, complexity might be split into complexity and sophistication. The criteria for assigning a value to, say, size can be reduced to a series of questions with weighted answers. Rules can then be established for determining size from the answers to these questions.

Examples of variables relating to project personnel (team members and users) are:

Ability (skill, training, experience in similar systems, compatibility, . . .)
Availability

Again, it is clear that these variables can be subdivided into several categories. An obvious division is by function (project leader, designer, . . .) or by organizational unit (DP, user department, . . .). Other variables that can be included are management style and method of organization. We omitted these because they probably do not vary from project to project and hence are probably not good predictors of the typical dependent variables.

By environment variables, we have in mind those related to the procedures used and to the facilities. Among these are:

Project methodology (method of estimating, planning, controlling, . . .; how standard, how formal, how well understood, . . .)

Development standards (method of design, coding, testing, . . .; how standard, how formal, how well understood, . . .)

System and operations (operating system used, experience with system, availability of test time, . . .)

In most cases, the environmental variables will be relatively stable and, therefore, will probably not be good predictors of project cost and time.

Data. Data is used for two purposes: to establish the relationships among the dependent and independent variables, and to make an estimate of the dependent variables for a particular project. It is the former use that we consider at this point.

After the dependent and independent variables have been selected, it is necessary to observe the values they assumed in past projects. Each past project yields a single observation for these variables. For example, if project cost is to be computed based on product size and product complexity, then there are three variables. The actual cost, size, and complexity on a given project are regarded as one observation on these three variables.

In collecting data on past projects, it is often necessary to reconstruct information from fragmentary project records, accounting data, and project deliverables. Adjustments are commonly required because data is usually not found in the form in which it is required. Judgment must be used as to how relevant the data is to current projects—the cost of producing a 650 or 1401 system has little relevance to the cost of a complex communications-based system. Less obvious is the fact that a major change in/ development technology—say, the introduction of top-down development and structured programming—may also vitiate past data for purposes of forecasting aspects of future projects.

Equations. Once sufficient data is in hand, it is a simple matter to use standard software packages to obtain regression equations relating the dependent variables to the independent variables. It is *not* at all simple to determine the significance of these equations. Interpretation of the output of statistical curve-fitting packages is not a do-it-yourself project unless you have the proper training. A few comments, however, can help to highlight some of the concerns that arise.

To derive significant equations, it is necessary to have sufficient data. At an absolute minimum, the number of observations must exceed the number of variables involved in the equation. For example, if cost is to be determined from product size and product complexity, there are three variables; therefore there must be at least four observations from past projects. This is the absolute minimum, and we would have little confidence in results unless there were many more observations than this.

Some estimating equations that are in use contain over 100 variables. To derive such an equation in the standard statistical manner would require data on at least 100 past projects. Most organizations have nothing like this amount of data to work with, certainly not on projects that are relevant to the type currently being undertaken by the organization. The use of extremely large estimating equations is probably based more on faith than on sound statistical principles.

An organization with 20 people in its development area might be expected to produce 5 or even 10 systems a year. After a couple of years, they might expect to have sufficient data to derive an estimating equation involving as many as 8 or even 10 variables. It is unlikely, however, that this many significant variables will be discovered with the available data. The reason for this is not hard to find.

The more variables there are to work with, the more likely it is that more than one variable will measure the same thing. For instance, programmer skill and programmer experience both relate to the ability of a programmer to perform his job. Variables that relate to the same thing tend to move in tandem; that is, when one increases, so does the other. But two variables that move precisely in tandem will not both prove to be significant in a single estimating equation. It follows from this that as an attempt is made to improve an estimating equation it becomes more and more difficult to find variables that make a significant contribution. Usually improvement can only be accomplished if much more data is available.

Of course, the phenomena just described can be viewed in another way. If it is difficult to find additional significant variables, it may well mean that reasonably good results can be obtained with only a few variables. This is not guaranteed, but it is a situation that often prevails; and certainly it is a situation to be desired.

Aside from considerations relating to data, in searching for estimating equations the form of the relationship between the dependent and independent variables must be explored. The most usual form that is considered is a *linear* relationship; that is, an equation of the form

$$y = a_0 + a_1 x_1 + a_2 x_2 + \cdots + a_k x_k$$

where y is the dependent variable and $x_1, \ldots, x_k$ are the k independent variables. This is only one of an endless variety of equations that might be hypothesized. For example, it might be observed that as system size increases, the system cost goes up even more rapidly. From this observation it might be proposed that system cost depends on the square of system size, or even on its cube. With so many possible relationships to choose from, how do you know which is best?

The answer is that you don't; moreover, you should not worry about which is best. What you should seek is a *satisfactory* equation—one that provides useful estimates. Surprising as it may seem, a linear equation frequently turns out to be quite satisfactory. The reason for this is that every equation can be approximated by a linear equation, and the approximation is adequate in a large number of cases. A further reason for using a linear equation has to do with the inherent difficulty of the estimating process. The quantities that are estimated are affected by a large number of variables. Most of these are never measured, and many of the rest can be measured only with minimal accuracy. This means that there is an inherent variability in the process that cannot be mastered without an unreasonable amount of data from past projects. Every equation is bound to omit many influencing factors, and every equation is bound to leave a certain amount of variability unaccounted for. In most situations, the inherent variability of the project process is such that the added benefit to be obtained from nonlinear equations is not warranted. Whether or not it is warranted in a particular situation will, of course, be revealed in the process of determining the estimating equation.

In this discussion, we have talked about using an equation to relate dependent and independent variables. If there are only two variables, one dependent and one independent, this equation can conveniently be expressed in graphic form. (Theoretically this could be done with more than two variables, but as a practical matter it does not work.) The first example in Section 13-10 is an instance of expressing a relationship in this way. It really does not matter which form is used because an equation relating two variables determines a graph and vice versa. Some people work with equations more easily than graphs, and some with graphs more easily than equations. To promote understanding, you should present an estimating relationship in whatever form is preferred by those who must use it. Better yet, present it both ways.

13-12 EXAMPLE OF COST ESTIMATING

Some of the ideas of this chapter can be illustrated by seeing how costs might be estimated at different points in a project by an hypothetical organization.

Phase 1.1. The estimate of total project cost in Phase 1.1 is developed subjectively. Members of the project team pool their experience and make a judgment based on their collective opinion. For important projects or in cases where opinions are likely to differ sharply, they formalize this process by using the Delphi technique.

To aid in making judgments, the team classifies projects as small, medium, or large. This classification, too, is subjective and not based on formal criteria. Typical costs for projects in these size classifications are shown in Table 13-3. (Note that the table does not include projects costing more than $250,000; projects exceeding that figure are fractured into subprojects. The table also omits mini projects.) If a project were judged, for instance, to be an average medium-size project, its cost would be estimated as $90,000. If it were judged to be medium size but above or below average, the cost would be adjusted up or down accordingly in the range from $30,000 to $150,000. All people involved with the project recognize that this initial estimate of cost is a ball park figure—it might be off as much as 50% or even 100%.

In the past, the organization has typically spent 15% of the total

Table 13-3
Range of Costs by Project Size

Project Size	Total Project Cost (thousands of dollars)
Small	1–30
Medium	30–150
Large	150–250

project cost in Phase 1.2. Thus, a preliminary estimate of the cost of that phase is obtained by taking 15% of the estimated cost of the total project. This preliminary estimate is adjusted up or down based on an assessment (at the standard task level) by the team of the actual work to be done in Phase 1.2. For instance, the preliminary estimate is adjusted upward if more interviews than usual are required or if the present system is poorly documented.

Phase 1.2. An estimate of total project cost is developed near the end of Phase 1.2 by applying the estimating formula

$$Y = 10 + 15X_1 + 7X_2 + 2X_3$$

where

Y = total project cost (in dollars)
X_1 = system characteristics
X_2 = personnel characteristics
X_3 = environment characteristics

Values are assigned to X_1, X_2, and X_3 by completing the questionnaires shown in Tables 13-4, 13-5, and 13-6.

(The hypothetical organization evolved the questions and weights shown in the questionnaires by using the Delphi method. Then they developed the formula by analyzing their past projects, following the procedure described in Section 13-11.)

The estimate obtained from the equation is compared with two other estimates. One of these is the total cost estimate developed in Phase 1.1. The other is the number obtained by dividing the actual cost of Phase 1.2 by 0.15. (This is what the total cost would be if, in fact, 15% of the total cost were expended in Phase 1.2. Note that the Phase 1.2 actual cost is almost all known at the time this estimate is made.)

The formula estimate is used for total project cost unless there is a great discrepancy between it and the other two estimates. If there is a discrepancy, an attempt is made to discover the reason and to make an appropriate adjustment. The confidence people have in the cost estimate at this stage is influenced by the degree of agreement among the three estimates of total cost.

In the past, the hypothetical organization has typically spent the same amount on Phase 1.3 as on Phase 1.2 (15% of the total cost). Thus a preliminary estimate of the cost of Phase 1.3 is 15% of the total project cost. This is adjusted based on an assessment of the actual work to be done in Phase 1.3, as judged by examining the standard tasks. It is also checked for reasonableness by comparing it with the actual expense of Phase 1.2.

Phase 1.3. The method of estimating total cost in this phase is the same

Table 13-4
Sample Assessment Form for an Hypothetical Organization

System Characteristics Assessment Form

1. How many functional areas of the organization   Score
   are involved with the project?
        ____ under 3   (0)
        ____ 3 or more   (1) ____

2. How many major subsystems in the system?
        ____ under 5   (0)
        ____ 5 or more   (1) ____

3. How many files?
        ____ under 5   (0)
        ____ 5 or more   (1) ____

4. Does this involve automation of an existing system?
        ____ yes   (0)
        ____ no   (2) ____

5. Is the system to be
        ____ batch?   (0)
        ____ on-line?   (3) ____

6. Is there a mandated project deadline?
        ____ no   (0)
        ____ yes   (2) ____

X_1 = Total = ____

Instructions:
1. Select one answer for each question.
2. Assign each question the score from the right column that corresponds
   to your answer.
3. Total these scores; this is the value of X_1.

Table 13-5
Sample Assessment Form for an Hypothetical Organization

Personnel Characteristics Assessment Form

1. Project Manager's level of experience: Score
   ____ very experienced   (0)
   ____ reasonably experienced   (1)
   ____ little or no experience   (2) ____

2. Project team's experience with the application area:
   ____ very experienced   (0)
   ____ reasonably experienced   (1)
   ____ little or no experience   (2) ____

3. User's experience with DP:
   ____ very experienced   (0)
   ____ reasonably experienced   (1)
   ____ little or no experience   (2) ____

4. Project team members will be full time on the project?
   ____ yes   (0)
   ____ no   (1) ____

5. There is need to hire additional people:
   ____ no   (0)
   ____ yes   (1) ____

6. There are unusual constraints on the availability of
   personnel (leaves, vacations, sickness, etc.):
   ____ not a problem   (0)
   ____ a problem   (1) ____

7. Relations between the project team and operations are:
   ____ not a problem   (0)
   ____ a problem   (1) ____

$$X_2 = \text{Total} = \underline{\quad}$$

Instructions:
1. Select one answer for each question.
2. Assign each question the score from the right column that corresponds to your aswer.
3. Total these scores; this is the value of X_2.

Table 13-6
Sample Assessment Form for an Hypothetical Organization

Environment Assessment Form

	Score
1. Additional hardware is likely to be:	
____ not required	(0)
____ a minor factor	(1)
____ a major factor	(2) ____
2. Additional software is likely to be:	
____ not required	(0)
____ a minor factor	(1)
____ a major factor	(2) ____
3. Constraints on resources (including test time) are likely to be:	
____ no problem	(0)
____ a problem	(1)
____ a serious problem	(2) ____
4. The project team must work in several locations:	
____ no	(0)
____ yes	(2) ____
5. Standards (including project methodology) are:	
____ good, well documented	(0)
____ weak	(1) ____
____ nonexistent and must be established	(2) ____

$$X_3 = \text{Total} = \underline{\quad}$$

Instructions:
1. Select one answer for each question.
2. Assign each question the score from the right column that corresponds to your answer.
3. Total these scores; this is the value of X_3.

as in Phase 1.2, but the details differ. Again a formula is used, but it is now based on more specific details about the product. Also, the estimate by formula is compared with previous estimates and with actual expenditures on the project to date. We omit the details.

Next phase costs are estimated as in Phase 1.2.

Phases 2.1 through 3.1. The estimate of total cost is altered after Phase 1.3 only if actual experience fails to match projections. There is no standard method for reestimating in these later phases; each project is treated separately.

Next phase costs are estimated as in Phase 1.2.

Phases 3.2 and 3.3. It is rarely necessary to alter an estimate in these phases. If alteration is necessary, it is based on the unusual circumstances surrounding the project.

13-13 SUGGESTIONS AND COMMENTS ON ESTIMATING

We have a number of suggestions and comments about estimating, some brief and some more extensive.

Make Several Estimates. At the risk of repeating ourselves, we want to stress the importance of making several estimates and comparing each with the others. There are two aspects to this. First, whenever possible, estimates should be made by employing different procedures. A projective estimate might be compared with a Delphi estimate of the same quantity, or an estimate might be made by using two projective techniques that rely on different input data. The second way to make several estimates is by progressively refining estimates. An estimate for a given phase is first made at an aggregated phase level; next this is refined to produce an estimate based on standard tasks; finally an estimate is made at the level of work units. As each refinement is made, it can be compared with the previous estimates.

Through making several estimates, there is a reasonably good chance of spotting really bad estimates. Looking at it another way, if several independent estimates yield similar results, one has much more confidence in one's estimate.

An Estimate Tends to be a Self-Fulfilling Prophecy. It has been stated that a transactional estimate is a self-fulfilling prophecy, and to some extent this statement holds for any project estimate. There is always a range of reasonable estimates, and a project team can adjust its efforts to make any estimate in this range *provided that* the estimate looks reasonable to the team and they have support to do their work the way they think it should be done. In other words, they must be motivated through seeing that the assignment is reasonable, and they must be allowed to exercise self-control of their work.

The fact that estimates tend to be self-fulfilling helps to underscore a point made earlier: An estimate is not a prediction of what will be. One estimates to be able to set reasonable goals. *The object of estimating is to enable performance to match the estimate rather than to have the estimate match performance.*

Effort is Easier to Estimate than Duration. The duration of a project depends not only on the work to be done but the resources. It is impossible to estimate the length of a project without making some assumption about how many people will be working on it. An estimate of project duration cannot be found by projecting the durations of past projects without making some adjustment for the resources available to all the projects.

There is another problem with estimating duration: a distinction must be made between project length and the calendar time required to complete the project. The latter depends on such factors as whether people are full time on the project, whether they will be pulled off at random for maintenance work, and whether the project gets delayed for a higher priority effort. It is difficult to predict how much the calendar completion date will be delayed because of project interference; usually it is necessary to estimate in terms of average delays on past projects.

One way to circumvent some of the problems in estimating durations is to make basic estimates in terms of effort. Effort for projects is more nearly comparable from project to project than is duration. The number of man-days of effort can be estimated by comparing the present project with completed projects, then durations can be estimated by taking resources into account, then the calendar completion data can be estimated by taking project interference into account.

An example of adjusting for nonproductive effort and for part-time workers is given in Sections 5-3 and 5-7.

Project Cost Depends on Project Duration. Having just implied that project length can be based on effort, we hasten to add that the relationship is far from simple. In discussing this relationship, we shall expand the discussion to consider all project costs (basically the cost of machine time as well as of personnel).

Projective estimates are always based on a tacit assumption that the project being dealt with is typical for the organization. If projects are always developed under severe time constraints, then this should be reflected in the data from past projects and should be incorporated automatically in the projective estimates. On the other hand, if special and unusual constraints are placed on a project, then past performance might not be a good indicator for the present project. This statement can be illustrated by describing the relationship between the time for development and the total cost of a project.

Many investigations have shown that the total cost of developing a project depends on the time allowed for the project.[4] As shown in Figure 13-7, there is a range of reasonable project durations for which the cost of development is essentially constant—the project might be done by five people in four months as easily as by four people in five months. But to complete a project in less than the normal time, it is usually necessary to increase costs. This increase comes about for several reasons. To bring the project in early, more people are added to the project; this means additional training, more time for communication, and additional planning. Premiums must be paid for special handling and overtime. When delays occur, such as machine failure, more people are delayed. And so on. As development time is shortened, costs rise until a point is reached at which they become infinite—no matter how much cost and resource are added, there is no way to cut the time below a certain minimum.

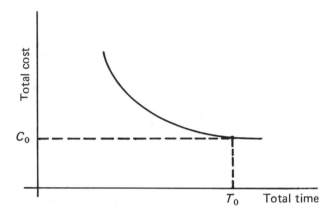

Figure 13-7. Time-cost relationship for a project

(If the time axis of Figure 13-7 were extended to the right, the curve should probably turn up. Extending a project beyond a reasonable time wastes resource and adds unnecessary cost to a project.)

An estimate for the cost of a project is based on the assumption (often made implicitly) that the project will have the accustomed time for development. The estimated cost and related time might be represented by C_0 and T_0 in Figure 13-7. If a mandate is issued to develop the project on a tighter schedule with significantly less time, then the estimated cost will un-

---

[4]For example, see an article by Alfred M. Pietrasanta in *On the Management of Computer Programming,* edited by George F. Weinwurm, New York, Petrocelli Books, 1970, page 83.

doubtedly prove to be too low—as the time is decreased, the cost will increase along the curve in the diagram. To get a realistic estimate of cost under the constraint of a shorter development period, it is necessary to increase the estimated cost; but many organizations do not acknowledge this fact. Many believe that the original estimate of cost is absolute and should hold regardless of additional constraints that are placed on the project. They don't adjust the estimate and then are surprised to learn that their ability to estimate is poor.

Another problem can be encountered, too. Even if an organization does recognize the need for an adjustment, they have difficulty making it. Most groups simply do not have enough data to draw the curve of Figure 13-7; consequently they do not have a reasonable procedure for adjusting estimates to reflect time constraints.

Time and cost are not the only major variables associated with a project; there is also product quality. If time is cut and costs are not allowed to rise, then the only alternative left is to sacrifice quality. This is usually done by curtailing the function to be delivered, by finding a way to phase the deliverable, or simply by skimping on workmanship. Mandating both time and cost almost guarantees poor product quality and high maintenance costs.

Estimates Can Be "Accurate" without Being Good. No matter how estimates are made, the question ultimately arises as to how accurate they are. Accuracy is usually measured by comparing the actual value with the estimate. Nobody expects the two to agree precisely, but actuals should be "close" to estimates "most" of the time. What is meant by "close" and "most" depends on the organization. For instance, one group finds that 75% of their projects come in within 10% of estimate, and they regard this as a satisfactory situation.

Of course, one way to have accurate estimates is to inflate them to the point where they are bound to be met. For example, transactional estimates might be self-fulfilling prophecies because there is so much "fat" in them that it is a simple matter to make them come true. One way to guard against this possibility is to use two estimating techniques; for instance, to use projective estimates to check transactional ones.

Suppose, then, that both projective and transactional estimates are made and that 95% of the projects are within 5% of the estimate. Is all well? Not necessarily. The fact that estimates agree and are "accurate" shows that projects are consistent, but it does not indicate how productive the organization is. An organization could do a consistently bad job taking twice the time they should on each project; but if they are consistently slow, they should be able to estimate their projects fairly well. Estimates will be accurate and in agreement, but performance is not what it should be.

(Perhaps the word "accurate" should never be used to describe an estimate for a project. "Accurate" has a positive connotation and suggests that all is well, yet we have just seen that estimates can be accurate even if productivity is low. Perhaps it would be better to say that estimates are "realized" consistently if estimates and actuals are usually close.)

To judge an estimating procedure, it is not enough to verify that estimates are consistently close to actuals or that several estimating techniques agree. To verify that an estimating technique is giving useful results, it is also necessary to look into the productivity of the organization. Not only is it important that the estimates be close to actuals, they must also be close to what other people in the industry are doing on comparable tasks. This check is needed because the time and resources for a project are a cost to the organization, and these costs must be in line with industry norms if the organization is to remain competitive with others. Even nonprofit organizations, such as government agencies, universities, and hospitals, should be concerned with productivity. They may not be faced with competition, but most have limited budgets and are interested in getting the most they can for their money.

To learn if productivity is reasonable, it is necessary to compare the organization with some outside group. One way to do this is to compare the organization's productivity with industry standards. These might be obtained from user groups, such as GUIDE or SHARE, or from previous work experience of some members of DP, or simply through discussion with other people in the data processing field. Knowledge of general industry standards for productivity should be part of the stock in trade of every data processing professional.

Some organizations ensure the productivity of their development groups by introducing competition. Many have the policy that users are allowed to contract for a system with an outside software shop if this can be done at a cost that is lower than the internal charge.

One organization tackled the productivity problem in a novel way. Internal DP did all project development, but specific portions of projects were put up at bid to members of the organization. Designers and programmers were asked to bid on how much they would charge to do specific tasks. The low bidder was given the job—and the money. If a worker didn't feel like working (and being paid), he didn't bid on any jobs. If he bid on several and won more than he could handle, he was allowed to subcontract some of the work to other employees. Reports are that the workers liked the idea. Even so, it is doubtful that many companies will adopt this approach.

In pointing out the importance of reviewing an organization's productivity, we do not want to overstress this issue. Attempting to achieve the maximum project productivity may, in fact, be counterproductive as far as the total organizational effort is concerned. Time and cost are always measured crudely, and attempts to maximize productivity almost always focus on the productivity of some small unit, such as the project, rather than the productivity of the entire organization. At times it may be much more important to the total organization for a project to have a schedule that will almost certainly be met rather than to have one that strives for minimum project cost. If many important functions and procedures are to be synchronized with the introduction of a new system, then the failure to meet the due date can have serious adverse consequences. In such a situation, a very tight schedule with no room for chance would be a mistake; and to make such plans simply to strive for maximum project productivity would be an error. As with so many aspects of projects, a balance must be struck—the question of project productivity cannot be ignored, and it cannot be overstressed.

The Average Estimate May Not Be the Best Estimate. Most books on estimating suggest that estimates be based on typical behavior or average behavior. If a project resembles many past projects in scope and resources and if the past projects took an average of ten months to complete, then most would say that the estimate for the new project should be ten months. But this might not be the best estimate. To understand why, let us go back to our discussion of random variation.

Based on the limited data we have when we make our estimate, we can only say that the completion time of a project will take a value in an interval and that some points in the interval are more likely than others. Suppose we use the average completion time for our estimate, as depicted in Figure 13-8. We recognize that our project can be completed before this time or after it, and we assume our estimate is such that the odds of these two events are about the same. But what is the cost to the organization in the two cases? If a project is completed early, it means that the product might sit around for a while before it is used. Also, it probably means some waste of resource; people on the project team would be available earlier than expected and it might be difficult to make adjustments so as to use their time effectively. It might even mean doing without some other product that could have been produced if the estimate had not been high. These are costs to the organization, but let us contrast these with the cost of a project that is completed late. Most DP projects interact with many functional areas of the organization. Frequently these areas must make extensive changes of their own to accommodate the DP project. They must alter procedures, convert data, train personnel, and make arrangements for installation and parallel operations. All of these changes are geared to the completion date of the project. If the project comes in late, the cost to the organization can be very high. The cost is not just that the benefits of the product cannot be realized on schedule, but it is also the cost of readjustment to cope with an unplanned situation.

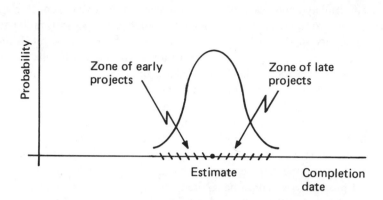

Figure 13-8. An estimate that balances probabilities

For the estimate shown in Figure 13-8, the chances of being early or late are about the same but the *costs* of being early or late are probably *not* the same. The risk associated with being late is probably greater than the risk associated with being early. A better estimate might be the one shown in Figure 13-9. Here the chance of a late project is lower than the chance of an early project. But we assume the estimate has been selected so that the costs of being early or late are about equal; thus the estimate balances the risks associated with early and late projects.

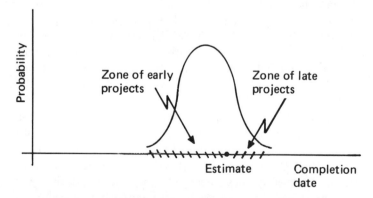

Figure 13-9. An estimate that balances risk

Estimating so as to balance risks becomes most important on large projects because these typically involve interaction of many groups. For such projects it is extremely important to lay out plans that can be achieved. Most project disasters were large projects that slipped behind schedule and went down hill from there. Has anyone heard of a large project that was a disaster because it came in way ahead of schedule? Probably not, because the cost to an organization of even a very large project coming in early is usually not great and certainly not catastrophic.

The concept of estimates that balance risks is a formal way of explaining what most project managers know intuitively: An estimate must have some slack in it. Most people know about random variation, although they might express it by saying, "You never can be sure . . ." or "Things usually go wrong. . . ." And they know that you need some slack to increase your odds of completing on schedule. They know from experience that the organization doesn't like late projects, and their job is to prevent them from happening. People may talk in terms of "adding fat" to an estimate or of using a "fudge factor." What they are really doing, however, is searching for an estimate that doesn't expose them to the problem of having an estimate too high to be acceptable or too low to be achieved with reasonable effort. What they are searching for is an estimate that balances risks.

There are some practical problems associated with risk-balancing estimates. One problem is that it can be an excuse for excessively high estimates. The cost of missing deadlines (early or late) is hard to measure. There is a temptation to overestimate the cost of late projects as a justification for high estimates. But estimates that are too high are self-defeating because the projects just won't be authorized. (Actually the tendency in many organizations is to underestimate in order to gain approval, then to ask for additional resources after management is committed.) A second problem is who adjusts for risk-balancing? There is a danger that estimates are adjusted at each level with the result that the final estimate is unrealistic. One way to avoid this problem is to require that all estimates be build on average numbers, and then to adjust for risk-balancing as a final step. A third problem is how to measure results. If all estimates are adjusted upward to balance risk, then most projects should come in early. How should a manager be judged who meets a goal that was set in such a way that it definitely *should* be met? Most organizations do not have an answer for this question, which is really part of a very general question: How does a person manage by objectives when he admits the existence of random factors that are outside management's control? This question is clearly worthy of a book in its own right, and no attempt at an answer will be given here.

13-14 A UNIVERSAL RULE

By now you might well be puzzled. We gave you some estimating tools; then suggested using several of these, which carries the clear implication that the tools might give different results. We said you should estimate effort, but then acknowledged that the trade-off between men and days is not constant. We suggested that estimates are self-fulfilling, but then suggested it is necessary to have an eye on risk while estimating. Why all the confusion and apparent conflict?

The answer is that in the final analysis an estimate is a judgment. There are some excellent tools that can help you produce good estimates, and there are some guidelines that can help you avoid major pitfalls. However, these tools and guidelines are there to supplement your judgment, not to replace it. Blind use of a formula can lead to disaster. Blind use of rules, too, can cause problems *except* for one rule that should invariably be followed: In estimating, always use common sense.

13-15 SUMMARY

- There is no easy way to estimate; it requires work to build an estimating procedure for an organization.
- An estimate should be judged by whether it is useful, not whether it is accurate.
- The field of probability and statistics provides a framework for understanding estimating; some important observations are:

    Estimating is based on a probabilistic model, not a deterministic one

    An estimate is a number in the likely range of the quantity being estimated

    Our confidence in an estimate depends on the size of the likely range of the quantity being estimated

    The more information we have on which to base an estimate, the smaller the likely range and the greater the confidence we have in the estimate

    The more relevant the information on which we base our estimate, the smaller the likely range and the greater our confidence

- To establish an estimating procedure, the first step is to standardize the project process, the second is to fix the class of projects to be considered, and the third is to devise specific procedures by:

  Determining the estimates required
  Selecting the estimating technique
  Determining the data requirements
  Capturing historical data
  Structuring the estimating procedure

- A scenario is an outline or description of a scene or situation; it can be used as a tool for long-range planning. A scenario of the future environment in which a system will operate can be used to estimate broad system parameters, such as utilization, cost of operation, and benefits.
- Transactional estimating is a method of estimating that takes the knowledge and experience of workers into account; it produces useful estimates and the motivation and commitment to meet them.
- Projective estimates require continuity in the project process and sufficient planning data from completed projects.
- The building of estimating equations requires specification of:

  Dependent variables
  Independent variables
  Equations relating the two types of variables

- Some suggestions and comments about estimating are:

  Make several estimates
  An estimate tends to be a self-fulfilling prophecy
  Effort is easier to estimate than duration
  Project cost depends on project duration
  Estimates can be "accurate" without being good
  The average estimate may not be the best estimate

- In estimating, always use common sense.

ESTIMATING—
THE DELPHI METHOD

14-1 ESTIMATING WITHOUT PLANNING DATA

At times estimates are required for a project when the methods of the previous chapter cannot be used. The problem usually stems from a lack of planning data. The most common reason for this is that no one has bothered to record historical data in a consistent manner, but there can be other reasons. The organization may be installing a new project methodology or making a significant change in an existing one, and this may make all historical data irrelevant. An influx of new personnel, particularly personnel with vastly different qualifications than in the past, can also invalidate past data. A significant change in the technical level of a project can have a similar effect. For example, an organization that is installing its first communications-based system may find that the data on traditional application projects does not help in estimating the new project. Still another reason why the projective technique cannot be used is that estimates are frequently required on future events that are unrelated to available historical information. For example, for design purposes it may be necessary to estimate the number of requests on a new system after it is operational for three years, and this probably cannot be done by simple projection.

If an estimate is required and all else fails, then the estimate must be based on personal opinion. People may speak of "pulling a number out of the air" or of using the WAG[1] method of estimating, but in effect they are making an estimate based on their own personal judgment. If people are serious about it and if their judgment is informed and professional, estimates

---

[1] Wild-assed guess. This term presumably is derived from the practice of divination by the spealbone or shoulder blade of *Equus asinus,* the wild ass of Africa. See scapulimancy in the dictionary.

based on opinion can be useful. The question arises: How can one get the most benefit from these informed opinions?

The first point to observe, in this direction, is that individual opinions are generally not as reliable as group opinions. Individual opinions tend to vary widely, which means that any one opinion has a high risk of being wrong. A group consensus is usually achieved through extreme views annulling one another with the result that the group opinion is generally fairly reliable.

The second point is that group opinion can be gathered in many ways, and that most of the traditional ways are subject to bias. The opinion of a group can be gathered through a series of informal one-on-one conversations with individual members of the group, through a committee meeting, or through a more formal conference or seminar. The one-on-one approach fails to generate true group interaction and, more seriously, is very susceptible to bias on the part of the person obtaining the information. The more usual way of gathering group opinion through meetings of one sort or another is subject to a number of pressures that can distort the result. Often a meeting is dominated by a loquacious individual who may not be the most knowledgeable. Frequently a shy individual will not speak up at a meeting even though he has key information; this is particularly true if the majority holds a contrary opinion. Even a strong person can be intimidated at a meeting attended by higher levels of management. An open meeting is not the best way to generate a free flow of ideas. In particular, an expert who has taken a public stand on an issue may find it difficult to back off even in the light of additional information. And, of course, personality conflicts may prevent a meaningful exchange of information in any open session.

The Delphi method is a structured means of group communications that tends to overcome the shortcomings of traditional meetings. This technique can be used to bring group opinion to bear on the problem of estimating. Our purpose in this chapter is to explain this tool.

14-2 INTRODUCTION TO THE DELPHI METHOD

The Delphi method, which is named after the ancient oracle of Apollo in Greece, is a method for the controlled exchange of information within a group. It provides a formal, structured procedure for the exchange of opinion, which means that it can be used for estimating. Some of the features of the method are:

It allows feedback of information to group members
It allows individuals some opportunity to assess group views

It allows some opportunity for individuals to make their opinions
  known to the group

It provides relative anonymity for individuals

The method was developed at the Rand Corporation in the early 1950s
as an offshoot of defense research. It was noted that there is a vast difference
in our society between the way we treat facts and the way we treat opinions.
The former are widely available in libraries, books, magazines, and so on. But
prior to the work of the Rand group, very little had been done to catalogue
opinions, and there was no formal technique for their exchange.

Since its conception, thousands of Delphi studies have been conducted
by governments, industry, and universities. The method is now a standard
tool to be considered whenever a consensus of experts is sought on a subject.
The method has been used for planning, budgeting, market research, and for
gathering estimates of current and historical data that is not otherwise available. Several large-scale Delphi experiments have been conducted to forecast
on topics of general interest, and the results of the studies have been widely
used.

When other methods of estimation fail, the Delphi method should be
considered as a way to obtain project data. It can be used to estimate such
aspects of the project as duration, resource requirements, risk, costs, and
benefits. If a planning data base is being newly created, the Delphi method
can be used to generate the "seed" data. The method can also be used to
estimate aspects of the deliverables, such as utilization rates, useful life,
acceptability, quality, and operational costs.

14-3 THE DELPHI GROUP

To conduct a Delphi experiment, a participating group and a person to
serve as a monitor are needed. The group should consist of experts on the
topic under discussion—people who by training, experience, or position are
qualified to have an opinion on the subject. There is evidence to suggest that
the higher the group's opinion of its own expertise, the better the results of
the experiment. At the same time, the group should be diverse. It is poor
practice to allow friends to recommend one another to the panel, because
there is a marked tendency for a group of friends to be all of the
same opinion.

The panel of experts must be committed to the study and must take its
job seriously. They must be prepared to devote sufficient time and thought;
otherwise the results may not be useful.

A panel should consist of at least ten people; with fewer than this, it is difficult to generate a meaningful exchange of ideas. Members can and should be drawn from the project team, operations, user groups, and others who are involved with the project. If it is hard to muster the required number of people, additional panel members can be drawn from parent organizations, trade groups, consultants, and others who are generally familiar with the type of questions to be considered.

A Delphi group need not be assembled in one location to conduct an experiment because all communication is done in writing. If the group is widely scattered or if meetings are hard to schedule, it is quite possible to conduct the experiment by mail. The problem of finding enough participants can sometimes be overcome by arranging the experiment so that people can do it at their own desks at times convenient to them.

The monitor is in charge of the experiment. He selects the panel and establishes the wording of the questions to be considered. He makes physical arrangements for the experiment and conducts it. If the group needs instruction, he introduces them to the Delphi technique, perhaps by making a practice run. During the experiment, he gathers and tabulates statistics, monitors responses that are generated, and presents appropriate information to the group. He communicates the final outcome of the experiment to the group.

The job of the monitor is difficult because it is easy for him to bias the results. One common reason for the failure of experiments is that the monitor imposes his views on the group, perhaps by subtle, unconscious actions or statements. The biggest job the monitor has is to maintain strict neutrality throughout the experiment.

14-4 OVERVIEW OF THE METHOD

There are many variations on the procedure to be followed in conducting a Delphi experiment. We shall describe one procedure that is relatively simple and that works. It is oriented toward a specific problem, namely, the estimation of parameters in a DP project. For example, it can be used to answer such questions as: How long will this project take if three people are assigned to it? What is the overall cost of this project? What is the worth of the information that will be supplied by the proposed system?

The questions posed to the group should require a quantitative answer—a duration, a cost, or some other number. One exception to this rule is easily handled; sometimes the question requires estimating a date, and the response of "now" or "never" is allowed because these can be placed in order along with numbers.

Most questions involving project estimates naturally lend themselves to quantitative answers. With a little practice, those few that don't can be revised to meet this requirement. For example, a question might be posed so as to require rating the importance of a topic on a scale from 1 to 10. (But be certain to state which is more important, 1 or 10!) Or a question might require assessing the probability of an event. Or a question might involve several factors that are to be ranked in order of importance.

The experiment is conducted in four rounds. Each round calls for a response from each group member. Each response contains an answer to the question, and it might also contain supporting reasons, as described below. The answer to the question is a number, which will be referred to as an *estimate* because of the nature of the question being asked. Responses are anonymous, and to achieve this the responses are made in writing. No names are afixed to the responses and it is important that group members not look at each other's answers. At the end of each round, the monitor provides the group with certain information. The tasks of the monitor and participants for the four rounds are summarized in Figure 14-1.

Before describing the four rounds in detail, we shall explain some statistical terms that will be used. Suppose that the responses to a question are arranged in order from the smallest to the largest. The smallest response is also called the *minimum* response, and the largest the *maximum*. The *first quartile* is the response such that at least 25% of the responses are equal to it or are less and at least 75% are equal to it or are greater. The *second quartile* or *median* response is such that at least 50% are equal to it or are less and 50% are equal to it or are greater. In other words, the second quartile or median is the middle-most response. The *third quartile* is the response such that at least 75% are equal to or are less than it and at least 25% are equal to it or are greater. Finally, the *interquartile range* is the range from the first quartile to the third quartile. It is a range that contains at least one-half of the responses.

All of this may sound complex, and it is stated in this way so as to be technically correct. The gist of it, and an approximately correct way to state it, is: Arrange the responses in order from the smallest to the largest. Count up one-fourth of the responses from the lower end—that is the first quartile. Then count up one-half the responses from the lower end—that is the second quartile. Then count up three-fourths of the responses—that is the third quartile.

To illustrate these concepts, suppose that there are 15 responses to a question as follows:

$$4, 6, 9, 5, 8, 2, 7, 3, 9, 6, 6, 8, 2, 5, 1$$

The first step is to order or rank them:

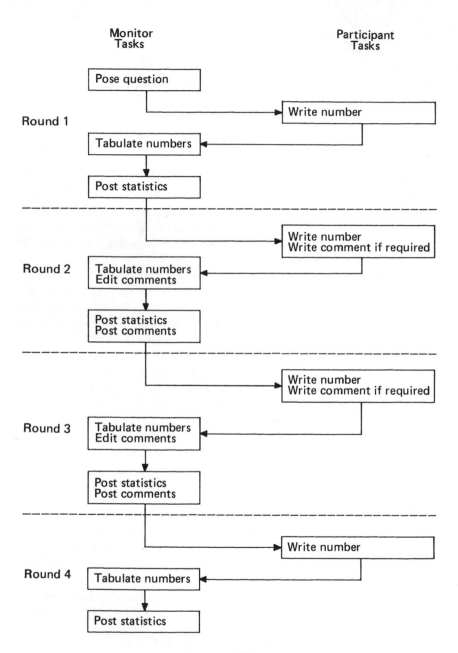

Figure 14-1. The Delphi rounds

1, 2, 2, 3, 4, 5, 5, 6, 6, 6, 7, 8, 8, 9, 9

One-fourth of 15 is 4 (after rounding), and the fourth response in order is 3. Thus the first quartile is 3. In a similar way the second quartile is 6, and the third is 8. The interquartile range is from 3 to 8.

Another statistical term used is *mode*; this is a response that is given most frequently. In the example above, 6 is a mode (we also say there is a mode at 6) because there are three responses of 6 and no other response is more frequent. A set of responses might have two or more modes. For instance, if the response of 1 in the above example were changed to 2, then there would be modes at 2 and 6 (three responses of each).

A further example of these terms appears in the next section.

The Delphi Process

A round-by-round description of the Delphi process is as follows.

Round 1. The monitor poses a question that requires a numerical answer, which will be referred to as an estimate. Participants respond to the question in writing. The responses are gathered by the monitor, tabulated, and analyzed. The monitor then gives the group the following information:

The minimum response
The maximum response
The first, second, and third quartiles
The interquartile range
The modes

Round 2. The monitor asks each participant to make a new response (estimate) to the question. This new estimate can be the same as the one the participant made in Round 1 or it can be different. (No one will know which it is except the participant—the system has no memory.) After making this new estimate, the participant is to compare it with the interquartile range presented to the group at the end of Round 1. If the new estimate is *outside* the interquartile range, the participant is to write a brief statement of his reason for his estimate. (The new estimate is outside the interquartile range if it is below the first quartile or above the third quartile.)

The monitor then collects a response from each participant. These responses consist of (1) the new estimate and (2) a reason for holding an extreme view *if* the new estimate is outside the Round 1 interquartile range.

The monitor tabulates the new estimates exactly as in Round 1 and presents the group the same kind of summary information as in Round 1, namely, the minimum, maximum, first, second, and third quartiles, inter-quartile range, and the mode (all computed, of course, from the Round 2 estimates).

Before presenting the reasons for extreme views to the group, the monitor should edit them to make certain that they do not reveal the identity of the writer. This requires careful judgments on the part of the monitor to avoid interjecting a bias.

After editing the written reasons, the monitor presents them to the group. This is best done by having the statements typed so as to avoid the possibility that handwriting might be recognized.

Round 3. This resembles Round 2 except that reasons are now given for an estimate inside the interquartile range.

The monitor asks each participant to make a new estimate. Then the participant is to compare the new estimate with the interquartile range given at the end of Round 2. If the new estimate is *inside* the range, the partici-pant should state why the arguments for the extreme views given at the close of Round 2 did not convince him. (Note: If the group is small, there may have been very few extreme views expressed in Round 2. In this event, the question in Round 3 can be altered to ask the participant why he holds a central view.)

The monitor collects all responses. He tabulates the new estimates and gives the group the same type of summary information as was presented in Rounds 1 and 2. After editing the written reasons, the monitor presents them to the group.

Round 4. The monitor asks for a new estimate; no reasons need be given. The new estimates are tabulated and summary statistics are presented to the group in the same manner as was done in the three previous rounds.

The estimates of Round 4 are the final results of the experiment. The median or second quartile from this last round is taken as the central group view on the question. The interquartile range gives some idea of the range in which the actual answer might be found. In addition, the spread of this range gives some indication as to the degree of consensus among the group on the question. The greater the spread, the less the consensus and the greater the risk associated with the median estimate.

14-5 AN EXAMPLE OF A DELPHI EXPERIMENT

A Delphi experiment was conducted with a group of 20 participants. This was the first experience any of the group had had with the technique. The group consisted of data processing people from many different organiza-tions. They were experienced people, all with many years in the business.

The question posed to the group was: How many years will it be before most companies use a formal DP project methodology? The answer was to be an integer 0, 1, 2, . . . or the word "never." An answer of 0 was understood to mean that most companies have such a methodology now. The group understood that the word *formal* has the meaning used in this book, that is, written, uniformly applied, and with written output.

Round 1. The estimates submitted in the various rounds are tabulated in Table 14-1. After analyzing the Round 1 estimates, the monitor supplied the group with the following information:

Minimum	0
First quartile	3-4
Second quartile	8
Third quartile	13
Maximum	Never
Interquartile range	4 to 13
Modes	0, 4, 9 (3 responses)

Round 2. The participants were asked to make a new estimate, to compare this with the interquartile range of Round 1, and to give a reason for their extreme view if their new estimate was less than 4 or greater than 13. By examining the new estimates as shown in Table 14-1, it can be seen that those without strong convictions tended to move their responses inside the interquartile range to avoid giving a reason. This action is quite usual.

Based on the new estimates, the group was supplied the following information:

Minimum	0
First quartile	4
Second quartile	7
Third quartile	10-11
Maximum	14
Interquartile range	4 to 10
Modes	4 (5 responses)

The reasons given for extreme views with the corresponding new estimates were supplied to the group. They were was follows:

Table 14-1
Responses for Four Rounds of a Delphi Experiment

Estimate	Number responding: Round 1	Round 2	Round 3	Round 4
0	///	//	///	///
1				
2	/			
3	/ ←1Q	/	/	
4	///	ЖТ ←1Q	//// ←1Q	ЖТ I ←1Q
5	/	/		/ ←2Q
6		/	//	//
7		←2Q	←2Q	
8	// ←2Q	/	/	/
9	///	////	///	//// ←3Q
10		←3Q		
11				
12	/	////	/// ←3Q	///
13	// ←3Q			
14		/	///	
15				
16	/			
. . .				
24	/			
. . .				
Never	/			

1Q = First quartile
2Q = Second quartile
3Q = Third quartile

New Estimate	Reason
0	Most companies have some sort of formal process now.
3	Since IBM seems to be behind the idea, it should happen soon.
0	Our organization has had a project methodology for several years.
14	The history of data processing shows that new ideas take a long time to develop. Since there are new shops starting all the time, I think it will take this long before the ideas are used by most people.

Round 3. The participants were asked to make a new estimate. If the new estimate is in the range from 4 to 10, they were asked to state briefly why (a) the arguments just supplied for the extreme position did not convince them or (b) why they held a central view. This choice of responses was allowed because there were so few reasons given in Round 2.

From the responses, the following statistical information was supplied to the group:

Minimum	0
First quartile	4
Second quartile	7
Third quartile	12
Maximum	14
Interquartile range	4 to 12
Modes	4 (4 responses)

Those who did not give reasons in Round 2 tended to be called on for reasons in this round. One person (new estimate of 12) gave a reason even though it was not required. (Remember, the 12 is to be compared with the interquartile range at the end of Round 2, not the numbers directly above.) It is not at all uncommon for this to happen when people are going through their first experiment.

The reasons given in Round 3 are as follows:

New Estimate	Reason
6	Changes in computer industry come fast (in comparison to general business changes); for example, the speed with

	which the whole top-down/HIPO/ structured code thing has been accepted.
4	This is when forecast.
6	Knowledge accumulates nonlinearly.
4	Many companies are in the process of adopting methods of formal planning. As methods are proven, will spread. Expect most to have it in four years.
9	I can't believe that the majority of companies now have a formal project methodology. This is based purely on personal experience. However, as more and more teleprocessing occurs, which affects not one firm but several, it will be a necessity.
9	Companies will not stay in business if not done soon.
4	Majority opinion, and I have held this view since Round 1.
8	Personal judgment and have not been convinced otherwise at this point.
9	Sticking with original decision, which seems close to norm.
4	Due to economical situations will be forced to formalize planning.
12	Progress is inevitable.

Round 4. The statistics supplied to the group on the basis of the Round 4 estimates are as follows:

Minimum	0
First quartile	4
Second quartile	5-6
Third quartile	9
Maximum	12
Interquartile range	4 to 9
Mode	4 (5 responses)

From this group's estimates, it would appear that most companies will use a formal DP project methodology in five to six years. This is not too likely to happen in less than four years, but most likely will take place before nine years from now. (Parenthetically, we might add that we have conducted experiments on this same question with many groups of DP people. The results are strikingly similar, which gives us added confidence in these estimates.)

A summary of the quartiles for the four rounds of the experiment is shown in Figure 14-2. This figure displays two characteristics that are frequently encountered with Delphi experiments. First, the interquartile range tends to narrow as the experiment progresses. Second, the median shifts rather steadily toward its final value. These shifts indicate that information is being exchanged and opinions are changing as a result of the experiment.

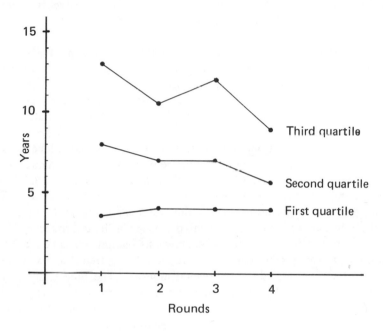

Figure 14-2. Quartiles for four rounds

14-6 ADDITIONAL COMMENTS

The question often arises as to whether it would be advantageous to continue a Delphi experiment beyond four rounds. This seems not to be worthwhile. Four rounds provide opportunity for extreme and central views to be aired, and additional rounds generally produce little new information. As a result, estimates generally do not change much if the experiment is continued past four rounds.

During an experiment, the monitor is often asked to clarify the question being considered. This should *not* be done. Part of the experiment involves bringing out differences in the interpretation of the question, and an experienced group will add clarifying comments to the reasons they submit in Rounds 2 an 3. For instance, the question considered in the previous section might elicit such comments as:

> "I interpret most to mean 50%, therefore . . ."
> "I assume most *American* companies . . ."
> "I take it the question refers only to reasonably large companies, say over 50 million in sales . . ."

From the comments that arise during the Delphi experiment, the monitor can determine just how much confusion the question generates. If it appears necessary, the question can be reformulated and a new experiment can be conducted. If trouble is anticipated with a question, it might even be worthwhile to run a small experiment to pretest the question before conducting the major experiment.

In training a new group in the Delphi method, it is a good idea to ask a factual question whose answer can be verified by looking it up somewhere. If everyone in the group is familiar with John, then "How old is John?" is a good beginning question—provided John is not sensitive about his age. The advantage of a factual question is that the group can compare their estimate with the actual answer and thereby gain confidence in the technique.

The experiment described in the previous section was conducted in a single session lasting about one hour. At the other extreme, an experiment can extend over several weeks or several months. The time schedule will depend partly on the physical location of the participants and partly on the amount of thought and work they are expected to put into the project. Explanations or reasons can be brief, as in the example we looked at, or they can be important studies in their own right.

For the experiment described, the participants were all seated in one room, and the written reasons given during Rounds 2 and 3 were read to the group rather than being typed and distributed. However, as mentioned above, participants can be located miles apart, and the various rounds can be conducted by phone or mail.

Some organizations have constructed terminal-based systems for conducting Delphi experiments. The project to establish such a system is not complex if the major hardware and operating systems are in place. One group set up such a Delphi system in less than a month. A terminal system is useful if:

The group is spread geographically
A written record of responses is desirable
The group is large
The organization wants to experiment with group communication through electronic media

The terminal system also helps to preserve anonymity provided there is a mechanism for the monitor to edit all verbal responses before they are distributed to the group.

The major cost of a Delphi experiment is the time of the participants and the monitor. Communication costs can be important if the experiment is conducted via an automated system.

In using the Delphi method, it is important to remember that it does not give a 20-20 view into the future. Its use and the interpretation of results should be viewed as something of an art rather than as an exact science. If a better method of estimating is available, then of course it should be used. But we know of some DP installations that have used the Delphi technique to do project estimating for over ten years. As a member of one of these groups said, "Our estimates aren't perfect, but they're a whole lot less wrong than they used to be."

14-7 SUMMARY

- Delphi is a method for controlled exchange of information within a group. It is more effective than traditional methods of exchange because it provides relative anonymity for individuals.
- The Delphi method can be used for estimating various aspects of a project. Its use should be considered when other estimating techniques cannot be used or when you want an independent check on estimates obtained by other techniques.
- To perform a Delphi experiment it is necessary to have a monitor and a group of at least ten people. Members of the group should have an informed opinion on the question being considered.
- A Delphi experiment is conducted in four rounds. The procedure for each round is simple, but highly structured.

15

NETWORKS–THEORY

15-1 HISTORY OF NETWORKS

The basic method for planning and controlling a development project is to break the total job into a number of activities or tasks, and to monitor these activities individually. This technique, which has been employed for centuries, is uncomplicated and easy to apply as long as the activities are few in number and follow one another sequentially. Problems arise with the technique, however, for a complex project consisting of a large number of interrelated activities. Then it becomes desirable to have some graphic method for representing the project so that one can see at a glance how the individual activities relate to the overall project.

One such technique is the *Gantt* or *bar chart,* which was invented around 1900 by Henry Gantt and is widely used to this day. As most readers know, a Gantt chart consists of a collection of horizontal bars plotted against a calendar scale. Each bar represents an activity. The beginning and end of the bar represent the scheduled start and finish dates of the activity, and the collection of all bars portrays a complete schedule for the project.

Gantt charts have been used extensively to plan projects and, with modifications to reflect actual dates, to monitor progress against plan. These charts are popular because they are easy to construct, and they serve as an effective tool for communicating the project plan to all involved groups. However, Gantt charts have certain inadequacies, and these become apparent when the charts are applied to complex projects. One problem is that Gantt charts fail to display interdependencies among activities. This can cause scheduling errors and, more important, can make it difficult to assess the impact that a change in one activity can have on the rest of the project. A related problem is the difficulty of modifying Gantt charts to reflect slippages of completion dates or other changes in plans.

During the late 1950s, attempts were made to discover methods for representing projects that would overcome the shortcomings of Gantt charts. These efforts resulted in two new planning tools: CPM (Critical Path Method) and PERT (Project Evaluation and Review Technique). These tools are closely related; both focus on the interdependence of activities and both represent a project as a *network* of activities.

In its original form, CPM was oriented toward the planning and control of a well-defined project that involved little uncertainty, such as might be encountered in the construction or process industries. For such a project, there is generally a relationship between the cost and time associated with each activity—by spending more on an activity, you can reduce the time required to complete it. At the same time, the total value of the project is generally increased if the project is completed early. CPM focused on this cost-time relationship and attempted to provide schedules that would maximize the economic worth of the project.

PERT, on the other hand, was originally oriented toward projects that were less clearly defined and involved considerable uncertainty. Such projects are typical of research and development efforts, systems engineering, and data processing. To cope with uncertainty, PERT incorporated three time estimates for each activity: an optimistic estimate, a pessimistic estimate, and a most-likely estimate. From these estimates, an expected completion date was computed for the project together with a variance, which could be used to estimate the probability that the project would be completed before or after the expected date.

Through the years, particularly as applied to DP projects, the distinction between PERT and CPM has tended to blur. In part, this has been due to the difficulty of obtaining the data required for the three time estimates of PERT or the time-cost analysis of CPM. In part the distinction has become blurred because managers have discovered that the core ideas of these two techniques were all they needed to control DP projects. What has emerged over the years is a technique that employs the common planning and scheduling procedures of PERT and CPM. This technique is sometimes referred to as PERT/CPM, but more usually it is simply described as a *network* technique. This technique is the topic of discussion in this chapter.

We should point out that the word *network* is used in DP in two entirely different ways. As just indicated, it is used to describe a method for representing a collection of related tasks for the purpose of planning and controlling a work process. But the word network is also used to describe a collection of interrelated communications paths—a so-called communications network. In this book communications networks will *not* be discussed. Whenever we use the word network, it is the planning, scheduling, PERT/

CPM, task-oriented management tool that we have in mind.

15-2 USES OF NETWORKS

Networks are used in performing many functions associated with a project. Some of these uses are as follows.

Planning. Networks are used to establish the overall plan for a project. This is done by listing all activities of the project and by showing the order in which these are to be performed. The list of activities should include not only DP tasks, but also those involving users, operations, vendors, and any other group associated with the project. On a large project, planning might entail the establishment of separate plans for these various groups and the integration of the separate plans into an overall network. Planning is not confined to the original effort, but continues throughout the project life as modifications are made to reflect the impact of slippages and changes.

The establishment of a project plan requires a careful analysis of the project and forces a discipline on the project planners. Many regard this discipline and systematic analysis as the most important benefit to be derived from the use of networks.

Scheduling. Based on the requirements for each activity, a network provides a simple procedure for establishing a time schedule for a project. It also provides a list of *critical activities* whose delay will impact the project completion date. The schedule for a project must be established in conjunction with an analysis of the project resource requirements. Frequently, schedules must be adjusted to accommodate mandated deadlines or constraints on resource availability. Also, updates in schedules must be made throughout the project life to reflect actual completion dates that differ from scheduled dates. A network provides a simple mechanism for making such adjustments.

Controlling. Control of a project revolves around the comparison of actual performance to plan. Networks play a role in this activity by providing the plan against which actuals are compared, and by providing a simple means of updating plans to accommodate revisions.

Communicating. Networks provide a documented description of project plans. Because of this, they are a convenient means for communicating project plans to all groups involved in a project. If warranted, various special groups can be provided with subnetworks that concentrate on their special portions of the project. Also, higher-level management can be provided with summary networks showing only the major aspects of the project.

Simulating. An important use of networks is that of project simulation. Most projects can be implemented in a variety of ways, and it is important for the project planner to select a plan that best fits the requirements of his organization. To do this, he must assess the impact on project duration and cost of such an action as a change in the order in which certain activities are performed. Or he must find the impact of a reassignment of resources among certain activities with resulting changes in activity durations. Such assessments can be made by simulating the changes—that is, by making the changes in the network and recalculating the project schedule. Properly used, this technique can result in substantially better project plans.

15-3 BASIC NETWORK DEFINITIONS

A network is composed of two basic elements: arrows and circles. An arrow represents an *activity* or *task,* which is some operation that consumes time and resources. A circle represents an *event* or *node,* and it marks the beginning or ending of an activity. An event can be thought of as a point in time; it does not call for an expenditure of time or resources. An activity is always drawn from one event, called the *predecessor event,* to another, called the *successor event.* The activity is the work required to progress from the predecessor event to the successor event.

As shown in Figure 15-1, an activity usually has a *description,* and events are assigned unique integer *event numbers.* These numbers need not be consecutive, but it is conventional to assign them in such a way that a predecessor event for an activity has a lower number than the successor event. The activity in Figure 15-1 can be identified by its description "CODE AND TEST MODULE" or, alternatively, by the designation "10,17" obtained from the numbers of the predecessor and successor events.

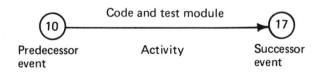

Figure 15-1. Example of an activity

An activity *B* is *dependent* on an activity *A* if *B* cannot be started until *A* is completed. It can be seen that activity *B* is dependent on activity *A* if the successor event of *A* is the predecessor event of *B.* In Figure 15-2, activities *B, C,* and *D* are all dependent on *A* and can be started only after *A* is completed. Event 2 of that diagram is called a *burst* event since it is the predecessor of more than one activity. In Figure 15-3, activity *L* is dependent on both *J* and *K.* Event 20 is called a *merge* event since it is the suc-

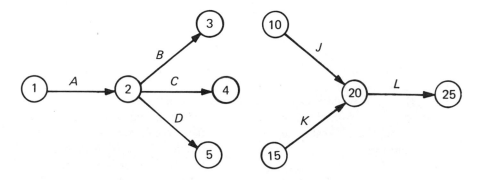

Figure 15-2.
Example of a burst event

Figure 15-3.
Example of a merge event

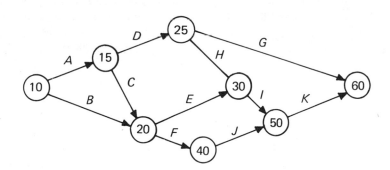

Figure 15-4. Example of a network

cessor of more than one activity. Clearly an event can be both a burst and a merge event.

A project can be decomposed into a collection of activities. Execution of the project is accomplished by executing these activities in some prescribed order. A *network* for the project is a collection of activities (arrows) and events (circles) that are linked together in such a way as to portray this order of execution. A typical network is shown in Figure 15-4. This diagram indicates that A and B can be started at the same time, C and D can be started as soon as A is completed, E and F can be started as soon as B and C are completed, and so on.

The terms predecessor and successor can be applied to activities as well as to events, but with a slightly different meaning. In Figure 15-4, activities *G, H, I,* and *K* are all called *successors* of activity D because they cannot be started until after activity D is completed. Activities G and H are *immediate successors* of D because they can be started immediately after D is completed. In the same way, $A, B,$ and C are *predecessors* of E, and I and J are *immediate predecessors* of K.

In Figure 15-4, we have followed the standard convention that calls for networks to be drawn so that all arrows have a general left-to-right orientation. From this it follows that the events on a network are roughly ordered in time sequence from left to right. It should be noted, however, that a network is *not* scaled to time. Thus the length of an arrow does not indicate the time required to perform the activity, and the placement of events is not strictly according to a calendar scale. For example, from Figure 15-4 alone it is not possible to determine if event 30 takes place before or after event 40. Unlike a bar chart, activities in the same vertical line need not be executed at the same point in time. It should be remembered that a network displays the sequence in which activities are to be performed, not the times that they are to be performed.

15-4 DUMMY ACTIVITIES

One additional concept is required to construct certain networks. To illustrate this, consider the activities listed in Table 15-1. In a network for this project, activities A and B can be started together, and activity C can be started at the completion of A. This much of the network can be drawn in only one of two ways: either activities C and B terminate at the same event, as shown in Figure 15-5(a), or they terminate at different events, as shown in Figure 15-5(b). But neither of these two possibilities is satisfactory. In the first case, activity D can be added by having it start from event 15 because D depends on both B and C. But it is not possible to represent activity E since

Table 15-1
A Collection of Activities

Activity Identification	Activity Description	Immediate Predecessor
A	DESIGN MODULE	—
B	PREPARE TEST DATA	—
C	CODE MODULE	A
D	TEST MODULE	B, C
E	DOCUMENT MODULE	C

that activity depends only on *C*. The situation is reversed in the second case. In figure 15-5(b) it is possible to draw activity *E* starting from event 20, but it is not possible to represent *D* because it depends on both *B* and *C*.

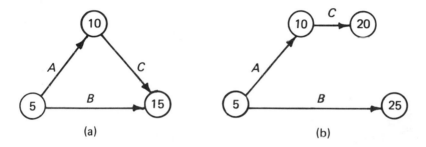

(a)   (b)

Figure 15-5. Two ways of representing activities *A, B,* and *C*

To resolve this dilemma, let us consider a new concept. A *dummy activity* is an activity that takes no time to accomplish and consumes no resources. It is used solely to indicate dependency in situations such as the above where the use of actual activities leads to complications. It is conventional to represent a dummy activity by an arrow with a broken line for a shaft.

It is possible to draw a network for the activities in Table 15-1 if we use a dummy activity. Such a network is shown in Figure 15-6, where activity *F* is a dummy. From the network it is clear that activity *E* has only activity *C* as an immediate predecessor. Activity *D*, however, has both *B* and *F* as immediate predecessors. From the fact that *C* is a predecessor of *F*, it follows that *C* is a predecessor of *D* as well. Moreover, since *F* takes no time, activity *D* can be started as soon as both *B* and *C* are completed. For this reason, it is convenient to say that *C*, too, is an immediate predecessor of *F*.

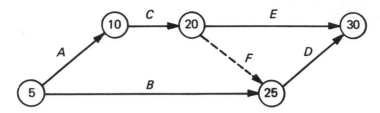

Figure 15-6. Network for the activities of Table 15-1

It is well to note the reason why it was necessary to introduce a dummy in Figure 15-6. The need arose from the fact that activities D and E had some immediate predecessors in common, but they did not have identical immediate predecessors. That is, both D and E depended on C, but both did not depend on B. This situation can be generalized: It is necessary to use a dummy activity in a network whenever there are two groups of activities that have some, but not all, of their immediate predecessors in common.

15-5 THREE RULES FOR NETWORK CONSTRUCTION

There is a second situation in which it is useful to employ a dummy activity. To illustrate this, consider a project consisting of activities A, B, and C with the property that A and B have no predecessors and C depends on both A and B. It is possible to represent the project by the network in Figure 15-7(a), but doing so can lead to a problem. If we refer to activity "10,20" in Figure 15-7(a), it is not clear if we mean activity A or activity B. Since there are many occasions when it is convenient to refer to activities by their predecessor and successor events, it is best to avoid this ambiguity. This can be accomplished easily by using a dummy and representing the project by the network shown in Figure 15-7(b), or by a similar network with the roles of A and B interchanged.

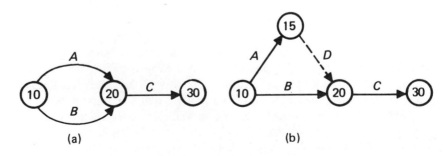

Figure 15-7. A use of a dummy activity

In the future, to avoid situations such as that shown in Figure 15-7(a) we shall observe the following rule:

RULE 1: Do not join two events with more than one activity.

To illustrate a second rule, observe the network in Figure 15-8. Notice that the dummy activity is not required. Presumably it was placed in the network to show that activity J depends on activity A. But this is automatic because J depends on H, which depends on G, which depends on C, which depends on A. It is amazing how often redundant dummy activities are placed in networks, particuarly in first attempts at representing complex projects. In the interest of economy we shall endeavor to abide by a second rule:

RULE 2: Avoid redundant dummy activities.

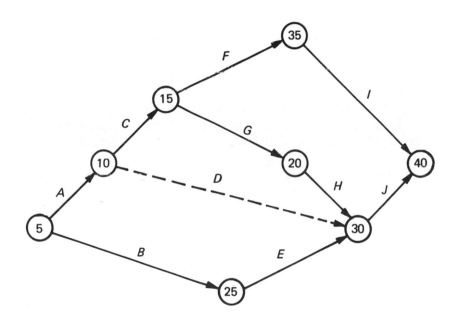

Figure 15-8. Example of a redundant dummy activity

Another problem that can occur in networks, particuarly in complex ones, is that of "looping." A *loop* in a network is a chain of activities that doubles back on itself; for example, activities *B*, *C*, and *D* of Figure 15-9 form a loop.

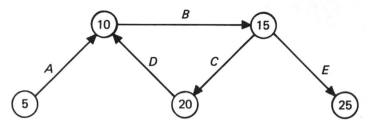

Figure 15-9. Example of a loop

Sometimes a loop is inserted in a network in an attempt to show that a sequence of activities must be repeated before going on. This, however, is an improper application of network concepts; the repetition should be shown by adding a second sequence of activities. More often, a loop appears in a network because of an oversight or an error. For instance, the duplicate event numbers in Figure 15-10 create a loop in the network.

Figure 15-10. Another example of a loop

In the next section, we shall study a technique that is used to generate a schedule for a network. That technique cannot be used, however, on a network that contains a loop. Therefore it is important to observe a third network rule:

RULE 3:   Avoid loops in a network.

15-6 SCHEDULING A NETWORK

Let us next consider the problem of *scheduling* a network—that is, the problem of establishing start and finish dates for each activity. To do this, we first assign a *duration* to each activity, which is our estimate of the time it will take to perform the activity. Durations are usually specified in days or weeks; days will be used for the examples in this chapter.

The estimation of activity durations is traditionally the most difficult part of network analysis and the part most subject to gross errors. For purposes of this chapter, we shall simply assume that duration estimates are at hand; the important topic of estimating is discussed at length in Chapters 13 and 14.

Early Start and Early Finish Times

The first step in scheduling is to compute an *early start* (*ES*) time and an *early finish* (*EF*) time for each activity in the network. As the names suggest, these are, respectively, the earliest possible time that an activity can be started and the earliest possible time that an activity can be completed. The *ES* and *EF* times are first computed for each *beginning activity,* that is, each activity with no predecessor. Next, the *ES* and *EF* times are computed for the immediate successors of the beginning activities, then for the immediate successors' successors, and so on until all activities have been considered. This procedure, which starts at the beginning of the network and works through to the end, is called a *forward pass* through the network.

Calculation of early start and early finish times is accomplished by observing two rules. The first rule is:

For each activity, *EF* = *ES* + Duration.

For instance, if an activity starts at time 0 and has a duration of 1, then it finishes at time 1. This calculation follows what might be thought of as an 8 A.M. to 8 A.M. schedule; if a one-day activity starts on day 0 at 8 A.M., then it is finished on day 1 at 8 A.M. (although actual work on the activity might have stopped at 5 P.M. on day 0).

The second rule has to do with the calculation of *ES*. If an activity has only a single immediate predecessor, then the *ES* for the activity is the *EF* of the immediate predecessor. This is in keeping with the rule in the preceding paragraph because if one thinks of the predecessor as ending at 8 A.M. on a given day, then the following activity can be started on the same day. But what if an activity has several immediate predecessors? Then the activity cannot commence until all of the predecessors are completed, which gives rise to the second rule:

The *ES* for an activity is the maximum of the *EF* times for *all* of its immediate predecessors.

This second rule, of course, does not apply to beginning activities, which have no immediate predecessors. To assign *ES* times to beginning activities, it is necessary to set a *starting date* for the entire project. This might be some scheduled date or it might be a baseline date that is established for planning purposes, which can be referred to as time zero. This starting date for the project then becomes the *ES* time for all beginning activities. For convenience, the project start time will be zero in all of our examples.

The procedure for making a forward pass through the network should now be clear. First, *ES* times are arbitrarily assigned to all beginning activities. Next, *EF* times are computed for these activities by applying the first rule. Then the second rule is applied to obtain the *ES* times for immediate successors. Their *EF* times are then obtained by applying the first rule, and so on. By applying the two rules alternately, it is possible to assign *ES* and *EF* times to all activities in the network.[1]

To illustrate these ideas, let us make a forward pass through the network shown in Figure 15-11. In that diagram, the number beneath each activity is its estimated duration.

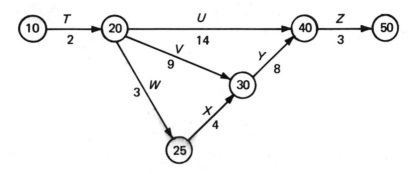

Figure 15-11. Example of a network

Activity *T* is the only beginning activity, and we take its *ES* to be 0. It follows that *EF* = 0 + 2 = 2 for *T*. Since *U*, *V*, and *W* can be started on the completion of *T*, we have *ES* = 2 for each of them. Next, *EF* = 2 + 14 = 16 for activity *U*, *EF* = 2 + 9 = 11 for activity *V*, and *EF* = 2 + 3 = 5 for activity *W*. We cannot yet schedule *Y* because all of its predecessors are not scheduled, but we can schedule *X*. For it, we have *ES* = 5 (the *EF* of *W*) and *EF* = 5 + 4 = 9.

Activity *Y* cannot be started until both *V* and *X* are completed. We have *EF* = 11 for *V* and *EF* = 9 for *X*, therefore *ES* for activity *Y* is 11, the larger of the two *EF*. Also, *EF* = 11 + 8 = 19 for activity *Y*. Finally, *ES* = 19 for *Z* (the maximum of the *EF* of *U* and the *EF* of *Y*), and *EF* = 19 + 3 = 22. These results are summarized in Table 15-2.

---

[1] Throughout the book schedules will be computed by using the rules just described. But it should be noted that some people employ an alternative computational scheme in which a one-day activity starts and stops on the same day, and an immediate successor cannot start until the next day. It makes absolutely no difference which scheme is employed as long as you are consistent.

Table 15-2
ES and EF for the Network of Figure 15-11

Activity	Duration	ES	EF
T	2	0	2
U	14	2	16
V	9	2	11
W	3	2	5
X	4	5	9
Y	8	11	19
Z	3	19	22

One result of a forward pass through a network is that it establishes a *completion date* for the project. This is the maximum *EF* time for all activities of the network, and it is the earliest date that the entire project can be finished. It may be, however, that the project has a *scheduled* or mandated finish date that differs from the completion date. In this event, it would be of interest to know how late the activities could be started and completed to meet this scheduled date. And even if the scheduled date is the same as the completion date, it might be that some activities could be delayed beyond their *ES* and *EF* dates without delaying the project. The next part of the scheduling process will assist us in exploring these and related matters.

Late Start and Late Finish Times

The second step in scheduling a network is to compute *late start* (*LS*) and *late finish* (*LF*) times for all activities. These are the latest allowable times that an activity can be started and completed, respectively. The procedure for accomplishing this is called a *backward pass* through the network, and it is just a forward pass in reverse. The *LS* and *LF* times are first computed for each *ending activity,* that is, each activity with no successor. Next, the *LS* and *LF* times are computed for the immediate predecessors of the ending activities, then for the predecessors' predecessors, and so on until the beginning activities are reached.

Rules for computing *LS* and *LF* are just the reverse of those used in the forward pass. The first rule relates *LS, LF,* and activity duration, but it is stated in a form useful for computation in a backward pass:

For each activity, $LS = LF - $ Duration.

The second rule recognizes that an activity must be finished no later than the earliest date on which an immediate successor must be started:

> The LF for an activity is the minimum of the LS times for all of its immediate successors.

If a scheduled date has been mandated for the project, this is assigned as the LF for all ending activities. In the absence of a scheduled date, it is customary to use the completion date for the project, which amounts to setting $LF = EF$ for the ending activities. In all of our examples, this practice will be followed unless otherwise stated.

Let us apply these concepts and make a backward pass through the network of Figure 15-11. For activity Z, we have $LF = EF = 22$ and $LS = 22 - 3 = 19$. Then $LF = 19$ for U and Y; and $LS = 19 - 14 = 5$ for U and $LS = 19 - 8 = 11$ for Y. From this, $LF = 11$ for V and X; and $LS = 11 - 9 = 2$ for V, whereas $LS = 11 - 4 = 7$ for X. Next, $LF = 7$ and $LS = 7 - 3 = 4$ for W. Finally, activity T must be finished no later than the latest times U, V, and W must be started. Thus the LF of T is 2, which is the minimum of the LS times of U, V, and W; and $LS = 2 - 2 = 0$ for T. Table 15-3 displays these results consolidated with the results of the forward pass. Table 15-3 also contains a column labeled "Slack," a subject discussed next.

Table 15-3
Schedule for the Network of Figure 15-11

Activity	Duration	ES	EF	LS	LF	Slack
T	2	0	2	0	2	0
U	14	2	16	5	19	3
V	9	2	11	2	11	0
W	3	2	5	4	7	2
X	4	5	9	7	11	2
Y	8	11	19	11	19	0
Z	3	19	22	19	22	0

15-7 SLACK ANALYSIS

The third step in scheduling a network is slack analysis. To describe this, some additional terminology will be introduced.

A *path* through a network is a sequence of activities that starts with a beginning activity and travels through a series of immediate successors until it terminates with an ending activity. The *length* of a path is the total time it takes to traverse the path; that is, the total of the durations for the activities on the path. In any network, there is a maximum to the lengths of all paths through the network. Any path whose length is equal to this maximum is called a *critical path*. Stated differently, a path is a critical path if there is no path in the network with a longer length. An activity is *critical* if it lies on some critical path.

(Note that we are carefully avoiding the statement that a critical path is *the* longest path. It is important to realize that there can be several critical paths in a network; in other words, several paths of maximum length. In this event, no one path in the network is longest, but there is no path longer than those that are critical.)

The length of a critical path is equal to the *project duration,* which is the difference between the project starting date and the project completion date. This length can also be described as the minimum time it takes to execute the project.

There are three paths in the network of Figure 15-11: path *T, U, Z,* path *T, V, Y, Z,* and path *T, W, X, Y, Z.* The lengths of these paths are 19, 22, and 20, respectively. This means that *T, V, Y, Z,* is critical. The length of this path, 22, is the time it takes to complete the project. This time can also be found from Table 15 3 as the difference between the early start time of the project, which is 0, and the early finish time, which is 22. It can also be found by taking the difference of the late start and late finish times for the project.

Certain facts make it important that critical paths be identified:

Slippage of an activity on the critical path results in slippage of the project completion date. In fact, a frequent cause of project delay is the failure to identify these critical activities that must be completed on time to avoid project delay.

Improvement of the total project duration is most responsive to improvements along a critical path. Sometimes a critical path can be redefined or the duration of a critical activity can be modified, and any such changes will be directly reflected in the total project length. Also, it is possible to lengthen noncritical activities without adverse effect on project duration. These facts are useful for planning purposes.

Critical activities are the ones most in need of management attention since their delay most impacts the project. Thus project monitoring should be concentrated on critical activities to achieve maximum benefit.

For a large project it is not practical to examine all paths through the network; therefore it is necessary to find some alternative procedure for identifying critical paths. Fortunately, there is such a procedure, and it is based on the dates assigned in the forward and backward passes. To describe it, the following definitions are made.

The *slack* of an activity is the number of days the activity can be delayed without delaying the project; that is, without delaying the LF date for any ending activity. From the definition of ES and LS it can be seen that

$$\text{Slack} = LS - ES.$$

Since $LF = LS + \text{Duration}$ and $EF = ES + \text{Duration}$, it is also true that

$$\text{Slack} = LF - EF.$$

Activities on the critical paths are those that can be delayed the least; therefore these are the activities with minimum slack. This means that in order to find the critical activities, we need only: compute the slack for each activity, find the minimum slack, and identify as critical those activities whose slack is equal to this minimum value.

Slack analysis is the calculation of slack, identification of critical activities, and investigation of groups of activities to see what effect their delay would have on the project.

An Example of Slack

Let us apply these notions to the network of Figure 15-11. The reader should verify that the entries in the column headed "Slack" of Table 15-3 have been computed according to their formula for slack given above. The minimum slack in this column is zero, and activities T, V, Y, and Z have slack equal to this value. It follows that these are critical activities, and the path they define is the only critical one in the network. This result, of course, agrees with our earlier analysis of this network.

From the slack listed in Table 15-3, we see that activity U can be delayed by three days without delaying the project. Also, activities W and X each have a slack of 2 so either can be delayed by two days. But notice that if *both* are delayed by two days, then activity Y cannot start until two days after its LS date, and this results in a delay of two days in the entire project. This leads us to the important observation: the slack of an activity is the number of days the activity can be delayed without delaying the project *pro-*

viding it is the only activity delayed. It is not possible to tell from examining the slack alone what would happen if two or more activities are delayed. For instance, U can be delayed three days and X can also be delayed two days with no harm to the project completion date. But to learn this it is necessary to examine the network for the project; it is not possible to draw this conclusion solely from the information in Table 15-3.

It is instructive to see how the above analysis is modified if a project has a scheduled completion date that differs from the project completion date computed in the forward pass. To illustrate this, let us recalculate the schedule for the network of Figure 15-11 using a scheduled completion date of 26 rather than the date $EF = 22$ that was used in Table 15-3. The results are given in Table 15-4.

Table 15-4
Schedule for the Network 15-11 with
Completion Date of 26

Activity	Duration	ES	EF	LS	LF	Slack
T	2	0	2	4	6	4
U	14	2	16	9	23	7
V	9	2	11	6	15	4
W	3	2	5	8	11	6
X	4	5	9	11	15	6
Y	8	11	19	15	23	4
Z	3	19	22	23	26	4

It can be seen that for each activity the slack in Table 15-4 is just 4 greater than the slack in Table 15-3. The minimum slack in Table 15-4 is 4, indicating that the project completion date (*EF* of activity Z) is four days before the scheduled date. Activities T, V, Y, and Z have slack equal to this minimum and as before, this indicates that they are critical activities.

Table 15-4 illustrated that the minimum slack in a network is positive if the scheduled completion date is after the project completion date; that is, if $EF < LF$ for the last activity on some critical path. In the same way, the minimum slack is negative if the scheduled completion is before the project completion date. The reader can construct an example to illustrate this by rescheduling the network of Figure 15-11 using $LF = 20$ for activity Z. It will be discovered that the critical activities have slack equal to -2. Negative slack for an activity simply means that the activity is behind schedule even if it is started as early as possible—a situation that is not unknown in actual projects.

15-8 CALENDAR DATES

The schedules presented so far have not been keyed to actual calendar dates, but for practical use of networks this is usually desirable. In theory this presents no problems; in practice it can be a tedious undertaking.

To illustrate the use of calendar dates, let us reschedule the network of Figure 15-11 with a starting date of 3/1/— and with scheduled date equal to project completion date. We shall assume an ordinary five-day work week with no special holidays. Assume that the calendar needed for this scheduling is shown in Table 15-5. The resulting schedule is shown in Table 15-6; the reader should verify its accuracy.

Table 15-5
Sample Calendar

March 19—

S	M	T	W	Th	F	S
				1	2	3
4	5	6	7	8	9	10
11	12	13	14	15	16	17
18	19	20	21	22	23	24
25	26	27	28	29	30	31

Table 15-6
Schedule for the Network of Figure 15-11

Activity	Duration	ES	EF	LS	LF	Slack
T	2	3/1/—	3/5/—	3/1/—	3/5/—	0
U	14	3/5/—	3/23/—	3/8/—	3/28/—	3
V	9	3/5/—	3/16/—	3/5/—	3/16/—	0
W	3	3/5/—	3/8/—	3/7/—	3/12/—	2
X	4	3/8/—	3/14/—	3/12/—	3/16/—	2
Y	8	3/16/—	3/28/—	3/16/—	3/28/—	0
Z	3	3/28/—	4/2/—	3/28/—	4/2/—	0

Two points are worth observing. First, note that activity T, a two-day activity, begins on 3/1/— and finishes on 3/5/—, two *working* days later. The EF for activity T can be found from the calendar by starting with 3/1/— and counting off two days, namely Friday the 2nd and Monday the 5th. All other dates can be found in a similar manner. Second, note that the slack for an activity must be calculated from the calendar. It cannot be found by simply subtracting the ES from the LS because a weekend might intervene. As an instance, note that activity X has 3/8/— for ES and 3/12/— for LS whereas its slack is 2.

The procedure of deriving a schedule directly from a calendar is slow and error prone, and an alternative technique is sometimes preferable. This consists of deriving a schedule based on consecutively numbered project days, as was done for Table 15-3, and then translating this schedule into one that has calendar dates. The correspondence between project days and calendar dates can easily be established by consecutively numbering each *working* day on a calendar, starting with 0 for the project start date.

15-9 BAR CHARTS

A schedule such as shown in Table 15-6 provides the planner with the data he needs to establish his project plan, but for many uses the information is not presented in the most convenient form. Usually it is desirable to reformat the information and to present it in the form of a Gantt chart. This facilitates the assignment of activities to individuals and the tying of project costs to accounting periods. A Gantt chart for the schedule of Table 15-6 is shown in Figure 15-12.

Various conventions can be followed in producing a Gantt chart corresponding to a network schedule. Let us discuss some we followed in the chart of Figure 15-12.

The first convention we followed is to omit nonworking days from the bar for an activity. This results in an "interrupted bar" but seems preferable to showing the activity scheduled on days, such as Saturdays and Sundays, when no actual work takes place.

A second convention has to do with the length of a bar for an activity. To explain this, recall that activity T has a duration of two days and is scheduled with $ES = LS$ on Thursday, March 1, and $EF = LF$ on Monday, March 5. This schedule follows the "8 A.M. to 8 A.M." rule. A case can be made for being consistent and extending the bar for activity T over the same period—that is, to show a bar from Thursday, March 1, through the following Monday (except for the weekend). This would result in a bar covering three working days and is at odds with the activity duration of two days. Since

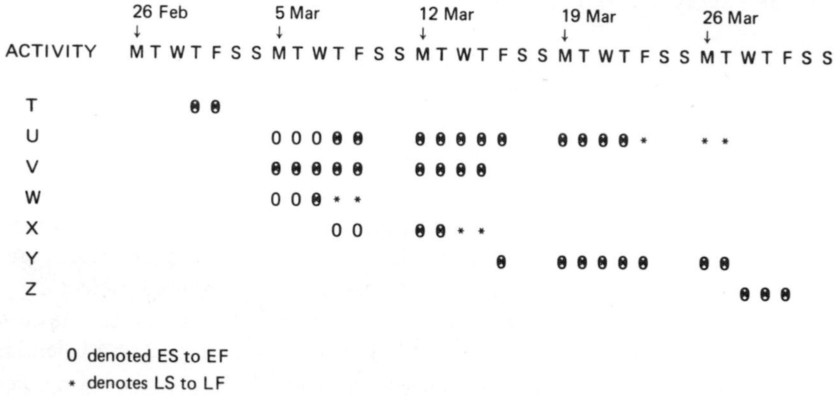

```
              26 Feb        5 Mar        12 Mar       19 Mar       26 Mar
                ↓             ↓            ↓            ↓            ↓
ACTIVITY     M T W T F S S M T W T F S S M T W T F S S M T W T F S S M T W T F S S

   T             θ θ
   U                         0 0 0 θ θ   θ θ θ θ θ   θ θ θ θ *     * *
   V                         θ θ θ θ θ   θ θ θ θ
   W                         0 0 θ * *
   X                           0 0       θ θ * *
   Y                                         θ       θ θ θ θ θ   θ θ
   Z                                                               θ θ θ
```

0 denoted ES to EF
* denotes LS to LF

Figure 15-12. A Gantt chart for the network of Figure 15-11

the actual work on the activity is probably confined to 9 A.M. to 5 P.M. (or thereabouts) on March 1 and 2, we elected instead to show a bar of length 2 extending only over these two days. We believe this to be less confusing than the first alternative.

A third convention we followed has to do with early start and finish versus late start and finish. We used the symbol 0 for the span from *ES* to *EF* and the symbol * for the span from *LS* to *LF*. For a critical activity, such as *T*, these symbols overlap completely and result in a bar consisting entirely of the symbol θ. This means that the critical activities for the project can be identified from Figure 15-12 at a glance. For a noncritical activity, such as *W*, the two spans are not identical. From the bar chart it can be seen that activity *W* can be started any time from the first 0 date (March 5) through the first * date (March 7) without delaying the project.

As we reflect on this difference in spans from *ES* to *EF* and from *LS* to *LF,* it becomes clear that we do not have just *one* schedule for a project but a *collection* of schedules depending on when we choose to start the various activities that have slack time. On some projects, such as heavy construction, we might actually be interested in scheduling activities on their *LS* dates. This would delay activities as long as possible, and it would result in maximum delay in the heavy investments that usually accompany such projects. If money is viewed as having a time value, this would result in lower finance charges for the project. With most DP projects, however, this finance charge is not a major concern. It is far more important to schedule activities as early as possible and to leave the slack as a cushion to help absorb unforeseen delays. Thus, to the extent possible, most DP projects are scheduled by using *ES* dates.

15-10 COMPUTER PROCESSORS

As we have seen, the scheduling of networks requires only basic mathematical skills, and it is quite possible to do this by hand if the network is not too large. Some believe that manual scheduling is possible with as many as 100 activities; but even a network of this size can require considerable time, particularly if frequent revisions are needed or if additional information is provided on such things as costs and resources. Moreover, many schedules are subject to error, which requires that additional time and effort be spent in verifying results. If a Gantt chart is required as well as a schedule, this also adds to the burden.

Network scheduling can easily be adapted to the computer, and dozens of processors are available to perform this function. The advantages of using a computer are familiar to DP personnel and include speed, accuracy, and standardization of procedures, formats, and content. But, of course, the overriding reason for using a computer in a particular instance is that it is the cost-effective way to do the processing.

Common Features

Network processors differ widely in their capabilities and characteristics, but there are certain features common to all. All processors have routines for the input of data, calculation of schedules, and output of reports. Required input for all processors is the network logic and the activity durations. Frequently, this is supplied by providing for each activity a description, duration, predecessor event, and successor event. Processor output includes a schedule for the network, usually arranged in an order selected by the user. Behind these basics, there is a wide variation in features such as the following.

Mode of Computing. Some processors operate in a batch mode, some in an interactive mode via a terminal.

Additional Dates. Some processors allow the input of scheduled dates and actual dates for activities. The user is allowed to specify if these dates should override the dates calculated in the forward and backward passes.

Editing Checks. Most processors perform certain edit checks on input data. Typical are checks for missing information, duplicate event numbers, and the presence of loops in the network.

Calendar Conversion. Many processors produce schedules with calendar dates rather than sequentially numbered project days. Processors vary in their ability to cope with flexible holidays and other nonworking days.

Network Integration and Consolidation. Frequently provisions are made for assembling networks from smaller components called subnetworks. Also, it is often possible to consolidate a network and to produce a summary network for higher level management. (Subnetworks and consolidated networks are discussed later in this chapter.)

Report Variation. Usually the user can control the order in which activities are listed in the schedule report. Typical options include chronological listing by *ES,* by *EF,* and so on; also, listing by slack or by special activity code.

Additional Reports. There is a wide range in reporting capabilities of various processors. Among the types of reports provided are Gantt charts, summary networks, summary Gantt charts, reports of major project events, and so on.

Although we are considering only network scheduling at this point, it should be noted that many network processors also interface with programs that can be used to plan and control project resources and costs. These programs provide reports on such things as resource assignments, resource utilization, and cost analysis.

Restrictions

The use of a computer processor for scheduling imposes restrictions that are generally not confining. Among these are the following.

Network Size. Limits placed on network size vary tremendously. Some processors place the maximum number of activities at about 100, some at 75,000, and some say it is unlimited.

Loops. Whether computing by hand or with a computer, a network cannot be scheduled if it contains a loop. There are processors built on a variation of the PERT/CPM procedure that address loops, but these are seldom used on DP projects.

Multiple Activities between Events. There is a split on this restriction. Some processors identify activities by predecessor and successor events, and in this case it is necessary to have no more than one activity joining two events.   Other processors identify activities by input sequence number or something similar, and then it is not necessary to impose the restriction. The restriction has been observed throughout this book because some processors do require it, it is easy to observe, and in our view it adds clarity to the networks.

i < j Event Numbering. Here again there is a split. Some processors require that a predecessor event be assigned a lower number than a successor event, some do not. The restriction has been observed for the same reasons as given in the previous paragraph.

Single Beginning and Ending Events. Some processors require a single beginning event and a single ending event, others do not. This restriction is not unnatural for most DP projects; usually a project is viewed as a series of activities between "project start" and "project end." Moreover, a project with multiple starts can always be reduced to one with a single artificial starting event by the use of dummy activities if this is necessary to accommodate the computer processor; a similar device can be used for multiple ends.

15-11 NETWORK INTEGRATION

The network for a large project can be complex and difficult to construct. Rather than establishing it directly, it is usually easier to divide the project into a number of major parts and to develop a network for each part separately. The division can be based on project phases, major functions, organizational responsibility, or any other natural break.

The networks for the major parts of a project are usually called *subnetworks.* Because of their reduced size, subnetworks are easier to construct and to maintain than would be an overall network for the entire project. Their relative simplicity also makes them a better vehicle for the communication of project plans. But the main advantage of subdividing the project is that each subnetwork can be developed by the people whom it most concerns. This adds realism to the project plan and helps to focus each group on its responsibilities.

Typically the subnetworks of a project are interdependent because the output from one subnetwork is required for another or because they compete for common scarce resources such as personnel or machine time. It follows that subnetworks cannot be scheduled independently but must be *intergrated* into a network for the entire project, which can then be scheduled in the usual way.

Network integration is accomplished through the use of *interface events.* These are events that appear in more than one subnetwork and are used as linkage points. An interface event must appear in all subnetworks affected, and its identification must be the same throughout. Usually interface events are shown on a network by some special symbol such as a square or rectangle.

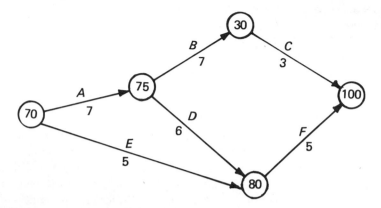

Figure 15-13. Example of a subnetwork

To illustrate network integration, let us consider the network shown in Figure 15-13. Standing by itself, the project has a duration of 18 days and a single critical path *ADF*. However, suppose this network and the network of Figure 15-11 are parts of the same project and interface through the common event 30. The integrated network is shown in Figure 15-14. It is easy to verify that the project duration for the combined network is 25 days and the (unique) critical path is *ABYZ*. That is, the combined network has a duration exceeding that of each subnetwork, and the critical path for the project weaves through both subnetworks.[2]

In Figure 15-14, all activities preceding event 30 in both subnetworks are predecessors for activities *Y* and *C*. A more usual situation is that certain activities in one subnetwork must be completed before some activities in another subnetwork can be started. To display such a constraint, it might be necessary to use dummy activities, as shown in Figure 15-15.

Both Figures 15-14 and 15-15 are examples of how subnetworks might be used within a project phase. For instance, in Figure 15-15 the top subnetwork might represent DP activities, and the bottom user activities. Incidentally, the interface events 100 and 200 are part of both subnetworks, and it is important from a management point of view to establish which organization has primary responsibility over these points.

---

[2] If a formal schedule is calculated for the network of Figure 15-14 by assigning the project duration as the *LF* for all terminal activities, then a single critical path *ABYZ* is obtained. However, if you let *LF* = *EF* for *each* terminal activity (as do some computer processors), then the additional critical path *ADF* is obtained. This difference stems from the fact that the combined network has more than one terminal event.

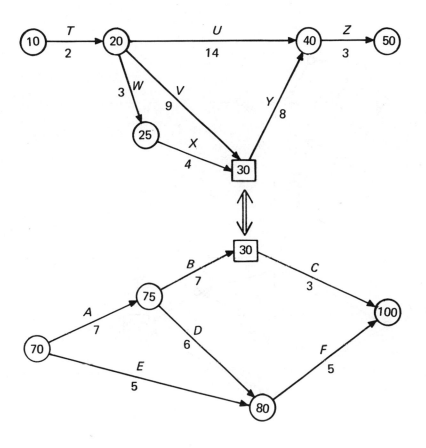

Figure 15-14. Integration of the subnetworks of figures 15-11 and 15-13

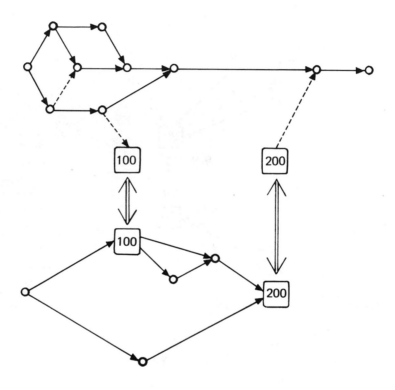

Figure 15-15. An example of interfaced networks

Two other uses of interface events are illustrated in Figures 15-16 and 15-17. The first, which is very common, illustrates the interface from project phase to project phase. In practice, this situation might not be treated as a formal integration of two subnetworks; instead the subnetworks might be handled separately, but the start date for the second subnetwork would depend on the finish date for the first. Figure 15-17 illustrates a more complex situation. In addition to the phase-to-phase interface, there is an interface to show an activity that bridges major project phases. An instance of this might be the wait time between the order of a piece of equipment (an activity in the first subnetwork) and its installation (an activity in the second).

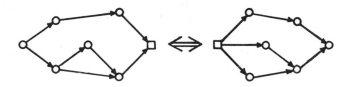

Figure 15-16. Phase-to-phase interface

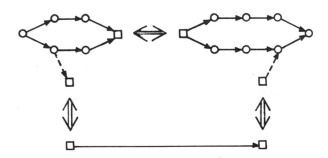

Figure 15-17. Interphase interface

15-12 NETWORK CONDENSATION

The amount of detail in a network for a project is a function of the use to be made of the network. At the project level where it is necessary to schedule in detail and to make individual work assignments, it is useful to work with a network that contains all of the basic activities for the project. This full level of detail, however, is not necessary for the DP Manager, who is interested only in tracking the major events of the project, and even less detail is required by higher-level management. Because of the dynamic nature of most projects, it is simply not feasible to satisfy these different requirements by maintaining separate networks at various levels of detail. But it is feasible to maintain the most detailed network and to derive the more aggregated networks from this by a process called *network condensation.*

Condensation of a detailed network is accomplished through the use of *checkpoint* events. These are events of the detailed network that are identified by management as important reference points for use in monitoring project progress. Examples of such key events are the completion of the design of a specific module, completion of a specific block of code, or completion of a specific unit of documentation. Checkpoint events are frequently identified in a network diagram by some special symbol; a triangle will be used in the examples given below.

Condensed networks are built around checkpoints and events that are initial or terminal—that is, events that do not have predecessors or do not have successors. In what follows, we shall assume that all initial and terminal events have been designated as checkpoints. This will simplify the discussion but will not in any way alter the outcome—it simply allows us to use the phrase "checkpoint events" instead of the more awkward phrase "checkpoint or initial or terminal events" in what follows.

Once checkpoints have been identified, a condensed network can be derived from the detailed network. The events of the condensed network are just the designated checkpoints of the detailed network, and the arrows in the condensed network are the *constraining paths* among the checkpoint events. These constraining paths are obtained in the following way.

For each pair of checkpoints in the detailed network, determine if they are joined by a direct network path, that is, by a path that does not pass through any other checkpoint. If so, the two checkpoints are joined in the condensed network by a constraining path. The *length* of this constraining path is taken to be the length of the longest direct path joining the checkpoints in the detailed network.

It should be noted that the arrow in a condensed network does not represent actual activities. It represents a path, and only certain longest paths are shown.

These concepts can be illustrated by considering the detailed network of Figure 15-18. Six checkpoints have been selected in this network and designated by the numbers 10, 20, . . . , 60. The condensed network based on these is shown in Figure 15-19. The reader should verify the lengths of the constraining paths in this network.

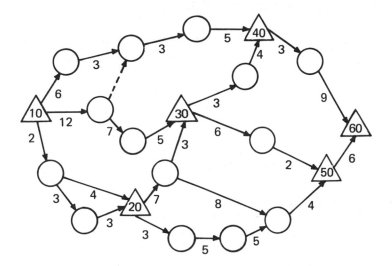

Figure 15-18. Detailed network

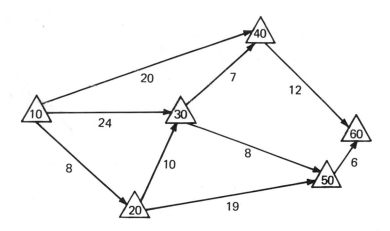

Figure 15-19. Condensed network

The process of consolidation can be applied repeatedly to produce networks that are more and more highly aggregated. Many computer processors have provisions for making consolidated networks; some will consolidate on as many as seven different levels.

15-13 RESOURCE REQUIREMENTS

It is important to observe that in the discussion up to now we have not taken resources into account. The schedule for a network and the total time to complete the project were computed without any mention of the resources required to perform the various tasks. In effect these computations were made as if infinite resources were available to the project. Since few projects operate in such an environment, it is time for us to discuss resource requirements and to see how these impact the above analysis.

The resources of a DP project can be grouped into categories in many ways. One might consider simply the two categories of people and equipment, or one might consider many resource categories, such as project leaders, analysts, designers, programmers, users, computer time, keypunch time, and so on. For each category that is defined, it is necessary to determine the resource requirements. We shall show how this is done for a single category, which will be referred to as people, but you should realize that the calculation illustrated must be made for each category that is used.

Determining Requirements

The first step in determining project resource requirements is to estimate resource requirements for each activity. In practice this is obviously not done independent of the estimate of the duration for the activity—the estimate that an activity takes so many days is based on an assumption about how much resource is assigned to it. Often it is possible to make adjustments and to shorten the duration by assigning more resource to the activity.

It is not enough for the Project Manager to know the resource requirements by activity, it is also necessary to know the total resource required each day on the project. A second step is to calculate this, and the procedure is quite straight-forward: For each day, determine the activities that are scheduled for that day, find the resources that are required for each of these activities, and add up these requirements. This calculation is facilitated by using a Gantt chart for the schedule, as illustrated below.

Let us reconsider the network of Figure 15-11, whose schedule is displayed in the Gantt chart of Figure 15-12. We assume that the actual project schedule is based on early start dates—that is, each activity is scheduled to commence on its early start date. Let us further assume that the number of people assigned to each activity of this network is as shown in Table 15-7.

To determine the number of people required on each day of the proj-

Table 15-7
Resource Requirements for the Network of Figure 15-11

Activity	People
T	3
U	2
V	3
W	2
X	4
Y	3
Z	2

ect, let us redraw the Gantt chart and indicate the scheduled dates for each activity by using the symbol for the number of people assigned to that activity. For example, activity T has three people assigned to it; therefore the bar for that activity is constructed by putting the symbol 3 under each of the two days that the activity is scheduled. Having indicated the schedule for each activity in this manner, the total number of people required on a particular day is easily found by adding the numbers in the column for that day. Results of this and the total people requirements for each day of the project are shown in Figure 15-20.

ACTIVITY	26 Feb ↓ M T W T F S S	5 Mar ↓ M T W T F S S	12 Mar ↓ M T W T F S S	19 Mar ↓ M T W T F S S	26 Mar ↓ M T W T F S S
T	3 3				
U		2 2 2 2 2	2 2 2 2 2	2 2 2 2	
V		3 3 3 3 3	3 3 3 3		
W		2 2 2			
X		3 3	3 3		
Y			4	4 4 4 4 4	4 4
Z					2 2 2
Total people	3 3	7 7 7 8 8	8 8 5 5 6	6 6 6 6 4	4 4 2 2 2

Figure 15-20. Total resource requirements for the network of Figure 15-11

Resource Constraints

To accomplish this project according to the given schedule, it is necessary to have eight people assigned to the project, at least during the period of peak activity. But what if only six are assigned? The usual answer in DP is to work overtime, but what if six people is an absolute maximum including overtime and all other adjustments to the resource availability? Then it is clear that the given schedule cannot be met, and it is necessary to adjust it.

The situation in this example is reasonably typical of what happens on an actual project (or on a phase within a project). As depicted in Figure 15-21, there is a tendency for scheduled resource requirements to start relatively low, build to a peak, and then taper off near the end of a project. For most projects, resource availability is more nearly constant. More often than not the resource requirements exceed the available resources near the middle of the project, as shown by the shaded area in the diagram. This mismatch indicates that the project cannot be accomplished according to the given schedule. One of two things must be done: either more resource must be allocated to the project (particularly during the period of peak demand) or a new schedule must be devised.

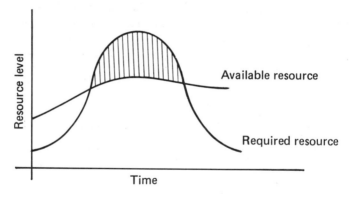

Figure 15-21. Resources for a typical project

Leveling by Adjusting

Slipping Activities. The process of adjusting a schedule to accommodate resource constraints is called *leveling*. There are many ways to level a network; one of these is to *slip* activities. Recall that we usually begin with a schedule based on early start dates; therefore it is not possible to move activities forward and start them earlier. However, it is possible to delay or slip activities. You first try to meet the resource constraints by slipping activities within their slack periods. If this is not possible, the slippage of activities will result in a delay of the project completion date. For instance, you should verify that in the example above the project completion date must be slipped by two days if no more than six people can be employed on any one day.

If it is necessary to slip one or more activities that are scheduled for a particular day, how do you choose which activities to slip? There is no standard answer to this question. What most people do is to use some rule that seems reasonable to them. For example, it is usual to select the activities to be slipped on the basis of slack. First, slip the activity with the greatest slack, then the one with the next greatest slack, and so on until the resource requirements are sufficiently reduced. The rationale for this procedure is that the larger the slack, the less critical the activity and therefore the less likely that the slippage will result in an unnecessary delay of the entire project. This statement is not 100% correct, but empirical evidence shows that it is close enough to the truth to be a useful rule of thumb.

Similar rules for picking the activities to be slipped are based on such criteria as:

ES, EF, LS, or *LF*
Duration
An assigned priority
Responsible department
Subnetwork membership
Random selection

Only the last of these criteria may need some explanation. It may seem a strange rule to say that if too many activities are scheduled for a given day, the activities to be slipped should merely be picked at random. But suppose this rule is followed for the entire project and a feasible schedule—one that meets resource constraints—is found. Then suppose this whole process is repeated and a second feasible schedule is found. And suppose the whole process is repeated several more times until a total of, say, ten feasible schedules are produced. Since all slippages were randomly determined, these ten schedules will generally have different completion dates—some good dates and some bad. At this point, simply select the schedule with the best completion date (shortest project duration) and throw away all other schedules. Chances are quite good that the selected schedule will compare favorably with one found by using some "rational" criteria, such as slack. The technique just described for finding a feasible schedule is essentially a simulation technique, and you may be familiar with it from other areas of computer applications.

Splitting Activities. Another approach to leveling a network is to *split* activities. By this we mean that an activity might be started, put aside for a period of time, and then completed when resources again become available. This approach works with many activities provided the interruption is not too long and alternate work assignments do not confuse people. But care must be taken. Some activities cannot be split; others can be split only at the cost of lengthening the activity duration to account for the time needed to pick up the activity after the interruption.

Network Processors. It is possible to formulate specific rules for applying the two techniques for leveling that we have discussed so far. These rules can be programmed so that the leveling can be done by computer. In fact, something like half of the commercially available network processors have associated programs for leveling networks. These leveling programs are usually relatively complex. If they are marketed separate from the network processor, as many are, it is not uncommon for the leveling program to cost as much as the basic network processor. Among the typical features of these leveling programs are:

> Activities can be classified into those that can be split and those that cannot

> The program user has a choice among several criteria for selecting activities to be slipped

> Many resource categories can be specified

> Resource constraints can be variable or cyclic

> Substitution of resources may be possible; for instance, senior programmers may be assigned in lieu of junior programmers

Leveling by Replanning

So far we have considered "mechanical" techniques for leveling—techniques that can be computerized. Some techniques that require judgment will be considered next. This means that these techniques cannot be computerized, but in most situations they offer a potential for securing much better schedules than can be found by simply slipping or splitting activities.

Replanning the Activities. One way to level a network is to replan the activities. For instance, an activity that was scheduled for five days with three people might be replanned to be done in four days with four people or, alternatively, in eight days with two people. Whether or not such a change is possible depends on the nature of the activity and the people; whether or not it is desirable depends on the total resource supply and demand. In most projects the replanning effort is an attempt to get more people on the activities near the beginning and end of the project and fewer on the activities that bridge the middle.

Replanning the Network. More general than replanning individual activities is the technique of replanning the network. This is an obvious approach to leveling, but one that is often overlooked. Once a network is drawn, it is often treated as if it were cast in concrete. This tendency is particularly noticeable when there is a processor to do the leveling function, because then the network tends to be pushed into the background. But most projects can be accomplished in a wide variety of ways, and the original network for the project is but one of many feasible sequences for the project work.

Sometimes a network schedule can be revised by replacing a series of activities by parallel paths. A network may call for activity G to follow activity E, as shown in Figure 15-22(a), but careful examination may show that this is not necessary. It may be policy or convention that led to the dependency, not actual task requirements. In such cases, the network might be improved by performing the two activities in parallel.

A more likely way to improve a network is to take advantage of *partial dependency.* Close examination of the tasks in Figure 15-22(a) may reveal that G does not depend on all of the work in activity E, but only part of it. It may be possible to subdivide E into activities E_1 and E_2 in such a way that G does not depend on E_2. This division might allow activities E and G of Figure 15-22(a) to be replaced with the configuration of E_1, E_2, and G shown in Figure 15-22(b). This network would allow activity G to commence earlier, and it is one way to take advantage of idle resources near the beginning of a project.

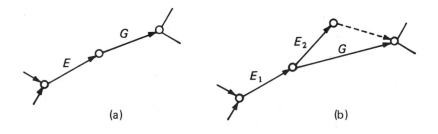

Figure 15-22. Example of partial dependency

15-14 PRECEDENCE DIAGRAMS

We have discussed networks in terms of PERT/CPM notation in which an activity is represented by an arrow. There is another notation, referred to as *precedence* diagrams or *activity-on-node* (AON) diagrams, in which the role of arrows and circles is essentially reversed. This notation will be discussed briefly to provide an introduction to it, but no attempt will be made to treat precedence diagrams in detail. If this is your first acquaintance with network concepts and you think you might be confused by new notation, then we suggest you simply skip the rest of this chapter and read it sometime later when you feel more at home with these concepts.

A precedence diagram is drawn with two constructs: rectangles and arrows. A rectangle is used to represent a task or activity, and an arrow is used to represent a constraint. Thus an arrow drawn from rectangle A to rectangle B means that activity A must be completed before activity B can be started.

Figure 15-23 shows a network in PERT/CPM notation, and Figure 15-24 shows the same network in precedence notation. An understanding of precedence notation can be gained by comparing these two diagrams.

Is it better to draw networks in PERT/CPM notation or in precedence notation? In our opinion it doesn't make much difference. The two notations have slightly different features, but basically they do the same job. Some things you might want to consider in evaluating the two notations are the following:

Familiarity. PERT/CPM notation is the older notation, and generally people are more familiar with it than with precedence notation.

Processors. Because PERT/CPM notation has been around longer, most of the commercially available network processors use it. However, there are a growing number of processors for precedence diagrams, and it is fast approaching the point where this is not a paramount issue.

Dummy Activities. An advantage of precedence diagrams is that there is no need for dummy activities. For instance, the dummy activity of Figure 15-23 does not appear in Figure 15-24.

Checkpoint Events. The selection of checkpoint events is a simple matter on PERT/CPM networks but not on precedence diagrams.

Interfacing Networks. This, also, is difficult to do with precedence networks.

Flexible Activity Relationships. An advantage of precedence diagrams is that they allow more relationships among activities than the simple dependency of PERT/CPM notation. Also, time lags for activities can be introduced more easily.

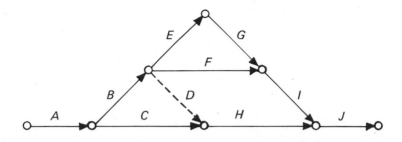

Figure 15-23. Example of a PERT/CPM diagram

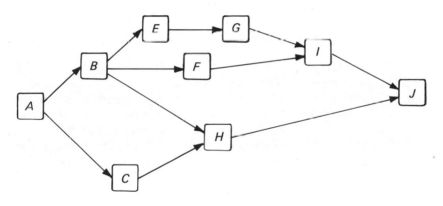

Figure 15-24. The network of Figure 15-23 drawn as a precedence diagram

The last three of these considerations need further discussion. First, the matter of checkpoint events. There is no standard way to show these on a precedence diagram (in fact, it is sometimes said that it cannot be done), but it is possible to invent a suitable notation. For example, let us use a broken rectangle to represent a *dummy* activity—an activity that consumes no resources and takes no time. Then a checkpoint after activity *G* and *F* and before activity *I* in Figure 15-24 can be represented by the dummy activity *D*, as shown in Figure 15-25.

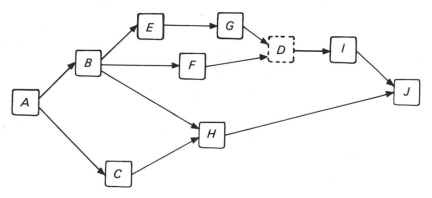

Figure 15-25. Example of a dummy activity

Although there is no standard convention, dummy activities can also be used for interface events. This allows you to interface precedence diagrams in a fairly obvious way. The problem, however, is that currently available processors for precedence diagrams do not have capability for handling this.

The last consideration that needs elaboration is that of the flexible relationships allowed by precedence diagrams. Figure 15-26 illustrates four possible constraints between the activities *S* and *T*. The end-to-start constraint is the standard one that is the basis of PERT/CPM networks. Instead of this, there might be a start-to-start constraint; that is, activity *T* cannot be started until activity *S* is started. The end-to-end and start-to-end constraints are interpreted in a similar manner. For each of these four possible constraints, it is possible to impose a *lag* between the activities. For example, it may be required that activity *T* cannot be started until three days after activity *S* is started; this would be depicted as in Figure 15-27. Processors for precedence diagrams allow all of the four possible relationships between activities and allow time lags on each of them.

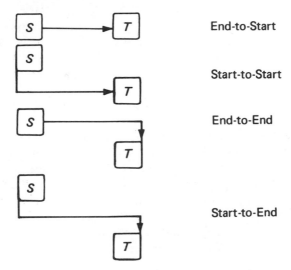

Figure 15-26. Precedence diagram constraints

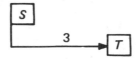

Figure 15-27. Time lag in a start-to-start constraint

In selecting between PERT/CPM and precedence notation, one additional factor should be considered. Recall the procedure used to determine
the work required to build an applications system. We started with a box
labeled "Accomplish Project." Through a series of decompositions, this box
was then replaced by nine boxes representing the nine primary phases of the
project. Then each of these boxes was decomposed into a number of boxes
representing the standard tasks, and so on. At each stage in this procedure,
the work to be done was represented by a box or rectangle. It can be argued
that it makes sense to continue this convention and to draw the network with
work represented by boxes or rectangles rather than switching to arrows.
This is a strong reason for using precedence notation for networks. Our
major reasons for not doing so is that it is less familiar than PERT/CPM
notation and fewer processors are equipped to handle it. In a few years the
situation might be quite different, and at that time we might well be advo-
cates of precedence diagrams.

15-15 FLOWCHARTS FOR CONCURRENT PROCESSES

We conclude this chapter, by shifting to a new topic—a topic that deals with the project *product* rather than the project *process*. We start our topic with some comments about flowcharting computer programs.

Most readers are familiar with the symbols and conventions for typical flowcharts. Not all, however, are familiar with notation used to flowchart concurrent processes, so let us review it.

Two processes are *concurrent* if their operations overlap (or interleave) in time. The term *parallel processes* is also used, and interest in such processes stems from the ability to do multiprocessing or multiprogramming.

Figure 15-28 shows the ANSI-standard flowchart representation of concurrent processes P_1 and P_2. The parallel lines above and below the two process boxes are the *limits of concurrency*. Execution is sequential as the top of the figure is entered, then P_1 and P_2 are executed concurrently. After both concurrent processes are complete, execution continues sequentially again at the bottom.

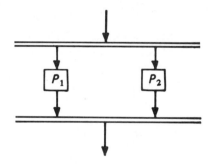

Figure 15–28. ANSI-Standard flowchart notation for concurrent processes

A more elaborate flowchart with many concurrent processes is shown in Figure 15-29. At this point you should stop and take a good look at Figure 15-29; make certain that you understand the multiprocess described by the chart. Once you have done this, rotate Figure 15-29 through 90° and compare it with Figure 15-24. You will observe that, except for obvious differences in the way the lines are drawn, the two figures describe the same collection of modules and the same ordering among them. In effect, the two describe the same parallel process.

The similarity of Figures 15-24 and 15-29 illustrates an important point: A project team can be viewed as a multiprocessor and a network as a flowchart of the concurrent project processes. Another way to state this is that both projects and concurrent processes involve parallel activities, and these activities can be depicted in essentially the same way. There are several

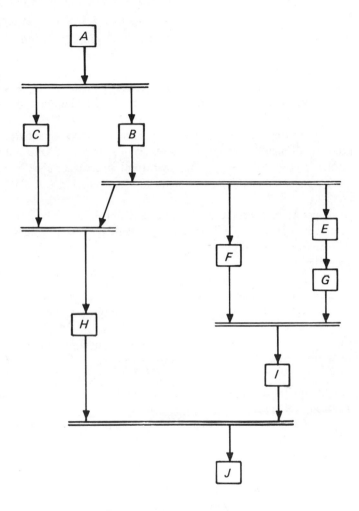

Figure 15-29. A flowchart

interesting consequences that follow from this observation:

> The similarity of projects and concurrent processes has a bearing on the question of whether to use PERT/CPM or precedence notation for project networks.

> The task of training people to use networks might be made easier if networks can be related to familiar flowcharting techniques.

> For both projects and concurrent processes, parallel activities may interact through use of shared resources or shared data. Procedures for resolving potential conflicts in concurrent processes might be used to resolve potential conflicts in projects and vice versa.

> Attempts to remove the restriction that networks cannot have loops have not met with great popularity. Perhaps better techniques will evolve from a study of the way loops are handled in concurrent processes.

> Problems of timing concurrent processes are similar to those of scheduling networks. This means that the scheduling algorithm for networks and, perhaps, scheduling processors might be used to advantage in planning concurrent processes. Critical path concepts might be used to guide the optimization of concurrent processes.

> Insight might be gained through a comparison of techniques for synthesizing networks and techniques for producing flowcharts. For example, the flowchart of Figure 15-29 would not arise through stepwise refinement, yet it seems a reasonable flowchart when viewed as the analogue of a project.

> Questions of "proofing" flowcharts and networks are similar and might be answered in a common way.

These observations point out some interesting areas for future development. More important for our purposes, they show that the view of a project team as a multiprocessor is both interesting and useful.

15-16 SUMMARY

- Networks are useful for planning, scheduling, and controlling project work and for communicating related management information to others. Networks can be used to simulate alternative plans and thereby help to promote the effective use of resources.

- Networks are simple, being built from a few basic constructs and rules. The fundamental purpose of networks is to display dependencies among activities; that is, to show the order in which activities must be done.
- A schedule can be obtained for a network by applying a simple algorithm. One result of this schedule is to identify critical activities —those activities whose delay will impact the project.
- There are a number of commercially available computer processors for doing network calculations.
- Techniques are available for combining related networks or for building condensed networks. These techniques are useful if several groups are doing project work or if networks are required for several management levels.
- Basic network scheduling does not consider resource requirements. To obtain useful schedules it is necessary to determine resource requirements and to adjust plans for resource constraints.
- Networks can be constructed by using PERT/CPM notation or precedence notation. There are pros and cons for each, which a prospective user should analyze.
- There are some interesting parallels between networks for projects and flowcharts for concurrent processes. These stem from the fact that a project team can be viewed as a multiprocessor.

NETWORKS–PRACTICE

16-1 INTRODUCTION

The network concept is a tool that can be used in managing a project. Like any tool, it must be used properly and only where applicable. Attempts at using networks several years ago could, unfortunately, often be likened to using a sledgehammer to drive in a tack. Worse yet, some attempts were more like driving in a tack with a hoe. Today the situation is vastly different because there has evolved a reasonably good understanding about how networks should and should not be employed. In this chapter some of these practical aspects of networking will be discussed.

16-2 USE OF NETWORKS

A planner should have considerable latitude in his use of networks if this tool is to be practical. All of the steps discussed in Chapter 15 need not be followed in every situation, and they should not be required by the project methodology. Rather, the methodology should encourage the planner to use networking in a manner that is acceptable to him and suitable for his project.

Some people believe that the effective way to use network concepts is simply to list the tasks and construct a network but not to follow through with formal scheduling and leveling. These people believe that the construction of a network forces them to think through just what work is required, and they find this discipline useful. However, they prefer not to become involved with the more formal aspects of planning when the work should be done.

Other people believe that a network should be constructed for a project

373

and that an original project schedule should be calculated. However, once the project is under way they prefer to do replanning and rescheduling by less formal procedures. These people like having an original schedule to work with, but they find they can adjust to a changing scene more easily without being encumbered by networks.

Some people use networks throughout the project. They draw up an original project schedule with the aid of network techniques. As tasks are completed, estimated completion dates are replaced by actual dates and the network is rescheduled. If problems arise at any point, the network might be used to simulate various possible solutions to find one that is most acceptable. These people believe that the full use of networks is the most effective way for them to do all of the planning and replanning required on a project.

Just how a planner chooses to use networks might vary with the stage of a project. For Phase 1.1 where there is little time and little parallel activity, he might apply the tool sparingly. But for Phase 2.2 where there are many people involved and considerable parallel activity, he might use a processor and make formal network calculations on a weekly basis.

There is no such thing as *the* right way to use networks—any way is right if it helps the planner to do his job.

16-3 PEOPLE AND PLANNING

A cardinal rule for the successful application of network planning is that it must involve the people who will be responsible for doing the project work. This is particularly true when detailed plans are being laid at the individual assignment level. The value of transactional estimating in obtaining meaningful task durations has already been discussed. However, it is equally important that those responsible for the work have a hand in preparing the list of tasks to be accomplished, the deliverables from the tasks, precedence constraints, checkpoint review points, and so on. Their insight can often prevent the omission of tasks or the construction of an impractical sequence of work.

It is equally important that management, too, be involved in network construction. If they fail to participate in the planning effort, they risk losing control of the project right from the start. Management involvement is also necessary to lend support to the concept of planning a project as opposed to the traditional laissez-faire approach. Project workers cannot be blamed for cutting corners on planning and control activities and for jumping right into coding if they perceive that management is not interested enough in the process to be involved.

The actual construction, scheduling, and revision of networks involve a fair amount of detailed work and, particularly if a processor is used, a certain amount of technical knowledge. This work is usually done by an individual who belongs to the project team, but it can be successfully accomplished in other ways. The important thing is to establish a routine that is compatible with the shop environment.

One large installation constructs and maintains networks on each project. There is one person in the installation who is an expert on networks and on the processor that is used to make all network calculations. His job is to act as a consultant to each project team. He gives advice and technical help in the construction and maintenance of their networks. Each week he collects revisions in plans and data on actual task completions, and runs this on the processor, and delivers the output to the teams. His job also entails the collection of historical records to aid in future network construction.

16-4 NETWORK COMPLEXITY

In one organization it was decided that all projects would be controlled by using networks. A standard was established to require that an early task on any project was the construction of a complete network for the entire job. This was to be done before any design or coding started; all subsequent work activity was to be guided by the network. As changes were required, the network was to be modified so that it would reflect the project accurately at all times.

This was the theory. In practice a detailed network was constructed at the beginning of each project and was used fairly successfully for a few weeks. But as a clearer idea of the system emerged, the number of changes in the network grew so rapidly that it was impossible for the network team to keep current. By midproject the network bore little resemblance to actual project developments—so great were the differences between project work and network description that it was difficult for an outsider to realize that the two were involved with the same system. Nevertheless, efforts to maintain the network were expanded right to the end of the project because the standard required a network!

Although extreme, the situation just described is not uncommon. People frequently attempt to construct one giant, detailed network to reflect all work activity. When change occurs, as it inevitably does, such networks are difficult and expensive to modify. Their cost soon far outweighs their benefits. For this reason, it is not uncommon to find that networks are used at the beginning of projects but are abandoned at the design and coding stages—just the place where they can be of most use because that is where the greatest amount of parallel activity takes place.

The proper approach to using networks involves the same basic tool that is behind all successful efforts at control: work breakdown. The complex should be subdivided into a number of smaller, more manageable pieces. Instead of building one large network, several smaller subnetworks should be built. Each phase should be described by a subnetwork, and on a large project consideration should be given to subdividing some phases along major functional lines. For instance, in Phase 2.2 one subnetwork might be constructed for the coding function, one for building user procedures, one for building the test system, and so on. These separate subnetworks must be integrated to provide a total phase network, but this is usually much easier to do than is the job of creating one large network of all activities. Moreover, if subnetworks are built along lines of responsibility, this has the effect of subdividing the phase into separate but interrelated subphases. This gives each responsible person his own subnetwork for use in planning and controlling his portion of the phase.

A critical factor in the effective use of networks is the choice of the level of aggregation, the level of detail in the network. Many people make the mistake of trying to build detailed networks long before the information is available to do so. Invariably this makes the system a millstone around the neck of the planner rather than a tool to help him with his job. There is no way, for example, that a detailed network can be built for Phase 2.2 (Build Product) back in Phase 1.2 (Specify Requirements) when the problem is first being formulated clearly. The proper way to build networks is by *successive refinement*. By this term we mean that a network is first built at a highly aggregated level, then it is replaced by a succession of networks each containing more detail than the one it replaces. For example, the way to plan for Phase 2.2 is to build an extremely simple network in Phase 1.2—perhaps a network with only one arrow to represent the entire phase. Then in Phase 1.3 when the problem is understood and the solution is being evolved, this aggregated network can be replaced with one having more detail—perhaps a dozen or two activities. But it is not until Phase 2.1 when the design is constructed that you really know what specific activities will be required in Phase 2.2. Thus it is not until the phase Design Product that you can build a detailed network of the kind that can be used for planning and controlling the phase Build Product of a project.

Some networks are used for preliminary design and planning of a project, others for implementation and actual assignment of work. A *design* network need not have the full detail of an *implementation* network. One of the biggest problems in planning a project is that of missing a major function —ordering of equipment or forms, site preparation, training of users, and so on. Quite often a missing function can be spotted more easily in a highly aggregated design network than it can be in a detailed implementation one. This is another reason for beginning a network at an aggregated level and adding more detail gradually.

In fleshing out a network, some people prefer to detail the critical paths more carefully than the noncritical ones. This follows the reasonable maxim that planning and control efforts should be concentrated on the most likely source of trouble.

Since highly aggregated networks are all that is required in the early phases of a project, it might be a good idea to make such networks a part of the Project Handbook. With minor modifications, these can then be used on most projects, and a good deal of planning effort can be saved.

16-5 NETWORK ACTIVITIES

Many comments about activities of a project have already been made in our discussion of standard tasks and work units. Those comments will not be repeated here, but you may wish to look back at Chapters 3, 4, 5, and 12 for a discussion of the definition, derivation, and characteristics of activities.

A common problem in working with networks is the omission of necessary tasks. Basic work is included, but it is not unusual to omit peripheral activities such as typing, reproduction, ordering of forms, and the approval of output. This problem can be lessened by constructing a list of standard tasks to be used in network planning. It can also be lessened by using peer reviews to examine all networks before putting them to use.

The bulk of the activities on a project are scheduled activities. These are to be performed at some specific point in the project. It is these activities that are represented in a network and on a project schedule. On a project, most of the discussion about project planning and control has to do with scheduled activities.

But some project activities are not scheduled. A prime example of this is much of the work that is done by the Project Manager. Take one specific task—the task of communicating with everyone to keep all project participants informed of project progress. This activity is important and can consume over half of the Project Manager's time. But it is not an activity that is scheduled to be performed at a specific point in the project. It cannot be planned by the device of a schedule, and it cannot be controlled on the basis of completed work. Yet it is a bona fide project activity that consumes important chunks of project resource. This means that it must be planned and controlled in some way, but how?

First, let us be clear what should *not* be done. Nonscheduled activities should not be represented on a network depicting project work. Sometimes an attempt is made to do this, and a nonscheduled activity is shown as an "umbrella" activity that spans the project from start to finish. The intent is to suggest that the activity parallels all others. But a network does not depict what goes on in parallel. It can only show what can *not* go on in parallel, that is, what must be done before something else can be accomplished. According to network rules, the "umbrella" activity can be done anytime— before, during, or after all the other activities. Clearly this does not represent reality, so nonscheduled activities should be left off the network.

By the same token, nonscheduled activities really have no place on a schedule except as a reminder that they are activities that will consume resource. An activity that is depicted on a project schedule is to be performed during a certain period of time. It has a definite start and a definite finish date. Although nonscheduled activities have a start date, most do not have a finish date except that they are done when the project is done.

The simplest way to handle nonscheduled activities is to isolate them and treat them separately from the scheduled activities. Resource (mainly people) can be dedicated to those activities, and this resource can be monitored separate from other project resource. By their nature, the resource required for nonscheduled activities tends to be relatively constant from week to week. Thus, a plan for nonscheduled activities amounts to a projection of the resource required to accomplish the activities, and control amounts to determining what was actually expended and checking that the required work was done.

16-6 DURATION ESTIMATES

Faulty time estimates are a major source of trouble in using networks effectively. Most of the trouble in this area stems from the failure to involve the people responsible for the work in the estimating process. Since this topic was discussed fully in Chapter 13, here we only reemphasize its importance.

A second source of estimating error is the failure to reconcile project times obtained from the scheduling algorithm with standard times derived from historical records. By this we mean the following. When the duration for a project phase, say Phase 2.2, is estimated near the beginning of a project, it is usually obtained from historical records. That is, the duration of the phase is taken to be the average Phase 2.2 duration for all past projects of a comparable size. This can be referred to as an *aggregated* or gross estimate for the phase duration. Later in the project, the duration for Phase 2.2 is obtained by estimating the duration of each activity and applying the scheduling algorithm. This might be called a *detailed* estimate of the phase duration. Of course, these two estimates are not expected to be exactly the same. However, if they are not roughly equal, the discrepancy must be explained.

Clearly there are many reasons why the aggregated and detailed estimates might differ. Perhaps this project has special aspects that make the aggregated estimate inapplicable—significant changes in personnel, implementation methodology, the amount of input and output formatting, the requirements for security, and so on. Perhaps the size of the detailed estimate points to potential problems—significant tasks have been overlooked, a poor network with insufficient parallel activity, individual task estimates significantly different from past experience, and so on. There is no simple answer as to why the two estimates differ, but a difference does signal a need for further investigation, a point that is sometimes overlooked.

A third source of error is to underestimate the time required for signoffs and approvals. This is a relatively simple activity, but it is one that is usually in competition for a very scarce resource: management's time. The time required for approvals can be shortened by careful planning and by giving management ample warning of the demands to be placed on them. But no matter how much planning is done, approvals usually take longer than expected.

There is another problem to look out for if a project is developed by the phased approach. The authorization of individual phases by the Project Selection Committee is an activity that takes place *between* phases. The activity, therefore, is not really part of the phase just completed nor the phase to be started. The time for this activity might be overlooked because it is not part of a phase duration. But this approval time is significant, and to overlook it is to underestimate project duration.

16-7 BUILDING THE NETWORK

Once the tasks have been defined, the network itself can be constructed in several different ways. Each of these ways is a trial and error procedure for synthesizing the separate tasks into a logical pattern that will yield meaningful work assignments and will accomplish the primary function of the project.

One method of constructing a network is to start by building a *precedence list,* which is a list of all network tasks in one column with matching predecessor tasks in another. The precedence list is usually obtained by asking of each item, in turn, what tasks must precede it in the network—that is, what tasks must be completed before the item in question can be started. The resulting list must be culled of items that are not immediate predecessors. For example, if T is a task, it might first be ascertained that items A, C, M, and Q are predecessors. But if C and A are also predecessors of M, they can be culled from the list of predecessors of T. Once the precedence list is obtained, a network can be constructed. The most natural way to do this is to start with all items that have no predecessors, then to adjoin items having only the first group as predecessors, and so on.

A second method of constructing a network is to omit a precedence list and to turn directly to a graphic representation. Some proceed in a *forward* direction: They begin by drawing a network with those items that can be accomplished at once, then they adjoin all items that can be undertaken after the first are completed, and so on. Some people believe it is more natural to construct a network in a *backward* direction. Here the questions are: What is the last thing that must be done to produce all deliverables? What comes just before the last? And so on.

One thing should be clear. A network is constructed in stages with much correction and change. For that reason, always use a large sheet of paper and a pencil with a good eraser. A chalkboard is even better.

If you draw a network for a collection of activities, don't be surprised to find that some lines cross. If this happens, you may be able to simplify the drawings by juggling the placement of items, but there is no guarantee of this. For some projects it is not possible to draw a network without crossing lines.

A shortcut to the construction of networks is to have standard networks for various phases.

Not long ago, the authors were approached by an individual who said, "My organization has adopted a formal project methodology. We use phased implementation, have formal output for each phase, phase reviews, the whole bit. We've even adopted standard networks for each phase, but we have a problem because some projects don't fit. How do we make all projects fit the standard network?"

The answer to the question of fitting all projects to a standard network is simple—you can't, and you shouldn't attempt it. Although it is helpful to have standard networks for each phase, it is folly to regard these as anything more than aids in developing a network for the specific project in hand. Even though there are basic similarities in projects, no two are exactly alike, and it is important to have enough leeway to adjust to individual differences. A project methodology must strike a balance between providing too much structure and providing too little. What is right for one organization may not be right for another, and what is right may change over time. But in any event, the methodology must be viewed as a framework, not a straightjacket.

Another way to obtain a network for a project is to modify the network from a similar project.

> One custom contract DP organization has required networks on each project for a number of years. They now have an extensive file on project histories. When a new project is undertaken, it is generally possible to construct a network for it by making minor modifications in the network of some similar previous project.

This story illustrates one of the major advantages of a standard approach to projects: It saves reinventing the entire wheel each time.

16-8 SCHEDULING

The actual scheduling of a network is a mechanical task, and it gives rise to no particular problems. We have just discussed the need to reconcile the computed network duration with historical figures; one additional point should be noted.

It is important to remember that the early finish date computed by using the scheduling algorithm is obtained under the assumption that *infinite resources are available.* That is, the standard scheduling procedure does *not* take resource constraints into account in any way, and the computed early finish date does *not* reflect the limited number of people and machine time available to the project. In practice this means that the computed early finish date can only be obtained by leveling the network to resource availability. This almost always results in stretching the original schedule. But the original schedule was only a mathematical abstraction; the leveled schedule is feasible and is one that the team can expect to meet.

More than one project manager has gotten burned by letting people see the early finish date for a project as computed by the scheduling algorithm. The burn hazard is especially great if a processor is used so that the early finish date is produced by the computer and is emblazoned neatly on a computer printout. Even when the early finish date is accompanied by a warning that it is, of course, based on an assumption of unlimited resources, somehow the caveat is forgotten over time and only the date comes back to haunt. So an absolutely basic rule is: Never discuss the project early finish date until the network has been leveled to meet resource constraints.

Incorrect attention to critical paths can also lead to problems, as the following story illustrates:

One project manager decided to use a network approach to planning, something he had never done before. After performing his calculations, he was horrified to discover that his most junior team member was assigned work that was sitting right on the critical path. Undaunted, the project leader decided to proceed, but vowed to watch the junior member like a hawk. And he did. He practically lived with the man. But his efforts were rewarded when the junior member's work came in right on schedule. Unfortunately, however, while spending all his time with the junior member, the project leader failed to notice that other parts of the project were lagging badly. The effect of this was that the project slipped its deadline by 30%.

The moral of this story is clear: Critical paths on a project are very likely to shift as work progresses. You cannot just "plan the work and work the plan," as some sources suggest. At times it is necessary to revise the plan to reflect a changed situation. It is a good idea to replan on a regular basis, say, weekly. In replanning, estimated task start and completion dates can be replaced by actual dates as they become available. Changes in durations and in the network itself can be substituted as the need is recognized. Revised schedules and revised estimates of slack will give the project team an up-to-date picture of project progress. The effort involved in reviewing plans on a periodic basis might be such that you might consider a processor for doing the calculations.

16-9 LEVELING

Leveling a network is another mechanical task. It is not a source of problems except that it involves a fair amount of work, particularly if several resource categories are used. A processor can assist with this work, but in a small shop, say one with fewer than 20 applications people, it might be difficult to cost-justify such a package. In this event resource constraints could be handled by some alternative method.

In one organization, resource constraints and task assignments are taken into account right at the beginning when a network is first constructed. To make this possible, the organization requires that a task be a job for one person. For control purposes, it further requires that the task be something that can be accomplished in from three to five days.

In constructing a network, the usual precedence constraints are observed, but care is also taken to see that each person is given job assignments that provide him with a clear pattern of work from project start to project completion. Network construction is aided by the convention that all tasks assigned to a given individual are shown on the same level of the network diagram. As an example, Figure 16-1 depicts a network with job assignments for three workers. Worker 1 is assigned tasks 1, 4, 7, and 10, which are shown on his level. The assignments for Workers 2 and 3 are shown similarly. Note that the question of resource constraints (as well as job assignments) is answered automatically.

16-10 SOME FINAL COMMENTS

It should be clear by now that the network concept is an important tool for project planning. But it is not a universal tool for all problems, and we might look at some of the restrictions faced in using it.

The concept of networking rests on the assumption that project tasks can be known in advance. This, of course, is not always the case. At the beginning, it may not be known if the project will involve building a system or buying and modifying one, and the tasks of the project will depend heavily on this determination. Within the testing phase it may be necessary to revise a certain module and its documentation, but this cannot be known until the tests are conducted and bugs discovered. Networks do not conveniently allow for tasks that depend in some way on the outcome of previous project tasks. There are several ways to compensate for this, but no way is entirely satisfactory.

If the contingency is a major one, such as the tasks resting on the make or buy decision, the best way to handle it is to withhold any detailed planning until the decision is made. Work cannot be planned until the objectives and deliverables are known. Of course, if time is a paramount consideration, it would be possible to build *two* sets of plans, one for build and a second for buy. But in most instances this could not be cost-justified, and it is best to await the decision.

Minor contingencies can be taken into account in various ways. First of all, standard estimates derived from past projects automatically include the normal contingencies that arise on any project because they arose in the past, so time for these contingencies should already be in the schedule. If unusual problems are expected, the prudent plan might include extra tasks for these— if they do not materialize, so much the better. Finally, most project leaders try to schedule work so the project contains some slack. They know that

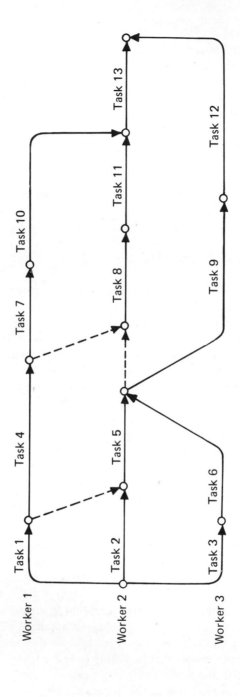

Figure 16-1. A network showing work assignments

Murphy's Law (If anything can go wrong, it will.) applies to projects, and they simply plan with this in mind.

A second assumption for effective use of networks is that each task has a clearly defined beginning and end. Admittedly this is not always the case. "Complete the first draft of a manuscript" certainly means different things to different people. It takes effort and experience to specify deliverables clearly, and the ideal is never realized. But at least the use of networks moves a group in the proper direction.

A more troublesome problem is the fact that tasks sometimes depend on one another in a complex way. Take coding and documentation. It may be possible to begin documentation sometime after coding has started, but the coding itself may be simplified if some of the documentation precedes it. In a similar way, specification of system requirements and interviewing of users are to some extent interdependent.

Interdependence of tasks can sometimes be handled by careful redefinition of the tasks. For example, since coding and documentation of modules are interdependent, it makes sense not to describe them as separate tasks, but to subdivide the project work according to program modules. In other cases it might be best simply to group tasks together; test a module and revise it might fall into this category. And sometimes you simply must live with the fact that the network doesn't describe the project as well as you might like.

Remember, a network of a project is a model of the project. As with any model, it is an idealized and simplified description of the real thing. The model does not contain all the complexity of the project—and therein lies its value. If the network were as complex as the project itself, it would be as hard to comprehend and probably just as expensive as the project. But because it is an abstraction and is concentrated on key elements, the network helps us to organize our thought and find our way through a project.

16-11 SUMMARY

- There is no such thing as *the* right way to use networks—any way is right if it helps the planner do his job.
- Successful application of network techniques requires that people who will do the work be involved in planning.
- For an effective use of networks, an overall network should be broken down into a collection of smaller subnetworks. Also, networks should first be built at a highly aggregated level and then successively refined until the desired level of detail is achieved.
- Planning and control of nonscheduled activities should be handled

separately from scheduled ones. Nonscheduled activities should not be included in a network.

- Estimates of activity durations can be improved by involving people responsible for work and by reconciling estimates from separate sources. Even so, care must be exercised to avoid underestimating time for sign-offs and approvals.
- A network can be constructed from a precedence list or by direct construction in a forward or backward direction.
- The network scheduling algorithm does not take resources into account. Therefore you should never use a scheduled project completion date until the network has been leveled to meet resource constraints.
- A network is a model of a project; it is an abstraction that concentrates on key elements.

17

PEER REVIEWS

17-1 INTRODUCTION

In common with other areas that employ knowledge workers, data processing has for years lacked a satisfactory method for checking the quality and accuracy of project work. Traditionally three basic tools have been used: self-review of work by individual workers, review by management, and testing of the product under lifelike conditions. None of these techniques has been very satisfactory. Individual workers have generally been too close to the work to see its flaws, and they have been reluctant to conform to the demands made upon them by rigorous self-appraisal. Management generally had time for only a cursory review of most project work, particularly when there were no standards to help make the work reasonably comprehensible to them. Testing serves only to verify the presence of an error, never its absence. Thus testing at best has been a means of showing that the number of errors shipped was not excessive.

Most would agree that the person best suited to review the work of a knowledge worker is a fellow knowledge worker—it takes one to know one. But to make review by one's peer workable, it is necessary to establish an environment in which natural fears and concerns on the part of the person whose work is being reviewed are replaced by the conviction he will benefit from the comments of his peers. Such an environment can be created by following a procedure known as the peer review.

A *peer review* is a structured review of project work conducted in a penalty-free environment by peers of the developer (reviewee). The purpose of a peer review is to detect errors in the product being reviewed. A peer review is the fundamental tool for checking the quality of project work, and its use results in a significantly better product.

Under the name "walk throughs," peer reviews were first introduced as a technique for examining the work produced during design and coding. However, reviews can and should be conducted on all output produced on a project, including project plans, specifications, architecture, design, code, test plans and results, and documentation.

17-2 CHARACTERISTICS OF PEER REVIEWS

Among the characteristics of peer reviews are:

Peer Reviews Are Formal. Material to be reviewed is documented, as are the issues raised during reviews and the final disposition of these issues. This formality forces all participants to take a definite position on the work being considered.

Peer Reviews Are Structured. They are scheduled in advance and are conducted according to a set pattern. All participants know their roles and the goals of the review.

Peer Reviews Are the Tool of the Reviewee. They are arranged and scheduled by the reviewee for the purpose of helping him produce error-free work.

All Work Is Reviewed. If peer reviews are used at all, then they must be used on the work of everyone from the most junior to the most senior member of the team. Thus, peer reviews are not a remedial tool for the inexperienced and underqualified but are a good work practice.

Peer Reviews Are Not Optional. They are part of the work effort, not an added feature. Peer reviews are a standard checkpoint on any job and are routinely used as part of the regular work effort.

Peer Reviews Concern Correctness, Not Style. It is not the function of the review to comment on the reviewee's manner of accomplishing the function as long as the result is correct. However, the review does concern compliance with standards and the clarity of the finished product.

Emphasis During Reviews Is on Error Detection. Reviews are used as a means of spotting problems but are not used to solve problems. This is the job of the developer, and the peer review does not relieve him of this responsibility.

Peer Reviews Are Psychologically Open. The atmosphere of a review must promote a nondefensive attitude on the part of all attendees. The intent is to encourage egoless work and an atmosphere where the reviewee is attempting to further the goal of the project team rather than to defend his own product.

Peer Reviews Are Not *a Tool for Employee Evaluation.* To promote an open atmosphere, management should not attend reviews and should not use the results of reviews to rate the reviewee. This is the most important rule about peer reviews. Failure to observe it inevitably turns the reviews from a useful tool for error detection into a useless, but costly, drag on the project.

17-3 THE REVIEW PROCEDURE

A peer review is always scheduled in advance, and it is slated to last from one to two hours. A much longer period than this is usually nonproductive because it is difficult to concentrate on detailed material beyond that limit. If additional time is required, subsequent reviews should be scheduled, or the work unit being reviewed should be subdivided. During periods of peak review activity, it is a good idea to post schedules of reviews in a central location to avoid the problem of scheduling a person for two reviews that are to meet at the same time.

The review is arranged and scheduled by the reviewee. This includes setting the time and place for the meeting, selecting and notifying attendees, booking the meeting room, and arranging for necessary supplies and equipment, such as a projector, easels, chalkboard, and pads (see Figure 17-1).

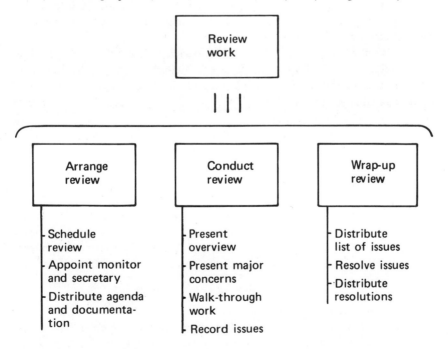

Figure 17-1. Tasks for a peer review

Including the reviewee, about three to six people are invited to attend a peer review, and attendance is by invitation only. The composition of the group might be specified by the organization's policies. For example, it might be specified that a review of coding requires the attendance of the reviewee, another programmer, a systems tester, and an outside expert who is familiar with the general type of work. It might also be specified that a trainee programmer be included as part of a training effort. Reviewers might be peers from areas other than that of the reviewee. For instance, work produced by someone from DP might be reviewed by users, auditors, data base administrators, Systems Assurance, Operations, or others as appropriate. Often it is a good idea to involve people who will be recipients of the output of work being reviewed, as this will give them a chance to study and correct what will eventually become their input.

As stated earlier, it is essential that management not be present at the review. This point will be discussed in Section 17-6.

A review should not be conducted by the reviewee, because he is too deeply involved with the subject of the meeting. Instead, the reviewee should appoint one of the group to moderate or chair the meeting. The reviewee also appoints one member of the group to be secretary for the review. For a small review, the secretary can be the same person as the moderator. The moderator and secretary should both be appointed far enough in advance of the meeting to have time to become completely familiar with their duties. These duties are described below.

It is up to the reviewee to distribute to each reviewer the agenda for the review and a copy of all work that is to be reviewed. This material should be distributed a minimum of two days prior to the meeting. Reviewers must become familiar with the material prior to the review; otherwise, the review is largely a wasted effort.

The mechanics of the review itself are generally as follows:

The moderator conducts the meeting and is responsible for keeping the discussion to the agenda and within the allotted time.

The reviewee begins the review with a brief overview of the work to be reviewed. This includes an explanation of the function to be accomplished, the inputs to the function, and the required outputs. It might also include an overview of the way in which the function is accomplished.

Reviewers are then called on, in turn, to express any major concerns with the work. This would include general comments on the accuracy, completeness, and quality of the product. At this point, minor problems are usually not discussed—they are brought up during the next step.

The reviewee then "walks through" the work step by step showing in detail how inputs are converted into outputs. As each component of the work is discussed, any reviewer with comments or queries raises them and briefly states his concern.

The secretary for the review records all issues and problems as they arise. These would cover errors, inconsistencies, discrepancies, ambiguities, incomplete or missing function, incorrect interface, and so on. Issues and problems are merely spotted and recorded during the review, and no attempt is made to correct them. It is up to the moderator to see that this rule is followed, and to focus the discussion on correctness rather than style.

After the review is over, it is up to the secretary to distribute to all attendees a list of all issues and problems raised at the review. The reviewee is responsible for correcting errors and resolving all problems and issues. After having done so, the reviewee notifies all attendees of corrections and modifications. If these are minor in nature, no further action is required. However, if changes are extensive a follow-up review is scheduled. The format for the follow-up review is the same as for the original review.

17-4 ADVANTAGES OF PEER REVIEWS

Experience using peer reviews confirms that people tend to do careful work if they realize it is to be reviewed by their peers. This means that peer reviews encourage work that is clear and precise—simple logic, understandable code, and material that can easily be read by others.

One function of a review is to check that there has been adherence to standards. Thus, if proper standards have been established for design, coding, and documentation, peer reviews will help to produce deliverables that are uniform. This, in turn, will be of great benefit when the product ultimately requires maintenance changes.

A closely related benefit is the significant improvement in quality that results from using peer reviews. Peer reviews of such matters as standards, estimating techniques, project plans, and control procedures result in improvements in the methodology used to accomplish the project. Peer reviews of the primary project output, such as design and coding, result in a lower number of errors in the finished product. In fact, peer reviews are so important that it is fair to state that they are the primary tool available today for assuring quality.

Not only do peer reviews help to catch errors, but their use on all project work helps to catch errors at the earliest possible time when the cost of correction is smallest and the impact on the project the least. An error detected during design is much easier to correct than the same error detected during coding, and it is 10 or 20 times easier to correct than would be the case if it were not detected until systems test.

Peer reviews are one means of promoting communication among all groups involved with the project, and they have proved to be particularly effective in keeping users abreast of project developments. Because reviewers must become familiar with the work they are to review, people tend to be aware of more of the project than just their small part. This acts as a positive motivator and often results in useful suggestions for improving the product.

All participants in a review gain skill and knowledge from examining the work of others. For this reason, peer reviews are sometimes used as a vehicle for training junior personnel. The opportunity to review the work of experienced developers should be contrasted with the usual entry-level training for programmers, which is the task of maintaining poorly written, poorly documented code. Certainly the former is the better guide as to how a job should be done.

Peer review can generate other benefits for the project. For instance, the involvement of testers in early peer reviews tends to result in better test designs. Also, in some instances the actual test data has been generated as a by-product of peer reviews. Another benefit is that peer reviews make for less dependence on machine testing, and this in turn allows a more flexible project schedule.

Finally, it should be pointed out that peer reviews fit well with other productivity techniques, such as top-down development and structured programming. All of these promote the clarity and accuracy of the finished product and concentrate on doing the job right rather than doing it over.

17-5 INTERNAL AUDIT CONSIDERATIONS

Peer reviews have an important bearing on one of the major concerns of internal auditors. To explain, let us review the traditional manner in which computer applications have been developed.

For years it was not at all unusual for a program or major module of a system to be assigned to a single individual for development. This individual was responsible for detailed design, coding, unit testing, and documentation of the module. Not uncommonly, the length and complexity of the code, to say nothing of the possessiveness of the developer, inhibited others from checking into the details of the program. Most installations today are running applications containing major segments of code that have been developed and reviewed by only the developer—and some of these programs involve sensitive areas such as payroll, accounts receivable, accounts payable, inventory, or employee benefits.

Internal auditors dread the thought that a program known to only one individual might contain "private code." An example would be code that directs all rounding values on payroll to the developer's own paycheck; or code that allows a fictitious order to be entered for shipment with no corresponding record to accounts payable; or code that tests to see if the developer's name is still on the payroll and, if not, directs the program to destroy a small, randomly selected portion of the data base.

Naturally, internal auditors are extremely interested in any procedure that can prevent such "private code" from entering the system. Their best defense would seem to be a requirement that every piece of design and all code that enters the system be reviewed in detail by someone other than the developer. Peer reviews obviously satisfy part of this requirement they ensure that approved modules can contain unauthorized code only through the collusion of several people. To ensure that the reviewed code is the code that actually enters the system, it is necessary to establish an additional control, possibly through some type of program librarian, but this is easily arranged.

Before leaving this topic, it should be pointed out that although the possibility of "private code" causes internal auditors to shudder, they also know it to be the sensational problem, not the typical one. Day in and day out, organizations lose much more through program error than they do through intentional fraud. Thus, internal auditors know that from their point of view the major benefit of peer reviews lies in the elimination of error. But they are also comforted by knowing that these reviews help to prevent the big surprises, too.

17-6 MANAGEMENT CONSIDERATIONS

Experience shows that problems arise if a management review is super-imposed on a peer review. This might happen either by direct management participation in the review or by insistence that the reports from the review be available to management. Either way, it changes the character of the peer review from one in which there is frank exchange of ideas to one of cautious expression or, worse yet, conscious backbiting. If the atmosphere becomes psychologically closed, peer reviews will probably not be neutral, but will have a decidedly negative effect on the project.

The number of problems and issues raised in a peer review is one of those statistics that must be viewed with some caution. In one installation, a group experimented with peer reviews of code. They held a series of seven reviews, each with an average of four participants and lasting an average of two hours. On learning that these 56 man-hours of effort had not uncovered a single bug, management decided that the peer reviews were definitely not cost effective! It was only when they were persuaded to compare the completed system with the typical product produced in their shop that they came to realize that the reviews had been eminently worthwhile as judged by the numbers of errors in the finished product.

If peer reviews are not to be used for appraising the developer, just how and when does management accomplish this? The proper way, most believe, is to hold him responsible for the final product after all checking and all peer reviews have been completed. When the developer completes the work activity, turns over the output, and certifies that it is complete and correct, then it is fair game to make a careful assessment. Was the product completed on time, within resources, and does it meet quality requirements? In short, the review of individual tasks should be conducted on a basis similar to that the project leader wants used on his own efforts.

As with most new tools, it is probably a good idea to introduce peer reviews in an evolutionary, not revolutionary, way. Success of the concept depends to some extent on the overall management style and philosophy. Peer reviews work best in an atmosphere that encourages teamwork and where individual workers are given considerable latitude in deciding how to accomplish their assignments. Peer reviews may not work at all in a more regimented atmosphere.

In introducing peer reviews, it is best to try the concept on a single project and to expand from there. Initial qualms about having work reviewed by others usually disappear as soon as people understand and accept the reasons for the reviews. Developers soon look upon peer reviews as an indispensible tool. This comes about partly because peer reviews are embedded in the work effort and are not an optional extra. In part, the acceptance comes from the realization that it is a standard for everyone on the project, not just a device to check on the work of junior people.

If problems develop in introducing peer reviews, wait a year or so before trying them again. But in the long run the concept should be introduced, because it is the primary tool for improving product quality.

17-7 SUMMARY

- A peer review is a structured review of work conducted in a penalty-free environment; its purpose is to detect errors.
- Some characteristics of peer reviews are:

  Peer reviews are formal
  Peer reviews are structured
  Peer reviews are the tool of the reviewee
  All work is reviewed
  Peer reviews are not optional
  Peer reviews concern correctness, not style
  Emphasis during reviews is on error detection
  Peer reviews are psychologically open
  Peer reviews are *not* a tool for employee evaluation

- The mechanics of peer reviews allow careful examination of the reviewee's work; errors are corrected by the reviewee after the review.
- Peer reviews are the primary tool for improving product quality. They also serve as an important device for communication and training.
- Because peer reviews involve others in the work of the reviewee, they help to meet audit requirements for separation of duties and thereby help auditors to sleep better at night.
- For peer reviews to be successful it is important that they not be contaminated by the management-appraisal process.

18

PROJECT CONTROL TOPICS

18-1 INTRODUCTION

In this chapter we shall discuss a number of project control topics not covered elsewhere. Each of these topics is important and could be discussed in much greater detail—several topics could reasonably be expanded into full chapters. Our decision to treat each topic briefly was based strictly on the need to keep this book to a reasonable size.

18-2 CHANGE PROCEDURE

We all know that change during a project is inevitable. No matter how excellent the methodology and no matter how hard one tries to anticipate all problems and to do everything right the first time, still changes will arise. Some of these will be mandated by factors well beyond the project group; for instance, the changes generated by new legal requirements, by a basic change in organizational policy, or by a shift in resources available for the project. Some will be optional, but desirable, changes brought about by such factors as an improved perception of the problem and its solution, by advances in technology, or by the impact of some other project. We simply must assume that changes will take place on a project and have procedures for dealing with them effectively.

Whatever its source, change is always disruptive and frequently costly. It calls for additional planning, and it impacts schedules and work assignments. The cost of change depends on its type and when in the project it is requested. As a rule, the later a change is made, the more costly it is. A change in specs during Phase 2.3 can cost many times what it would cost to make the same change in Phase 1.3. The cost of change also depends on how well it is managed. Controlled change has some impact on a project, but uncontrolled change can be a disaster. It can seriously impact the schedule and budget; worse yet, it can result in a demoralized staff, a dissatisfied user, and a product of poor quality.

A good project methodology curbs the impact of change in two ways. First, it reduces the number of changes that are requested. It is one thing to admit that change in inevitable, it is another to invite change through improper procedures. Many of the features of the methodology discussed in this book have the effect of reducing the need for change. These include:

> A logical pattern of work; for example, requiring completed specifica-
> cations before design and completed design before coding
> Formal documentation
> Adequate reviews
> Emphasis on individual responsibility and self-control

It is easy to extend this list, and you might find it worthwhile to do so.

A second way that a good methodology curbs the impact of change is by providing a procedure for evaluating proposed changes and for implementing those changes that prove to be worthwhile. The purpose of this section is to discuss such a *change procedure.*

Characteristics of a Change Procedure

What we call a "change procedure" is frequently referred to as "change control." We believe that this term should be avoided because it is widely misunderstood. To many people, use of word "control" suggests that change should be held in check or prevented; they look on a change-control procedure as a device for inhibiting change. In fact, some change is highly desirable and should be encouraged. What is required is a procedure for selecting worthwhile change and implementing it in a satisfactory way. "Change procedure" seems to be a better term for this.

The procedure for handling project changes should be standardized and applied uniformly to all projects. It should be part of the methodology documented in the Project Handbook. A standard procedure for all projects is important because change involves the commitment of resources and might impact schedules, therefore it is not just a project responsibility. A standard change procedure is also important from a training perspective. It is much easier to promote understanding if there is one standard procedure uniformly applied to all projects.

The contents of a change procedure are typically as follows:

Purpose of the procedure
Definition of change
Responsibility for change management
Procedures for
      Initiation of change
      Evaluation of change
      Approval of change
      Implementation of change
      Documentation of change[1]

We shall comment on some of these topics. An example of a change procedure appears in Appendix C.

As we use the term, a *change* is any alteration in baseline data. *Baseline data* is any data from approved documents that were input to the project or were output of a previous phase—that is, any phase prior to the one in which the request for change is made. Another way to state this is that change is any alteration in a document that flows between upper management and the project. (Note that we are not including change to data that flows within a phase, a topic that will be discussed briefly near the end of this section.)

Managing the Change Procedure

Change is usually managed by the Project Manager. It is his duty to explain the procedure to people, to collect requests for change, to apply the evaluation and approval procedures, to see that change is implemented properly, and to keep everyone informed.

Initiating Change. Change can usually be initiated by anyone who sees the need. Requests are submitted on standard forms and evaluated by the Project Manager and appropriate user representatives. Just who should be the user representatives can sometimes be a serious problem. We assumed there was a single representative for users in the change procedure of Appendix C, but often this cannot be achieved. If several users originally signed-off on a baseline document, then probably they will all want to sign-off on a change to that document. Such a practice can introduce lengthy delays on a project; one way around this problem is to appoint a Project Administrator (see Section 18-8).

---

[1] It is our belief that implementation of change *includes* documentation of change, but to emphasize the importance of documentation we are listing it as a separate step.

Evaluating Change Requests. Part of the evaluation procedure usually involves classifying changes as minor or major. This distinction is made to facilitate the processing of change requests. A minor change can be made upon the agreement of the Project Manager and the users. This means that it must be a change that does not impact the due date, budget, or scope of the project. Any change that alters any of these is a major change, and it must be approved by the Project Selection Committee. It is easy to measure changes in due date and budget, but it is hard to describe and measure changes in scope. Hard or not, it must be done. The change procedure cannot allow an important function to be added or dropped without approval of upper management, even if the alteration can be made within original time and resource constraints. The Project Manager and user cannot change the scope of the project on their own.

Implementing Change. Upon approval, change is implemented and documented. Notice of the change should be distributed to all project people so that baseline documents can be updated. Information on implemented changes should also be included in the Phase Report when the current phase is completed. This allows upper management to update their baseline documents. It also allows them to monitor the change process; for example, they can check to see that a major change isn't creeping in as a sequence of minor changes.

All change requests should be logged, and a record kept of their disposition. The originator of a request should be informed of its disposition; this is particularly important for requests that are denied because he will not learn about them in any other way. A sure way for a person to be turned off is for him to hear absolutely nothing about a suggestion he has taken the trouble to submit.

Benefits of a Change Procedure

The most important benefit that results from an effective change procedure is that the right product is produced. One of the biggest mistakes that can be made is to continue a project in one direction after it is recognized that a change is justified. At first glance a project team might look good if it brings a project in on time, within budget, and meeting original specs. But if organizational requirements have changed since the original specs were formulated and the product is not timely, the project might really be a failure. An effective change procedure encourages worthwhile change, and it attempts to have this change introduced as early in the project as possible.

An organization reaps many other benefits from an effective change procedure. Approved changes are installed in an efficient manner with minimum cost and disruption. The change procedure provides an audit trail so that changes in baseline documents can be traced easily. The change procedure adds to product quality by helping to maintain design integrity and documentation standards. And an effective change procedure reduces confusion and lost effort, which are sometimes major sources of irritation to project workers.

Making a Procedure Effective

No matter how good the procedure is, it won't be effective unless it is used properly. Two points are worth mentioning here. First, change requires time and resource, and allowance must be made for these. Major changes are no problem because their authorization provides for changes in resources and schedules. Minor changes, however, are absorbed into the original plan. The need for minor changes must be anticipated and time and resource for them built into plans. If an estimate is made at the project or phase level, then the time and resource data on past projects should include a normal amount of minor change. This means that the statistics for past projects should not have to be adjusted to allow for normal minor change on the current project. However, if more than normal minor change is anticipated, this should be allowed for in making plans.

How change is handled at the Work Plan level depends on the way records have been kept on past projects. One way to do this is to charge all change to a specific (nonscheduled) standard task. Historical data on this standard task will then suggest how much effort should be allowed for change in a typical Work Plan.

A second point for proper use of a change procedure, is the need to create a suitable atmosphere. The change procedure is easier than most to circumvent; all it takes is a private agreement between, say, a designer and a user. This can be done with the best of intentions—just an attempt to build the product the user requires. To prevent such unauthorized changes it is important that all people connected with the project understand the purpose of the change procedure and the need for it. Compliance usually follows understanding.

Interpretation Procedure

Up until this point we have been discussing changes in baseline data. Sometimes, however, it isn't a change that is required, but an interpretation. What seems clear when a document is written and approved causes confusion

later on. It is necessary to agree on a meaning and to see that this is uniformly applied; this requires an *interpretation procedure.* For an example of
such a procedure, see Appendix C.

Change Within a Phase

In this section we have been concerned primarily with changes in baseline data. There is another type of change that must be controlled: change in
data that flows within a phase. For example, suppose a module is coded in
Phase 2.2, unit tested, and declared to be finished. Later in that same phase
a bug is discovered in this code, and it must be corrected. Such a change does
not involve baseline data; therefore it is not covered by the change procedure
of the project methodology.

Change within a phase must be managed by the Project Manager. He
can handle this as he sees fit because it does not impact other groups—it is
part of the effort required to build the phase deliverables. This is *not* to suggest that within-phase change is a trivial matter or that no standard procedures should be established for dealing with it. We merely say that it is the
Project Manager's choice. One approach he might take is to establish a
within-phase change procedure that parallels the standard change procedure
except that evaluation by users and approval by upper management can be
omitted.

18-3 PROJECT SECURITY

DP security is a very urgent topic. Most readers are aware of such
problems as the need to prevent unwarranted access to DP systems, the need
to provide audit trails so that transactions can be traced, and the need for recovery capability after system failure. But most concern about security
focuses on the system during its operational phase; surprisingly little attention is directed toward securing the system during the development stage.
Obviously this should also be a concern, and security standards for an organization should cover it too.

Project security standards are of two types: those that pertain to the
development process itself, and those that pertain to the product being built.
Standards for the process should establish who has responsibility for project
security. They should also address such topics as the project back-up and
recovery procedure in the event of disaster, procedures for preventing unauthorized work or change during development, and control of sensitive
project documentation. Security standards for the product might be in-

cluded as part of the product specifications or might be established more generally in installation guidelines. Product security standards pertain to characteristics and features of the product that will be important once it is operational.

Security of a DP project is a large and vital topic, part of the general topic of data processing security. Although project security will not be discussed in detail, it is important to mention how certain features of a good project methodology do promote project security.

An authorization and approval procedure and a documentation procedure provide for direct control of assets. Planning and control procedures help provide for appropriate use of assets.

The phased approach to projects allows a checkpoint and restart procedure for projects, thereby aiding in disaster control.

An important control technique is separation of duties—planning work so that no one person can control a vital aspect. Properly used, peer reviews can be used to achieve such separation. For example, if vital design or code is reviewed by peers and if the reviewed material is secured by a librarian, then no one person can control the material.

An emphasis on documentation and on careful adherence to change procedures provides an audit trail for all project products. This helps to eliminate the danger of unauthorized change.

Most security losses stem from carelessness rather than fraud. Thus the emphasis on quality that permeates a good methodology is probably the best security feature of all.

18-4 REVIEWS

A *review* is an examination of various aspects of a project by a group. Informal reviews go on all the time; in this section we are concerned only with reviews that are planned and structured. (Such formal reviews include peer reviews; see Chapter 17 for an expanded discussion of this topic.)

Classification of Reviews

Reviews can be classified as *technical* reviews or *business* reviews depending on the aspect of the project being examined. A technical review examines such questions as: Are the objectives technically feasible? Are there reasonable procedures for producing the product? Is the work output of satisfactory quality? Is work output understandable, complete, and correct? A business review examines such questions as: Are the product objectives justifiable from a business point of view? Are there sufficient resources for producing the product? Are there reasonable plans and controls for the project? Are necessary skills available? A technical review tends to concentrate on the product, a business review on the production process. A technical review tends to concern quality and to be qualitative, a business review tends to concern time and resource and to be quantitative. Of course, many reviews cover both technical and business aspects. Nevertheless, this classification is a useful one because it helps to fix more clearly the objective of a particular review.

Reviews can also be classified by how often they are held. Some types of reviews are held frequently, perhaps on a weekly basis. Some are held only if the project shows signs of serious trouble. In general, the more frequently a type of review is held, the less formal the review and the shorter its duration.

An important way to classify reviews is by the sponsor of the review—that is, the person or group who is calling the review and who is its primary beneficiary. A review of the project team's work that is called by the Project Manager is one thing, a review of the same material called by upper management is another. The first review tends to be a self-examination and might concentrate on discovery of error; the second tends to be an appraisal and might concentrate on presenting material in the most favorable light. It is a mistake to assume that the tone and results of a review are independent of who is sponsoring it. Almost never is it possible to kill two birds with one stone—to have genuine self-examiation in a setting where the individual could be appraised. A review is either an examination or a report, not both.

The foregoing remarks should suggest that a review is a tool that can be used in various ways. Reviews vary in scope, objectives, participants, frequency, formality, and so on. In Appendix D we have described six types of reviews that might be conducted by an organization. Those descriptions will provide you with a good example of how the review tool is used. Remember, however, that those descriptions are only examples; before using them it will be necessary for you to tailor them to the needs of your organization. And to do this it is important for you to understand some basic concepts about reviews.

Basic Concepts

A review is a group activity. The basic premise behind reviews is that several heads are better than one. Detection of error is more likely if examination is by a group rather than by one individual. A comprehensive view of a phase is best obtained from a group—no one person can be familiar with all facets of such a complex undertaking. A review is a structured method for pooling knowledge; it provides information that would be difficult to obtain in any other way.

A review is not a forum for solving problems, but it is used to identify problems and to fix responsibility for problem resolution. In general, a review is conducted to discover facts, to analyze them, and to make recommendations. More specifically, a review is conducted for reasons such as:

To determine status; to compare actual results with plan, and to monitor progress

To identify problems and to fix responsibility for resolving them

To solicit recommendations for improvement

To obtain information for making decisions

To assess quality; to assess adherence to standards and specifications

To report to management; to present a comprehensive view of the project

To communicate with people involved with the project

To educate people involved with the project

To motivate the project team

The project methodology specifies general review procedures, and these are documented in the Project Handbook. Review procedures cover such topics as: types of reviews to be conducted, guidelines for the frequency of reviews, responsibility for reviews (sponsors), and required review reports. The methodology does not specify just how and when (except for phase reviews) reviews will be conducted for a specific project. It is the responsibility of the Project Manager to see that the time and cost of reviews are included in project estimates, and it is the responsibility of sponsors to conduct reviews as required.

The sponsor of a review is responsible for making all arrangements. He must pick the reviewers, schedule the review, and conduct it. (See Appendix D for the procedure for a phase review; other reviews follow similar steps.) Reviews should be scheduled in advance as part of the regular work process; this helps to avoid the suggestion that the review is a vote of no confidence in the reviewee.

A review would ordinarily be conducted by three or four reviewers, although there could be a dozen or more for an important review. Reviewers should be skilled in the topic being reviewed and should be at least as knowledgeable as the reviewees. Some reviews are *internal,* in that the reviewers are members of the project team; others are *external.* The boundary between internal and external reviews need not be drawn too carefully; a team might invite some nonmember to review their work and still maintain an essentially internal review. The main distinction between internal and external reviews is: Is the review a self-examination or an appraisal; are we doing it or are they? This is a question that might arise, for instance, when the review is conducted by a Systems Assurance Group (see Section 18-7). Is Systems Assurance primarily a partner or primarily a representative of upper management? Should it arise, this question must be resolved.

An internal review is usually somewhat informal. Generally there is not a need for much background information because all participants are familiar with the project. An internal review concentrates on highlighting present problems and checking to see that past problems have been resolved satisfactorily.

An external review is more structured. Generally there is a need to present background information on the project. The review often takes the shape of a status report by the reviewee with questioning and probing by the reviewers in their attempt to understand and evaluate.

To be effective, a review must result in a report that contains the findings and an action plan for resolution of identified problems and opportunities. This report must be produced in a timely manner. The report goes to the sponsor of the review; ordinarily he should distribute it to all participants in the review. The sponsor might also decide to distribute the report to others (for instance, upper management), but this decision should be made and announced to all participants before the review is donducted.

A review can be considered as a project, and from this perspective it is clear that it must have:

> A clearly defined purpose and objectives
> Clearly specified inputs
> An effective process for review, including
>> A sponsor who understands his function and performs it
>> Qualified reviewers
>> Advanced distribution of relevant data
>> An appropriate agenda that is followed
>> A follow-up plan
> Documented output, consisting of
>> Report of findings
>> Action plan

A review is likely to be successful if all of these ingredients are present.

18-5 PROJECT ASSESSMENT

Closely related to reviews is the concept of project assessment—a review of the way the methodology was used on a project. Project assessments promote product quality by helping to provide for a better project process.

The assessment process was discussed in Section 5-5. Before making an assessment, you should define what you mean by a good methodology. The list in Section 8-6 should help you to do this.

Project assessments are a tool for improving the project methodology. But that tool will be ineffective unless there is some person in the organization who has responsibility for maintaining and improving the methodology. This person should establish a procedure for collecting and evaluating project assessments and for implementing changes that are appropriate (see Section 8-7).

18-6 RESPONSIBILITY GRID

The typical DP project is a complicated undertaking that involves many functional areas of the organization. Various groups work on different aspects of the project; work might be assigned and monitored by several people; work done by one functional area might be subject to approval by another. In such a situation it is important to know just who is responsible for what, and a tool for making this clear is the responsibility grid.

A *responsibility grid* is a matrix that shows the involvement of various groups in the tasks of a project. To construct a grid it is necessary to know three things: (1) the tasks to be performed, (2) the groups that are involved with these tasks, and (3) the types of involvement to be shown. An example will show how these are related.

Suppose that an organization wants to show three types of involvement with any task. One is that of managing the task. This type of participation means planning, assigning, and controlling the task; it also means being directly answerable to upper management for the task. A second type of involvement, which might apply to some tasks, is to review the completed work. This type of participation would not be the review that is part of the management control function, but a special examination similar to those discussed in Section 18-4. The review involvement might carry with it sign-off authority over the work; this authority would mean that the work could not be considered finished until the reviewers gave their written approval. The third level of involvement is that of performing work on the task other than the work of management and review. This is the involvement of doing direct work, support work, providing input data, and so on.

A responsibility grid using these three types of involvement is shown in Figure 18-1. In that figure, the tasks to be performed are listed in a column, and the various groups are listed in a row across the top. For each task, letters are inserted in the relevant columns to show the type of involvement of corresponding groups. For instance, the entries on the fifth row of the grid show that the Project Team is responsible for doing and managing the task and that the User Department and Data Management are responsible for reviewing it.

The three types of involvement shown in Figure 18-1 are not the only ones that might be used. The involvement we called "review" might be subdivided to distinguish a sign-off involvement from other examinations. The work involvement might be divided to show major or minor work roles or to show classes of work, such as direct and support. Care must be taken, however, not to have too many categories; most organizations do not go beyond five. Also, a careful definition must be given of each type of involvement so that everyone knows, for example, the difference between major and minor work roles.

Tasks	Project Team	User Dept.	Data Mgt.	Operations	...
Task 1	M/W				
Task 2	M	W		R	
Task 3	W		M/W		
Task 4		M/W			
Task 5	M/W	R	R		
.					
.					
.					

M = Manage
W = Work
R = Review

Figure 18-1. A responsibility grid

Speaking of clarity, we should point out that we use the term "responsibility grid" with some qualms. This term and the similar term "responsibility matrix" are becoming fairly standard in our industry, and we are going along with this trend. But the grid does not show *responsibility* so much as *involvement,* and the term "involvement grid" might be more appropriate. Involvement is a fairly straightforward concept; a person either has something to do with a task or he does not. Responsibility, on the other hand, is a complicated concept. One complicating factor is that each person is responsible for his own work. This means that everyone who is involved with a task has responsibility; an attempt to depict actual responsibility for tasks would show a grid full of responsibility symbols. Another complicating factor is that responsibility is like athlete's foot—you can pass it on to someone else, but that doesn't mean you're rid of it. The Project Manager is usually responsible for a project. He can assign responsibility for parts of the project to others; but if anything goes wrong with one of those parts, he is still held accountable. An attempt to depict responsibility for an actual work task would indicate the project worker, the Project Manager, the DP Manager, the Project Selection Committee, and everyone else up the chain of command. Because of complications such as these, a responsibility grid usually shows only the direct responsibility to upper management (part of the "manage" involvement); other types and levels of responsibility must be described separately.

The responsibility grid is a tool that can be used in different ways. For instance, grids can be constructed at different levels of aggregation. At one level the tasks might be project phases and the groups might be major functional areas; at a more detailed level a grid might show standard tasks and might subdivide some major functional areas into different groups, say, management and workers. Responsibility grids can also be constructed for different purposes. A standard responsibility grid can be included as part of the Project Handbook; this would be a general guide for projects and would be used to alert various areas to their typical involvements. For a particular project this standard grid could be adjusted to reflect the requirements of the particular project; the resulting special-purpose grid would fix involvement for the project and would be used in making actual assignments for the Work Plan.

Benefits of a Responsibility Grid

The most obvious reason for constructing a responsibility grid is that it makes explicit the involvement of various groups in the project. It prevents misunderstandings, and it helps prevent things "falling between the stools" because each thought the other was taking care of it. It helps to avoid "border disputes" where each group tries to push responsibility on the other. A responsibility grid is an excellent tool for communicating with users and others, and it can be used to point out just how heavily project success depends on them.

But there are other reasons for building grids. Construction of standard responsibility grids for the Project Handbook is an interesting and worthwhile effort. You will discover that the true meaning of each standard task and the true method of interfacing among functional areas become much more clearly defined during the discussions that lead to the standard grids.

If the Project Handbook has the blessing of upper management, as it should, then the existence of standard responsibility grids in the Handbook can help gain the cooperation of reluctant users. They can see from the standard grid that it is expected that they will be involved in the project and, moreover, are responsible for part of it.

Examination of a responsibility grid can reveal potential project problems. A task that nobody is managing is a clear indication of trouble. Just as bad is a task for which two or more groups are responsible—shared responsibility often means no responsibility. If a grid shows a large number of sign-offs, it might indicate an unnecessarily complex approval procedure and might portend bureaucratic delay. If all standard tasks are managed by the project team, it might indicate that "user involvement" is more of a slogan than a fact.

A tendency in many organizations is for the Project Manager to serve as a coordinator of a "task force" composed of people from various groups. More and more the Project Manager has no direct management authority over many of the people who must do the project work. In such situations clear recognition of responsibility for individual tasks takes on an added importance, and the use of responsibility grids is particularly rewarding.

If you are introducing the concept of responsibility grids into an organization, you should realize that this can be a substantial undertaking. Building a responsibility grid really means fixing part of the mission or charter of the different groups within the organization, and to do this will probably require upper management involvement. One practical way to build grids is to start by recording present practice and to introduce desired change in an evolutionary way.

18-7 SYSTEMS ASSURANCE

A recent development in data processing is the emergence of special groups for promoting quality and productive work. These will be referred to as Systems Assurance Groups, although they are sometimes known as Quality Assurance Groups or some similar name.

Because Systems Assurance Groups are relatively new, at present there is no industry standard for their function. Several versions of their duties have been encountered. For our discussion we shall describe these as:

To perform a project audit function
To perform a quality control function
To perform a management review function
To be a consultant to the project team

Each version of these duties will be discussed.

An audit function is an assessment of a project to learn if it is designed so as to safeguard organizational assets and to see that the assets are used in an effective manner. It is an assessment made on behalf of upper management. In most organizations the group doing this is known as the (Internal) Auditing Department. If there is no Auditing Department, this function is sometimes called Systems Assurance. Instances of using the term in this way are not too common and are at odds with fairly standard terminology; therefore we believe that this use of the term Systems Assurance should and will disappear. (For further discussion on auditing, see Chapter 19.)

By "quality control" we mean the function of inspection, discovery, and removal of error. It is an after-the-fact review to detect and remove error, but not to prevent it. Many organizations have DP groups that perform this function, and many of these are called Systems Assurance Groups. We prefer not to use the term in this way; if a group is performing a quality control function, it should be called a Quality Control Group or Quality Assurance Group. It should be pointed out, however, that quality control as we have defined it is *not* the correct way to promote quality. We much prefer the concept of Systems Assurance as described below.

The two remaining versions of the duties of Systems Assurance are quite similar. Both involve regular review and assessment of the project; both aim at preventing errors rather than after-the-fact detection. The primary difference between the two is that: In one case the Systems Assurance Group is a representative of management, in the other it is an outside assistant to the project team. This distinction is extremely important; it influences the way Systems Assurance is used and the impact and acceptance it has. Many organizations view Systems Assurance as an arm of management. In our opinion, and many share our view, the function of Systems Assurance should be to act as a consultant to the Project Team. But each organization with a Systems Assurance Group must make its own decision as to which function best fits their shop.

Function of Systems Assurance

The basic purpose of Systems Assurance, whether it represents management or acts as a consultant, is to provide an independent assessment of the project at key points. This assessment covers both the technical and business aspects of the project. Usually the assessment is made by conducting a formal review—a Systems Assurance Review would resemble the description of a Phase Review in Appendix D. If Systems Assurance is viewed as a consultant to the team, they might also be called on for less formal meetings and for advice in handling difficult situations.

The project methodology should specify points in the project where review by Systems Assurance is required. For instance, it might specify that such a review is required at the end of Phase 1.2 when requirements have been determined, at the end of Phase 1.3 when architecture and major plans are complete, at the end of Phase 2.1 when the design is complete, and at the end of Phase 2.3 when the system is built and tested. Alternatively, Systems Assurance might be required to conduct all phase reviews, in effect serving the role of upper management as far as the project team is concerned.

In assessing a project, Systems Assurance would check to see that work to date has been done properly and that reasonable plans exist for the future. They would examine such questions as:

> What is the project status?
> Are estimates realistic? Do they allow for contingencies?
> Are plans complete? Realistic?
> Is there a reasonable procedure for tracking and control?
> Are risks identified and contained?
> Are resources adequate?
> Are project goals well defined? Technically feasible?
> Are project products complete? Do they adhere to standards?

Members of the Systems Assurance Group should be highly experienced and familiar with both the technical and business side of projects. They must be able to assess, advise, and communicate well. They must have the confidence of people on the project teams and upper mangement. They must also be people who understand that the Project Manager is in charge of the project and that he cannot be undercut. In short, it takes an unusual individual to perform the Systems Assurance function properly. But if the function is performed properly, it is an effective tool for promoting quality and productive work.

18-8 USER INVOLVEMENT

For success, the user must be involved with the project. No book on the management of projects would be complete without that statement. But with today's complex systems, we can't usually speak of *the* user—there are many users. An on-line order entry system might well involve sales, production, inventory control, warehousing, shipping, and accounting; plus, of course, data management, auditing, and security. All of these are users. The problem isn't just to get all of them involved, but to coordinate their activities and to get them to agree among themselves. If the Project Manager must deal with each user individually and if he must mediate disputes among users, then he won't have enough time for his primary activity, which is to manage the project. If each user must approve all project plans and sign-off on all deliverables, the project can bog down in needless delay.

One way to solve the problem of user involvement is to appoint a *Project Administrator*. This is a person who represents all users and serves as the interface between the Project Manager (representing the project team) and all user departments. The Project Administrator should have the responsibility and authority to act for all users in project-related matters. Among his duties are:

Assist with planning—to provide user input for planning, to approve plans, to communicate plans to users

Assist with project work—to keep users informed, to provide user workers as required for tasks, to arrange interviews, to resolve disputes among users, to represent users in resolving issues with the project team

Monitor change—to act for users in administering the change procedure

Review output—to conduct user reviews, to represent users at other reviews as required

Approve output—to secure approvals from users, to approve output for them

A Project Administrator is particularly useful if the project work is being done by an outside contractor. Then the Project Administrator also administers the contract. He represents the organization in interpreting contract provisions and stipulates that contract provisions have been met.

Use of a Project Administrator can be criticized as establishing a barrier between the users and the project team—just one more layer of bureaucracy. Improperly used, it can be that. But the use of a Project Administrator takes a large burden of work off the Project Manager and allows him to do his major job. It provides users with a focus for project-related matters and relieves them of many project details. It provides at least one person outside the project team who has a comprehensive users' view of the entire system, and thereby it helps to maintain the architectural integrity of the system.

These benefits mean that, if properly used, a Project Administrator can expedite projects, improve productivity, and promote quality.

18-9 SUMMARY

- The Project Handbook should include a change procedure, which describes the steps in the initiation, evaluation, approval, implementation, and documentation of changes in baseline data.
- Many features of a good methodology promote project security.
- A review is a group activity designed to examine business and/or technical aspects of a project. Adequate reviews are necessary on any project.
- A responsibility grid makes explicit the involvement of various groups in a project.
- Systems Assurance is a special group for promoting quality and productive work through regular review and assessment. Their emphasis is on prevention rather than detection of error.
- A project with many user groups can simplify problems associated with user involvement through use of a Project Administrator.

19

AUDITING A
PROJECT METHODOLOGY

19-1 THE CONCEPT OF AN AUDIT

After all of this discussion of project methodology, readers will certainly have asked themselves: What are we doing right in our shop? What are we doing wrong? What should we be doing that we aren't? The only way to answer such questions is to make a thorough examination of present practice. This means an assessment or audit of the present project methodology.

An audit is a structured review and is ordinarily undertaken for the purpose of determining the quality of present methods and for learning if it is desirable to introduce new concepts or to improve existing ones. It is a logical first step in any effort at improvement. In this book only the audit of project methodology will be discussed, that is, an audit of the system used to build a system. Management aspects of a project that are people oriented—such as hiring, job assignment, goal setting, motivation, and evaluation—will not be considered. Although the general management philosophy does have a profound influence on the methodology used on a project, an attempt to cover both areas would take us far beyond the scope of this work. Also, in assessing current practice it is probably best to separate the two issues so that each, in turn, can be given the emphasis it deserves. Another topic not considered at this point is an audit of the project deliverables, the products for which the project was established. This is omitted because the review of these products is an integral part of the project itself, and it has already been discussed.

An audit is conducted to answer questions of three types:

Is there a formal methodology? If so, what is it?
What, in fact, are people doing? How does this compare with the

formal methodology?
Are procedures (formal and/or actual) good?   Are there any specific
suggestions for improvement?

In brief, the object is to determine: What do people say they do? What do
they do? What should they do?

19-2 THE AUDIT TEAM

The Internal Audit Department of an organization periodically conducts audits of DP and, among other things, assesses the procedures used to
develop applications. The review we have in mind, however, is different in
nature. First, it is conducted primarily for the benefit of DP. The audit
reports will ordinarily go to the Project Manager or the manager who initiates
the review. The audit is an internal review conducted for the purpose of
improving performance; this view helps to avoid some of the hang-ups that
often accompany a review by Internal Audit. Second, it is generally more
specific and more detailed than the typical Internal Audit review. It should
be conducted by people who are familiar with the project process and who
have more knowledge of DP project methodology than does the average
internal auditor.

The audit should be conducted by a small team—from one to three
people. It is difficult for most people to make a critical assessment of something they are closely involved with, and for that reason it is best that members of the audit team not be part of the group whose methodology is being
reviewed. This is not always possible. If the review covers a specific project,
it is usually possible to select auditors who are not on the project team; but
if the review covers the methodology used throughout a DP Department, it
may be difficult to find qualified non-DP people to conduct the review.
Rather than to use people who are too close to the methodology, the answer
might be to obtain the services of a qualified outside consultant.

The people selected for the audit team should be good interviewers.
Much of the effort on the review will consist of obtaining information through
discussions with people. It is important that the auditors possess tact, that
they can build confidence, and that they can ask good questions and listen
to the answers. Second, at least one member of the team should have a good
knowledge of project methodology. This is needed to help direct the investigation and also to provide a standard against which current practice can be
measured.   Third, the members of the audit team should be sufficiently
mature and experienced to be able to make meaningful suggestions and

recommendations to management. The credibility of the audit report will in large measure depend on the credibility of the individuals on the team.

19-3 THE AUDIT

An audit is a project. All comments and statements of the preceding chapters apply to an audit. The methodology described also applies, but in a simplified form, of course.

In particular, an audit project requires a clear scope and objective. The reason for the review and expected benefits should be stated in writing. The reports to be generated, the distribution of these reports, and the uses to be made of them should be specified before the project is started. The scope should indicate if the review is for the methodology of a specific project or the general project methodology used throughout the DP Department. The scope should be in keeping with the resource limitation, which is usually anywhere from 5 to 15 man-days of effort.

An audit project needs clear authorization. As with any project, this is necessary to assure that sufficient resources are allocated and authorized for the review. But this is relatively unimportant because the resource requirements are so small. The real reason to have authorization is to give the reviewers the authority to talk with all the people who are involved with projects. Many of these people are outside DP, so an authorization from DP management might not be sufficient to secure the full cooperation that is required. Instead, the review should be sanctioned by a high-level authority. This person should initiate the review with a letter to concerned parties asking for their cooperation in the review effort. This makes everyone, including the review team, realize the importance of the effort.

Inputs to the audit function are the authorization, proper resources, and specification of required deliverables. The major output is the Audit Report. This is a report of the important findings and the answers to the questions of Section 19-1. One possible outline for the Audit Report is shown in Table 19-1.

In addition to the Audit Report, an output of the audit project should be a Project Completion and Assessment Report (Phase 3.3 report). As with any project, this summarizes the experience of the project itself. Among other comments, it should contain the record of actual vs estimated time and cost, major problems encountered, observations concerning the methodology, review plans and tools (such as checklists), and any recommendations for future reviews. The Project Completion and Assessment Report will be useful when it comes time to plan subsequent audits.

Table 19-1
Audit Report—Sample Table of Contents

I   Summary of findings and recommendations
II   Main body
   1. Purpose of review (scope and objectives)
   2. Methodology of the review (interviews, observations, examination of documents, statistical analyses, etc.)
   3. Sources (organizations contacted, documents reviewed, etc.)
   4. Conclusions and recommendations
       a. Description of present methodology
       b. Description of present practice
       c. Specific recommendations
III Appendix (data, list of interviews, documents, etc.)

19-4 THE AUDIT PROCESS

The chart in Figure 19-1 provides a decomposition of the audit function to a second level. Because it is a small project, it is unlikely that further decomposition is useful.

In formalizing the review, it is necessary to list the specific tasks to be performed and to establish the sequence in which these are to be performed. The concepts of networking are helpful in doing this, but it is probably not necessary to establish a formal network. If there are, say, three people on the project, there can be at most three parallel activities actually being performed at the same time. More likely there will be fewer because one of the main reasons for having several people on the project is to give them an opportunity to discuss things among themselves. With so little chance for parallel activity, it is not necessary to adopt very formal planning techniques. Nevertheless, a schedule should be established and progress should be monitored to make certain that the review does not lag.

Training the auditing team can be an important task, particularly if this is the first review that has been conducted by any of the members. If assistance is required for this, an excellent reference on the general topic of auditing is a book by Lawrence B. Sawyer.[1]

---

[1] *The Practice of Modern Internal Auditing,* Orlando, FL, The Institute of Internal Auditors, 1973.

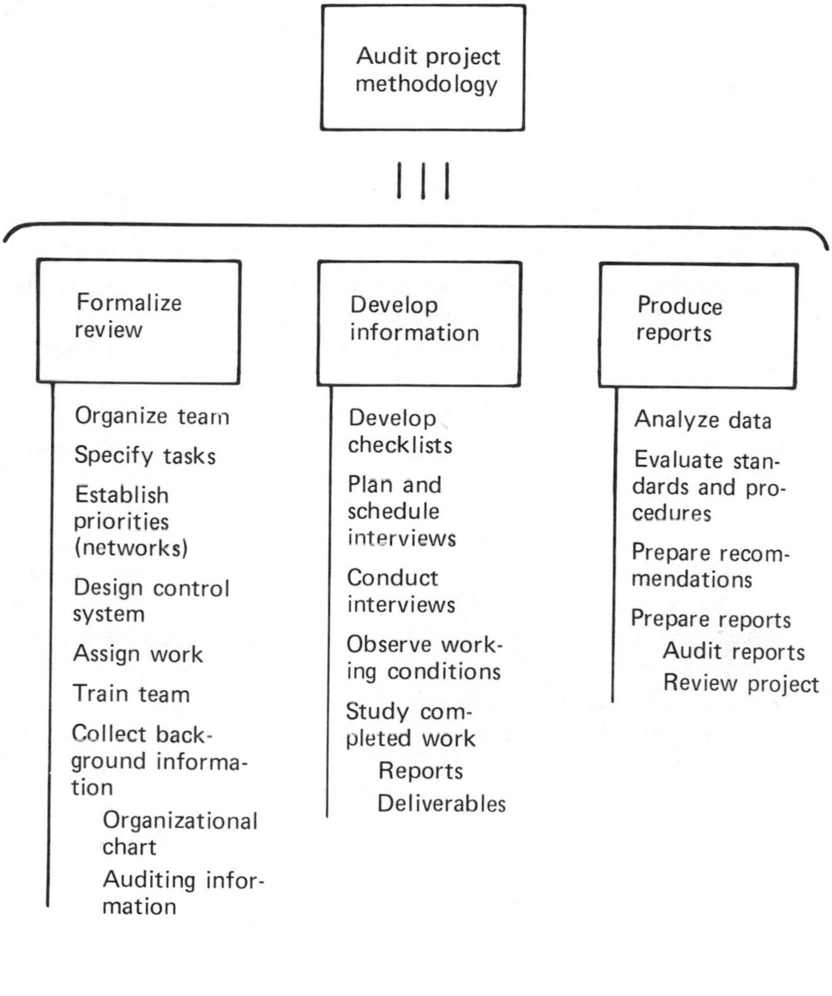

```
              ┌─────────────────┐
              │  Audit project  │
              │  methodology    │
              └─────────────────┘

                     │ │ │
```

Formalize review	Develop information	Produce reports
Organize team	Develop checklists	Analyze data
Specify tasks	Plan and schedule interviews	Evaluate standards and procedures
Establish priorities (networks)	Conduct interviews	Prepare recommendations
Design control system	Observe working conditions	Prepare reports
Assign work	Study completed work	Audit reports
Train team	Reports	Review project
Collect background information	Deliverables	
Organizational chart		
Auditing information		

Figure 19-1. Phases and standard tasks for an audit of project methodology

419

The audit team must develop the information to answer the three basic questions near the end of Section 19-1. Since formal methodology means written methodology, it can be ascertained by gathering and examining relevant documents, such as policy statements, practice and procedures manuals, standards manuals, project handbook, and project control system documentation.

Actual practice can be ascertained in part through the examination of documentation for completed projects and in part through observation of actual work practice. Another important way to determine what people are actually doing and what they think of the procedures is by asking them. The audit team should interview all the people who are involved with projects or the output of projects, including project team members, Operations, technical support, DP management, user departments, the data base manager, the security officer, and the audit department. Interview questions should be thought out in advance and written down in a so-called checklist. Construction of such a list can be very time consuming, and the process can be shortened by examining the checklist in Appendix D for ideas. That list, however, should be viewed only as a general guide and not one that can be used without modification by any organization.

Some suggestions for conducting interviews are the following:

Interviews should be scheduled in advance and should last at most an hour or so

Begin the interview by stating its purpose and the general topic to be covered

Don't waste time on nonbusiness topics; stick to the agenda

Use the checklist questions as a guide; improvise and add impromptu questions as required; do *not* read questions, but have list well enough in mind to talk informally and from memory

Listen; don't be so wrapped up in the next question that you fail to hear the answer to the question just asked

Ask opinions; ask for recommendations for improvement

Keep note taking to a minimum during the interview

Keep the discussion informal, yet businesslike

At the conclusion, let the interviewee know you appreciate his time and cooperation

Document the interview right after it is over

To produce reports it is necessary to summarize the information that has been gathered, but the most important thing is to make judgments about what has been recorded. The existence of formal procedures is not important —what is important is the quality of the procedures. To judge this it is necessary to compare existing procedures and practices with a standard. The methodology described in this book will serve as such a standard, and it is reasonable to make specific recommendations based on ideas of the sort presented here. Other standards for comparative purposes can be gleaned from knowledge of the methodology in other organizations, trade publications, and the literature on project methodology.

Remember that there is no such thing as *the* right way to do projects. Some methodologies work better than others, and what is good in one environment might not be good in another. What is important is to make specific suggestions for adapting reasonable and successful ideas to the conditions that prevail in your organization.

19-5 INTERNAL AUDIT CONSIDERATIONS

We have already indicated that the Internal Audit Department has a stake in evaluating a project methodology, so this is as good a place as any to make a few remarks concerning the role of the internal auditor and his involvement in the project process.

The image most people have of an auditor is that of a man wearing a green eyeshade who is busy counting the pencils. This image stems from the traditional function of internal audit: To act for top management to assure that the organizational assets are properly preserved. In recent years the internal auditing profession has moved to expand this traditional function in two ways that have a significant impact on DP. First, they have come to recognize that data is an important organizational asset and that they must assure its protection. This obviously has tremendous significance for the types of systems that are built by DP and the controls to be embedded in them. The second and more far-reaching expansion of their traditional function is that internal auditors now believe that it is not sufficient to know that assets are protected, but it is also important to know that the assets are properly employed. As this relates to DP projects, it means that the Internal Audit Department is concerned that proper procedures are in place to assure that DP is developing useful applications and is doing so in an effective manner. Thus, Internal Audit is concerned that there is an effective project selection process and an effective methodology for accomplishing projects.

To what extent will Internal Audit delve into the details of the project process? This obviously depends on the organization. At present it varies all the way from a cursory, inefficient examination to a full-blown effort by extremely knowledgeable individuals. The norm that will probably evolve is an investigation on a reasonably aggregated level to ascertain that the problem is being handled properly by the DP Department. To describe this level more precisely, let us examine the view that internal auditors presently tend to take.

According to Sawyer,[2] whose book is a standard reference for the internal auditing profession, an audit of a project methodology should ascertain that there is:

An effective selection process
Active user participation
Segregation of duties
Design and programming standards
Authorization and approval at each major phase
Sufficient testing
Effective control over conversion
Effective change procedure

Most DP people would agree that this list of requirements is reasonable; if anything, it is not comprehensive enough. Most would add that a project methodology should also ensure such things as:

An adequate planning and controlling process
Adequate risk assessment and control
Effective participation of operations, technical support, data management, security, and internal audit
Sufficient training and education
Adequate documentation and communications

The concerns of the internal auditor are sensible and are among the concerns of DP management but do not go as far or in as much detail. If DP evolves a project methodology that meets its own requirements, then it is likely that the methodology will also meet the requirements of Internal Audit. This means that the concern some DP personnel have about the involvement of internal auditors in the DP Department is really not warranted.

The Internal Auditor as a User

While discussing the internal auditor, a few comments should be made about his involvement in the project itself. Internal Audit is likely to have a direct stake in the project deliverable. One reason for this is that most products are involved with the assets of the organization, and to safeguard these assets it is necessary for the auditor to investigate th eproduct. Systems for

---
[2] Op. cit., pages 254-256.

assets it is necessary for the auditor to investigate the product. Systems for payroll, billing, order entry, inventory, and so on all directly or indirectly control the movement of assets. For such systems, internal audit must be convinced that the proper controls have been installed to prevent unauthorized or incorrect use, to enable recovery, and to build an audit trail for individual transactions.

A second reason for Internal Audit's interest in project deliverables is that they are likely to be users of the system. Much of the data that Internal Audit needs to perform its function is generated by data processing systems, and it is important to make certain that this data is captured and preserved in a form most useful to audit personnel. An example will illustrate this. It is not uncommon for salesmen to have discretion to shade the standard price for a product if, in their opinion, this action is warranted. Thus, a system for order entry would necessarily have provisions for nonstandard prices to be used in transactions. Internal Audit would be interested in knowing how frequently nonstandard prices are allowed, which salesmen grant these most frequently, and which customers get the favored treatment. Although generated by the system, this information is ordinarily not captured; but if the system builders regard Internal Audit as one of the system users, it is possible to meet their requirements along with those of the primary user.

For the reasons just given, Internal Audit realizes they should be involved with building the system. At the same time, they recognize a dilemma. If Internal Audit helps to build the system, how can they audit it? For many years this question bothered the auditing profession because of their strong tradition favoring separation of duties. Many felt it was a clear violation of this principle for auditors to review systems after being partly responsible for building them. But the alternative to involvement in the project is to repair finished systems in order to retrofit audit requirements; for systems of any size, this is prohibitively expensive. Realization of this cost led the audit profession to their present position, which is to become heavily involved with system specification and acceptance test but to preserve their independence by having little or no involvement with system design and coding.

Practice will vary from organization to organization, but most auditors do not want to be involved with Phase 1.1 of a project. This is too early. A large number of proposals will be killed during the Phase 1.1 review, and Internal Audit does not want to waste time on these.

The primary input from Internal Audit should come during Phase 1.2. This is the point where they should specify their controls and special requirements. If you are working on a project that involves organizational assets in any way and if the internal auditors are not involved during Phase 1.2, then you owe it to yourself and your organization to get them involved.

Delay in receiving their input can only mean costly changes later on.

Internal Audit is likely to require sign-off privileges at the end of Phase 1.3. This gives them an opportunity to verify that the proposed system will fulfill their requirements and a chance to voice any objections they might have.

During Phases 2.1, 2.2, and 2.3, Internal Audit will frequently be involved only in preparations for testing the system. They may decide to combine their testing with that of the user, or they may decide to test separately. In any event, they must make provisions to test the finished system for compliance with the Internal Audit requirements. Testing itself will ordinarily take place during Phase 3.1; and, if all is well, Internal Audit will then sign-off on the finished product.

In most installations, the involvement of Internal Audit in the affairs of DP is fairly recent. Auditors and DP personnel are still getting to know one another; habits and attitudes have yet to solidify. Many DP Departments have yet to decide how they should regard this newcomer. Our opinion is the following.

As far as project deliverables are concerned, the auditor should be treated the same as any other user. His satisfaction is just as important as that of any other user, and it is gained by obtaining clear specification of requirements and then meeting them. As far as the project methodology is concerned, the auditor should be regarded as having concerns that basically parallel those of DP. Some concerns, such as those for product and project security, might go beyond usual DP requirements, but they are certainly compatible and are in keeping with the organizational goals that both groups pursue. Therefore, the most reasonable attitude is that of partners striving together in a common cause.

When it comes to broader issues, most DP people have not yet realized that the internal auditor can be a powerful ally. It is generally forgotten that Internal Audit reports very near the top of most organizations, and because of this they can achieve things that DP by itself cannot. Often DP sees the need for essential controls or procedures but is unable to convince the organization of their importance. In such situations, it should be remembered that DP's concerns might well be shared by Internal Audit; their support might be just the added push that is needed to get the organization moving.

19-6 SUMMARY

- An audit of a project methodology is designed to answer three questions:

What is the formal project methodology?
How do people actually accomplish projects?
What should be the formal project methodology?

- An audit by DP is for internal DP use; it is complementary to any audit that might be conducted by the Internal Audit Department.
- An audit is a project. With modification, the methodology of this book can be applied to such a project. An audit should be formally authorized and should have a clear purpose and objective. It should produce an Audit Report and an assessment of the project itself.
- Because of their responsibility for safeguarding the organization's assets and for seeing that these are used in an effective manner, the Internal Audit Department is concerned with the quality of an organization's project methodology. Their requirements for a methodology are consistent with those of the DP Department.
- For most projects, the Internal Audit Department should be viewed as one of the system users. In particular, the system requirements should reflect the needs of Internal Audit, and the acceptance test should show that these needs have been met.

20

QUALITY

20-1 INTRODUCTION

References to quality pervade this book. Every chapter references the topic directly or indirectly. Yet we have waited until the very last to discuss the topic in detail, and you may well wonder why. The reason is that many of the comments to be made about quality are based on the assumption that you are thoroughly familiar with the project process, the need for quality, the way that quality is monitored, and other basics. What we will do here is to make some general observations and to discuss some of the subtleties of quality.

Of all the aspects of work that are to be controlled, the most elusive is quality. This is because quality is quite different from time, personnel, equipment, and money. These other aspects are inputs to the production process whereas quality is an output or a result, and for any process it is usually easier to control inputs than outputs.

In spite of this basic difference, our discussion of quality will in part parallel that of other aspects of work. With, say, time we discussed planning, observing, comparing, and adjusting as required. These same topics will be discussed for quality but, as you shall see, there are several complicating issues that must also be aired.

20-2 WORKER PERFORMANCE

Most of us have heard of someone who bought a car that was a lemon; the bolts were not tightened properly, parts were left off, cables were not connected correctly, and on and on. Yet someone else may have gotten very good service from a car of the same model and year. The two cars were built in the same factory to the same specifications and standards: the big difference was the quality of the workmanship that went into them. The same kind of situation can take place in DP. Two project teams can be given identical assignments, identical facilities, and identical standards; yet they can produce products of significantly different quality because of a difference in worker performance.

These examples show that in discussing quality a distinction must be made between the setting of objectives for quality and the achieving of them. We must distinguish between the quality of what is supposed to be done and the quality of what is actually done—between planned quality and actual quality. Quality objectives and quality worker performance are independent concepts; it is possible to have high-quality objectives with high- or low-quality performance, and to have low-quality objectives with high- or low-quality performance.

Projects should have both high objectives for quality and high worker performance. Most of this chapter pertains to quality objectives, but first we want to say something about quality and worker performance.

The quality of worker performance meets with quality objectives through the employee appraisal process. In an organization that manages by objectives (MBO), performance objectives are established for workers. These objectives describe what is to be done and set a standard or quality level that is to be achieved. Then work results are reviewed to determine if work has been completed and if it has been done according to quality standards. In some organizations the task of appraising workers falls to the Project Manager. In others it is not his job, but he must provide important input to the process. In either event, the Project Manager must be acquainted with the art of giving appraisals to workers.

Worker appraisals will not be discussed here because there is already a vast literature on the topic to which you can turn. Most of this literature is general and is not aimed specifically at projects. However, this should cause no trouble because most projects present no special problems. The only situation that might require special assistance is where the project team includes people who do not report to the Project Manager or his superior for purposes of appraisal and compensation. But these situations typically arise in large organizations where professional help is available to give needed guidance.

The only other point we wish to make about appraisals has to do with the need for improved standards. In many organizations, worker appraisals are made in a very subjective way. There are few formal standards and employee ratings are based largely on the manager's opinion. Increasingly this practice is being questioned because it allows discrimination, either conscious or unconscious. Under the impetus of equal opportunity and other legislation, attempts are being made in many organizations to make the appraisal process less subjective. A key step in this process is the establishment of meaningful quality objectives against which completed work can be measured. But there are many other aspects of projects that bear on the appraisal process, such as clear job definitions, well-defined outputs of tasks, and clear patterns of responsibility. The need to give equal opportunity to all workers is just one more reason for establishing formal performance standards and an effective project methodology.

20-3 PRODUCT QUALITY AND PROCESS QUALITY

Some typical questions that pertain to quality include:

Does the deliverable meet performance requirements?
Does user documentation meet requirements?
Have coding conventions been observed?
Are there sufficient reviews in the project?
Is the new system a significant improvement over the one it replaces?
Is the user satisfied?

Although they all pertain to quality, these questions are fundamentally different; no two are about exactly the same subject. Realization of this leads to an important observation: Quality is a composite concept. There are many facets to quality, many different topics that have something to do with it. And the many facets of quality have different characteristics. Some are obvious and easy to assess; some are subtle and illusive. Some are formally acknowledged; some are understood, but not discussed. The many facets of quality and their different characteristics have a lot to do with the problems we encounter in controlling this aspect of work.

The facets of quality can be grouped into two clusters: those facets that pertain to the product and those that pertain to the process. This grouping allows us to think of quality as having two basic dimensions, product and process. Product quality is the dimension that has to do with the delivered product; it pertains to project selection, product specifications, operational performance requirements, maintenance requirements, user reactions, and so on. Process quality is the dimension that has to do with the project or the process used to build the product; it pertains to the project methodology and the various standards for work.

There is no question that the quality of the product is important. This is one of the primary requirements of a project; and it is usually stressed by stating that the task of the project team is to deliver a quality product, on time, within budget. But our interest in a quality process is quite different. We really do not desire this because it is good in its own right, but because of the beneficial influence we believe it to have on the quality of the product or on the time and resource required to produce it. This is an important point, which we shall return to in Section 20-5. Now, however, let us explore the relationship between the quality of the product on the one hand and the quality of the process on the other.

To have a quality product it helps to have a quality process, but this alone is not sufficient. For example, the best process will not overcome the defect of a poor choice of projects by the Project Selection Committee or incorrect specifications from the user.

On the other hand, it is possible to produce a quality system with a production process that is not of high quality and with mediocre workmanship. This can be accomplished in the same way that, say, quality shirts can be produced in an inefficient plant with poor workers. In such circumstances, the key to quality output is an extensive quality-control system to uncover errors and to have them corrected before the product is shipped to end users. As most factories have learned long ago, this approach to quality products is expensive and time consuming. Moreover, as demand increases, the expense of finding and repairing errors rises more rapidly than the volume of work; it is almost as if the organization were on an ever-quickening treadmill. Instead of spending money on correcting errors, a more profitable way to obtain quality output is to spend money on the prevention of errors—that is, to improve the quality of the production process and the workmanship. Manufacturing plants learned long ago that improving the process and training people to do the job right the first time is the way to obtain quality output at the lowest total cost.

The traditional approach to quality products in DP has been that of inspection, discovery of error, and correction; in other words, the quality of the final product has been achieved by screening out mistakes. The modern trend is toward improving the quality of the production process and the quality of worker performance—toward the prevention of error. Much of the methodology discussed in this book is aimed at this goal.

20-4 MEASURING QUALITY

Another complicating feature of quality is that it cannot easily be quantified. Of course, some facets of quality are not a problem; for example, performance standards involving response time or processing volume relate to quality and clearly these can be measured. But most facets are difficult or impossible to quantify, and certainly there is no general measure that can be assigned to product quality or to process quality. This feature of quality sets it apart from the other aspects of work that we control. All others can be monitored by counting or measuring in fairly standard units. Indeed, it was not even necessary for us to discuss how, say, time was to be measured because it was automatically assumed to be in terms of days or weeks or some other equally familiar unit. But for quality, no such standard yardstick exists. This means that before we talk of planning and controlling for quality, we must first discuss how it is to be measured.

Various attempts at quantification have been made in the past. The quality of the product has been measured by the number of bugs per thousand lines of delivered code, or the ratio of maintenance cost to development cost. Measures of the production quality include the number of test shots per module and the number of changes per module. But all such measures are incomplete; they focus on certain facets of quality and ignore others. Much research needs to be done in this area before a meaningful, widely accepted measure is likely to evolve.

Even when measures do exist, they sometimes fail to indicate clearly which dimension of quality they are measuring. The number of bugs per thousand lines of delivered code might be considered as a measure of product quality, but it might also be considered as a measure of the production process. The number of changes per module sounds like a measure of the production process, but some might regard it as a predictor of product quality. In most cases it would take controlled experiments and careful analysis to be able to attribute an improvement in a measure to the proper dimension of quality. It would be useful, however, if such a distinction could be made because it would indicate whether improvements in quality could best be made by adjusting the process or the product requirements.

Another problem arises with such measures as we currently have for the quality of products. Most existing measures can be applied only after the product is installed and is in operation; therefore they provide little help in our efforts to control for quality during the building process. Perhaps this will not be such a problem when products are assembled in a more uniform fashion; after all, the quality of a car is measured largely by its performance, and this does not prevent reasonable control for quality during production. But when a software product is viewed by its creators as a custom job, as is often the case now, it is difficult to establish formal correlations between performance and aspects of production.

At present, quality is generally not assessed by assigning it a numerical rating. Instead, we attempt to decide whether the quality of a product or a process is acceptable or not, whether it meets requirements or not, whether we pass on it or reject it. That is, quality is assessed by comparison to approved criteria or benchmarks; quality is acceptable if and only if it compares favorably to these criteria. Thus, quality assessment is generally a "go/no-go" decision.

Quality Criteria

Criteria for quality emerge from three sources: product specifications, formal standards, and professional opinion. The first two of these are usually documented in writing; the third is usually informal but is, nevertheless, real and important.

Product specifications already have been discussed in detail, so they will not be discussed at this point.

Most organizations have standards, but there is considerable variation in their extent and the degree to which they are documented. Standards will be discussed in the next section.

The third source of criteria for quality is professional opinion, and its importance should not be underestimated. Specifications and standards often fail to cover such important topics as the criteria for choosing the architecture, the maintainability of the system during operation, and the robustness of the system—that is, its reaction to minor blows. Decisions involving these and other important topics often rest on the judgment of professionals.

Professional opinion is almost entirely undocumented and a matter of subjective judgment. Judgment is always individual; but it might be influenced by a group, as in a peer review or a Delphi exercise. Judgment is usually applied informally, although a structured process such as the Delphi technique might be used to advantage in some cases.

Part of professional opinion stems from industry norms. This leads to such criteria as the requirement that the new system be leading edge (some say bleeding edge) or that it involve a certain type of technology. And it also leads to requirements that the new system perform at least as well as the system it replaces, or that the new system perform as well as similar systems already in existence.

Professional opinion also stems from the personal standards of project personnel and users, and these standards can be technical or aesthetic. Indeed, one of the important reasons for training and education of professionals is to build their personal conception of what constitutes quality work.

20-5 FORMAL STANDARDS

Standards are established as one set of criteria for quality. They are established for both dimensions of quality—product and process. Some standards clearly relate to a single dimension, some to both. The only reason to classify standards by dimension of quality is to be aware of likely implications when establishing the standards.

Criteria for the quality of deliverables include: development standards (analysis, design, programming), product documentation standards, and test standards. Operational performance criteria might be established as standards or might be included with the specifications for individual projects.

The first written standards adopted by most organizations have to do with the primary development activities. Standards for design might cover the techniques to be used, such as HIPO diagrams and flowcharts, and such topics as nomenclature conventions, data formats, flowchart symbols and file ID. Programming standards might specify structured programming conventions, languages to be used, and procedures for error routines, checkpoint and restart routines, security measures, and audit routines. Other standards in the development area might specify such procedures as top-down development or program proofing.

Standards for product documentation cover the system description and user documentation. The former should cover manual and automated procedures and requirements such as narrative descriptions, HIPOs, flowcharts, decision tables, and listings. These standards are closely related to development standards, as the previous paragraph reveals. User documentation standards should cover requirements for describing how the system is operated and employed. It should cover requirements for preparation of input, output descriptions, run books, error-correction procedures, and so on.

Standards for testing should indicate the general philosophy of testing, including such matters as who does the testing, the extent of user involvement in systems test, and the role of the audit department and operations. The standards should also specify the extent of testing required; for example, the fact that documentation, manual procedures, operations procedures, and so on are to be tested in addition to the developed software. The requirements for regression testing might also be indicated.

Standards that relate to the quality of the process make up the project methodology and are documented in the Project Handbook. These standards are the major topic of this book and need no elaboration here. See Section 4-2 for basic features of a project methodology.

In Section 8-6 we listed what we believe to be features of a good methodology. But it is natural to ask: How do we determine if a feature in a methodology is good or bad? How do we decide what standards we *should* set for the process? Let us explore these questions.

Suppose we are considering the addition of a separate procedure to our methodology. How would we justify it? How would we decide if it is worthwhile? The answer is we would have to look at the result of using the procedure. There are many intermediate things we could inspect, but in the final analysis we must see if the procedure enhances the quality of the product or if it makes more effective use of time and resources. We must look to these because the goal of projects is stated in terms of product quality, project time, and project resources—there is no other standard of measure. (Of course, we are assuming that other factors, such as employee satisfaction, will make themselves felt on these project goals.)

In the abstract, process quality is measured by its effect on product quality, project time, and project resources. In practice, it is nearly impossible to make careful measurements to determine the effect on these of each process procedure. Therefore, in practice we usually establish quality standards for the process that we *believe* will make for quality products or more effective use of time and resource—things we believe will lead to easier use, less missing function, fewer bugs, and so on. We try to measure the effect on project goals whenever possible, but by necessity we must base many decisions on our personal professional opinion. For example, it might be difficult to prove the benefit of, say, a formal change procedure on project goals. Such a procedure is usually not installed in isolation but is included along with other enhancements to a project methodology, and it is hard to attribute recognized benefits to specific procedures. Nevertheless, we would install the change procedure because in our professional opinion it will help us to produce quality products and to use time and resources more effectively.

One final point about standards: An organization should establish standards for their standards—that is, they should establish requirements that standards be simple, clear, and essential. The best way to do this is to require that all standards be reviewed before adoption by those who will be affected by them, and to follow this with periodic reappraisals to learn if standards are still effective. Bad or outdated standards are often worse than no standards.[1]

20-6 MANAGING FOR QUALITY WITHIN A PROJECT

We said in Chapter 3 that for each aspect of work that is controlled we must plan performance, observe actual performance, compare actual with plan, and adjust as required. Let us see how this applies to quality.

---

[1] A *Wall Street Journal* article (April 19, 1978) reported on some problems women weightlifters encounter because standards for weightlifting competitions were established before women were involved with the sport. At one contest, four women were weighed nude before three male officials because rules required contestants to be weighed nude. In other contests women have worn athletic supporters because the standards required all contestants to wear them.

Planning for quality within a project is aimed at meeting or exceeding the criteria for quality discussed in Section 20-4. To achieve this goal, it is necessary that all people connected with the project be aware of these criteria and that it is part of their job to meet them. To promote this awareness it might be necessary to establish a Training Plan. The only other explicit planning that is required is to establish a schedule of reviews for tracking quality. Because reviews typically cover more aspects of work than just quality, it is customary to call the output of the planning process a Review Plan. Thus, planning for quality does not result in a separate document that reasonably could be called a Quality Plan.

For quality, the observation of performance is combined with a comparison to plan. This is because the observation amounts to checking to see if standards have been met or not. Information on performance comes from a variety of sources, including: review reports, checkpoint reports, work unit completion reports, test reports, trouble reports, and informal reports.

Most of these reports are described and formats are specified in the organization's Project Handbook. However, the last class of reports—informal reports—are often oral and unstructured. This source of information is invaluable and must not be stifled. In building a control system always remember that the formal structure cannot provide all the information needed for sensible management. There is always the unusual, the unexpected, or the out of the ordinary situation that must come to management's attention. One of the hardest problems in building a control system is to establish a formal structure, which is absolutely essential for managing the work, without restraining the informal exchanges that no project can do without.

We have already indicated that quality differs from other control elements because it has to do with the project as well as the product and because of the problem with its measurement. Quite frequently there is another difference that has to do with the provisions for making adjustments in case actual performance does not measure up to plan. Usually the responsibility for making limited adjustments in time or resource schedules is lodged with the Project Manager; but it is not unusual for the Project Manager to delegate responsibility for the monitoring of quality to special groups. Thus, it is not uncommon for there to be groups for monitoring change, architectural integrity, or other facets of quality. The existence of such groups bears witness to the fact that quality is the most difficult aspect of work to plan and control.

20-7 THE QUEST FOR QUALITY

It is difficult to strive for quality on just a single project. For quality it is necessary to have understanding, standards for work, and a reasonable project process; and it is a chore to establish all of this for an individual effort. Much of the activity related to the achievement of quality should precede the project—it should be part of a DP Department's on-going quest for quality. This activity should have the full support of upper management, who should make their support apparent by adopting a quality policy similar to the one given in Appendix C.

The task of building appropriate tools should be recognized by DP management for what it is—a project in its own right. By treating the development of standards and an implementation methodology as a separate project it is possible to establish a rational, uniform procedure that can be applied across the board. The cost of such a project can be amortized over many development projects, and this should justify the effort. But more importantly, the uniform procedures that result from such a project make interproject comparisons meaningful. This uniformity is an essential prerequisite to improved project estimates and to meaningful standards of accomplishment.

A second important step that should be started early and should be an ongoing DP Department activity is that of motivation and education for quality. This effort should concentrate on two fundamental messages. The first is: *Quality is everybody's job.* The only way to produce a quality product is to achieve quality at each and every step in the production process, and it is up to each person related to the project to see that his contribution measures up to expectations. Quality is not just a question of quality coding, but it requires a quality problem definition, quality architecture, quality design, quality documentation, quality management—quality throughout.

The second important message is: *Do it right the first time.* Certainly it takes longer and costs more to take the time to do a proper job of designing or coding or planning, but this time is saved many times over through the reduction of effort spent on rework. The message of doing it right the first time is extremely difficult to put across. Often it means changing deeply ingrained work habits, and people resist this with great tenacity. The argument usually encountered is that "everybody" knows DP work is different and that it is not possible to build complex systems without a certain amount of trial and error. This argument ignores the growing number of successful applications that have been delivered without errors. But more importantly, it ignores the fact that the only way to attain quality is to adopt an attitude that quality work *is* possible, that it is within our power to do things correctly the first time. This attitude is becoming essential as both the complexity of systems and the demand for reliability accelerate.

Of course, the task of managing for quality does not stop with standards and education. It is necessary to monitor results regularly by using such tools as postinstallation audits, user reports, and operations reports. It is also necessary to make regular adjustments to improve performance. Quality is achieved by a series of small steps, not by one giant leap.

20-8 SUMMARY

- A discussion of quality should distinguish between the objectives for quality and the quality of worker performance.
- Quality has two dimensions: the quality of the project product and the quality of the project process used to produce the product.
- It is difficult to quantify quality. Therefore we usually assess quality by comparison with certain criteria; we say the quality criteria have been met or have not been.
- Criteria for quality emerge from three sources:

    Product specifications
    Formal standards
    Professional opinions

- Product specifications establish criteria for products. Formal standards establish criteria for products and for the production process.
- Criteria for the production process are measured ultimately by the impact they have on product quality, project duration, or project resources.
- Most of the activity related to the achievement of quality should precede individual projects; largely this activity consists of establishing proper standards and providing proper education.
- Three important messages concerning quality are:

    Quality is everybody's job
    Do it right the first time
    Quality is achieved by a series of small steps, not by one giant leap

APPENDICES

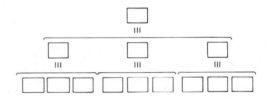

APPENDIX A: THE STRUCTURE OF PROJECT WORK

A-1 INTRODUCTION

In this appendix we detail the project work described in Chapters 3 and 4.

The material that follows has two uses: to support and amplify the text and to provide a base for the identification and description of the phases in your own project methodology. While this material is reasonably complete, our phases and their descriptions must be adapted to your particular organization to be usable. Our major assumptions are summarized as follows:

The organization has identified levels of control with well-defined tasks and responsibilities

Project work proceeds only upon management approval and authorization of the phase

Modern development techniques and technology are used throughout the project

A change procedure has been established and input documents reflect approved changes

Individual responsibility and self-control, transactional processes, teams, MBO, etc., and all they imply are used effectively by the organization

Our analysis of project work will use the techniques of function analysis described in Chapter 12.

441

A-2 PROJECT CHARACTERISTICS

Formal Definition of a Project

A project is a formally established, single-time work effort with these characteristics:

An established, definite start date
A well-defined purpose and scope
A well-defined end product
Specific product performance specifications
A formally stated cost and benefit basis
An established, definite project end date

Functional Definition of a Project

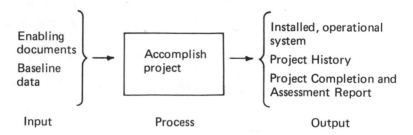

Input   Process   Output

Purpose of a Project

The purpose of a project is to provide an economically justified response to the opportunity or requirement identified in a DP Project Proposal.

Objectives of a Project

The objectives of a project are:
1. To evaluate the DP Project Proposal and to determine an appropriate response to it
2. To develop a business assessment of the proposed response
3. To develop and install a fully tested system for an approved response

Comments

There are two types of projects: mandated and discretionary. In general, project procedures treat them the same. A major difference is in the business assessment. Both reduce the funds available for additional investment.

Discretionary projects are investments and are treated as such; the DP system developed is expected to provide a measurable benefit that is above a preestablished minimum return on investment. In addition, the payback period is usually determined and considered.

Mandated projects are required by law. The DP System produced must meet requirements and allow for foreseeable changes in the requirements. These projects represent "pure" costs that should be minimized. They reduce the funds available for investment without providing a return on the money spent.

A-3 THE FIRST-LEVEL BREAKDOWN OF PROJECT WORK

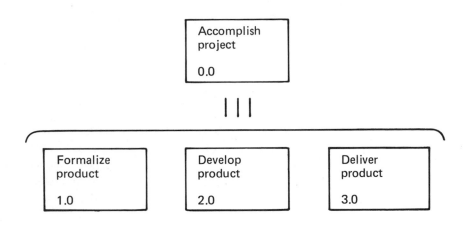

Subfunction 1.0: Formalize Product

Purpose:

To define an appropriate system in response to a DP Project Proposal.

Objectives:

1. To study the DP Project Proposal and to formalize the requirements.
2. To develop and evaluate alternative responses and to select the alternative best meeting system and business requirements.
3. To establish an appropriate system development plan.

Subfunction 2.0: Develop Product

Purpose:

To provide a complete, tested system as defined and approved.

Objectives:

1. To design the system as defined and approved.
2. To provide appropriate tests and test procedures.
3. To build and integrate the system.
4. To test the completed, integrated system.
5. To detail Acceptance Test and Installation Plans.

Subfunction 3.0: Deliver Product

Purpose:

To install an operational, user-accepted system.

Objectives:

1. To obtain user acceptance of the tested system.
2. To complete installation of the accepted system and to place it in productive operation.
3. To transfer the system and its documentation to the Systems Group.
4. To close the project by completing and submitting:
   The Project History File
   The Project Completion and Assessment Report

Comments

Deliverables have been omitted because they can be obtained by consolidating the deliverables described in Section A-4.

Project methodologies usually do not document this first level of work breakdown. However, this work subdivision is logical and is implicit in most "phased" methodologies. We have used this breakdown as an aid in the logical determination of phases (the second-level breakdown). You will frequently find these first-level subfunctions useful in writing or talking about projects or project methodologies. Also, they are useful in adjusting a methodology for use with small projects.

A-4 PHASES—THE SECOND-LEVEL BREAKDOWN OF PROJECT WORK

Subfunction 1.0: Formalize Product

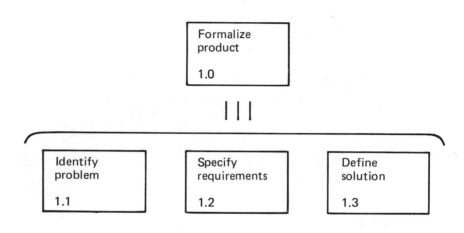

Subfunction 2.0: Develop Product

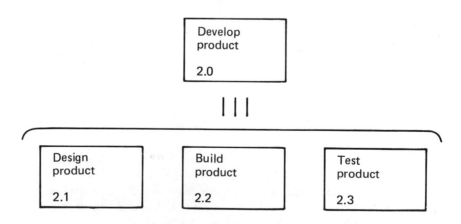

Subfunction 3.0 Deliver Product

```
          ┌─────────────┐
          │ Deliver     │
          │ product     │
          │             │
          │ 3.0         │
          └─────────────┘
               │ │ │
    ┌──────────────────────────────┐
┌──────────┐   ┌──────────┐   ┌──────────┐
│ Accept   │   │ Install  │   │ Transfer │
│ product  │   │ product  │   │ product  │
│          │   │          │   │          │
│ 3.1      │   │ 3.2      │   │ 3.3      │
└──────────┘   └──────────┘   └──────────┘
```

Format for Phase Descriptions

The phase descriptions are presented in the following format:

PHASE NAME: The name and number identifying the phase.

PURPOSE: The reason the particular phase is being performed.

OBJECTIVES: Specifically what will be accomplished during the phase. Only major objectives associated with the primary phase deliverables are shown.

STANDARD TASKS: The standard tasks are listed separately for convenience (see Section A-5).

DELIVERABLES (Outputs): Only major outputs are listed; intermediate and minor outputs are not shown. Phase deliverables are listed according to the following classification:

  1. Specific: (These are outputs unique to the phase; they are associated with the purpose of the phase.)
        Target systems
        Support systems
        Plans, specific and named
        Reports
  2. General: (Management-oriented reports common to all phases.)
        Project business reports
          Report to Management
          Project Plan (initial or updated)
          Phase Plan (next phase)
        Project Workbook (initial or updated)
        Phase Completion and Assessment Report

Comments: Phase inputs can be classified as follows:

  1. Enabling documents
  2. Baseline data (contained in baseline documents) as modified by the Change Procedure
  3. The Project Workbook (except Phase 1.1)
  4. The Phase Plan (except Phase 1.1)

We have not shown inputs in our phase descriptions because our analysis into sequential subfunctions assumes that the output from one subfunction becomes the input to the next.

Phase 1.1: Identify Problem

Purpose:

A brief study of the opportunity or requirement identified in a DP Project Proposal conducted to establish purpose, scope, and bounds of the project.

Objectives:

1. To identify the specific area of concern and to agree on the general purpose, scope, and bounds for the proposed project.
2. To prepare the initial project business reports.
3. To establish the Project Workbook.

Deliverables:

Specific:

Identification Report

General:

Project business reports
 Report to Management
 Project Plan (initial)
 Phase 1.2 Plan
Project Workbook (initial)
Phase 1.1 Completion and Assessment Report

Phase 1.2: Specify Requirements

Purpose:

> To make a formal, comprehensive determination of the proposed system requirements.

Objectives:

> 1. To complete the documentation of the present system.
> 2. To produce a precise statement of system requirements.
> 3. To prepare the general reports to management.

Deliverables:

> Specific:
>
> > Documentation of the present system
> > System Requirements Specification Report
> > Training Plan (initial)
>
> General:
>
> > Project business reports
> >   Report to Management
> >   Project Plan (updated)
> >   Phase 1.3 Plan
> > Project Workbook (updated)
> > Phase 1.2 Completion and Assessment Report

Phase 1.3: Define Solution

Purpose:

To select a recommended approach for satisfying the identified system requirements and to specify the external design for the selected alternative.

Objectives:

1. To define and evaluate alternative ways of meeting the systems requirements as specified.
2. To select a recommended alternative and to prepare the System Architecture Report (external design)
3. To determine the resources required to build the recommended system.
4. To prepare the general reports to management.

Deliverables:

Specific:

System Architecture Report
Summary of Alternative Architectures Considered
Training Plan (updated)
Plans and Orders for Purchased Items (initial)

General:

Project business reports
Report to Management
Project Plan (updated)
Phase 2.1 Plan
Project Workbook (updated)
Phase 1.3 Completion and Assessment Report

Phase 2.1: Design Product

Purpose:

> To produce the internal design of the selected system and to define the support requirements.

Objectives:

> 1. To produce the internal design of the system as defined and approved.
> 2. To initiate development of all test systems.
> 3. To produce support plans and packages required.
> 4. To prepare the general reports for management.

Deliverables:

> Specific:
>
>> System Design Specifications
>>> Program Specifications
>>
>> Test Plans (initial)
>>> Program
>>> System
>>> Acceptance
>>
>> Support Systems Specifications and Plans
>> Documentation Plan
>> Plans and Orders for Purchased Items (updated)
>> Location and Site Plans
>> Conversion Plan
>> Installation Plan
>> Training Plans (updated)
>>> Project team
>>> Users
>>> Operations
>
> General:
>
>> Project business reports
>>> Report to Management
>>> Project Plan (updated)
>>> Phase 2.2 Plan
>>
>> Project Workbook (updated)
>> Phase 2.1 Completion and Assessment Report

Phase 2.2: Build Product

Purpose:

To build and integrate the system.

Objectives:

1. To provide a complete system ready for system test.
2. To complete the System Test Package.
3. To produce support plans and packages required.
4. To prepare the general reports for management.

Deliverables:

Specific:

Complete, integrated system, ready for system test
  Programs
  Procedures
  Documentation
  Purchased items
Unit and Program Test Reports
Training Completion Reports
System Test Package
  Data
  Programs
  Test cases
  Procedures
  Script
  Sample results of test runs
Acceptance Test Plan (updated)
Documentation Plan (final)
Plans and Orders for Purchased Items (updated)
Location and Site Plans (updated)
Conversion Plan (updated)
Installation Plan (updated)
Training Plans (updated)
  Project team
  Users
  Operations

General:
  Project business reports
    Report to Management
    Project Plan (updated)
    Phase 2.3 Plan
  Project Workbook (updated)
  Phase 2.2 Completion and Assessment Report

Phase 2.3: Test Product

Purpose:

　　To produce a complete, tested system.

Objectives:

　　1. To provide a complete, tested system ready for Acceptance Test.
　　2. To complete the Acceptance Test Package.
　　3. To produce support plans and packages required.
　　4. To prepare the general reports to management.

Deliverables:

　　Specific:

　　　　Complete, tested system (including corrections and updated
　　　　　　documentation)
　　　　System Test Report
　　　　Training Completion Report
　　　　Training Package
　　　　Acceptance Test Package
　　　　Location and Site Plans (final)
　　　　Training Plans (final)

　　General:

　　　　Project Business Reports
　　　　　　Report to Management
　　　　　　Project Plan (updated)
　　　　　　Phase 3.1 Plan
　　　　Project Workbook (updated)
　　　　Phase 2.3 Completion and Assessment Report

Phase 3.1: Accept Product

Purpose:

To obtain user acceptance of the system.

Objectives:

1. To obtain user acceptance of the system as tested.
2. To complete the conversion and installation packages.
3. To prepare the general reports for management.

Deliverables:

Specific:

Accepted system
Acceptance Report
Conversion Package
Installation Package
Training Completion Report

General:

Project business reports
   Report to Management
   Project Plan (updated)
   Phase 3.2 Plan
Project Workbook (updated)
Phase 3.1 Completion and Assessment Report

Phase 3.2: Install Product

Purpose:

To install the completed, tested, accepted system.

Objectives:

1. To complete site preparation.
2. To install the system.
3. To complete all conversion activities.
4. To complete all training.
5. To prepare the general reports for management.

Deliverables:

Specific:

Installed, operational system
Installation and Conversion Completion Report
Training Completion Report

General:

Project business reports
   Report to Management
   Project Plan (updated)
   Phase 3.3 Plan (standard plan)
Project Workbook (updated)
Phase 3.2 Completion and Assessment Report

Phase 3.3: Transfer Product

Purpose:

To complete the project.

Objectives:

1. To transfer the system and its documentation to the Systems Group.
2. To produce a usable Project History File.
3. To prepare the Project Completion and Assessment Report.
4. To close the project.

Deliverables:

Specific:

System File
Project History File
Project Completion and Assessment Report

General:

(none)

A-5 STANDARD TASKS

In Chapter 3 the standard task was defined as the smallest unit of work with a unique accounting number. As discussed in the text, there are many types of standard tasks: management, technical, administrative, clerical, scheduled, unscheduled, etc. How are standard tasks identified? Is there a unique or "best" list? The answers to these and related questions are important to the organization creating its own project methodology.

Is there a unique list? No. There are many possible lists, each associated with the method of identification and the individual making the identification. Is there a "best" list? Yes and no. There may be a "best" list for a specific situation, but, in practice, it will seldom be found. An organization will frequently find one list more *useful* than others because it "fits" the organizational situation better. For example, such a "better" list might provide accounting data in a manner more acceptable to the accountants or to management.

How are standard tasks identified? There are four techniques that can be used. Each can provide lists of satisfactory utility, although quite different in nature. They are:

1. *Function analysis.* This is the technique for the definition and analysis of functions described in Chapter 12. Such an analysis will produce a list of standard tasks generic in nature, complete, and extensive. In general, the lists produced will not contain the unscheduled tasks.

2. *Historical analysis.* If the organization has access to a reasonable amount of historical data (their own or from a similar organization), careful analysis will usually produce a satisfactory list of standard tasks.

3. *Major deliverables.* In developing its project methodology, an organization concentrates on the identification of deliverables, both products and documents, that must be produced. The identification of standard tasks with major deliverables produces useful lists, controlled in length, and keyed to the work required to provide the work products desired.

4. *Mixed.* As the name implies, this technique is a mixture of the above techniques.

We use the fourth technique in developing our list of standard tasks presented below.

What should be the degree of aggregation of the list of standard tasks? This question can only be answered by considering the organization and the *people* who will use data provided by the methodology being developed. The methodology must provide the level of detail needed or expected by the individuals involved in controlling the project and, at the same time, remain practical and simple enough to be used by the people doing the actual work. Our list is very aggregated. The indented items are subtasks that could become the basis for a more detailed list of standard tasks if desired (they are also useful as an aid in defining work units). When developing a project methodology, we suggest you start at the aggregate level and add detail based on your actual experience. Also, remember that the level of detail does not have to be the same for each phase.

The Nonscheduled Standard Tasks

Manage project
    (excludes scheduled tasks and the management of change)
Manage change
    (includes logging, evaluation, replanning, and tracking of change)
Implement approved change
    (includes all nonmanagement work required to implement an approved change)
Perform support tasks
    (includes travel time, attending meetings and reviews, training, studying, and other)
Administer project
    (includes clerical tasks and administrative tasks)

The Scheduled Standard Tasks Common to All Phases

Develop action plans
    Analyze input documents
    Prepare Work Plan, schedule, and budget
    Assign work
    Orient team
Prepare general outputs
    Prepare Phase Plan for the next phase
    Update Project Plan
    Prepare Report to Management
    Update Project Workbook
    Prepare Phase Completion and Assessment Report

Phase 1.1: Identify Problem

Standard Tasks:

Develop action plans (see common tasks)
    (a minimum activity utilizing a standard Work Plan)
Develop Identification Report
    Search literature
    Interview involved people
    Define project purpose, scope, objectives, and contraints
    Prepare Identification Report
Prepare general outputs (see common tasks)

Phase 1.2: Specify Requirements

Standard Tasks:

Develop action plans (see common tasks)
Gather data
    (include present and proposed system)
    Schedule interviews
    (include users, DPD, user's user, others)
    Conduct and document interviews
Describe present system
    Observe present system
    Analyze performance of present system
    Prepare written description of present system
Develop System Requirements Specification Report
    Detail purpose, scope, and objectives of the proposed system
    Define inputs and outputs
    Define system interfaces
    Determine system impact
    Describe performance and quality requirements
    Obtain necessary approvals and concurrences
Evolve plans
    Prepare Training Plan (initial)
Prepare general outputs (see common tasks)

Phase 1.3: Define Solution

Standard Tasks:

Develop action plans (see common tasks)
Formulate alternative solutions
   (include building new system, modifying existing system, buying a
   package, doing nothing)
Select recommended solution
   Evaluate identified alternatives
      (include reason why this alternative was selected; reasons why
      other alternatives were rejected)
   Obtain approvals and concurrences
Develop System Architecture Report
   Detail system specifications
      (include structure, hardware, software, data base requirements,
      interface, impact, test requirements, security and audit require-
      ments)
   Determine resource requirements
      (include people, money, machine time, skill requirements, train-
      ing requirements)
   Obtain necessary approvals and concurrences
Evolve Plans
   Prepare purchased items requirements
   Update Training Plan
Prepare general outputs (see common tasks)

Phase 2.1: Design Product

Standard Tasks:

Develop action plans (see common tasks)
Develop System Design Specifications
    (include HIPOs, flowcharts, tables as required; specify hardware, software, and site requirements; define program requirements including modifications to programs obtained from vendors; specify procedures; define operator actions; design and order forms; design screen formats)
    Define the computer system
    Determine the noncomputer system
Determine Support System Specifications
    Define Test Plans
    (include Program Test, System Test, and Acceptance Test)
    Determine training requirements
Evolve Plans
    Develop Test, Documentation, Purchased Items, Location, Site, Conversion, and Intallation Plans
    Update Training Plan
Prepare general outputs (see common tasks)

Phase 2.2: Build Product

Standard Tasks:

Develop action plans (see common tasks)
Build system
    Develop computer system
        (include code, integrate, and test modules; document system)
    Develop noncomputer system
        (include the identification, development, and documentation of all procedures)
Build System Test Package
    (include data, programs, test cases, sample test outputs, procedures, and scripts)
Prepare Training Completion Report
    Conduct training
    Produce Training Completion Report
Evolve Plans
    Update Test, Documentation, Purchased items, Location, Site, Conversion, Installation, and Training Plans
Prepare general outputs (see common tasks)

Phase 2.3: Test Product

Standard Tasks:

Develop action plans (see common tasks)
Produce System Test Report
    Conduct all system tests
    Correct system and update documentation
    Prepare System Test Report
Develop Acceptance Test Package
    (include test cases, test data, expected test results, and test script)
Perform training tasks
    Develop training packages
    Conduct planned training
    Prepare Training Completion Report
Evolve Plans
    Update Location, Site, Conversion, and Installation Plans
Prepare general outputs (see common tasks)

Phase 3.1: Accept Product

Standard Tasks:

      Develop action plans (see common tasks)
      Produce Acceptance Report
         Conduct all acceptance tests
         Correct system and update documentation
         Prepare Acceptance Report
      Build Conversion and Installation Packages
         Verify delivery of purchased items
         Prepare script for conversion and installation
      Prepare Training Completion Report
         Conduct planned training
         Produce Training Completion Report
      Prepare general reports (see common tasks)

Phase 3.2: Install Product

Standard Tasks:

      Develop action plans (see common tasks)
      Prepare Installation and Conversion Completion Report
         Install and convert system
            (include completion of site preparation and hardware installation;
              install programs; convert data and procedures; test system)
         Produce Installation and Conversion Completion Report
      Perform training tasks
         Conduct planned training
         Prepare Training Completion Report (final)
      Prepare general reports (see common tasks)

Phase 3.3: Transfer Product

Standard Tasks:

      Develop action plans
         (A minimum activity utilizing a standard Work Plan.)
      Prepare Systems File
      Prepare History File
      Prepare Project Completion and Assessment Report

APPENDIX B:
BASIC DOCUMENTS

B-1 INTRODUCTION

As discussed in Chapter 7, effective communication is vital to project success. An essential part of a successful project communication system is a well-defined set of *formal* project documents. The Project Handbook describes these documents and the methods and procedures to be used on all the organization's projects. The Project Workbook is really a filing, update, and distribution system to deal with the documents and products produced on each project. These two fundamental documents are outlined in some detail. We have more briefly outlined selected documents relating to the product and the project that are not outlined in the text.

B-2 THE PROJECT HANDBOOK—A GENERIC TABLE OF CONTENTS

1. Preface

>   Source of the Handbook
>   Tells who authorized and who prepared the Handbook
>   Distribution of the Handbook
>   Tells who is to receive the Handbook and describes the distribution mechanics
>   Control information
>   Identifies the current contents of the Handbook and gives dates of the versions
>   Standards for the Handbook
>   Describes the format of the Handbook and tells how it will be updated

2. Contents

*3. Foreword

>   A signed letter from the sponsor of the Handbook

4. Introduction

>   Comments on a project methodology
>   What it is
>   Why it is needed
>   Benefits to various groups
>   Comments on this Project Handbook
>   What it is
>   Its scope of applicability
>   Relation to other organizational documents
>   Manager's Manual
>   Other standards and procedures

5. Organization Overview

>   General organization
>   Mission
>   Basic policies
>   Business trends

---

*Part of our base methodology (see Appendix C-6).

> Data Processing Department
> > Mission, purpose
> > Policies
> > Interfaces with other functional areas
> > Trends

6. The Project

> Basic definitions
> > System and DP system
> > System, project, and operation and maintenance life cycles
> > Characteristics of a project
> *Project Proposal and Selection Procedure
> > The project as a business investment
> > The process
> > Selection criteria

*7. Project Phases

> Definition and purpose of phases, standard tasks
> Individual phase descriptions
> > Purpose and scope
> > Objectives
> > Outputs
> > Standard tasks

8. Planning Work

> Relation of standard tasks to a specific project
> Responsibility grids
> *Definition and purpose of work units
> *Action plans
> > Purpose
> > List of action plans
> > Standards for action planning

9. Doing work

> Management procedures
> > Estimating
> > Cost and benefit analysis
> > Assessing and controlling risk

---

*Part of our base methodology (see Appendix C-6).

References to related documents
Standards for work performance
Standards for the project product
Standards and procedures of related functional areas
Definition and role of the Project Administrator
Definition and role of Systems Assurance
The Data Processing Audit function and its role
Project security

10.   Controlling Work

Control requirements (by organizational level)
*Tracking procedures

*11.   Reviewing Work

Purpose and types of reviews
Individual review descriptions
Purpose and scope
Sponsor
Objectives
Guidelines

*12.   Reporting Completed Work

Definition and purpose of reports
Individual reports
Purpose
Contents
When completed, by whom
Distribution

*13.   Change Procedure

Definitions
Baseline documents
Change
Interpretation
Need for change and for monitoring change
Details of the Change Procedure
The Interpretation Procedure

---

*Part of our base methodology (see Appendix C-6).

14.   Accounting and Administrative Procedures

       Definition and purpose of procedures
       Description of accounting procedures
       Description of administrative procedures
             Time reporting
             Requesting support services
             Requesting supplies
             Requesting capital expenditures
             Other

15.   Approval Procedures

       Phase approval procedures
       Project approval procedures

*16.   The Project Workbook

       Purpose
       Responsibility
       Structure of the Workbook
       Update procedure
       Distribution
       Disposition

17.   Adjusting Procedures to Project Size

       Purpose of adjusting procedures
       Size classifications
       Adjustment for each size classification

*18.   Methodology Management Procedure

       Need for maintaining the methodology
       Who is responsible for monitoring the methodology
       Change procedure for the project methodology

19.   Glossary

       The standard DP and business vocabulary of the organization,

---

*Part of our base methodology (see Appendix C-6).

including abbreviations and acronyms

20. Appendix

     Sample forms
     Tables
     Examples

21. Index

B-3 THE PROJECT WORKBOOK—A GENERIC TABLE OF CONTENTS

Note: The Project Workbook is defined in the Project Handbook. It provides continuity across the phases. Within a category, documents are filed by phase.

1. Table of Contents

2. Project Documentation

    Enabling documents
      DP Project Proposal
      Statements of
        Funds allocation
        Work authorization
        Work assignment
    Resources
      Organizational data
      Personnel data (isolate private data)
        Availability
        Individual profiles
          (experience; training; restrictions)
      Facilities
      Equipment
    Plans
      Project Plans
      Phase Plans
      Action Plans
        Work
        Organization
      Facility
      Change
      Training, internal
      Training, external
      Tracking and reporting
      Review
      Documentation
      Approval
      Other
    Reports
      Weekly time

Completion and Assessment
   Work
   Phase
   Project
Exception
Checkpoint
Reviews
Systems Assurance
Audits
Periodic
Change History
(*Note:* Approved changes are filed with the document affected in addition to being filed here.)
Requests
Evaluation Reports
Disposition
Interpretation Requests
Interpretation Notices

3. Products and Product Documentation

Requirements
System Description
Data Requirements
Procedures
Products

4. Accounting and Administration

Administration
   Rules for work, travel, etc.
   Procedures unique to this project
   Reports
Accounting
   Standard cost data
   Special procedures for time and expense reporting
   Budgets
   Expense reports
   Payroll
   Computer usage reports
   Other

5. Correspondence

> (*Note:* This includes documentation of meetings, phone calls, and conversations that result in decisions.)
>> Users
>> Audit
>> Security
>> Data Administration
>> Legal
>> Operations
>> Systems and Procedures
>> Personnel
>> Vendors
>> Consultants
>> Others

6. Glossary

> (*Note:* Terms, both technical and business, abbreviations, and acronyms unique to this project are listed.)

B-4 THE DP PROJECT PROPOSAL

The Project Proposal is the formal document that starts a development effort. It is prepared by an authorized person and submitted to the Project Selection Committee for evaluation.

Purpose:

To identify an organizational opportunity, requirement, or need and to initiate its evaluation by the Project Selection Committee.

Outline:

DP Project Proposal identification
Department identification
Functional areas affected
Description of the opportunity, requirement, or need
Primary objectives of the requested system
Potential costs
Potential benefits
    Contribution to the organization
    Source of expected benefits
Constraints or limitations
Desired completion date
Authorization signatures

B-5 SOME SPECIFIC REPORTS

In this section some of the specific reports that are produced on a project will be outlined. Outlines for such major deliverables as designs, programs, and test plans will not be provided because those documents are project dependent.

Identification Report

Note: The Identification Report is the primary deliverable from Phase 1.1. Due to the time constraints of this phase, this report should be simplified as much as possible. Perhaps it could be in the form of a document designed to fill in the blanks.

Purpose:

To provide a formal definition of the opportunity, requirement, or need identified in the DP Project Proposal and to begin the business analysis of the proposed project.

Outline:

Project identification
Department identification
Project description
    Why this project?
    The business situation
Background, general description
    Current environment
        Procedures
        Problems
        Trends
    Scope of the proposed project
        Exclusions
System objectives
Constraints
    (people, time, money, risk factors)
Approvals

Documentation of the Present System

Note: This document will be an updated, verified version of current system documentation if it exists.

Purpose:

To provide a verified base for system analysis and for new system definition.

Outline:

Project identification
Department identification
Current business environment
    Department mission, objectives, and plans
    Staffing and general department structure
    Procedures
    DP systems used
    Physical layout
For current systems, describe:
    Functional capability of the system
    Dataflows
    Files: structure, volumes, and usage
    Controls and special considerations
    Impact analysis
    Interfaces with other systems
Analysis of current operations and costs
    Work distribution
    Performance measurements and productivity
    Personnel and their costs
    Maintenance costs
    Other costs
    Total operating costs
Current and anticipated problems
Approvals

System Requirements Specification Report

Purpose:

To provide a precise functional definition of the system to be built.

Outline:

Project identification
Department identification
Background, purpose, and scope of the project
    Describe the business problem to be solved
    Detail all requirements to be met by the new system
Complete functional definition of the new system
    Business functions included, excluded
    Detail inputs and outputs
Control requirements
Define interfaces, boundaries, and constraints of the new system
Comprehensive impact analysis of the new system
    (include Users, User's User, Operations, Audit, Data Management,
    others)
Performance and quality requirements
Other specific exclusions from the new system
Approvals

System Architecture Report

Purpose:

> To describe the system recommended to meet the requirements identified in the System Requirements Specification Report.
>
> To detail the resources and support effort necessary to build and install the recommended system.

Outline:

> Project identification
> Department identification
> General description of the selected alternative
>   Describe possible levels or versions of the system
> System structure
>   Hardware and software environment
>   Describe fallback configuration
>   System flows
>   Description by function
>   Layouts and descriptions of all reports, CRT screens, input documents, special forms
>   Data base requirements
> Detail interfaces with other systems
> Detail manual (noncomputer) procedures
> Detailed impact analysis for this system
> System limitations
> Potential for system growth
> Requirements for development and installation
>   Resources
>   (people, money, time, machine time, other)
>   Additional hardware and software required
>   Support requirements
>   Documentation system
>   Library system
>   Planning and control system
>   Test requirements
>   Site requirements
>   Conversion and installation requirements
>   Training requirements
>   Project personnel
>   User and Operations personnel
> Acceptance criteria
> Approvals

Summary of Alternative Architectures Considered

Purpose:

> To inform management of the alternatives considered and provide data
> that will help them evaluate the recommendations.

Outline:

> Project identification
> Department identification
> General description of the alternative (for each alternative)
>> Summary of the cost and benefit analysis for the alternative
>> Advantages and disadvantages of the alternative
>> Primary reasons this alternative was not chosen

B-6 PROJECT BUSINESS REPORTS

Collectively, these reports provide management with the data they need to make decisions about the project being reported. The report to Management provides a brief summary of the project to date and contains the project team's recommendations. The Project Plan summarizes project performance to date and shows projected cost and time to completion. The Phase Plan is a detailed look at the cost and time for the next phase (summarized in the Project Plan).

Report to Management

Outline:

>   Project identification
>   Department identification
>   Brief project description
>   (any significant changes from the previous reports)
>   Status report
>   Performance to date
>   (actual versus estimate)
>   (cost and time by completed phase)
>   Projected cost and time to completion
>   (by phase and for the total project)
>   Cost and benefit analysis (updated)
>   Risk analysis (updated)
>   Potential problems
>   Recommendation
>   (proceed, modify, or abort)
>   Signatures

Phase Plan

Outline:

Project identification
Department identification
Identification of the phase
Purpose, scope, and objectives of the phase
Summary information
    Completion date for the phase
    Total man-hours for the phase
    Total machine-hours for the phase
    Cost for the phase
Detailed data
    Schedule by standard task
    Schedule of personnel required by skill category
        (weekly basis or more aggregate)
    Schedule of machine requirements
        (weekly basis or more aggregate)
    Budget
Other data
    Service requirements
        (administrative, clerical, support, etc.)
    Other special requirements
Potential problems
Preparation and authorization data (dates, signatures, etc.)
Approvals

Project Plan

Outline:

    Project identification
    Department identification
    Identification of the phase being completed
    Purpose, scope, and objectives of the project
    Summary information:
        Completion date of the project
        Project cost
            Phases completed (actuals)
            Phases to come (estimates)
            Total
        Major changes from the previous Project Plan
    Detailed information
        (by phases; actuals for completed phases and estimates for future phases)
        Completion date
        Man-hours by skill categories
        Machine time
        Cost
    Other information
        Significant service requirements (by phase)
        Other special requirements (by phase)
    Potential problems
    Preparation and authorization data (dates, signatures, etc.)
    Approvals

B-7 ASSESSMENT REPORTS

The Phase Completion and Assessment Report is prepared at the end of each phase (except Phase 3.3). These reports provide input for the preparation of the Project Completion and Assessment Report and are included in that report. The project report is included in the Project History File as a summary. It provides input data for those responsible for assessing and improving the organization's methods and procedures.

The purpose of these reports is to assess project performance and provide data that will:

Aid in planning future projects
Lead to improvement of the project methodology
Help evaluate the performance of new tools and techniques

Phase Completion and Assessment Report

Outline:

Project identification
Department identification
Brief project description
Phase description
Work environment
Comparison: Phase Plan versus Work Plan
(comparisons of duration, people-hours, machine time, and costs; explanations of significant deviations)
Comparison: Work Plan versus Actuals
(modifications to the Work Plan caused by approved changes; comparisons of duration, people-hours, machine time, and costs; explanations of significant deviations)
Other observations
Significant deviations from the standard project methodology
Suggested new standard tasks
Valuable new techniques
Problems
Other suggestions
Management summary
Signatures and date

Project Completion and Assessment Report

Outline:

Project identification
Department identification
Project description
Summary of the work environment
Summary of the project change history
Summary of cost data
   (original estimates plus modifications caused by changes versus
   actuals)
Summary of observations
Comprehensive management summary
All Phase Completion and Assessment Reports
Signatures and date

APPENDIX C: MISSION, POLICIES, AND PROCEDURES

C-1 INTRODUCTION

In Chapter 1 a project methodology was defined as a formal collection of explicit and referenced definitions, principles, policies, methods, procedures, and practices dealing with how an organization's DP projects will be accomplished and specifying how this process interfaces with other organizational processes. In Chapter 7 (also in Appendix B) the Project Handbook was discussed as part of the formal documentation of the organization's project methodology.

Here, we are concerned with the part of the methodology documented in the Project Handbook. We believe the Handbook should be as small as possible consistent with the needs of the organization. This is especially true when the Handbook and the methodology it documents are being introduced. While, in theory, everything an organization does should have a documented procedure, in fact, this is impractical. Excessive formalization is restrictive and can hinder progress. Remember that a good methodology has provisions for adding essential procedures found missing and that excessive procedures can kill the possibility that the organization's personnel will accept and follow the methodology.

The Handbook is a procedure, a way of doing work, with pointers to standards for work performance. It is, also, a collection of procedures and pointers to procedures. These procedures are modified by the policies and standards of the organization. In this appendix the mission of the Data Processing Department and the essential policies and procedures of a base methodology will be discussed.

C-2 MISSION AND GOALS OF THE DATA PROCESSING DEPARTMENT

Specific purpose is the key to organization success. An organization's mission statement identifies this purpose. It should concentrate the organization's activities on the products or services provided.

Many DP Departments started without a mission statement and continue to operate without one. After all, "everybody knows what the DP Department does." In practice it isn't clear that "everybody knows" and especially the DP Department itself. Further, as DP matures, the role of the DP Department has changed. The mission of the DP Department should give the department sufficient scope to allow it to provide the support function that modern business requires. Data processing is a generic activity that takes place throughout the organization, not just in the DP Department. The DP Department cannot and does not do it all, but the DP Department can help all areas perform their own data processing activities more effectively. And, in today's environment with the growing use of small, dispersed systems, the DP Department can provide a central, unifying point for an organization's data processing activity. It can consult on procedures, standards, sources of equipment and services, and even provide central processing facilities where appropriate. The DP Department could become the focal point for an organization's development of a long-range data processing requirements plan—something long overdue in many organizations.

A sample mission statement and goals for a modern Data Processing Department are presented below. In Appendix C-3 the basic policies needed to support this expanded mission of the DP Department are discussed.

Mission of the Data Processing Department

The Data Processing Department is a functional unit within the organization specifically created to facilitate the data processing activities of the organization. The mission of the Data Processing Department is to ensure that:

Appropriate data processing services are provided for the organization
Data is properly managed
Compatibility of systems and procedures is maintained

Goals

The general goal of the Data Processing Department is to assure that the organization's data requirements are met in a manner consistent with basic policies and economic justification. Specific goals are:

To provide uniform methods, procedures, and standards for the identification, selection, development, and operation of all data processing systems

To develop and maintain short- and long-range projections of the organization's data requirements and the systems that will be required to meet these requirements

To operate a central DP facility as authorized by management

To assure the quality of all DP systems and the integrity of organization data

To create an environment that fosters organization awareness and professional growth

In short, the mission and goals of a modern DP Department are to help the organization provide the right data, in the right form, to the right people, at the right time, and at an acceptable cost.

C-3 POLICIES

According to the dictionary, a policy is "a plan or course of action, designed to influence and determine decisions." While an organization will have many policies in effect, there are five fundamental policies frequently overlooked. These five policies should influence the data processing systems the organization builds, and, if nothing else, keep the organization from breaking one of the growing numbers of laws governing the use of data and data processing equipment. Here an example is presented of each of these five policies. These policies are best stated at the organization level. If they are not written there, however, the Data Processing Department should write them.

Quality Policy

This organization is committed to quality and to the concept of error-free products. Quality is an organization and an individual responsibility. To further this policy, management will ensure that:

The organization measurement and evaluation system rewards quality performance

Definitions and measures of quality are established

Work standards and procedures are established that promote quality products

All personnel receive proper training in concepts, methods, and procedures for producing quality work.

Comments. This policy establishes quality as a primary goal of the organization and makes each individual accountable for producing quality work. It means that a DP Department must introduce methods, procedures, and techniques that foster quality systems. Further, management and professionals must be trained to understand and use these tools and techniques effectively. "Right the first time" is a reasonable goal.

Data Policy

Data is to be considered a primary organization resource. As such, systems and procedures will be established to ensure that:

Legitimate and appropriate data for reporting, planning, controlling, and operating are captured

Stored data is as complete, current, and accurate as can be economically justified

Maximum availability of such data is attained consistent with economic justification and with the organization's policies of Privacy, Security, and Audit.

Comments. This policy establishes data as a controlled resource—similar to cash. It provides the basis for an organization having a position of "data controller." A data policy is required if an organization wants to manage its data as it does other resources. It is essential if an organization wants a well-managed, effective distributed data processing system and the benefits such a system promises.

Privacy Policy

Privacy is both an implied and a legal right of the individual. This organization will comply with both the letter and the intent of the body of law governing the use of private data and will act to further the legitimate interests of individual privacy. To further this policy the legal department will:

Obtain information regarding existing and potential laws
Interpret intent and impact of these laws to all areas affected
Work with internal audit to ensure compliance with such laws
Keep the entire organization informed of the current status of privacy
   laws and of the effect these laws will have on them

Comments. Privacy laws cover the legal individual. This means business organizations, government agencies, and institutions are included as well as people. This policy will help keep an organization in compliance with law and, further, publicly demonstrate the organization's commitment to the ethics and morality of data privacy.

The phrase "body of law" is used because passed legislation, court decisions, executive decrees, agency regulations, and contracts must all be considered. Reference is made to potential laws because changes in the laws can impact systems that are installed. Every effort should be made to anticipate such changes while a system is being developed. Further, the "body of law" is multiplied by the number of places an organization does business. Each city, county, state, and country has its own laws; and these laws are not consistent or compatible.

Security Policy

An appropriate economic basis for the justification of security measures will be established. Consistent with this measure, appropriate security systems and/or subsystems will be provided to deal with established exposures and comply with legal requirements. This includes, but is not limited to, protection for:

Money, inventory, tools and equipment, and supplies
Business systems and procedures
Appropriate organization data

Comments. Data is essential for successful organization performance. It is at least as valuable as cash, and it must be protected. Frequently organizations put their security dollars into highly visible security systems without evaluating the contribution the investment will make to the organization's real security needs. This policy establishes the basis necessary for an organization to manage its security on a realistic and businesslike manner. Further, this policy helps the organization meet its commitment to protect private data as specified by privacy laws.

Audit Policy

Systems and procedures will be provided with appropriate subfunctions to facilitate the proper activities of the internal and the external auditors in an economically justifiable manner. This includes, but is not limited to, systems and procedures for:

Data capture on transaction processing so auditors can properly reconstruct a transaction

Providing visibility of controls and adequate data to demonstrate compliance with these controls

Visibility of systems and appropriate demonstration of their integrity

Visibility of data and appropriate demonstration of data integrity

Comments. Computer crime is growing and must be prevented. The Audit Community is under growing pressure to help prevent computer crime and fraud. This policy provides an environment that will help protect an organization's data and will enable the auditors, internal and external, to perform their jobs.

C-4 THE CHANGE PROCEDURE

Changes can, will, and should occur during a project. Contrary to popular opinion, change is not a problem—what is a problem is uncontrolled change. By uncontrolled change we mean changes that occur without a business justification or an appropriate adjustment of the resources and time allocated to the project. Since change is both inevitable and desirable, organizations must learn to manage change; this means learning to justify changes on a business basis and, upon approval of a change, to make the appropriate adjustment in the resources required to accomplish a project.

The Change Procedure is one of the most important procedures in the organization's project methodology. It must be written carefully and managed properly. Remember, the purpose is to manage change, not prevent it. The procedure must help, not hinder, the development process.

Project Change Procedure

Purpose:

To establish formal procedures for requesting a change, evaluating change requests, and implementing approved change requests.

Responsibility:

The Project Manager will be responsible for managing the Change Procedure.

General:

1. *Baseline documents* are documents that are subject to this change procedure. These are the documents that have been submitted to controlling agencies for approval and whose content have been approved. This includes the original Project Proposal and the various phase outputs that arc submitted to management for approval.
2. A *change* is any addition, deletion, or modification to the content of any baseline document of the project.
3. The interface for all change requests will be the Project Manager for the project team and a designated individual, who will be called the Project Administrator, for the user departments.
4. Changes will be classified by the Project Manager as major or minor. A *minor* change is a change that can be made without altering the purpose, scope, objectives, or resources required for implementing the project. Any other change is a *major* change.
5. All change requests will be processed by the procedures described below.

Procedure:

1. A change request can be initiated by any person involved with the project. This is done by completing a Change Request (CR) form containing a description of the proposed change and the reasons for the change. Completed CRs should be approved by the initiator's manager before being submitted to the Project Manager for processing.
2. Completed CRs will be logged by the Project Manager in the Project Change Log and all changes in the status of the request will be entered in this log.

3. The Project Manager will classify changes as major or minor.

4. Minor changes will be evaluated by the Project Manager and the Project Administrator. If both approve, the change will be implemented.

5. The Project Manager will assess the impact of proposed major changes on the project's purpose, scope, objectives, and resource requirements. This impact will be documented in a Project Amendment Report. This report must be approved by the Project Manager and the Project Administrator before the change itself is considered.

6. Upon approval of the Project Amendment Report, the Project Manager and the Project Administrator will evaluate the proposed major change. If both approve, the proposed change will be submitted to the Project Selection Committee for consideration.

7. The Project Selection Committee will approve or reject the requested change. Their decision is final. If the committee approves the change, it will be implemented. Their approval is also the authorization to alter the project purpose, scope, objectives, and/or resources as described in the Project Amendment Report. It is also the authorization to make related changes in the project Work Plan and any other affected plan.

8. In case of dispute between the Project Manager and the Project Administrator, changes in dispute (major or minor) will be submitted to the Project Selection Committee for arbitration. The Committee's decision is final.

9. Copies of approved CRs are filed in the Project Workbook with the baseline documents affected. Copies of the approved change will be distributed to all personnel affected.

10. The disposition of all proposed changes will be recorded in the Project Change Log. Rejected CRs will be filed in the Rejected Change Request File.

11. The originator of a Change Request will be notified of the final disposition of the request.

C-5 THE INTERPRETATION PROCEDURE

Project Interpretation Procedure

Purpose:

> To establish a procedure for clarifying ambiguities in project documents
> (a supplement to the Change Procedure).

Responsibility:

> The Project Manager will be responsible for managing the Interpretation
> Procedure.

General:

1. See the Project Change Procedure for basic definitions.
2. An *interpretation* of a baseline document is a clarification of document content to remove ambiguities or inconsistencies in the document. Usually an interpretation will have no impact on the schedules or resources required for the project.

Procedure:

1. An interpretation request can be initiated by any person involved with the project. This is done by completing an Interpretation Request Form (IR) and submitting it to the Project Manager.
2. IRs will be logged by the Project Manager in the Project Interpretation Log and all changes in the status of the request will be entered in the log.
3. Interpretation will be made by the Project Manager in conjunction with the Project Administrator and other personnel affected. The interpretation will be documented in an Interpretation Agreement.
4. An Interpretation Agreement must be approved by both the Project Manager and the Project Administrator. In case of unresolved requests, upper management will resolve the issue.
5. Approved Interpretation Agreements are logged by the Project Manager and filed in the Project Workbook with the baseline document that it clarifies. Copies of the Interpretation Agreement will be distributed to all personnel affected.
6. If an approved Interpretation Agreement will impact the schedule or resource requirements of the project, the Project Manager will

initiate a Change Request based on the agreement. This Change Request will be processed in the normal manner and, if approved, result in the appropriate resources being allocated to the project.

7. On final disposition of the IR, the originator of the request will be notified of its disposition.

C-6 PROCEDURES—A BASE SET

In Chapter 4 we discussed some 20 different procedures that might be included in a project methodology. If you were to introduce such a comprehensive set of procedures at one time, you could overwhelm your organization. The procedures we consider to be basic and essential for productive project work are:

Authorization Procedure
Project Proposal and Selection Procedure
Project Planning Procedure
Tracking and Reporting Procedure
Change Procedure
Interpretation Procedure
Methodology Management Procedure

In practice, the other procedures will be used even though their description is informal. As your organization gains experience with the base methodology, additional procedures of importance will be identified and added formally to the methodology.

Because of their fundamental importance, the Change and Interpretation Procedures have been described in detail. The other procedures in our base list only will be outlined. For each procedure, the purpose, responsible person, and general contents will be given.

Authorization Procedure (Outline)

Purpose:

> To provide a uniform, business-based process for the justification, funding, and authorization of all project work and resource expenditure.

Responsibility:

> General management establishes this procedure, and it is monitored by Internal Audit. This procedure delegates specific project authorization authority to:
> > The Project Selection Committee
> > The Purchasing Department
> > Department Managers
> > Project Managers
>
> These areas establish their own procedures and operate within the limits of their delegated authority.

Content:

> The general procedure establishes:
>
> > What must be authorized
> > Who may fund and authorize project work (with pointers to specific procedures)
> > How project purchase requests are processed
>
> This procedure establishes the principle that all project work and expenditures must be authorized and are subject to audit.

Project Proposal and Selection Procedure (Outline)

Purpose:

> To ensure that the data processing systems built and installed are cost-effective and meet a business need.

Responsibility:

> The chairman of the Project Selection Committee will manage this procedure and ensure that it conforms with the Authorization Procedure.

Content:

> This procedure provides for four distinct activities:

1. Project Proposal
   Describes who may propose a project, what data must be provided, what approvals are required, and where proposals are submitted.

2. Project Selection and Authorization
   Defines the business basis for project selection. Describes the process of project funding and work authorization. Provides for separate authorization of Phases 1.1 through 2.1 and a final authorization for project completion following Phase 2.1. This procedure provides for rejecting or redirecting a project at each evaluation point.

3. Project Monitoring
   Provides procedures for monitoring the selected project as work progresses. Provides procedures for evaluating changes and providing additional funds and resources for approved changes. Provides for rejecting or redirecting a project if its business basis changes.

4. Postinstallation Evaluation
   Provides procedures for evaluating the performance of installed systems to determine the actual benefits obtained from the system. Using this and other data, provides for the evaluation and improvement of the project selection process.

Project Planning Procedure (Outline)

Purpose:

> To ensure that appropriate project plans are prepared, maintained, and that these plans are consistent in content, method of preparation, and effectiveness.

Responsibility:

> The Project Manager will manage this procedure with the approval of Systems Assurance (or some other designated monitoring agent).

Content:

> This is a collection of procedures. The total number of procedures will depend on the number of plans your organization requires. A minimum set of plans includes:

> Phase Plans
> Project Plan
> Action Plans
>   Work Plan
>   Work assignments
>   Schedules
>   Budget

> For each plan there should be a procedure describing:

> The purpose and content of the plan
> Guidelines for the preparation and maintenance of the plan

Tracking and Reporting Procedure (Outline)

Purpose:

> To ensure that project work progress is reported regularly and uniformly.

Responsibility:

> The Project Manager will manage this procedure.

Content:

> Defines the types of reports to be provided and who will provide them
>
> For each report the procedure specifies:
>
> > Purpose
> > Content and format
> > Frequency of the report
> > Distribution
>
> Defines the performance summary that will compare planned performance to actuals

Methodology Management Procedure (Outline)

Purpose:

> To provide a process for the continuous evaluation and updating of the organization's project methodology to ensure its usability and effectiveness.

Responsibility:

> Management will designate a person to be responsible for methodology evaluation and improvement.

Content:

> Describes the procedure to be used to assess methodology effectiveness at the end of each phase and at the end of each project
>
> Defines the procedure for submitting suggestions or questions about the methodology
>
> Establishes procedures for evaluating assessment reports and other suggestions for improving the methodology, determining appropriate changes, and introducing these changes into the methodology. This procedure would include validation of significant changes in methods or procedures
>
> Establishes publication standards for the Project Handbook
>
> Defines who will receive the Project Handbook and how distribution, including updates, will be made

APPENDIX D: FORMS, REVIEWS, GUIDES, AND CHECKLISTS

D-1 FORMS

A form is a way of defining a procedure. It specifies what data is to be recorded and in what format. A form can specify how data will be processed and even where completed data will go. And it can say who is responsible for completing the form and when. Thus, a good form is a simple, easy way to specify and communicate a procedure.

But beware, forms and their design can make or break your project methodology. Three common pitfalls in the use of forms are:

Mistaking a collection of forms for a comprehensive project methodology
Providing an excessive number of forms
Providing improperly designed forms

In all of these cases, the forms will defeat their purpose. They will misdirect effort, cause people to work around the procedure (form), or—worst case—create a negative reaction in project team members to the point where crea-tive, productive work is hampered. A few good forms, however, will greatly simplify project work.

What is a good form? It is a form of such purpose and design that the people who use it will:

Understand what data is to be provided
Understand why the data is wanted
Believe the data requested is useful
Be able to provide the data in a simple, straightforward way
Feel the data requested is not being gathered to control them

Thus the organization and the forms designer producing a form face four major problems:

1. Creating a work environment where people feel the control effort is really aimed at the control of work, not workers
2. Determining the minimum amount of data required to assure proper project control
3. Defining a minimum number of forms to collect this data
4. Designing forms that are convenient for people to use

When detailed data is required, it should be collected by a special program. A form is a basic communication tool. Each form should carry clear identification of the purpose of the data recorded and the project to which the data refers. The clear identification of all work is vital for effective data collection. Every project should be uniquely identified with a name and an official abbreviation of the name. This abbreviation, combined with a unique number, should be the project identifier. The project identifier combined with the phase number, the standard task number, and the unique work unit number can identify all assigned work. These numbers can be used in establishing the planning data base.

Weekly progress reporting is important for proper project tracking and accounting. Each member of the project team must provide time and work performance data so that project control can be maintained. Unfortunately, this usually means that the team members are completing many different forms, often at different times (weekly time report, work completion reports, individual progress report, to name a few). To further complicate the reporting process, time often must be reported to the nearest tenth of an hour (six minutes). Combine this with poorly designed forms and you create resistance in individuals. They will complete the forms, but often the data provided is questionable.

We suggest combining these separate reports into a single report, which we call the Consolidated Weekly Report. This report provides all essential data on one form. Time data should be recorded to the nearest half hour. Collect only data needed to meet legal requirements, make cost allocations, and supply management with data essential to overall project control. We have included a sample Consolidated Report. This sample form could be modified to show the date work started on a work unit and an estimate of the hours required to complete the work.

A base set of forms for you to consider follows.

DP PROJECT PROPOSAL page 1 of 2

To: Project Selection Committee

From: ______________________________

____

What activities or functions will the proposed project deal with?

____

____

____

____

Is the proposed system required by law? When? ______________

____

How will the proposed system help the organization? Include an estimate of potential benefits and their source: ______________

____

____

____

____

____

What will be the effect of doing nothing? ______________

____

____

____

What are the estimated development costs? ______________

____

____

____

Exhibit D-1. DP Project Proposal

Name of the system: _____

_____

List the major goals or objectives of the proposed system:

_____

_____

_____

_____

Identify all areas of the organization affected by the system:

_____

_____

_____

_____

Describe any system constraints or limitations:

_____

_____

_____

_____

Signature of preparer: _____

Date: _____

Approval: _____

Title: _____

Date: _____

Exhibit D-1. (Continued)

WORK ASSIGNMENT

Work unit identification: Project name and identification:

_____   _____

_____   _____

Person assigned (indicate percent of work time):

_____

Others assigned (indicate percent of work time):

_____

_____

Work unit description (include deliverables and constraints):

_____

_____

Prerequisite work units—identification:

_____

_____

Completion criteria: _____

_____

	Planned	Actual
Man-hours:		
Work days:		

	Planned	Actual
Start date:		
Completion data:		

Agreement on Assignment: Agreement on Completion:

Person assigned   Date   Person assigned   Date

_____   _____

Manager   Date   Manager   Date

_____   _____

Exhibit D-2. Work Assignment

511

WORK PLAN

Prepared by: _____   Project: _____   Revision: _____

page ____ of ____

Date: _____

Work Unit Name and Identification	Person Assigned	Start Date		Completion Date		Work Days		Man-hours	
		Plan	Actual	Plan	Actual	Plan	Actual	Plan	Actual

Exhibit D-3. Work Plan

CONSOLIDATED WEEKLY REPORT Week ending: _____

Name: _____   Employee number: _____

Project Work

Work Unit Identification	S	S	M	T	W	T	F	Total	Date Completed

Total [ ]

Other Project Work

Other Total [ ]

Project Total [ ]

Nonproject Work

Nonproject Total [ ]

Weekly Total [ ]

Exhibit D-4. Consolidated Weekly Report

513

Explain missed target dates (if any): _____

_____

_____

Briefly state next week's plan: _____

_____

_____

_____

_____

Problems:
    Status of previously identified problems: _____

_____

_____

_____

    New problems and recommended solutions: _____

_____

_____

_____

Other comments: _____

_____

_____

_____

_____

Signature: _____ Date: _____

Reviewed by: _____ Date: _____

Exhibit D-4. (Continued)

PROJECT CHANGE REQUEST

CR Number: _____

Project name: _____   Date submitted: _____

_____

Project identification: _____

Description of the proposed change:

_____

_____

_____

_____

Why is this change needed?

_____

_____

_____

_____

What would be the effect if this change were rejected?

_____

_____

_____

_____

Submitted by: _____

Approvals: _____

_____

Disposition: _____

_____

Exhibit D-5. Project Change Request

515

Project Name: _____ Date: _____

Project Number: _____ Report Number:____

Manager: _____

Work Summary:

	Plan	Actual	Variance
Work Units—Starts:			
Work Units—Completions:			
Work Days:			
Man-hours:			

Explain variances of over ten percent: _____

_____

_____

_____

Manpower Status: _____

_____

_____

_____

Technical Status (include product quality): _____

_____

_____

_____

Estimate to complete phase; project: _____

_____

_____

_____

Exhibit D-6. Project Status Report

Summary of next month's plan: _____

_____

_____

_____

_____

Problems:

    Status of previously identified problems: _____

_____

_____

_____

_____

    New problems and planned solutions: _____

_____

_____

_____

_____

Other comments: _____

_____

_____

_____

_____

Signature: _____   Date: _____

Systems Assurance: _____   Date: _____

Dept. Manager: _____   Date: _____

Exhibit D-6. (Continued)

(Organization identification) Title:	Page ___ of ___ Date _____
Project Identification:	Author _____

Note: This is a general purpose blank form that can be used for a variety of things, such as narrative descriptions, diagrams, etc. It could be stocked in blank and ruled form.

Exhibit D-7. General Purpose Form

D-2 REVIEWS

Six types of reviews might be used to monitor work and project progress. These are the Peer, Periodic, Checkpoint, Technical, Phase, and Audit reviews. Because of the fundamental importance of the Peer Review, it is discussed in detail in Chapter 17. In Chapter 18 the general reasons or objectives of reviews are discussed and specific ingredients for successful reviews are identified. These ingredients are:

> A clearly defined purpose and objective
> Clearly defined inputs
> An effective review process (formally stated)
>> A sponsor who understands his function and performs it
>> Qualified reviewers
>> Advanced distribution of relevant data
>> An appropriate agenda that is followed
>> A recording secretary
>> A follow-up plan
> Documented output, consisting of
>> A report of the findings
>> An action plan

In this appendix we will describe these six reviews assuming that the review as conducted contains these ingredients.

A word of caution: reviews are important for project success but they can be overdone. Remember, too many reviews with too many sign-offs can prevent project progress. There should be sufficient reviews to ensure problem recognition but not so many that project progress is prevented.

Peer Review

Purpose:

To detect error in the work product and to ensure product quality

Scope:

Covers the output of a specific work assignment

When held:

Toward the end of a work assignment; more than one review may be held for some assignments

Sponsor:

The developer

Duration:

Usually one or two hours not including preparation time

Reviewers:

The developer's peers who have appropriate knowledge and experience and others as selected by the sponsor

Reviewee:

The developer

Discussion.   A Peer Review should be conducted for each critical task of the project.   The review should follow a formal procedure, although the process should be conducted in a relaxed and informal manner.   These review sessions may be chaired by a neutral party, such as Systems Assurance, if it is helpful and not threatening.

The Peer Review should be considered the tool of the developer.   In general, management should not attend these review sessions.   Their presence tends to make the review appear as part of the appraisal process, not a tool to help the developer.

All work output should be reviewed, but the Peer Review is too costly for most work output.   For the less critical work output, a structured self-review procedure should be constructed to aid the developer in the analysis of his work output.   This process should attempt to bring the discipline of the Peer Review to the self-review process.

Periodic Review

Purpose:

To determine project status, discover problems, and inform the project team of the current project status

Scope:

Includes all aspects of the project, concentrating on current status and problem identification and resolution

When held:

Regularly scheduled at fixed intervals appropriate to the specific project (weekly, monthly, etc.)

Sponsor:

Project Manager

Duration:

Usually one or two hours not including preparation time

Reviewers:

The project team

Reviewees:

The project team

Discussion. This review is a progress report to the project team. It is informal and relaxed. Update reports by all team members improve everybody's awareness of the project purpose and progress. General discussion improves the informal communications on the project. All areas of the project are reviewed. The status of previously identified problems is determined. Any new problems are identified and plans are made to deal with them.

For a large project using multiple teams (including multiple locations), the reviewees would be the separate team leaders. Each team should have local reviews in preparation for the project review. Each team should receive a status report for the entire project upon completion of the project review.

Properly used, the Periodic Review can be a powerful unifying, motivating, team building, and educational project force.

Checkpoint Review

Purpose:

> To review project performance and to assess project status after the completion of a selected set of work units

Scope:

> Reviews the work product and performance against plan to validate current project plans

When held:

> At key points marked by the completion of a selected set of work units whose output could severely impact the technical assumptions or business case for the project

Sponsor:

> Project Manager or Systems Assurance

Duration:

> One-half to one or more days as required to complete the impact assessment

Reviewers:

> Project team, Systems Assurance, and possibly outside consultants

Reviewees:

> Developers of the work products being reviewed.

Discussion.   This review is used to validate project plans after the completion of a significant amount of work.   Not all projects have such key points.   Where such reviews are warranted, they can provide management with needed information early in the development process.   This review is formal but conducted in a relaxed and informal way.   Discussion should be encouraged because it will enhance the understanding of the project.

Checkpoint Reviews for large projects are handled in the same manner as described for the handling of Periodic Reviews on large projects.

Technical Review

Purpose:

> To ensure the technical quality and the architectural consistency of the system being developed

Scope:

> Includes the technical aspects of the project to be the point of the review

When held:

> As scheduled by the sponsor, at the end of a phase, or upon completion of a significant segment of work

Sponsor:

> Upper management, Systems Assurance, or the System Architect

Duration:

> One to five days depending on project size

Reviewers:

> Nonteam technical experts

Reviewees:

Project Manager, selected team members, and involved users

Discussion. This review is primarily held to ensure the architectural integrity of large systems being built by separate groups. It is used on smaller projects where the level of technical innovation is exceptionally high.

This is a formal review covering all aspects of the project. Work products to date are evaluated and their impact on project objectives assessed. Module interfaces and data consistency are evaluated. Standards and system performance are reviewed.

Phase Review

Purpose:

> To evaluate the phase outputs and assess project status

Scope:

> Covers all aspects of the project, technical and business, with emphasis on the phase just completed

When held:

> Upon completion of a phase

Sponsor:

> Upper management

Duration:

> One to five days depending on project size

Reviewers:

> Upper management, nonteam experts, Systems Assurance, and user representatives

Reviewees:

> Project Manager, selected team members, and involved users

Discussion. This is a comprehensive review. It validates the current phase outputs and assesses the project, both technically and from a business viewpoint. This review amounts to a presentation and evaluation of the Project Business Reports prepared during the phase just completed.

This is a formal review. All aspects of the project are reviewed. Normally both technical and business aspects of the project are considered equally. For large projects it is convenient to isolate the technical analysis in a separate Technical Review (discussed separately), which should be completed prior to the Phase Review.

Audit Review

Purpose:

> To make a detailed review of project performance and the current work product so as to validate the technical assumptions and the business case for the project

Scope:

> A complete review of all aspects of the project

When held:

> Upon request of anyone concerned with the project who believes a major problem is going unresolved

Sponsor:

> Upper management

Reviewers:

> A special panel consisting of members from upper management, senior DP specialists, consultants, and users; no one associated with the project in any way.

Reviewees:

> Project Manager, the project team members, users, Systems Assurance, and any others directly associated with the project.

Discussion. The Audit Review is seldom held. It is a drastic action. The outcome of the review can severely change a project and frequently results in the personnel involved having their careers impacted.

This review considers all aspects of the project. It is a very formal process; the atmosphere is seldom relaxed. It is a threatening situation for the personnel being reviewed. The intent of the review is to determine if the project is on a sound basis and, if not, what must be done to put it on a sound basis if it is to be continued. Recommendations frequently include changes in personnel and management.

D-3 GUIDES AND CHECKLISTS

Reviews are a significant part of the project communication process. Proper preparation for a review requires a great deal of effort. As mentioned in Chapter 18, a review can be considered a project. It should receive the same careful consideration and planning as any other project. To help you plan and conduct your reviews, we have:

> Prepared a guide for conducting a Phase Review using the techniques of Function Analysis (see Chapter 12) and expressed it in structured English
>
> Prepared a general guide for conducting any type of review using the type of description used in Appendix A to present the standard tasks for the phases
>
> Developed a checklist of questions to consider when preparing for and conducting a review
>
> Developed a checklist of questions to consider when preparing for and conducting an audit

Each professional involved with a project is responsible for making adequate preparation for the reviews that they are involved with. These checklists will help in this preparation. These checklists assume that a formal project methodology exists and is being used. The checklists are not exhaustive. They should be supplemented with additional questions appropriate to the situation and to the organization.

A special note about the term "audit." It is used for certain types of reviews, but there is no single standard for how the term is used. Audits tend to be formal and complete. They usually are conducted by people outside the area being reviewed. But aside from these characteristics, there are differences from organization to organization, or even within an organization, as to what an audit is. These are some of the ways that term is used.

Internal audit routinely conducts spot checks to assure compliance with procedures and policies and to assure that they are reasonable. Such reviews are called audits, and it is this type of review that was discussed in Chapter 19.

There is another type of audit, and it is this that was outlined in Appendix D-2. In many organizations there is a procedure for reviewing a project if serious problems surface or are suspected. Such reviews are called audits; they are conducted by specially constituted audit teams. Audits of this type are threatening to the people being audited, and they must be conducted with professional competence and understanding.

A third type of audit is a review of the project development process of an organization, such as was discussed in Chapter 8. This type of audit can be performed by internal or external personnel. The purpose of this review is to evaluate the project methodology and to recommend changes as required.

Our checklist can be used to audit a project's performance, to look for specific problems, or to evaluate a project methodology. The Questions for Reviews in the other checklists are useful and should be considered, but the Questions for Audits are more specific to the needs of audits.

A Guide for Conducting the Phase Review

0.0   Review Phase

1.0   Prepare for review (part of phase activity)
      Select coordinator (to make arrangements)
      Select and notify reviewers
         Appoint chairman, recording secretary
      Select and notify reviewees (Project Manager, team members, etc.)
      Negotiate schedule
      Inform reviewers
         Provide review agenda
         Provide review data
         Brief reviewers (about known problems, special constraints, politics, special situations, etc.)
      Prepare review site
         Obtain room
         Equip room (visual aids, projectors, etc.)
         Arrange refreshments (coffee, etc.)
         Arrange security
      Prepare additional materials (handouts, graphics, etc.)
      Arrange clerical support

2.0   Conduct review
      Discover facts
         Present project status to reviewers
         (Include purpose of the review, general **description** and background of the project, review the business status of the project, review the technical status of the project, identify any additional requirements, open questions)

Analyze findings
(Include discussion of findings, identification of problems, determination of responsibility for problem resolution)
Make recommendations

3.0   Finalize review report
Prepare report
(Include drafting of the report, reviewing the draft with the Project Manager, preparation of the final report)
Distribute report
(To all reviewers and reviewees)
Assess review procedure

A Generalized Guide for Conducting Reviews

Prepare for the review
Select and notify reviewers and reviewees
(Identify chairman and the recording secretary)
Negotiate schedule
Provide data required for the review
Prepare review site
Arrange support services
Conduct review
Present review
Answer questions
Identify problems and fix responsibility for problem resolution
Summarize findings
Report review results
Prepare report
Distribute report
Assess review procedure

Questions for Reviews—A Checklist

Business-Related Questions about Plans:

Are there appropriate plans for the phase or project?
Are the plans consistent?
Do estimates appear realistic?
Has a contingency allowance for rework been made?
Have holidays, vacations, illness, etc., been taken into account?
Is funding adequate? Do cost estimates include travel and living expense if it will be required?

Has project security been provided for and included in the estimates?

Do plans include time for reviews, approvals, etc.?

Is there a mandated completion date? What adjustments were made to accommodate this date?

Are responsibilities clearly defined and assigned for all tasks?

Are the resources required readily available?

Are the physical facilities provided adequate?

Is available administrative and clerical support adequate?

Are testing facilities adequate?

Is the project size normal for the organization?

Is there in-house experience with similar projects?

Will new hires be required? Experienced? Are they available?

Are project team members qualified for the work?

Have training requirements for the project team been considered? For the user? For others?

Are project team members full time on the project? If not what problems will this cause? Has this been allowed for?

Is the project management provided adequate? Experienced? Full time?

Is the project methodology being followed? If not, what are the differences and why?

Is the methodology too restrictive? Too vague?

Is the user actively involved? Does the user understand the required involvement? Has a project administrator been appointed? Are user-DP relations good?

Are there any special political problems that might impact this project?

Is the project organization reasonable? Are communications free and open?

Does this system require special equipment, software, a new physical site? Are proper plans made to provide for such vendor items?

Have adequate plans for conversion and installtion been made?

Business-Related Questions about Project Performance to Date

What is the status of the project? Are all required deliverables present? Are they complete?

Do actual costs compare favorably with planned costs?

Have previously identified problems been solved? Was there unexpected impact?

What are the new problems? Has responsibility for dealing with known problems been clearly assigned?

Has the review process uncovered problems not identified by the project team or its management? What prevented the team from finding these problems?

Are there any signs of personnel problems (excessive absenteeism, increasing rate of turnover, etc.)?

Is the Project Manager decisive? Are his decisions effective?

Is there interference from other work (maintenance, mini projects)?

Is the change procedure being followed? Is the number of change requests excessively high?

Have all sign-offs and approvals been obtained? Are these approvals firm?

Is the user involved and aware of the current project status?

Are there undocumented oral agreements with the user or anyone else connected with the project?

Is upper management aware of the current project status?

Have phases started out of sequence or other unusual activities occurred?

Technical Questions Related to Quality

Is the statement of project purpose and scope adequate?

Is the specification of system requirements clear and unambiguous?

Is the system technically feasible?

Are the project objectives still valid?

Is there adequate user input into the product specifications?

Does the design call for new equipment?

Does the design call for new, untested software products?

Have privacy, security, and audit matters been taken into account in the design?

Were modern techniques used in the design of the system? Programming?

Have adequate plans been developed to ensure the architectural integrity of the system as designed?

Is testing to be done by a separate test group?

Are technical standards (design, code, etc.) being followed?

Is the documentation complete? Understandable? Accurate?

Are the primary deliverables of satisfactory quality?

Do the products meet the requirements?

What improvements can or should be made to this system?

Have appropriate technical and operational reviews and sign-offs been received from Operations? Legal? Internal Audit? Data Management? Other concerned areas?

Questions Concerning Project Selection Procedures

How are projects proposed? Initiated?

Are projects well defined?

Is there a formal cost/benefit evaluation? A well-documented procedure for determining costs and benefits?

Who establishes development priorities?

Who allocates funds for projects? Authorizes work?

Are the present systems (installed and under development) balanced among using groups for the best interests of the organization?

How far ahead are applications planned? How is the need for system redo determined?

How do the organization's DP systems compare with the average systems installed in their industry?

Questions Concerning User Involvement

To what extent do users participate in problem definition? Problem solution? Testing?

What is the project involvement of Operations? Security? Data Management?

What is the involvement of Internal Audit in system specification? Testing? Postinstallation evaluation?

Do the External Auditors become involved in any way? How?

How good are communications between the project team and the various other constituencies of the organization?

What is the easiest user group to work with? Why?

What is the hardest user group to work with? Why?

What do users think of the systems they have operating? Of their projects? Of the development group? Of Operations? Of Auditors? Of Data Management?

Who has responsibility for development and conversion of user procedures? Documentation? Data? Do all parties agree on these responsibilities?

Who is responsible for training users? Operations? Others affected by the project?

Questions Concerning Planning and Control

What plans are made for the project? How are they validated? By whom?

Is there a procedure for updating plans?

Is the project accomplished in phases? What are the phases?

How are project estimates made? By whom? How are these estimates validated? By whom? Are the estimates reviewed by the project team?

How are milestones selected? Are they unambiguous? Are they uniform in size?

When are overall resources allocated for the project?

Is there a formal project control system?

> If YES:
>> Is it automated? Should it be?
>> How well does it work? Is it effective?
>> Is the same control system used for all projects?
>>> If not, describe the differences.
>> Is the control system evaluated regularly? By whom? How? What is the procedure for modifying it?
> If NO:
>> What measures are taken to assure that project targets are met?

How is completed work reported? Are the reports clear, complete, and accurate? Is sufficient management information available? Is too much detail provided?

What happens when deadlines or targets are missed?

Questions Concerning the Project Change Procedure

Is there a documented change procedure? Does it make provisions for processing requests for clarification and interpretation of existing documents? Are the procedures followed?

Who initiates change requests? Who approves change requests? Who authorizes the change to be made?

Who evaluates the impact of change? What is the frequency of change requests?

Are the resources allocated to the project altered to reflect the effect of approved changes?

How is change documented? How are team members affected by a change notified?

Is change a problem? In what way? Any suggestions to correct the problem?

Questions Concerning Quality

Has quality been defined? What is the definition?

What steps are taken to ensure product quality?

Does the individual team member use the peer review? Should peer reviews be used? What prevents their use?

Is the individual responsible for the quality of work produced? How is this responsibility communicated to them?

Is there any incentive to "clean up" programs? What is it?
What provisions are there for backing up completed work?

Questions Concerning Documentation

Is there a Project Handbook? What is its content? How is it maintained? Who is responsible for its maintenance? How are changes in the methodology entered into the book? How are development teams notified about changes?

Is there a Project Workbook? What is its content? How is it maintained? Who is responsible for its maintenance? How are changes entered into the book? How are team members notified about changes?

Is there a standards manual? What is it content? Is one planned? (The above questions apply here also.)

How is project documentation controlled? Does the system work? Is documentation a problem? What are the problems?

Should the documentation system be automated?

Questions Concerning Testing

What is the system test procedure? Acceptance test? Are the procedures documented?

For system test:
Is there a separate test group? Should there be one?
Who establishes test data? Who verifies test results?
Who keeps test files? Should there by a librarian?
What testing aids are used?
Is adequate machine time available? Properly scheduled?
Are programs adequately tested? Are back-up procedures tested? Manual procedures? Operating procedures? Documentation?
Can test procedures be improved? How?

For acceptance test:
Is this the user's test? Does the user plan and conduct the test?
Who provides technical support for the user?
(Many questions unders sytem test should be reviewed.)

Questions Concerning Installation and Conversion

Is new equipment or supplies required? Have they been defined and ordered? Was the order placed early enough to ensure timely delivery? Is there a fall-back plan in case of nondelivery?

If new space is required, has it been planned? Contracts let? Communications arranged? Move arranged?

How are new applications installed? Is the installation properly planned? Has operations been notified? Trained?

Who "tunes" new systems? What are the plans for maintenance of new systems? Are maintenance responsibilities assigned and documented?

How is data converted? When? By whom? Who audits the conversion? Is there an adequate recovery system in case of data loss?

What other changes must be made? How are they identified? Who is responsible for this identification? Who assigns responsibility for making the identified changes?

Questions Concerning Working Conditions

Is there adequate work space? Conference space? Storage space? Provisions for security?

Is there satisfactory light? Temperature? Noise level? Privacy? Safety?

Is the level of administration and clerical support adequate?

Are there adequate supplies? Reference materials?

Questions Concerning Completed Work

(These questions relate to earlier stages of a particular project and/or to recently completed projects.)

Were all required documents and deliverables completed?

Were all necessary authorizations and approvals obtained?

Were all procedures and standards adhered to? If not, why not?

Does the documentation fulfill its purpose?

How do the actual times and costs compare with those planned? If major differences exist, explain why. Does the estimating procedure need improvement? How?

Did the deliverables meet specifications? If not, what were the discrepancies?

Questions Concerning the Methodology

Is the project methodology satisfactory? Does it require:
  Phased or incremental authorization and approval of a project? Phased
    commitment of resources?
  An effective feasibility study?
  Effective participation of user and other involved parties?
  A business-based justification of a proposed project?
  Effective standards?
  Adequate risk assessment and control?
  Comprehensive impact analysis?
  An adequate planning and control process?
  Adequate system and acceptance testing?
  Effective conversion and installation procedures?
  Sufficient training and education?
  Adequate communication? Documentation?
Do standards specify the use of modern productivity techniques (such as
  structured programming, top-down development, etc.)?
Is financial reporting adequate? Is there a realistic charge-back system?

Some General Questions

Are the fundamental policies regarding quality, data, privacy, security, and
  audit in place? Are these policies observed?
Do work assignments clearly define the result expected? Is responsibility
  and accountability clearly defined?
How large is the project team? Does it have the right mix of skills and
  experience?
Do outside jobs interfere with the project? Is this causing problems that
  will delay the project or affect quality?
Describe the training provided for the project team. Is additional training
  needed? Is there training for individual development as well as for project
  requirements?
Describe the training for users. Is additional training needed?
How does the project group learn of hardware or software changes that might
  impact the project?
What are the security provisions on the project? What is done to back up
  programs? Documentation? What is done to prevent unauthorized
  modifications? Are there additional security measures that should be
  instituted?

What problems have been encountered on the project? Other recent projects?

When does the project team's responsibility end? How do they know when they are through?

Any suggestions for improving the project methodology?

Define the project roles of the Project Manager, Project Administrator, Systems Assurance, and Internal Audit.

BIBLIOGRAPHY

BIBLIOGRAPHY

The following list is intended to be a useful rather than an exhaustive bibliography. Only items that will be most helpful in developing your understanding of projects are included. All items are classified by subject matter, and books are rated as to their relevance to project management, according to the following codes.

M	General management	*	Good
DP	DP project area	**	Excellent
T	Technical or special topic	***	Must reading
G	General or miscellaneous	△	Reference work

BOOKS

Ackoff, R. L., *A Concept of Corporate Planning.* New York: John Wiley and Sons, 1970. — M **

Archibald, R. D. and R. L. Villoria, *Network-Based Management Systems (PERT/CPM).* New York: John Wiley and Sons, 1967. — T △

Aron, J. D., *The Program Development Process.* Reading, MA: Addison-Wesley Publishing Company, 1974. — DP **

Brandon. D. H. and M. Gray, *Project Control Standards.* New York: Brandon/Systems Press, 1970. — DP *

Brooks, F. P., *The Mythical Man-Month.* Reading, MA: Addison-Wesley Publishing Company, 1975. — DP **

Christopher, W. F., *The Achieving Enterprise.* New York: AMACOM, 1974. — M **

Crosby, P. B., *Quality is Free.*   New York: McGraw-Hill Book   M
Company, 1979.   ***

Dolotta, T. A. et al., *Data Processing in 1980-1985.*   New York: DP
John Wiley and Sons, 1976.   **

Drucker, P. F., *The Age of Discontinuity.*   New York: Harper and   M
Row, 1969.   ***

————, *The Effective Executive.*   New York: Harper and Row,   M
1967.   **

————, *Management: Tasks, Responsibilities, Practices.*   New   M
York: Harper and Row, 1974.   ***

Grindley, K. and J. Humble, *The Effective Computer.*   New York: DP
AMACOM, 1974.   **

Grossman, L., *The Change Agent.*   New York: AMACOM,   M
1974.   **

Hanan, M., J. Cribbin, and H. Heiser, *Consultative Selling.*   New   G
York: AMACOM, 1973.   **

Herzberg, F., *Work and the Nature of Man.*   New York: The World   M
Publishing Company, 1966.   *

Hice, G. F., W. S. Turner, and L. F. Cashwell, *System Development*   DP
Methodology, Revised Edition.   New York: North-Holland   *
Publishing Company, 1978.

International Business Machines Corp., *Managing Application*   DP
Conversion Projects.   Armonk, NY: IBM Corporation, 1978.   ***

————, *Managing the Application Development Process.*   Armonk,   DP
N.Y.: IBM Corporation, 1977.   ***

Lakein, A., *How to Get Control of Your Time and Your Life.*   New   G
York: The New American Library, 1973.   *

Linstone, H. A. and M. Turoff, eds., *The Delphi Method.*   Reading,   T
MA: Addison-Wesley Publishing Company, 1975.   △

Martin, J., *Security, Accuracy, and Privacy in Computer Systems.*   DP
Englewood Cliffs, NJ: Prentice-Hall, 1973.   **

Maslow, A. H., *Motivation and Personality.*   New York: Harper and   M
Row, 1954.   *

McClelland, D. C., *Power: The Inner Experience.*   New York: M
Irvington Publishing, 1975.   **

McGregor, D., *The Professional Manager.*   New York: McGraw-Hill   M
Book Company, 1967.   ***

Metzger, P. W., *Managing a Programming Project.*   Englewood Cliffs, DP
NJ: Prentice-Hall, 1973.   **

Sawyer, L. B., *The Practice of Modern Internal Auditing.*   Orlando, T
FL: Institute of Internal Auditors, 1973.   △

Sperry, L., D. J. Mickelson, and P. L. Hunsaker, *You Can Make It*   G
    Happen. Reading, MA: Addison-Wesley Publishing Company,   **
    1977.
Steiner, G. A., *Top Management Planning.* New York: Macmillan   M
    Publishing Company, 1969.   △
Weinberg, G. M., *The Psychology of Computer Programming.* New   DP
    York: Van Nostrand Reinhold Company, 1971.   *
Wiest, J. D. and F. K. Levy, *A Management Guide to PERT/CPM.*   T
    Englewood Cliffs, NJ: Prentice-Hall, 1968.   *

PERIODICALS

Behavioral Science Newsletter, Whitney Industrial Park, Whitney   M
    Road, Mahway, NJ 07430.
Business Week, 1221 Avenue of the Americas, New York, NY 10020.   G
Communications of ACM, 1133 Avenue of the Americas, New York,   DP
    NY 10036.
Computerworld, 797 Washington Street., Newton, MA 02160.   DP
Computing Surveys, Association for Computing Machinery, 1133   DP
    Avenue of the Americas, New York, NY 10036.
Data Management, DPMA, 505 Busse Highway, Park Ridge, IL 60068.   DP
Data Processing Digest, 6820 La Tijera Boulevard, Los Angeles,   DP
    CA 90045.
Data Processor, IBM Corporation, 1133 Westchester Avenue, White   DP
    Plains, NY 10604.
Datamation, 1801 S. La Cienega Boulevard, Los Angeles, CA 90035.   DP
EDP Analyzer, 925 Anza Avenue, Vista, CA 92083.   DP
EDPACS, Automation Training Center, Inc., 11250 Roger Bacon   T
    Drive, Suite 17, Reston, VA 22090.
Forbes, 60 Fifth Avenue, New York, NY 10011.   G
Fortune, 541 North Fairbanks Court, Chicago, IL 60611.   G
Harvard Business Review, Soldiers Field Station, Boston, MA 02163.   M
IBM Systems Journal, Armonk, NY 10504.   DP
Journal of Systems Management, 24587 Bagley Road, Cleveland,   DP
    OH 44138.
Management Review, 135 West 50th Street, New York, NY 10020.   M
Sloan Management Review, MIT, Cambridge, MA 02139.   M

INDEX

INDEX

Leon W. Ellsworth   Claude W. Burrill

ABOUT THE AUTHORS

Claude W. Burrill and **Leon W. Ellsworth, Jr.,** are senior staff members at the IBM Systems Science Institute. They have worked together for many years doing research, consulting, and teaching in a variety of management areas. In 1972 they became interested in improving the methods for data processing application development projects. This book is the result of their extensive development and validation efforts.

Dr. Burrill began his work with computers in 1955. He has a Ph.D. in mathematics, was a Fulbright scholar, and has published numerous books. Mr. Ellsworth began his work with computers in 1953. A leader in data processing education since 1952, he has degrees in physics, electrical engineering, and education.

Both authors are experienced managers and are principals in Burrill-Ellsworth Associates, Inc.

Burrill-Ellsworth Associates, Inc.
26 Birchwood Place
Tenafly, N.J. 07670